On Becoming a Psychotherapist

On Becoming a Psychotherapist

The Personal and Professional Journey

Edited by

ROBERT H. KLEIN
HAROLD S. BERNARD
VICTOR L. SCHERMER

OXFORD
UNIVERSITY PRESS

2011

OXFORD

UNIVERSITY PRESS

Oxford University Press, Inc., publishes works that further
Oxford University's objective of excellence
in research, scholarship, and education.

Oxford   New York
Auckland   Cape Town   Dar es Salaam   Hong Kong   Karachi
Kuala Lumpur   Madrid   Melbourne   Mexico City   Nairobi
New Delhi   Shanghai   Taipei   Toronto

With offices in
Argentina   Austria   Brazil   Chile   Czech Republic   France   Greece
Guatemala   Hungary   Italy   Japan   Poland   Portugal   Singapore
South Korea   Switzerland   Thailand   Turkey   Ukraine   Vietnam

Published by Oxford University Press, Inc.
198 Madison Avenue, New York, New York 10016
www.oup.com

Oxford is a registered trademark of Oxford University Press

Library of Congress Cataloging-in-Publication Data

On becoming a psychotherapist : the personal and professional journey / edited by Robert Klein,
Harold Bernard, Victor Schermer.
     p. ; cm.
   ISBN 978-0-19-973639-3
   1.   Psychotherapists—Attitudes.   2.   Psychotherapists—Psychology.   3.   Psychotherapy—Vocational
guidance.   4.   Psychotherapy—Study and teaching.   5.   Career development.   I. Klein, Robert H.
II. Bernard, Harold S.   III. Schermer, Victor L.
[DNLM: 1.   Psychotherapy.   2.   Motivation.   3.   Personality Development.
4.   Professional Role—psychology.   5.   Vocational Guidance.   WM 420 O575 2011]
   RC480.5.O492 2011
   616.89'14—dc22   2010020132

9 8 7 6 5 4 3 2 1
Printed in the United States of America
on acid-free paper

This book is dedicated to all psychotherapists who have labored courageously to become the best we can be.
We are especially grateful to the many teachers, supervisors, colleagues and patients who have contributed to our own personal and professional development.

Foreword

Psychotherapy is praxis, not a *gnosis*. The practice of psychotherapy draws upon talent, knowledge, experience, attitudes, values, and the freedom to employ these in the service of the patient and the treatment. This is difficult (Freud suggested "impossible") and therapists, like therapy itself, are always in the process of becoming, never complete. Further, like psychotherapy itself, the process of becoming a therapist is the essence; the product has significance only insofar as it reflects the process that created it. This book, by directing our attention to those processes that create psychotherapists, marks the beginning of a new chapter in the study of psychotherapy.

There are many books about psychotherapy—what it is, how to do it, how it works, whether it works, and the several theories or schools that guide its practice. Their number and popularity attests to the ongoing struggle of psychotherapists to think about what they do, and how and why they do it.

There are fewer books about those who conduct psychotherapy, the psychotherapists. This is one of those books. Psychotherapists, like everyone else, are more comfortable looking outside rather than inside, at their patients or at their work rather than at themselves. This is a book in which psychotherapists do look at their colleagues and at themselves, at how they came to be and at what difference it makes. It is striking how, as they talk about their students and colleagues in rather abstract terms, they return repeatedly to personal stories about themselves, the experiences that led them to their being the kinds of therapists that they have become. It is not surprising that gifted therapists find the most powerful version of what that want to say in the specific and concrete rather than the general and the abstract, for that is what is most powerful in psychotherapy as well.

The process of becoming a therapist is viewed from many perspectives within these pages. We learn of the personal background, critical developmental events, traumas, mentoring relationships, personal therapy, supervision, didactic teaching, and clinical experience. The contributors to this book also discuss new developments in the field, tensions between the ancient art and the emerging science; between the most traditional psychoanalytically-based models and the more specific, focused and research-based techniques developed in recent years.

In a way the very existence of this volume marks an important turning point in the evolution of the profession of psychotherapy itself. In the beginning therapy was seen as an expert applying knowledge about psychology and psychopathology to the study and treatment of patients. The knowledge was about the patient; the treatment situation was simply the context in which it was applied and the therapist was the expert who applied it. However, it soon became apparent that the results, the efficacy or effectiveness of the treatment, depended upon more than the psychological and psychopathologic understanding of the therapist. The focus of interest broadened, to encompass the therapeutic process as well as the patient and psychopathology. Understanding the events in the treatment became as or more important that understanding the patient's struggles in life.

Once again there has been a broadening of interest, with the change marked by this volume. The events in treatment are created by the therapist as well as by the patient, and we therefore direct our gaze to the therapists as well as to the patient and the treatment. The editors of this volume have assembled a group of gifted guides as they lead us along this new path. We have much to learn and far to go, but most important, we have taken that first step.

Robert Michels, M.D.
Walsh McDermott University Professor of Medicine and University
Professor of Psychiatry
Weill Medical College of Cornell University
New York, NY

Preface

This book has been a long time in the making. Collectively we, the editors, have been treating patients in psychotherapy for more than 100 years. In addition, education, training, and supervision have all been mainstays of each of our careers, during which we have worked with thousands of trainees and fellow professionals from the various mental health disciplines. One of us (RHK) recently received the Award for Outstanding Contributions to the Field of Group Psychotherapy from the National Registry of Certified Group Psychotherapists, and served for many years as the Director of Education and Training at the multidisciplinary Yale Psychiatric Institute. Another of us (HSB) has been supervising trainees from all the mental health disciplines for more than 30 years, and directed the group psychotherapy training program at NYU/Bellevue Medical Center for 14 years. The third co-editor (VLS) is the author and editor of many highly regarded books and articles about psychotherapy, and has been responsible for the training, education, and supervision of therapists in numerous settings in the United States and worldwide.

As a result of being deeply immersed for many years in both clinical work and the educational process, we have witnessed significant changes in the field of mental health, and psychotherapy in particular. To say that things have changed dramatically over the years regarding the practice of psychotherapy would be an understatement! The patients we currently see for treatment are different from those we typically saw 40 years ago. Many are treated psychopharmacologically, either exclusively or in tandem with psychotherapy. Increasing numbers of those seeking psychotherapy no longer fall into the "neurotic" or "worried-well" categories. Instead, many present with complex problems that include histories of substance abuse, trauma, dual diagnoses, and longstanding, often profound interpersonal problems. Successful treatment now poses new challenges for psychotherapists and often requires additional special training.

Furthermore, the treatment process itself has changed substantially. Not only have a plethora of different theoretical models emerged and developed, but therapy is now routinely provided in different settings, including hospitals and agencies, not primarily in private practice offices, not just face-to-face but via telephone and the Internet, and for different lengths of time (mostly short-term, as compared to the longer-term, open-ended intensive treatment that used to be much more prevalent than it is today). In addition, psychotherapy is now delivered by a different, broader variety of mental health professionals, not just by psychiatrists, psychologists, social workers, and nurses. There are more women providers as the field undergoes increasing "feminization," and fewer psychiatrists are conducting psychotherapy, as more rely upon medications as the treatment of choice. Most importantly, the entire field is subject to the influence of managed care, with its emphasis on cost containment. Along with these developments have come increasing demands from insurance companies, consumers, and the federal government for accountability: psychotherapy must demonstrate that it is evidence-based and that it works. New and extensive bodies of research data are rapidly accumulating that require attention and incorporation into practice by psychotherapists. When one considers the promising advances that have been reported in neuroscience and biochemistry along with those involving psychotherapy paradigms and research, the information explosion is truly staggering.

Each of these factors has changed the face and the process of psychotherapy. Indeed, one would be hard-pressed these days to speak about psychotherapy in general when even the fundamental generic model of psychotherapy—psychodynamically based psychotherapy—has itself changed substantially. No longer is the patient alone viewed as the troubled object of study by a neutral, detached, and objective psychotherapist. Instead, we are practicing in an era marked by increasing awareness that understanding the person of the therapist is crucial to understanding and effectively making use of the co-constructed therapeutic relationship and process. The selection of our title for this book, which emphasizes both the personal and professional aspects of psychotherapist development, is testimony to how much our thinking has shifted.

In view of these developments, we believe that it would be worthwhile to pause, reflect, and take stock of where we have been during the developmental journeys that have characterized our own careers and those of our respected colleagues who have contributed to this book. All of us, particularly at this point in our travels, would like to be able to give back something of value based upon our accumulated years of experience that will help to better prepare the next generation of clinical practitioners. Our collective hope is that we may have learned a thing or two along the way that is worth sharing.

The background and primary orientation of the co-editors is psychodynamic and group-oriented. But like most other seasoned clinicians, we are eclectic in our practice and utilize our knowledge of many different approaches and modes of intervention in our day-to-day work. The specific target audience for this book encompasses directors of training, clinical supervisors, and the broad spectrum of psychotherapists who lean toward a dynamic, holistic, and developmental understanding of the personality and of treatment. More generally, we believe this volume will be of interest to the many thousands of practitioners who are interested in understanding more about how they have become the therapists they are, and what they might do to further develop their competency. The book may also find a wider audience among the many laypersons, patients, and former patients who are interested in what makes therapy and therapists "tick." The authors we have chosen to include in this volume are clinicians who subscribe to the belief that even if treatments are relatively brief, and even if compelling scientific evidence of their efficacy cannot yet be cited, we must still make an attempt to treat the whole person and not just one or more isolated symptoms. Our working assumption is based upon the notion that psychotherapy occurs within an interpersonal context and fundamentally rests upon the development of a relationship between human beings.

While the factors we will be considering go beyond the realm of formal training, what we learn will certainly have implications for the preparation of practitioners who are preparing to take on the challenging role of psychotherapist. What are the crucial components of an effective approach to training, and how can they best be transmitted to developing professionals? Is there a particular sequence that works best? Are there additional elements that now need to be incorporated into clinical training (e.g., how can psychotherapists be trained to incorporate research developments into their clinical practices)? How can we promote increased sensitivity and awareness of ethical, cultural, and diversity considerations? And where is the field headed? Given our interpersonal, dynamic, holistic framework, what new challenges can we anticipate and prepare developing psychotherapists to cope with in the future?

In the concluding chapter of the volume, we will attempt to integrate the various contributions made by chapter authors in an effort to move toward a comprehensive theory of psychotherapist development. We will endeavor to identify particular phases of therapist development, and the challenges that need to be met at each phase. The authors will pay special attention to what is involved in the process by which psychotherapists learn how to make the most effective use of their selves, not just their theory and technique, in the treatment process. The goal will be to develop a set of generalizations about personal experiences and professional training that are relevant to a wide variety of psychotherapists. Our authors have been chosen because of their expertise, whether in the area of psychodynamic psychotherapy broadly defined, cognitive-behavioral approaches to treatment, and/or psychotherapy research on treatment process and outcome as well as evidence-based practices. The ultimate goal is to contribute to what is known about how to best prepare the next generation of clinicians to successfully practice the craft of psychotherapy, which continues to be an amalgam of art, science, and interpersonal relatedness.

Contents

Contributors   *xv*

1. Introduction   *3*
   Robert H. Klein, Harold S. Bernard, and Victor L. Schermer

2. Growing Up to Be a Good Psychotherapist, or Physician—
   Know Thyself!   *29*
   John O'Leary

3. The Mentoring Relationship: Co-creating Personal and
   Professional Growth   *49*
   Robin G. Gayle

4. The Place of Didactic Preparation in the
   Therapist's Development   *69*
   Victor L. Schermer

5. The Role of Clinical Experience in the Making
   of a Psychotherapist   *94*
   Jerome S. Gans

6. Psychotherapy Supervision and the Development
   of the Psychotherapist   *114*
   Molyn Leszcz

7. Up Close and Personal: A Consideration of the Role of Personal
   Therapy in the Development of a Psychotherapist   *144*
   Suzanne B. Phillips

8. The Psychotherapist as "Wounded Healer": A Modern Expression
   of an Ancient Tradition   *165*
   Cecil A. Rice

9. Has the Magic of Psychotherapy Disappeared? Integrating Evidence-Based Practice into Therapist Awareness and Development   *190*
    Debra Theobald McClendon and Gary M. Burlingame

10. Becoming a Cognitive-Behavioral Therapist: Striving to Integrate Professional and Personal Development   *212*
    Edmund C. Neuhaus

11. Psychotherapy Research: Implications for Optimal Therapist Personality, Training, and Development   *245*
    Shannon Wiltsey Stirman and Paul Crits-Christoph

12. Conclusions: A Phase-Specific Model for Psychotherapist Development   *269*
    Robert H. Klein, Harold S. Bernard, and Victor L. Schermer

Index   *303*

Contributors

Harold S. Bernard, Ph.D.
Clinical Associate Professor of Psychiatry
New York University School of Medicine

Gary M. Burlingame, Ph.D.
Professor of Psychology
Brigham Young University

Paul Crits-Christoph, Ph.D.
Professor of Psychology in Psychiatry
University of Pennsylvania

Jerome S. Gans, M.D.
Associate Clinical Professor of Psychiatry
Harvard Medical School

Robin G. Gayle, Ph.D.
Associate Professor of Psychology
Department of Counseling Psychology
Dominican University of California

Robert H. Klein, Ph.D.
Lecturer, Department of Psychiatry
Yale School of Medicine

Molyn Leszcz, M.D.
Psychiatrist-in-Chief, Mount Sinai Hospital
Joseph and Wolf Lebovic Health Complex
Professor and Head, Group Psychotherapy
University of Toronto Department of Psychiatry

Debra Theobald McClendon, Ph.D.
Brigham Young University

Edmund C. Neuhaus, Ph.D.
Assistant Clinical Professor of Psychology
Department of Psychiatry
Harvard Medical School
Clinical Associate Psychologist, McLean Hospital

John O'Leary, Ph.D.
Faculty and Supervisor
William Alanson White Institute

Suzanne B. Phillips, Psy.D.
Adjunct Professor of Psychology
C.W. Post Campus
Long Island University

Cecil A. Rice, Ph.D.
President
Boston Institute for Psychotherapy

Victor L. Schermer, M.A.
Executive Director
Study Group for Contemporary Psychoanalytic Process
Founding Director
Institute for the Study of Human Conflict

Shannon Wiltsey Stirman, Ph.D.
Department of Psychiatry
University of Pennsylvania

On Becoming a Psychotherapist

1

Introduction

Robert H. Klein, Harold S. Bernard, and Victor L. Schermer

How does someone become a psychotherapist? What sort of education and training, life experiences, and professional experiences are necessary to become a competent psychotherapist? Do certain childhood experiences, or some combination of genetic endowment and personality traits, equip one to become a more effective and successful psychotherapist? Is there a common path that psychotherapists follow in their development? These are issues of significant interest to both the mental health professional community and to the public that relies on the quality of its services. Because of the rapidly changing health care environment, these issues have become increasingly salient and require thoughtful consideration. Our goal in this volume is to comprehensively explore the many experiences that therapists have over the course of their lifetimes, both personal and professional, that contribute to their professional identities as practicing psychotherapists, a process that we construe as an ongoing lifetime endeavor that ends only when the practitioner ceases to practice.

To achieve our aim of exploring the process of how therapists develop into the clinicians they become, we have made an effort to deconstruct the process—that is, to identify what we understand to be the key developmental experiences that most therapists go through in their professional evolution. We are well aware that this process is highly individualized, and that there is enormous variation between and among therapists as to what influences are most important in their development. However, we also believe there are certain influences that virtually all clinicians experience that inevitably have an impact on how they develop as therapists.

The issues we have chosen to explore will be addressed in a series of chapters written by acknowledged experts in our field. Our authors all draw upon their experience and expertise, as well as their personal reflections. Wherever possible, they incorporate findings from relevant empirical research into their chapters, and highlight ethical, cultural, and diversity issues. Let us briefly describe the influences we have decided to highlight in this volume.

First, we will take up the influence of early life experiences. Freud's early writings alerted us to the lifelong impact that early life experiences have on

3

how our lives unfold, and there has never been any serious refutation of this notion; in fact, it is at this point a universally accepted truism. We will then look at therapists' experiences with mentors and other role models. Most of us meet people along the way who make deep impressions on us, and whose influence we look back upon as having been formative in our becoming who we become. We often meet such people well before we embark upon a particular professional course.

Once we have embarked on the road to becoming a therapist, and sometimes even before (that is, in undergraduate courses), we begin our didactic preparation for becoming a practicing clinician by taking courses and reading about such things as normal development, psychopathology, and even approaches to treatment. This continues in graduate training, where there is typically some time spent in the classroom before actually beginning to see patients. Of course this varies from profession to profession: often psychiatric residents begin seeing patients before spending much time on didactic preparation. But the typical sequence is to do some didactic preparation before entering the clinical fray.

What comes next is our beginning encounters with actual patients. Such encounters almost always have great influence on how we develop as clinicians: the experience is usually very challenging, and can easily be traumatizing. We move on from a consideration of these early clinical encounters to a discussion of the developing clinician's experiences in supervision. Here we will focus not only on early supervisory experiences, but also on supervision throughout one's professional career. Most clinicians have experiences with multiple supervisors over the course of their careers, at least some of whom are usually pointed to as formative as clinicians reflect on how they have developed into the therapists they have become.

We then take up the question of the influence of personal treatment on the development of the therapist. While some specialty approaches to psychotherapy (e.g., psychoanalysis) require their candidates to undergo personal treatment, training programs in psychiatry, psychology, social work, and the related disciplines typically do not. Nevertheless, a high percentage of mental health professionals in training, and subsequent to training, voluntarily avail themselves of the opportunity to experience personal treatment, often more than once, over the course of their careers (see Chapter 7). For those who do, the experience is almost always an important influence on how they develop as therapists. We then move on to a consideration of the therapist as "wounded healer." There is a widespread notion that therapists enter the field in order to resolve their own personal issues. We do not necessarily subscribe to this notion, but we do believe that *everyone* sustains wounds over the course of a lifetime, and that therapists need to deal with their wounds if they are going to be successful in their professional roles.

Next we take up a recent development in our field that has begun to influence all practitioners, and that is likely to have increasing influence in the years ahead: the increased emphasis on evidence-based treatment.

For many of us, we have been practicing without clear and objective evidence that what we are doing is effective. We adapt to this reality in different ways, of course, but now that there is increasing pressure to provide such evidence, we are all confronted with the need to come to grips with this in some way, if only internally. We then turn to a consideration of cognitive-behavioral therapy (CBT), the approach to treatment that has been most responsive to the increased emphasis on evidence-based treatment. This chapter will highlight the ways in which CBT is different from psychodynamically oriented treatment approaches, but also how they overlap. It will permit us to examine in greater detail differences between the developmental pathways available for both CBT and psychodynamically oriented clinicians. Finally, we provide an overview of the status of empirical research in our field that bears upon changes in current and future clinical practice patterns. This will lead us into our concluding chapter, in which we will summarize the insights and contributions of our authors, put forth a general model of psychotherapist development, and make suggestions about therapist growth and well-being garnered from what we have learned by shepherding this book to its conclusion.

Our efforts to identify and explore the essential components of how psychotherapists become the practitioners they are will not be limited only to an examination of their formal education and training, but will also include consideration of their lives, careers, practices of psychotherapy, and patterns of self-care and personal growth. We will attempt to shed light on how these components are effectively organized and integrated, and address the current controversies that surround what constitutes the optimal set of experiences for the developing psychotherapist. The challenges facing practitioners in the contemporary health care environment will be examined in terms of their implications for psychotherapist selection, education, supervision, practice, and continued professional growth, and with an eye toward delineating what mitigates for and against good treatment outcomes.

Literature Review

When compared to the research on psychotherapies, research about psychotherapists is relatively limited. (In 1997, for example, *Clinical Psychology: Science and Practice* presented a special series entitled: "The therapist as a neglected variable in psychotherapy research.") The literature in the area of psychotherapist development is even more sparse. Some authors have provided biographical or autobiographical accounts of well-known analysts (Gay, 1988; Jung, 1989; Strozier, 2001). A few contributions have appeared on the evolving professional self (Cross & Papadopolous, 2001; Kottler, 2003; Mahoney, 2001; Skovholt & Ronnestad, 1995). Others have focused on how one becomes a "master" therapist (Jennings & Skovholt, 1999; Skovholt & Jennings, 2004); the frequency and value of personal treatment for the psychotherapist (Bike et al., 2009; Brenner, 2006; Freudenberger, 1986; Geller et al., 2005; Norcross, 2005; Penzer, 1984); and the process of adopting a theory that works for the particular therapist (Truscott, 2010). Conscious and unconscious motives for practicing psychotherapy have been described (Ellis, 2005; Farber et al., 2005; Mahrer, 2005; Norcross & Farber, 2005; Orlinsky, 2005; Reppen, 1998; Sussman, 1992), as has the importance of psychotherapist resilience (Skovholt, 2001). Bergin and Garfield's *Handbook of Psychotherapy and Behavior Change* has contained in each edition (1971, 1994) an extensive compilation of research on therapist variables and their relationship to outcome in psychotherapy. Specific therapist characteristics thought to promote effective treatment outcomes have been the subject of extensive investigation (Bergin & Garfield, 1971, 1994; Crits-Christoph et al., 1991; Garfield & Bergin, 19781978, 1986, 1990; Lambert, 2004; Norcross, 2002a, 2002b). Therapist use of self (Basescu, 1990), the personal life of the therapist (Guy, 1987), therapist self-care (Baker, 2003; Norcross, 2000), and attempts to identify what creates and sustains commitment to the practice of psychotherapy (Dlugos & Friedlander, 2001; Miller, 2007) have all received considerable attention. Efforts have also been made to examine the therapist as wounded healer (Millon et al., 1986; Rippere & Williams, 1985; Sherman & Thelan, 1998; Stadler, 1999) and to explore therapist burnout (Deutsch, 1984, 1985; Edelwich & Brodsky; 1980; Maslach, 1982, 1986; Maslach & Leiter, 1997). In recent years, ethical and professional issues facing therapists have been receiving increased attention (Brabender, 2006; Cottone & Tarvydas, 2003; Pope & Vasquez, 1991; Truscott & Crook, 2004; Welfel, 2002). So, too, is the importance of recognizing and effectively dealing with multicultural issues, including race, ethnicity, and gender (APA, 2002; Baruth & Manning, 2003; Brinson & Cervantes, 2003; Comas-Díaz, 2005; Debiak, 2007; Fish, 1996; Markus, 2008; Pope-Davis & Coleman, 2001; Robinson & Howard-Hamilton, 2000; Sue & Sue, 1999). Several recent series of journal articles describe the journeys that practitioners have taken over the course of their professional lives (Bernard, 2008; Rhead, 2006).

Only a few contributions, however, have specifically dealt with the evolving professional self (e.g., Belson, 1992; Dryden & Spurling, 1989; Farber, 1990; Goldfried, 2001; Kottler, 1986, 2003; Orlinsky & Ronnestad, 2005; Orlinsky et al., 2005; Skovholt & Ronnestad, 1995). Of these, Orlinsky & Ronnestad (2005) have produced by far the richest and most comprehensive work in the field. Through their use of a detailed questionnaire, they collected self-reports from nearly 5,000 psychotherapists from countries worldwide at different points in their careers. Initiated in 1989, they then studied therapeutic work and professional growth for 15 years as a cooperative enterprise under the auspices of the Society for Psychotherapy Research. Their research clearly underscores the important contribution made by psychotherapists to clinical outcomes. It also attempts to determine whether patterns of professional work and development can be identified, and whether these are similar across professions.

With regard to professional development *per se*, innumerable didactic curricula have been developed by all of the disciplines involved in the teaching and training of mental health professionals that specify the body of knowledge that needs to be mastered to become an effective psychotherapist. But few if any authors have attempted to provide a volume that effectively integrates both professional and personal development. Moreover, no one has yet examined the matter of psychotherapist development in the current socioeconomic and cultural context, which is characterized by both an emphasis on brief, cost-efficient, evidence-based treatment and a growing body of theory and research that suggests that more attention needs to be devoted to the person of the psychotherapist in order to better understand treatment process and outcome.

This volume seeks to address the need for an integration of what is involved in the development of the psychotherapist at both the personal and professional levels. Among the matters that will be considered is how the training of mental health professionals should be affected by the increased recognition of the importance of the therapist's person to treatment outcome; how to integrate our understanding of the personal and professional experiences that developing psychotherapists have with the formal training they receive; and how the shifting cultural context affects the demands and challenges facing psychotherapists today. Ultimately our field would do well to have a comprehensive and generalizable model for therapist growth and development. Our intention is to address these various needs.

Why Now?

We believe this volume is timely for a number of reasons. First, as you see from the literature review we have provided, there has not been a great deal of work published about the topic of therapist development. While we all go through a developmental process, we are often not aware of how the various influences we discuss in this volume are affecting us cumulatively. Also, we believe that those who are charged with shepherding therapists in training through the developmental process will find this book valuable in thinking about how they structure their training programs to facilitate optimal therapist development.

A second, equally important rationale for organizing this book now is that there has been a fundamental evolution in our field in the direction of greater appreciation for the contribution of the therapist's person to the treatment process. The notion of the therapist as a "blank screen" onto whom the patient projects his or her transferences, to be interpreted by a neutral, objective and non-contributing therapist, is all but passé. The emerging consensus over the past few years is that therapists are active co-participants in the interpersonal field that develops between them and their patients (Aron, 1996; Mitchell, 1988). This "intersubjective" approach has been gaining increasing attention and support (Fosshage, 2003; Ogden, 1994; Stolorow & Atwood, 1992). It follows that the more we know about therapists as persons, and the process of development that has led them to bring what they bring to the therapeutic encounter, the more we will know about what ultimately transpires in the consultation room. It is noteworthy that this consensus extends even to many therapists who practice CBT and other approaches that follow manualized protocols (see Chapter 10). The particulars of the nature and extent of the therapist's influence on the unfolding treatment process are just beginning to be fleshed out in research, but the general sense that the therapist's contribution is profound is increasingly held to be beyond dispute—thus the importance of understanding as much as we can about who therapists are and how they become the practitioners they become.

Finally, therapists are facing many new pressures as psychotherapeutic practice continues to evolve. Later in the chapter we will briefly describe some of the sociopolitical, scientific, and theoretical developments that are having an impact on contemporary practice. The pressures exerted by managed care companies and the increased emphasis on evidence-based treatment are prodding therapists to justify what they are doing. The economic pressures that impinge on both therapists and patients profoundly affect the treatment experience as well. We need to know as much as we can about how these matters influence what therapists bring to their therapeutic encounters. In sum, the more we know about the person of the therapist, the more we will know about the process of therapy and what individual practitioners and training programs can do to facilitate optimal therapist development.

Factors Impinging on Contemporary Therapeutic Practice

There can be little doubt that we live in an age of rapid, kaleidescopic change, with shifting realities and priorities. We believe it is especially timely to assemble this volume since the entire health care field has been undergoing enormous change. As this chapter is being written, the U.S. Congress is struggling to come to terms with proposed legislation that would fundamentally change the way health care is practiced and paid for in this country, a topic deemed to be of the highest priority by the Obama administration. Among the critical questions that are being addressed in the current debate are: Can we make health care available to all, or at least to a greater number of people than we do currently? If so, how will it be paid for? Can we create a "public option"? How will quality of care be affected by the changes that are being contemplated? Will we establish a two-tier health care system in which only the wealthy or privileged will be able to gain optimal care? Stakeholders in this important discussion include, among others, health care consumers, health care providers, insurance companies, administrators, actuarial cost-benefit analysts, and of course politicians, who seek both to represent their constituencies and to be re-elected. Many powerful and well-organized voices are being heard during the debate. We hope that those of the poor, minorities, immigrants, the elderly, and the historically underrepresented will also be heard. Precisely whose interests will be best served remains to be seen. But no matter how these issues are addressed and resolved, the answers will have a profound impact on the nature, availability, quality, cost, and delivery of mental health services.

In the following sections we want to briefly identify and highlight those specific factors that have affected mental health and have had the most significant impact on the practices of those who become psychotherapists. Specifically, we will address the issues of managed care, the increased prevalence of short-term psychotherapy and manualized treatment, advances in neuroscience, changes in psychopharmacology, the changing patient population, differences in services and providers, accountability and evidence-based treatment, and changes in psychodynamic theory that underlie much of the psychotherapy that practitioners currently offer their patients.

Managed Care

Any clinical professional who currently practices psychotherapy or who is preparing to enter the field as a provider must take into consideration the complex and influential reality of managed care. In most managed care operations, case managers now determine what practitioners are permitted to do, with whom, and for how long. Clinician treatment plans must be approved, mandated treatment reviews are required, treatment results must be documented in clearly measurable terms, and any form of treatment that extends beyond a short time period must be preauthorized. The days when long-term, uncovering, insight-oriented treatment would be covered by health insurance are over. Five years of psychoanalysis has largely been replaced by five sessions of approved care. Treatment geared to promoting self-awareness and establishing more authentic, gratifying human relationships is a hard sell today. Managed care companies apply continual pressure to keep all forms of treatment brief and cost-effective. At the same time as this pressure is being exerted by the managed care industry, our culture has put more and more emphasis on achieving immediate results, so there is pressure for quick results from consumers as well. Instant food, instant housing, instant information, instant gratification, and instant treatment are often what seem to be desired.

Short-Term Psychotherapy and Manualized Treatment

Developments in the theory and practice of short-term psychotherapy seem to reflect this uniquely American perspective. Various models of short-term individual (e.g., Davanloo, 2001; Mann, 1973; Sifneos, 1987) and group psychotherapy (e.g., Budman et al., 1996; Klein, 1985; MacKenzie, 1997) have appeared in the literature over the past half-century. For the most part, these short-term approaches advocate addressing more limited treatment goals with a more narrowly defined patient population. Of particular interest here is the fact that these approaches lend themselves more easily to research than do longer-term treatments. More recently, short-term approaches have been bolstered by the development of what have been called "manualized" treatment approaches, which attempt to provide a clear set of instructions for the therapist to apply in conducting more time-limited forms of intervention. In large part, the impetus here is to make the process of psychotherapy more objective and standardized, and to make it easier to train successful, competent therapists. Implicit in this effort is the notion that all therapists are equal and interchangeable, and that the method of treatment, not the person of the therapist or his or her relationship with the patient, is critical for producing change.

Advances in Neurosciences

At the scientific level, the practice of psychotherapy has also been influenced significantly over the past two decades by advances in the areas of neuroscience and biochemistry. As a result, we have begun to fashion a more complex view of human development, and, therefore, the treatment of illness or disorders. To view psychiatric disorders as purely biologically determined, and not significantly influenced by experience, is now considered an overly simplistic, reductionistic view. Recent findings in neuroscience indicate that interactions with the environment, especially interactions with other people, have a direct impact on the structure and function of the brain (Siegel, 1999; Siegel & Hartzell, 2003). One need not choose between biology versus experience, or mind versus brain. Understanding brain/mind functioning and the flow of energy and information in the brain requires an understanding of how human relationships can affect neuronal activity, organization, and function. Mental health treatment, therefore, must consider biological and experiential factors as well as their reciprocal influence upon one another.

Changes in Psychopharmacology

In conjunction with these developments, as the biochemical/biological components of various symptoms and diseases are being more clearly identified, we have witnessed a veritable explosion in psychopharmacological treatments. While it is not our purpose here to review these advances, it is important to note that new and reportedly more effective medications with fewer side effects are available for treating a host of different disorders. Furthermore, advances in psychopharmacology have paved the way for significant reduction of the disabling symptoms that, in past years, often prevented or significantly interfered with patients' capacities to make successful use of psychotherapy (e.g., patients suffering from psychosis, obsessive-compulsive disorder, bipolar disorder, or severe depression). Such patients, when properly medicated, are now more frequently amenable to psychotherapy.

This proliferation of medications, however, has also ushered in new problems. Thus, for example, these medications are now being prescribed not only by psychiatrists, but also by primary care and other non-psychiatric physicians, advanced practice nurses, and so forth, many of whom have only limited experience in using these medications to deal with difficult-to-treat clinical situations. As a result, complications not infrequently arise in treatment when a prescribed medication does not work as hoped for. Patients are often referred for treatment to a mental health professional only after unsuccessful treatment attempts have been made by the patient's primary care physician.

In addition, successful use of medications may have paved the way for unrealistic wishes, on the part of patients, clinicians, and insurance companies, that medication alone will be sufficient, and that a short-term, cost-effective solution can be easily found. Such beliefs are maintained even though studies involving random controlled trials repeatedly confirm that the combination of medication and psychotherapy is more effective than either alone in treating a variety of psychiatric disorders (e.g., Eddy et al., 2004). Providing only psychotherapy without at least raising for consideration with the patient the potential use of medications may soon be construed as malpractice. The opposite, of course, may also hold true: simply providing medications without considering psychotherapy may be viewed as untenable.

Even so, one cannot turn on the television without being bombarded by a spate of commercials advertising one or another new medication that is good for whatever ails us. Many of these medications are for treating psychiatric problems. Possible medication side effects and complications are carefully listed and consumers are, of course, reminded to talk to their doctors about whether such medications are right for them. Nevertheless, the overall impression conveyed is that most psychiatric problems, especially depression and anxiety, can be successfully treated by some form of medication.

It is important to note in this regard that the impressive advances made in the field of psychopharmacology do not reduce the importance of psychotherapy. Even when treating those disturbances now thought to have a biological basis, "talking therapy" remains a cornerstone of what mental health professionals have to offer (Engel, 2008). Each of these sets of symptoms or disorders has significant personal and interpersonal antecedents and clearly has profound consequences for one's present life. Anyone who has suffered from, treated, or lived with a patient suffering from an affective or anxiety disorder, for example, will attest to the fact that these disorders disrupt and negatively affect all those involved with the individual struggling with the problem. In fact, most people come into treatment seeking help with how they are feeling about themselves and their interpersonal relationships, not simply relief from their symptoms. After all, it is a human being who is experiencing these problems. The best health professionals treat the person, not the symptom or the disease. Furthermore, medications themselves are prescribed within an interpersonal, relational context. In fact, one might argue that the therapeutic relationship is crucial in determining the success of a treatment intervention, even when that intervention is primarily or exclusively psychopharmacological.

Practicing psychotherapists, therefore, need to remain aware of the increasing array of available medication options, and must possess some understanding of their indications and contraindications for use, as well as their benefits and limitations. Psychotherapists must also be prepared to work collaboratively with other health care providers.

The Changing Patient Population

Another factor that continues to affect the journey of becoming a therapist is the changing nature of who comes for treatment. Psychotherapists are no longer simply treating the "worried well." YAVIS syndrome (young, attractive, verbal, intelligent, and successful) patients seems to be in far less abundance. Instead, mental health professionals are being asked to treat more and more people with complex, hard-to-treat disorders, including substance abuse, dual diagnoses, eating disorders, and severe personality disorders. These individuals come not just from the white, upper-middle class, but from all walks of life, with different cultural backgrounds, and varying levels of education, verbal ability, and psychological mindedness. They, therefore, pose new challenges for clinicians. Older, more traditional models for conducting psychotherapy are often not relevant in working with these patients. In addition, clinicians themselves are much more diverse, and they, like the patients they treat, bring with them into the consulting room their own beliefs, values, and cultural traditions. Furthermore, many clinicians are moving beyond the consulting room into the community. Planning, implementing, and evaluating post-disaster mental health interventions is becoming an area of heightened concern for many professionals. Worldwide dissemination of intervention protocols requires a much more sophisticated recognition and appreciation of cultural differences. Furthermore, helping patients dealing with sudden and overwhelming loss, complicated grief and depression, and post-traumatic stress disorders is stressful for therapists and requires additional training, a new set of skills, and different levels of supervision and support for treaters (Klein & Phillips, 2008; Klein & Schermer, 2000; Saakvitne & Pearlman, 1995).

Different Types of Services and Providers

With the increasing demand for mental health services has come increased competition in the marketplace. More and more people are presenting themselves as "therapists," regardless of their training. Even though licensure and certification requirements are becoming more stringent for some professions in some states, this trend is more than offset by the proliferation of people who hold themselves out to be helpers in one way or another. New fields are evolving as offshoots of more traditional psychotherapy, such as "life coaching." Anyone seeking psychotherapy quickly realizes that various types of "therapy" are practiced by mental health professionals as well as others who do not necessarily have a background in the social and natural sciences. Many of these "therapists" are not subject to state licensure requirements, nor are they necessarily part of any national professional regulatory organization. Modes of delivery for psychotherapy are also undergoing significant change. One can currently be treated, for example, by telephone (Simon et al., 2004, 2009) or via the Internet (Christensen et al., 2004; Griffiths & Christensen, 2007; Horgan et al., 2007; Kessler et al., 2009), not just in a professional office. Computer-aided psychotherapies are being used with increasing frequency (Marks et al., 2007; Marks & Cavanaugh, 2009). However, in our view and for the purposes of this volume, the term "psychotherapy" refers to face-to-face treatment provided by helping professionals trained in the traditional mental health disciplines of psychiatry, psychology, social work, and nursing. This includes directive and non-directive mental health counselors in a variety of specialties; psychoanalysts and analytic therapists; cognitive and behavioral therapists; group therapists; family therapists; gestalt therapists and transactional analysts; and those with psycho-spiritual or faith-based emphases. The preparation and training of all such psychotherapists includes exposure to empirical research as well as theory, and careful consideration of ethical, cultural, and diversity issues associated with the practice of psychotherapy.

Accountability: Evidence-Based Practice

Concurrent with these developments, there has been a much broader, rapidly growing national trend, fueled by multiple sources (e.g., the federal government, consumers, providers, and insurance companies), that reflects an increasing emphasis on accountability. The crucial question/challenge being raised is: Does psychotherapy work, and *can it be "proven"*? Practitioners are being asked to demonstrate the efficacy of what they are doing—that is, to prove that psychotherapy works (Burlingame & Beecher, in press; Klein, 2009). This escalating pressure has given rise to increasing demands for "evidence-based" practice. Treatments that are evidence-based have been demonstrated to be effective utilizing scientific criteria (Burlingame et al., 2004a, 2004b). Both the Rosalynn Carter Symposium on Mental Health Policy (2003) and the President's New Freedom Commission on Mental Health Final Report (2004) formally endorsed evidence-based practice. Each maintained that effective services and supports validated by research found their way too slowly into practice. They suggested that a premium be placed on rapidly incorporating evidence-based practices as the bedrock for clinical mental health services. Treatment approaches that fail to do this and/or cannot demonstrate through systematic research that they are efficacious may well fail to qualify for reimbursement, and may in the future even be regarded as unethical.

Despite these admonitions, considerable ambiguity, confusion, and controversy have continued to surround the notion of evidence-based practice (Bohart et al., 1998; Chambless & Ollendeick, 2001; Norcross et al., 2005). Although the term "evidence-based" is frequently used to confer the mantle of scientific legitimacy and respectability on particular interventions, it is often unclear what this term actually means. On the most fundamental level, what constitutes acceptable "evidence," and at what levels of specificity should it be required (Burlingame & Beecher, in press)? Are we talking about empirically supported treatments, or what were previously called empirically validated treatments? The American Psychological Association has used the notion of "evidence-supported treatments" based on randomized clinical trials, widely regarded as the "gold standard." In contrast, should evidence-based treatment conform to generally accepted "practice guidelines" (e.g., Bernard et al., 2009), a more descriptive than prescriptive approach suggested by the American Psychiatric Association? Demonstrating "efficacy" requires randomized controlled trials, the hallmark of drug studies, while "effectiveness" rests on studies conducted under naturalistic conditions. With regard to psychotherapy practices, nearly 80% of the studies demonstrating efficacy are based upon cognitive and/or behavioral approaches (Burlingame et al., 2004b). Psychodynamic and humanistic approaches remain underrepresented (Wampold, 2001). Does that mean that it is much more difficult to demonstrate the efficacy of such treatment approaches, or that they are of more limited value (Leichsenring, 2005; Wampold, 2007)? In addition, since most research is about pure outcome without consideration given to relevant process variables, it is virtually impossible to determine what specifically accounts for change. Might most of the variability in reported success rates be attributable not to the particular technical model under investigation, but to common factors across different approaches, or to differences in the quality of the patient–therapist alliance (Ahn & Wampold, 2001; Frank & Frank, 1991; Hubble et al., 1999; Kazdin, 2005)? Impassioned debates continue to be waged about precisely how to define and measure "success" in treatment: From whose perspective? At what points in time? Measuring symptom change is certainly considerably easier than attempting to define and measure changes in the quality and depth of self-understanding or interpersonal relationships. Precisely how these issues will influence the ways in which psychotherapy will be practiced going forward and, therefore, how practitioners need to be trained, remains to be seen.

Changes in Theory

An additional compelling reason for doing a book on psychotherapist development at this point in the evolution of our field has to do with recent theoretical advances in the area of psychodynamic treatment that have empha-sized that the psychotherapist is not simply a blank screen upon whom the patient projects his or her problems. Rather, these theories maintain that the person of the psychotherapist is a crucial contributor to the treatment of patients. Of particular importance in this regard is the growing interest in intersubjective and relational models of treatment, which have as their prem-ise the notion that psychotherapy is a co-creative process between therapist and patient. As such, the person of the therapist is a crucial contributor to, and determinant of, the success of a treatment experience. These theoretical advances have been supported by a growing body of evidence in the form of both research and clinical experience that has shown that the therapist-as-person has a profound impact on treatment outcomes above and beyond his or her training and theoretical orientation (e.g., Garfield & Bergin, 1990; Lambert, 2004; Luborsky, 1992; Norcross, 2002a, 2002b). From the current intersubjective and relational perspectives, the therapist's own experience, attitudes, and unconscious processes interact reciprocally and mutually with those of his or her patients, so that the effectiveness of treatment depends crucially on the nature and quality of the therapeutic relationship and the "match" between therapist and patient. Thus far, therapy has by and large put its "microscope" on the patient and his or her psychopathology, but it is clear that more needs to be known about what the therapist and the therapeutic interaction bring into the equation. If this volume adds to our knowledge of what is involved in the development of the therapist's persona, and how we can promote increased awareness on the part of the therapist regarding the nature of his or her contribution to the treatment process, we will have accomplished our purpose.

Implications for Therapist Training and Development

What, then, are the implications of these factors that currently affect the process of becoming a psychotherapist? How might they affect or fundamen-tally change the education and training, as well as the long-term professional and personal growth, of practitioners? What can we expect the next genera-tion of clinical practitioners to be facing, and how can we best prepare them to function effectively?

Several preliminary suggestions can be made, each of which will be explored, developed, and augmented in the chapters that follow. To begin with, it seems clear to us that psychotherapists need to develop and maintain flexibility and range in their modes of intervention, a firm grasp of their limi-tations and biases, and an awareness and appreciation of what other mental health professionals have to offer. It is clear that psychotherapists as a group will continue to be called upon to provide treatment to an increasingly broad range of patients, many of whom are difficult to treat. They will be asked to do so using a variety of strategies and techniques, applied under a variety of circumstances, in a variety of settings. For example, treatment is needed not only for the "worried well," but also for patients with complex dual diagnoses. In such clinical situations, being able to work (conjointly and) collaboratively with professionals from other disciplines is essential to ensuring quality of care. *It will be incumbent upon clinicians to remain sensitive to sociocultural differences.* Furthermore, whether one is treating a patient and/or a family on an inpatient or outpatient basis, or providing help following a disaster to organizations and communities, one must remain aware of what is possible to accomplish and what is not.

It is safe to assume that the influence of managed care, with its preoccupation with cost-effectiveness, and the demand for accountability, in the form of the increased demand that treatments be evidence-based, are not likely to diminish in the near future. Hence, psychotherapists will need to have available within their treatment arsenals short- as well as long-term treatment strategies and methods. Furthermore, such practices will need to be based on empirical research, or they may not be covered by insurance, and might even be considered unethical.

While no single psychotherapist can necessarily master all of these elements so that he or she can provide effective care to the full range of patients no matter what the circumstances, each will need to be well schooled in multiple approaches to treatment, without being casually eclectic. A core set of fundamental beliefs, values, and ethical standards will be needed to anchor this level of flexibility. Furthermore, whatever form of treatment he or she provides, it will be essential to understand the significant contribution of the therapist's self as person to the interpersonal process of psychotherapy. Increased self-awareness will also be needed to determine what patients, methods, and theories of psychotherapy one can work with effectively. Making this determination will require the integration of personal and professional development. The task of integrating the personal and the professional, in our view, can best be accomplished by therapists engaging in personal psychotherapy.

From this perspective, it is also clear that the knowledge base for the next generation of psychotherapists will need to expand. Psychotherapists, for example, will need to know more about developments in neuroscience and psychopharmacology. They also will need to become sophisticated consumers of research on psychotherapeutic process and outcome. They will need to learn how to make use of new approaches that appear to be promising. Positioning oneself to be equipped to incorporate into one's arsenal those approaches supported by research will become increasingly important.

At a broader level, psychotherapists in the next generation will need to be trained to manage the stress of the occupation, adapt to changing circumstances, and maintain their core identities and values—all while learning to make a living! Three central lifelong challenges must be repeatedly faced by all psychotherapists: (1) how to remain sufficiently open to permit new learning/growth as a person and as a professional; (2) how to most effectively use oneself in the treatment process; and (3) how to maintain resilience, arrive at a viable balance between professional and personal concerns, and continue to function in a committed, vibrant, and authentic fashion.

Stages of Therapist Development

One area of interest that we plan to investigate is whether we can identify stages of therapist development. Apart from the contributions of Ronnestad and Skovholt (2003) and Orlinsky & Ronnestad (2005), relatively little systematic research has been conducted in this area. Nevertheless, we believe that it is worth having a closer look to try to determine how professional psychotherapists develop over their careers, and how that developmental process affects both their personal and professional lives. Is there a discernible pattern to such development? Can common features be identified? How important are certain aspects of development? Is there an optimal sequence that should be followed to become an effective and successful psychotherapist? If, for example, we can outline a series of developmental stages, each of which contains a specific task or set of tasks to be negotiated and mastered, it may be possible to draw some important implications for therapist selection, education, and training and for therapists' future growth, development, and sustainability.

In this connection, it is important to acknowledge that we will be working with a limited database from which to draw generalizations. Our efforts to postulate a theory of therapist development will not be based upon a large stratified sample drawn from multiple countries (Orlinsky & Ronnestad., 2005). Rather, our data will largely be gleaned from those who have contributed to the available literature (e.g., Sussman, 1992, 1995, 2007), plus self-reports, reflections, and observations gathered by our own chosen group of authors, each of whom has taught, supervised, and/or treated many psychotherapists over the years. Our hope is that these sources of information, coupled with our own experiences, will enable us to formulate some useful hypotheses about the complex nature and interrelatedness of professional and personal development for psychotherapists.

Integrating Personal and Professional Experiences

One of the issues we are addressing in this volume is how personal and professional experiences become integrated in the developing therapist. As indicated, we will be exploring the influence of therapists' early life experiences on their professional development, as well as their relationships with mentors and other role models, the wounds they experience as they go through life, and the personal treatment they engage in. At the same time, we will be looking at the professional experiences developing therapists have, including the didactic preparation they engage in, their early clinical experiences, and their supervisory experiences both during training and thereafter. It is of course impossible to specify precisely how all of these various experiences influence how therapists develop, at least in part because it is undoubtedly different for different people, but our contention is that these experiences have great mutual influence on the developing therapist, and are usually important contributors to how therapists ultimately come to work.

This brings up the whole issue of "clinical intuition." What exactly is it? Some people see it as "flying by the seat of one's pants," the notion being that there are some people who have excellent inherent intuition about things, while others presumably do not. While there may well be innate differences along this dimension between people entering the mental health field, our conviction is that intuition is not random; rather, it is developed and cultivated (Lomas, 1993). We believe that one's intuition is in fact informed by our cumulative developmental experiences at both the personal and professional levels. Our life experiences, our clinical experiences, what we learn in supervision, what we learn about ourselves in our personal treatment, and our didactic preparation all come to inform what is called our "intuition." Thus, an important premise of this volume is that understanding as much as we can about the formative influences on developing therapists will help us demystify the concept of "intuition" and help us understand what influences contribute to becoming an effective clinician.

Life is an ongoing learning experience. Everything that we experience potentially contributes to what we learn about ourselves and the lives of those with whom we come in contact, both in the professional context and in every other aspect of our lives. At the most obvious level, developing therapists have personal relationships of all kinds, from which they have the opportunity to learn about what happens when people attempt to relate to each other. All therapists experience the wide array of affects that inevitably arise as we go through life: anxiety, fear, sadness, and even despair. It is our contention that those who learn and grow from these experiences are likely to be more effective therapists than those who do not. As therapists have come to appreciate the reality that they contribute a great deal to the dynamic that unfolds between them and their patients, it has become clear how important it is for us to understand as much as we can about how a developing therapist's personal experiences contribute to the kind of professional he or she becomes.

The Concept of the "Good Therapist"

Implicit in our exploration of the developmental trajectory for therapists are notions about what makes for a good therapist. This of course is a complicated and layered question. For a comprehensive discussion of research findings linking specific therapist characteristics with successful therapeutic outcome, the reader is referred to Garfield and Bergin's *Handbook of Psychotherapy and Behavior Change* (1990). Is it even reasonable to posit that there is such a thing as a "good therapist"? Given the variety of approaches to treatment that exist, as well as the enormous variability among patients who present for treatment, perhaps it is more accurate to say that there are many kinds of good therapists, and that a good therapist for some kinds of patients may be quite different from a good therapist for other kinds of patients.

And yet perhaps it is possible to identify certain characteristics that most people would agree are part and parcel of what is necessary to be a good therapist, regardless of the theoretical approach employed. For instance, we would suggest that certain interpersonal skills are necessities for all good therapists. An example would be the ability to understand the experience of others. This is certainly difficult to measure, but that does not mean that it is a meaningless statement. The phenomenological experience of those who present themselves for treatment needs to be accurately understood if therapy is to have any chance to succeed.

A closely related interpersonal skill that characterizes all good therapists is the ability to communicate empathy in a way that is credible and can be taken in. Patients who experience their therapists as being able to feel, and vicariously experience, what they are going through in their lives have a much better chance of finding treatment beneficial than those who do not.

To be able to understand and empathize with their patients, therapists need to get outside themselves. Countertransferential feelings get induced in therapists all the time; the difference between good therapists and those who are less so is the ability of the former to recognize and keep in check what is evoked in them, to not enact their emotional experiences but use them in the service of understanding their relationships with those they treat, and to keep their focus on what they are learning about their patients' experience of their lives.

Once a patient's life experience is well understood, and credible empathy is communicated in an ongoing fashion, the question is how this material is massaged so that treatment becomes a transforming experience. A premise of this book is that good therapists need to find ways to utilize their personas toward this therapeutic end. It is not simply a matter of applying therapeutic technique for the betterment of our patients. Rather, it is a matter of entering a two-person field (or multi-person field, if one is working with a group, couple, or family) and utilizing oneself in the therapeutic relationship in such a way as to create a space from which the patient can emerge transformed. Thus, good therapists are ones who incorporate what they have learned from others into an approach in which they utilize their selves and their sensibilities in their efforts to effectively relate to their patients. This premise is not one shared just by psychodynamically oriented therapists; as you will see in Chapter 10, it is one to which an increasing number of cognitive-behavioral therapists subscribe as well.

Much more can be said about what constitutes a good therapist. For instance, good therapists are willing to acknowledge error and learn from their experience. They recognize that one never "arrives" at a final point in the developmental process; rather, one must continue to learn, evolve, and grow as long as one continues to do the work. They remain humble in the face of the enormous challenge of playing a role in effectuating change in those who come to them for treatment. We hope to shed further light on the question of what constitutes a good therapist as we explore the developmental journey that therapists take as they evolve into the clinicians they become.

Organization of this Volume

In organizing the chapters you will be reading as you proceed through this volume, we have tried to take a more-or-less sequential approach, taking up issues as they typically emerge in the developing clinician's unfolding life. Having said this, we are well aware that different individuals have experiences that occur at different points in their lives. For instance, some clinicians might have an experience with a mentor or other kind of role model that shapes them early in their life experience, while others might have such an experience much later in their development. Nevertheless, there is a logic to how we have arranged this volume. Let us describe the chapters you will be reading in the order in which we have sequenced them.

We begin with the chapter on early life experiences. The author of chapter 2, John O'Leary, PhD, is a supervisor and faculty member at the William Alanson White Institute, a well-regarded psychoanalytic institute in New York City. He brings an analyst's sensibility to his depiction of the contribution of early life experiences to therapist development, acknowledging the contributions of genetics and environmental influences on the developing clinician as well. His focus on psychological-mindedness and resilience is a useful antidote to those who focus on the wish to master unresolved conflicts as the main reason most therapists enter the field.

We then move on to a chapter on the influence of mentors and other role models. As acknowledged above, this kind of experience can occur at almost any point in a clinician's development, but many do point to early life experiences with such people as formative in their development. Robin Gayle, PhD, MFT, is a psychology professor in California and has done a great deal of writing in this area. Dr. Gayle's focus is not so much on the characteristics of mentors and other role models, which obviously are vastly different for different people, but rather on the way in which the relationship between the mentor and mentee unfolds. She underscores that these relationships afford the mentee the opportunity for a relational and intersubjective experience that can serve as a model for the quality of relationship therapists seek to establish with their patients.

Chapter 4 focuses on the didactic preparation that beginning clinicians typically go through before they begin to work with patients. We are well aware that this too differs from setting to setting, and from discipline to discipline. But for the most part didactic preparation precedes initial clinical encounters. Victor L. Schermer, MA, LPC, CAC, a private practitioner in Philadelphia and one of the editors of this overall volume, has undertaken to write this chapter. He presents us with a comprehensive discussion of the variety of forms that didactic preparation takes, as well as the role it plays in overall clinician development.

Jerome S. Gans, MD, then takes up the area of the early clinical experiences that all developing clinicians have, and the disproportionate influence they invariably have on therapist development. In Chapter 5 Dr. Gans, an Associate Clinical Professor of Psychiatry at Harvard, does a masterful job of describing some of the conundrums that beginning clinicians often encounter when they start treating patients. He articulates a set of critical tasks to be faced, and then identifies a series of desirable traits that clinicians will ideally emerge with that set them on the road to becoming effective therapists.

Beginning clinical experiences are almost always accompanied by clinical supervision, so Chapter 6 takes up the complexities of the supervisor–supervisee relationship, and the outcomes that ideally emerge from these experiences for the developing clinician. Molyn Leszcz, MD, FRCPC, a Professor of Psychiatry at the University of Toronto, describes a model of supervision that aims to facilitate trainees' synthesizing an identity that balances their professional and personal selves. While he draws a clear distinction between supervision and psychotherapy, he puts forth a model that is highly personal, and emphasizes the transmission of the core values of the field of psychotherapy, the crucial importance of the clinician being able to self-reflect, and the central importance of establishing relationships with patients that are respectful and have boundaries.

Chapter 7 focuses on the personal treatment that a high percentage of therapists choose to engage in, often for a combination of personal and professional reasons. Personal treatment is typically not required in generic therapist training programs, though it certainly is in specialty training programs such as psychoanalysis. Nevertheless, there is evidence that a high percentage of developing clinicians voluntarily enter into treatment. Suzanne B. Phillips, PsyD, ABPP, CGP, FAGPA, an Adjunct Professor of Psychology at Long Island University, describes the enormous number of benefits that can derive from a successful personal treatment experience, particularly in terms of the recognition of the importance of the person of the therapist in the therapeutic encounter. She describes what developing clinicians can learn from their own treatment experience: an awareness of how much a therapist's reliability and commitment facilitates the treatment process; the central importance of a therapist's warmth and empathy; the crucial importance of a therapist's patience and tolerance; the opportunity to see that therapy can work;

and increased self-awareness, self-esteem, and openness to genuine human relating.

In Chapter 8 we then turn to the idea of the therapist as "wounded healer." Cecil A. Rice, PhD, co-founder and president of the Boston Institute for Psychotherapy, elaborates this idea, starting from the premise that wound-edness is universal, and that what distinguishes good therapists is their will-ingness, and even desire, to acknowledge their scars, to understand them as well as they can, and to live with them in a self-aware fashion. He argues that unrecognized woundedness is an impediment to the healing process.

We then take a turn in the direction of discussing one of the most momentous developments in the field of psychotherapy in some time: namely, the increasing emphasis on evidence-based practice. Along with the increas-ingly pervasive presence of managed care, with its profound impact on how clinicians practice, the focus on evidence-based practice confronts therapists with a new set of challenges, and coming to terms with it is appropriately construed as a developmental challenge. Debra Theobald McClendon, PhD, and Gary M. Burlingame, PhD, both from Brigham Young University, address this phenomenon and describe their approach to evidence-based practice (which they call "practice-based evidence"), placing it within the larger con-text of evidence-based practice and elaborating its many potential benefits.

When we organized this volume, we were keenly aware that the authors we were inviting to write chapters were all from the world of psychodynamic treatment, broadly defined. We came to see this as a limitation, and decided that we would do well to include a chapter on another widely-used approach to treatment: cognitive-behavioral therapy (CBT). Edmund C. Neuhaus, PhD, ABPP, an Assistant Clinical Professor of Psychology at Harvard, agreed to write the chapter, and more specifically to address the question of whether and how the utilization of the therapist's person is important in the practice of CBT. As we learned from working with Dr. Neuhaus, this is a controversial matter in the CBT world. You will see from reading his contribution that there is an increasing view among CBT practitioners that the person of the CBT therapist is indeed an important contributor to the treatment experi-ence, even when the treatment that is being delivered is manualized.

Finally, we have a chapter on the status of psychotherapy process and outcome research, and its implications for therapist development. Shannon Wiltsey Stirman, PhD, currently a Clinical Research Psychologist in the Women's Health Sciences Division of the National Center for PTSD in Boston, and Paul Crits-Christoph, PhD, a Professor of Psychology at the University of Pennsylvania, have written just such a review, and offer a variety of ideas about therapist development that emanate from the current state of knowledge in our field.

The book concludes with a chapter by the co-editors of the volume in which we summarize and integrate the salient points made in each chapter of the volume, propose a model for therapist development, and offer a set of recom-mendations for therapist selection, training, lifelong learning, and self-care.

References

Ahn, H., & Wampold, B. E. (2001). Where oh where are the specific ingredients? A meta-analysis of component studies in counseling and psychotherapy. *Journal of Counseling Psychology*, 48, 251–257.

American Psychological Association. (2002). *Guidelines on Multicultural Education, Training, Research, Practice and Organizational Change for Psychologists*. Washington, D.C.: Author.

Aron, L. (1996). *A Meeting of Minds: Mutuality in Psychoanalysis*. Hillsdale, NJ: Analytic Press.

Baker, E. K. (2003). *Caring for Ourselves: A Therapist's Guide to Personal and Professional Well-Being*. Washington, D.C.: American Psychological Association.

Baruth, L., & Manning, M. L. (2003). *Multicultural Counseling and Psychotherapy: A Lifespan Development* (3rd ed.). Pacific Grove, CA: Brooks/Cole.

Basecu, S. (1990). Tools of the trade: The use of self in psychotherapy. *Group*, 14, 157–165.

Belson, R. (1992). Therapist burnout. *Family Therapy Networker*, p. 22.

Bergin, A. E., & Garfield, S. L. (Eds.) (1971). *Handbook of Psychotherapy and Behavior Change* (1st ed.), New York: Wiley.

Bergin, A. E., & Garfield, S. L. (Eds.) (1994). *Handbook of Psychotherapy and Behavior Change* (4th ed.), New York: Wiley.

Bernard, H. S. (Ed.). (2008). On becoming a group therapist: Personal journeys. *Group*, 32, 93–144.

Bernard, H., Burlingame, G., Flores, P., Greene, L., Joyce, A., Kobos, J., Lesczc, M., MacNair-Semands, R., Piper, W., McEnaeny, A., Feriman, D. (2009). Clinical practice guidelines for group psychotherapy. *International Journal of Group Psychotherapy*, 58(4), 455–542.

Bike, D. S., Norcross, J. C., & Schatz, D. (2009). Processes and outcomes of psychotherapists' personal therapy: Replication and extension 20 years later. *Psychotherapy Theory, Research, Practice, Training*, 46:1, 19–31.

Bohart, A. C., O'Hara, M., & Leitner, L. M. (1998). Empirically violated treatments: Disenfranchisement of humanistic and other psychotherapies. *Psychotherapy Research*, 8, 141–157.

Brabender, V. (2006). The ethical group therapist. *International Journal of Group Psychotherapy*, 56(4), 395–414.

Brenner, A. M. (2006). The role of personal psychodynamic psychotherapy in becoming a competent psychiatrist. *Harvard Review of Psychiatry*, 14(5), 268–272.

Brinson, J., & Cervantes, J. (2003). Recognizing ethnic/racial biases and discriminatory practices through self-supervision. In J. A. Kotter & W. F. Jones (Eds.), *Doing Better*. New York: Brunner/Routledge.

Budman, S. H., Demby, A., Soldz, S., & Merry, J. (1996). Time-limited group psychotherapy for patients with personality disorders: Outcomes and dropouts. *International Journal of Group Psychotherapy*, 46, 357–377.

Burlingame, G. M., & Beecher, M. (2008). New directions and resources in group psychotherapy: introduction to the special issue. *Journal of Clinical Psychology*, 64(11), 1197–1205.

Burlingame, G. M., & Beecher, M. (in press). Models of evidence-based group treatment: What's available? *Journal of Clinical Psychology*.

Burlingame, G. M., MacKenzie, K. R., & Strauss, B. (2004a). Small group treatment: Evidence for effectiveness and mechanisms of change. In M. J. Lambert (Ed.), *Bergin and Garfield's Handbook of Psychotherapy and Behavior Change* (5th ed., pp.647–696). New York: Wiley.

Burlingame, G. M., MacKenzie, K. R., & Strauss, B. (2004b). *Evidence-Based Group Treatment: Matching Models with Disorders and Patients.* Washington, D.C.: American Psychological Association Press.

Carter Center (2003). Rosalynn Carter Symposium on Mental Health. Retrieved January 21, 2005, from www.Cartercenter.org.

Chambless, D. L., & Ollendick, T. H. (2001). Empirically supported psychological interventions: Controversies and evidence. *Annual Review of Psychology, 52,* 685–716.

Crits-Christophe, P., Baranackie, K., Kurcias, J. S., Luborsky, L., McClelland, T., et al. (1991). Meta-analysis of therapist effects in psychotherapy outcome studies. *Psychotherapy Research, 1,* 81–91.

Christensen, H., Griffiths, K. M., & Jorm, A. F. (2004). Delivering interventions of depression by using the Internet: randomized controlled trial. *British Medical Journal, 328*(7434), 265.

Comas-Díaz, L. (2005). Becoming a multicultural psychotherapist: the confluence of culture, ethnicity, and gender. *Journal of Clinical Psychology, 61*(8), 973–981.

Cottone, R. R., & Tarvydas, V. M. (2003). *Ethical and Professional Issues in Counseling* (2nd ed.). Upper Saddle River, NJ: Prentice Hall.

Crits-Christoph, P., Barananckie, K., Kurcias, J. S., Carroll, K., Luborsky, L., McLellan, T., et al. (1991). Meta-analysis of therapist effects in psychotherapy outcome studies. *Psychotherapy Research, 1,* 81–91.

Cross, M. C., & Papadopoulos, L. (2001). *Becoming a Therapist: A Manual for Personal and Professional Development.* UK: Routledge.

Davanloo, H. (2001). *Intensive Short-Term Dynamic Psychotherapy.* New York: Wiley.

Debiak, D. (2007). Attending to diversity in group psychotherapy: an ethical imperative. *International Journal of Group Psychotherapy, 57,* 49–59.

Deutsch, C. J. (1984). Self-reported sources of stress among psychotherapists. *Professional Psychology: Research and Practice, 15,* 833–845.

Deutsch, C.J. (1985). A survey of therapists' personal problems and treatment. *Professional Psychology: Research and Practice, 16,* 305–315.

Dlugos, R. F., & Friedlander, M. L. (2001). Passionately committed psychotherapists: A qualitative study of their experiences. *Professional Psychology: Research and Practice, 32,* 298–304.

Dryden, W., & Spurling, L. (Eds.) (1989). *On Becoming a Psychotherapist.* London: Tavistock/Routledge.

Edelwich, J., & Brodsky, A. M. (1980). *Burn-out.* New York: Human Sciences Press.

Eddy, K. T., Dutra, L. Bradley, R., & Westen, D. (2004). A multidimensional meta-analysis of psychotherapy and psychopharmacology for obsessive-compulsive disorder. *Clinical Psychology Review, 24,* 1011–1030.

Ellis, A. (2005). Why I (really) became a psychotherapist. *Journal of Clinical Psychology, 61*(8), 945–948.

Engel, J. (2008). *American Therapy: The Rise of Psychotherapy in the United States.* New York: Gotham Books.

Farber, B. A. (1990). Burnout in psychotherapists: Incidence, types, and trends. *Psychotherapy in Private Practice, 8*(1), 35–44.

Farber, B. A., Manevich, I., Metzger, J., & Saypol, E. (2005). Choosing psychotherapy as a career: why did we cross that road? *Journal of Clinical Psychology*, 61(8), 1009–1031.

Fish, J. M. (1996). *Culture and Therapy*. Northvale, NJ: Aronson.

Fosshage, J. L. (2003). Contextualizing self psychology and relational psychoanalysis: Bi-directional influence and proposed syntheses. *Contemporary Psychoanalysis*, 39, 411–448.

Frank, J. D., & Frank, J. B. (1991). *Persuasion and Healing: A Comparative Study of Psychotherapy* (3rd ed.), Baltimore, MD: Johns Hopkins University Press.

Freudenberger, H. J. (1986). The health professional in treatment: Symptoms, dynamics and treatment issues. In C. D. Scott & J. Hawk (Eds.), *Heal Thyself: The Health of Health Care Professionals*. New York: Brunner Mazel.

Garfield, S. L., & Bergin, A. E. (Eds.) (1978). *Handbook of Psychotherapy and Behavior Change* (2nd ed.). New York: Wiley.

Garfield, S. L., & Bergin, A. E. (Eds.) (1986). *Handbook of Psychotherapy and Behavior Change* (3rd ed.). New York: Wiley.

Garfield, S. L., & Bergin, A. E. (Eds.) (1990). *Handbook of Psychotherapy and Behavior Change* (4th ed.). New York: Wiley.

Gay, P. (1988). *Freud: A Life for our Time*. New York: Norton.

Geller, J. D., Norcross, J. C., & Orlinsky, D. E. (Eds.) (2005). *The Psychotherapist's Own Psychotherapy: Patient and Clinician Perspectives*. New York: Oxford University Press.

Goldfried, M. R. (Ed.) (2001). *How Therapists Change: Personal and Professional Reflections*. Washington, D.C.: American Psychological Association.

Griffiths, K. M., & Christensen, H. (2007). Internet-based mental health programs: a powerful tool in the rural medical kit. *Australian Journal of Rural Health*, 15(2), 81–87.

Guy, J. D. (1987). *The Personal Life of the Psychotherapist: The Impact of Clinical Practice on the Therapist's Intimate Relationships and Well-Being*. New York: Wiley.

Horgan, C. M., Merrick, E. L., Reif, S., & Stewart, M. (2007). Internet-based behavioral health services in health. *Psychiatric Services*, 58(3), 307.

Hubble, M. A., Duncan, B. L., & Miller, S. D. (1999). *The Heart and Soul of Change: What Works in Psychotherapy*. Washington, D.C.: American Psychological Association.

Jennings, L., & Skovholt, T. M. (1999). The cognitive, emotional and relational characteristics of master therapists. *Journal of Counseling Psychology*, 46, 3–11.

Jung, C. (1989). (Ed. by Aniela Jaffe). *Memories, Dreams, and Reflections*. New York: Vintage Books.

Kazdin, A. E. (2005). Treatment outcomes, common factors, and continued neglect of mechanisms of change. *Clinical Psychology: Science and Practice*, 12, 184–188.

Kessler, D., Lewis, G., Kaur, S., Wiles, N., King, M., Welch, S., Sharp, D. J., Araya, R., Hollinghurst, S., & Peters, T. J. (2009). Therapist-delivered internet psychotherapy for depression in primary care: a randomized controlled trial. *Lancet*, 374(9690), 628–634.

Klein, R. H. (1985). Some principles of short-term group psychotherapy. *International Journal of Group Psychotherapy*, 35, 309–330.

Klein, R. H. (2009). Toward the establishment of evidence-based practices in group psychotherapy. *International Journal of Group Psychotherapy*, 58(4), 441–454.

Klein, R. H., & Phillips, S. (Eds.) (2008). *Public Mental Health Service Delivery Protocols: Group Interventions for Disaster Preparedness and Response*. New York: American Group Psychotherapy Association.

Klein, R. H., & Schermer, V. L. (Eds.) (2000). *Group Psychotherapy for Psychological Trauma*. New York: Guilford Press.

Kottler, J. A. (1986). *On Being a Therapist*. San Francisco: Jossey-Bass.

Kottler, J. A. (1999). *The Therapist's Workbook: Self-Assessment, Self-Care, and Self-Improvement Exercises for Mental Health Professionals*. San Francisco: Jossey-Bass.

Kottler, J. A. (2003). *On Being a Therapist* (rev. ed.). San Francisco: Jossey Bass.

Lambert, M. L. (2004). *Bergin and Garfield's Handbook of Psychotherapy and Behavior Change* (5th ed.). New York: Wiley.

Leichsenring, F. (2005). Are psychodynamic and psychoanalytic therapies effective? A review of empirical data. *International Journal of Psychoanalysis*, 86, 841–868.

Lomas, P. (1993). *Cultivating Intuition: An Introduction to Psychotherapy*. New York: Jason Aronson.

Luborsky, L. (1992). The Penn research project. In D. K. Freedheim (Ed.), *History of Psychotherapy: A Century of Change* (pp. 396–400). Washington, D.C.: American Psychological Association.

MacKenzie, K. R. (1997). *Time-Managed Group Psychotherapy: Effective Clinical Applications*. Washington, D.C.: American Psychiatric Association.

Mahoney, M. J. (2001). Behaviorism, cognitivism and constructivism: Reflections on peopleand patterns in my intellectual development. In M. R. Goldfried (Ed.), *How Therapists Change: Personal and Professional Reflections*. Washington, D.C.: American Psychological Association.

Mahrer, A. R. (2005). What inspired me to become a psychotherapist? *Journal of Clinical Psychology*, 61, 957–964.

Mann, J. (1973). *Time-Limited Psychotherapy*. Cambridge, MA: Harvard University Press.

Marks, I., & Cavanaugh, K. (2009). Computer-aided psychological treatments: Evolving issues. *Annual Review of Clinical Psychology*, 5, 121–141.

Marks, I., Cavanaugh, K., & Gega, L. (2007). Computer-aided psychotherapy: Revolution or bubble? *British Journal of Psychiatry*, 191, 471–473.

Markus, H. R. (2008). Pride, prejudice and ambivalence: Toward a unified theory of race and ethnicity. *American Psychologist*, 63, 651–670.

Maslach, C. (1982). *Burnout: The Cost of Caring*. Upper Saddle River, NJ: Prentice Hall.

Maslach, C. (1986). Stress, burnout and workaholism. In R. R. Killburg, P. E. Nathan, & R. W. Thoreson (Eds.), *Professionals in Distress*. Washington, D.C.: American Psychological Association.

Maslach, C., & Leiter, M. P. (1997). *The Truth About Burnout*. San Francisco: Jossey-Bass.

Miller, B. (2007). Innovations: psychotherapy: what sustains commitment to the practice of psychotherapy? *Psychiatric Services*, 58, 174–176.

Millon, T., Millon, C., & Antoni, M. (1986). Sources of emotional and mental disorders among psychologists: A career perspective. In R. R. Killburg, P. E. Nathan, & R. Thoreson (Eds.), *Professionals in Distress*. Washington, D.C.: American Psychological Association.

Mitchell, S. A. (1988). *Relational Concepts in Psychoanalysis*. Cambridge: Harvard University Press.

Norcross, J. (2002a). Empirically supported relationships. In J. C. Norcross (Ed.), *Psychotherapy Relationships That Work: Therapist Contributions and Responsiveness to Patients* (pp. 3–16). New York: Oxford University Press.

Norcross, J. C. (2000). Psychotherapist self-care: Practitioner-tested, research-oriented strategies. *Professional Psychology: Research and Practice*, 31, 710–714.

Norcross, J.C. (Ed.) (2002b). *Psychotherapy Relationships That Work: Therapist Contributions and Responsiveness to Patients*. New York: Oxford University Press.

Norcross, J. C. (2005). The psychotherapist's own psychotherapy: Educating and developing psychologists. *American Psychologist*, doi: 10.1037/0003-066X.60.8.840.

Norcross, J. C., Beutler, L. E., & Levant, R. F. (Eds.) (2005). *Evidence-Based Practices in Mental Health: Debate and Dialogue on the Fundamental Questions*. Washington, D.C.: American Psychological Association.

Norcross, J. C., & Farber, B. A. (2005). Choosing psychotherapy as a career: beyond "I want to help people." *Journal of Clinical Psychology*, 61(8), 939–943.

Ogden, T. H. (1994). The analytic third: Working with intersubjective clinical facts. *International Journal of Psycho-Analysis*, 75, 3–19.

Orlinsky, D. E. (2005). Becoming a psychotherapist: a psychodynamic memoir and meditation. *Journal of Clinical Psychology*, 61 (8), 999–1007.

Orlinsky, D. E., Norcross, J. C., Ronnestad, M. H., & Wiseman, H. (2005). Outcomes and impacts of the psychotherapist's own psychotherapy: A research review. In J. D. Geller, J. C. Norcross, & D. E. Orlinsky (Eds.), *The Psychotherapist's Own Psychotherapy: Patient and Clinician Perspectives*. New York: Oxford University Press.

Orlinsky, D. E. & Ronnestad, M. H. (2005). *How Psychotherapists Develop*. Washington, D.C.: The American Psychological Association.

Penzer, W. N. (1984). The psychopathology of the psychotherapist. *Psychotherapy in Private Practice*, 2(2), 51–59.

Pope, K. S., & Vasquez, M. J. T. (1991). *Ethics in Psychotherapy and Counseling: A Practical Guide for Psychologists*. San Francisco: Jossey-Bass.

Pope-Davis, D. B., & Coleman, H. L. K. (2001). *The Interaction of Race, Class, and Gender: Implications for Multicultural Counseling*. Thousand Oaks, CA: Sage.

Reppen, J. (Ed.). (1998). *Why I Became a Psychotherapist*. New Jersey: Jason Aronson.

Rhead, J. (Ed.) (2006). Psychotherapy as calling, way of life, spiritual path, and political philosophy. *Voices*, 42, 1–85.

Rippere, V., & Williams, R. (Eds.) (1985). *Wounded Healers*. New York: Wiley.

Robinson, T. L., & Howard-Hamilton, M. F. (2000). The convergence of race, ethnicity and gender. Upper Saddle River, NJ: Merrill.

Ronnestad, M. H., & Skovholt, T. M. (2003). The journey of the counselor and therapist: Research findings and perspectives on professional development. *Journal of Career Development,* 30, 5–44.

Saakvitne, K. W., & Pearlman, L. A. (1995). *Trauma and the Therapist*. New York: Norton.

Sherman, M. D., & Thelan, H. M. (1998). Distress and professional impairment among psychologists in private practice. *Professional Psychology: Research and Practice*, 29, 79–85.

Siegel, D. J. (1999). *The Developing Mind*. New York: The Guilford Press.

Siegel, D. J., & Hartzell, M. (2003). *Parenting From the Inside Out*. New York: Jeremy P. Tarcher/Penguin.

Sifneos, P. (1987). *Short-Term Dynamic Psychotherapy, Evaluation and Technique* (2nd ed.). New York: Springer-Verlag.

Simon, G. E., Ludman, E. J., & Rutter, C. M. (2009). Incremental benefit and cost of telephone care management and telephone psychotherapy for depression in primary care. *Archives of General Psychiatry*, 66(10), 1081–1090.

Simon, G. E., Ludman, E. J., Operskalski, B., & Von Korff, M. (2004). Telephone psychotherapy and telephone management for primary care patients starting antidepressant treatment: a randomized controlled trial. *Journal of the American Medical Association*, 292(8), 935–942.

Skovholt, T. M. (2001). *The Resilient Practitioner: Burnout Prevention and Self-Care Strategies*. Boston, MA: Allyn & Bacon.

Skovholt, T. M., & Jennings, L. (Eds.) (2004). *Master Therapists: Exploring Expertise in Therapy and Counseling*. Boston, MA: Allyn & Bacon.

Skovholt, T. M., & Ronnestad, M. H. (1995). *The Evolving Professional Self: Stages and Themes in Therapist and Counselor Development*. New York: Wiley.

Stadler, H. A. (1999). Impairment in mental health professionals. In E. R. Welfel & R. E. Ingersoll (Eds.), *The Mental Health Desk Reference* (pp. 413–418). New York: Wiley.

Stolorow, R. D., & Atwood, G. E. (1992). *Contexts of Being: The Intersubjective Foundations of Psychological Life*. Hillsdale, NJ: Analytic Press.

Strozier, C. (2001). *Heinz Kohut: The Making of a Psychoanalyst*. New York: Farrar, Straus & Giroux.

Sue, D. W., & Sue, S. (1999). *Counseling the Culturally Different*. New York: Wiley.

Sussman, M. B. (1992). *A Curious Calling: Unconscious Motivations for Practicing Psychotherapy*. New Jersey: Jason Aronson.

Sussman, M. B. (1995). *A Perilous Calling: The Hazards of Psychotherapy Practice*. New York: Wiley.

Sussman, M. B. (2007). *A Curious Calling*. New Jersey: Jason Aronson.

The President's New Freedom Commission (2004). Final report. Retrieved January 21, 2005, from www.mentalhealthcommission.gov.

The therapist as a neglected variable in psychotherapy research [Special series] (1997). *Clinical Psychology: Science and Practice*, 4, 40–89.

Truscott, D. (2010). *Becoming an Effective Psychotherapist: Adopting a Theory of Psychotherapy That's Right for You*. Washington, D.C.: American Psychological Association.

Truscott, D., & Crook, K. H. (2004). *Ethics for the Practice of Psychology in Canada*. Edmonton, Alberta, Canada: University of Alberta Press.

Wampold, B. E. (2001). *The Great Psychotherapy Debate: Models, Methods and Findings*. Mahwah, NJ: Erlbaum.

Wampold, B. E. (2007). Psychotherapy: The humanistic (and effective) treatment. *American Psychologist*, 62, 855–873.

Welfel, E. R. (2002). *Ethics in Counseling and Psychotherapy*. Pacific Grove, CA: Brooks/Cole.

2

Growing Up to Be a Good Psychotherapist, or Physician—Know Thyself!

John O'Leary

What inborn and acquired characteristics predispose an individual to become an effective, ethical and successful psychotherapist?

Is there a discernible developmental path, or a common base of experience, that suggests suitability for the impossible profession?

How might both predisposition and experience bear upon selection, training, and supervision of a new generation of therapists?

The answers to these questions require arduous pursuit of a moving target. A good psychotherapist is, obviously, the complex product of genetic endowment, environmental influence, and life experience. All the traits a therapist brings to training are further shaped by decades of socialization as student, patient, supervisee, and practitioner. The profession itself is in flux, undergoing tremendous shifts in theory and application, not to mention the demographics of patients and practitioners alike (Orlinsky & Ronnestad, 2004). To define and measure effectiveness in a significant sample of therapists over the continuum of their careers is a huge and costly undertaking. Even more daunting is the attempt to generalize meaningfully across the spectrum of contemporary theoretical persuasions and treatment modalities. The very idea of a "good therapist," and "good—for *whom?*" is open to argument.

This chapter makes no promise to settle it. This is, rather, a meditation on a number of topics the profession has long been criticized for avoiding. The discussion will be animated by other therapists' disclosures from informal interviews conducted by the author, and excerpts from published interviews such as the following from *How I Became a Therapist*:

> *It is consistent with my avowed skepticism to be skeptical of the usual explanations of how one becomes anything... I like to think that I have become what I always was. My historical tradition is a variety of Jewish freethinking with an outsider's sense of irony and play, a lack of conviction about authority, and a traditional entitlement to question what I am told...*
>
> (Reppen, 1998, p. 213)

The powerful example of self-scrutiny offered by Freud did not extend from the personal to the psychotherapeutic community at large. Therapists are at times willing, indeed eager, to disclose their own process and experience as professionals in a collegial way; however, the challenge of producing systematic, controlled, and quantifiable research has not been met.

The Research Dilemma

In a retrospective study, Fussell and Bonney (1990) noted that "Given the importance of the psychotherapist's personality in the treatment process, there has been relatively little empirical examination of the childhood experience of psychotherapists" (p. 506). The need for such research was apparent some 60 years before Michael Sussman (1992) wrote, "The influence of the therapist's personality and motivation on the therapeutic process remains a relatively neglected area of inquiry" (p. 4). This statement also appears in the second edition of his fine book, *A Curious Calling*, published 15 years later.

For a profession dedicated to self-examination, the failure to fully examine itself suggests, perhaps, a level of avoidance and denial. Psychotherapists, like patients, use such defenses to protect their egos. After years of training and practice, countless hours in personal therapy and supervision, and with an image to uphold, it may be hard for therapists to admit to residual difficulties in living. Unwillingness to keep probing the shifting substrata of motivation may indicate fear that the shoes of the wounded healer may fit their own feet.

If professionals tend to avoid the topic, others do not. Public perception of therapists has been shaped by considerable media attention that casts a humorous but decidedly negative light on the reasons for choosing the career, and hints at unresolved personal pathology continually affecting work with patients (Gabbard & Gabbard, 1999). Motives of profit and popularity continue to mitigate against accurate portrayal of the mental health profession in film and TV. As Orchowski (2006) observes, "stereotypes of cinema psychotherapy are unflattering to say the least" (p. 507).

A focused and thorough effort to study why people become therapists and how those reasons affect their work would enhance credibility, and invigorate both theory and practice. The implications for the selection, training, and supervision of candidates and for effectiveness, burnout rate, and ultimate career satisfaction are profound. Even more important, for psychotherapy to flourish in the new century, it is critical to promptly address the increasingly multicultural nature of a patient population that, so far, a largely mono-cultural population of clinicians has been expected to treat. Cultural competence, perhaps the primary professional issue of our time, is just beginning to have a major influence on training, practice, and research.

We must never stop our studying, learning from the insights of others, not as sycophants, or as ideological dilettantes, but always integrating, enriching, deepening our own understanding of what it is to be human. In effect, I am still becoming a psychotherapist now at the age of 70, and anticipate the process will go on for as long as I do.

(Reppen, 1998, p. 147)

Developmental Considerations

Fussell and Bonney (1990) addressed weaknesses they perceived in previous research, specifically the inappropriate choice of comparison groups, and the use of students as subjects. They compared early developmental histories of 42 psychotherapists and 38 physicists, median aged mid-forties, all of whom had worked in their fields for a minimum of 5 years, using instruments largely dependent on self-report. The empirical data supported the hypothesis that resolution of early childhood issues such as parent/child role reversal, abandonment, and family dysfunction results in an increased capacity for empathy and might relate to the choice to become a helping professional. The study concluded: "The childhood of psychotherapists involved pain but to a degree that enhanced, not extinguished, their continuing interest in people" (p. 509). The authors suggested that unresolved pain might impede empathic development, even hamper the ability to apply basic therapeutic strategies appropriately. Common sense would lead anyone to these unstartling conclusions.

This solid and straightforward study illustrates a central problem: research must of course have limitations. When the object of study is so complex, those very limitations can undercut the validity of findings or render them simplistic. These authors limited their study to the exploration of childhood experience at the expense of any given traits and qualities that might be in the mix, a major constraint. It should also be noted that, in contrast to the external objectivity of physicists, therapists are highly sensitized to early trauma. Constant immersion in subjectivity reinforces a way of seeing, and therefore *reporting*, psychic pain. Comparison groups of therapists of different theoretical persuasions, instead of physicists, might have made this study more convincing.

In an effort to map out a developmental trajectory for potential therapists, Ronnestad and Skovholt (2003) performed a cross-sectional and longitudinal study. They engaged 100 counselors and therapists as subjects, and applied results to a descriptive six-stage model of professional development. The lay helper, they said, guided mostly by commonsense conceptions of helping others, typically projects personal solutions for problems encountered. Identification, sympathy, and empathy are not yet clearly defined at the beginning helper stage. Subsequently, pressure to excel and avoid error may adversely affect the advanced student. The therapist engages in a deeper exploration into theory, profession, and self in the novice stage, to be followed by experienced and senior professional stages, when a clinical niche is found. With luck, wisdom follows.

These stages mark a long individuation process in which theory-bound approaches become more flexible, assured, and internal. The counselor/therapist relies on accumulated expertise in a slow, erratic learning trajectory that entails considerable anxiety but eventually becomes manageable. Through self-reflection and exposure to a widely varied client population, the practitioner achieves "a realignment from self as hero to client as hero." Optimal development, Ronnestad and Skovholt propose, depends on movement "from therapist/counselor power to client power" (p. 19).

This robust longitudinal study exemplifies the gold standard for research. The weakness of any stage theory, however, lies in the presumption of a tidy sequence that all too often disintegrates in the real world, where things rarely follow a linear path. For example, compelling interest in theory may come much later (or earlier) in the maturational process than the authors propose. They also did not consider how inborn traits and characteristics develop in a therapist over the course of the stages they define.

I absolutely rely on career inventories for vocational work with adolescents and college students interested in the helping professions. I don't think anybody else does. They're a great help.

(From informal interviews conducted by the author)

A Cross-Disciplinary Perspective

Since the 1940s, there has been a massive effort in the field of vocational psychology to show how professions differ from one another in terms of key traits. This research appears abundantly in the literature directed to vocational psychologists. It is, however, unread and underutilized by most psychotherapists (Whitfield et al., 2009). These solid and fruitful studies compare response patterns on standardized test items of established professionals such as psychologists (the segment that reports enjoyment in the profession) with those of the test-taker. Relevant to this discussion, there is considerable research (Holland, 1997; Loner & Adams, 1972) with fairly large sample sizes carried out using the Strong Interest Inventory and the Myers-Briggs Temperament Indicator (Sullivan & Hanson, 2004).

While this research is largely correlational, it provides useful outlines of personality pertaining to psychiatrists, psychologists, and social workers. Studies employing the Strong Interest Inventory find that members of the three professions have commonalities. They are attracted to the social professions by the underlying emphasis on helping. They share an interest in science (an investigative aspect) and the light it can shed on human personality and mental illness. There is, across the social professions, common evidence of delight in putting things together in new and interesting ways, a kind of puzzle solving (an integrative aspect), and additionally a theory-oriented, creative, or artistic bent.

Research with the Myers-Briggs Temperament Indicator also points to an intuitive-feeling pattern in psychologists. There is an orientation toward interpretation, seeing the big picture and grasping larger consequences. Myers-Briggs also identifies a strong academic or intellectual focus, although those who practice psychotherapy are found to make decisions largely on the basis of feelings, their own and those of other people.

Clearly, these assessment tools could and should play a more significant role in the identification of suitable candidates for careers in psychotherapy. It is only a small cross-disciplinary step to the field of vocational psychology. For this writer, inclusion of its valuable research contributions would be just the beginning of a meaningful dialogue with more distantly related disciplines and across wider theoretical divides.

I hope you don't just write about all the terrific things that made us become analysts, our curiosity, empathy and resilience. I hope you talk about the voyeuristic piece to it that allows entry to the darkest parts of a person's soul. And another thing is the narcissism. Where else do you get permission to examine all the feelings inside of you as the patient talks? You get to think constantly about yourself. Hopefully we do it to the benefit of the patient.

(From informal interviews conducted by the author)

The Importance of Conscious and Unconscious Factors

A Curious Calling (Sussman, 1992, 2007) remains one of the best recent explorations of the topic at hand. Using traditional paradigms for interpretation of nine therapist profiles, Sussman examines motivation through the prism of drive theory, oedipal resolution, self theory, and the theory of object relations. He looks only for the generally darker and *unconscious* aims, and the role pathology may play in choice of career, as well as the possible impact of these motivations (resolved or unresolved) in the analytic setting.

Sussman's thoughtful study reinforces the view that desire to resolve inner conflict is a powerful motivator to enter the profession. Understanding and mastery of these issues through analysis and clinical practice are found to contribute greatly to professional success. Failure to deal adequately with pathology that underlies career choice, or successful denial of it, can lead to malpractice and abuse. These conclusions, too, are unsurprising.

However, Sussman's suggestion that the psychological reasons for becoming a therapist are akin to those that lead a patient to seek it offers a breath of fresh air. He explores a level playing field where analyst and patient struggle with identical issues and conflicts. His presentation is remarkable in its sense of normality; it humanizes and demystifies the therapist.

The subjects in the small sample group demonstrate a familiar range of developmental experience. They report over- or under-protective parenting, family dysfunction, abandonment, depression and self-esteem issues, and early exposure to therapy. Their paths through training and career suggest relatively mild levels of pathology. While Sussman focuses on the unconscious motivations that could lead to trouble, any reader can identify with the personal histories of his subjects, and would feel at ease in the consulting room of any one of them.

Sussman's (1992) quest for pathology is modulated as well by a balanced and intersubjective view of the therapeutic relationship. He says, "The analyst is no longer the detached observer, but rather a co-participant whose behavior and personality shape the transference paradigm. Transference and countertransference, in fact are viewed as reciprocally generating and interpreting each other" (p. 10). Not all clinicians embrace this view.

Sussman (1992) dates his own curiosity about the profession to his first encounter with a therapist: "Why has he chosen this odd sort of work," he asks, "and what exactly does he get out of it?" (p. xiii). This points to the main problem in his approach. The moment this question arises, the days of innocence are numbered. Driven by innate desire to "figure things out," the nascent clinician is soon pressured to get things conscious, fast. How useful is it to rely on reports of unconscious motivation from therapists, much less compare them with reports from physicists, surgeons, or financial advisors who do not plumb their psyches as part of training for their professions?

Firmly directed in a quest for unconscious motivation at both ends of the career trajectory, Sussman also does not give sufficient credence to reasons readily available to consciousness. What about traits and characteristics like intelligence, or the determination to get through graduate school? What about altruism, curiosity, and emotional intelligence, the qualities often collectively referred to as psychological-mindedness? This writer argues that the picture is incomplete without examination of the innate traits and the *conscious* factors that contribute to psychological-mindedness.

> *As I look back today I fail to see any Euclidean straight line to my present day theoretical and clinical conceptions.*
> (Gerald Chrznowski, cited in Reppen, 1998, p. 64)

A Spectrum of Traits and Characteristics

An abundance of personal narrative in the literature attempts to put a human face on the practical, visceral aspects of clinical work, as well as the more conceptual issues pertaining to early development that Sussman deals with. A primary example is *Why I Became a Psychotherapist*, by Joseph Reppen (1998). He includes both the famous and the unknown, all still-living subjects, and focuses rather narrowly on conscious motivation to practice. The reports group in distinct categories, telling in themselves. Two prominent therapists in this group express doubt that it is possible to determine the reasons for choice of the profession, one reason for this being given in the quote from Chrznowski above.

Many therapists in Reppen's book appear to have overcome particularly difficult childhoods. The shadow of the Holocaust hangs over many of these personal histories. A large group of subjects report that they consider themselves better therapists because of early traumatic experience or illness in the family. One discloses that the "sense of vulnerability has been a major source of my love of learning, doing, and teaching psychoanalysis, and has always rung out as a critical counterpoint to what some others might easily misunderstand simply as a very ambitious wish to achieve and be admired" (p. 105).

Another group Reppen singles out immersed themselves in theory to escape their early problems; many found refuge in literature. As one respondent puts it: "I wonder if this is one of the unconscious motives that is involved in becoming a therapist—intimacy and emotionally intense interactions but with safe and clear boundaries, to use Hoffman's terms" (p.70). Strong mentors played an important role for many clinicians. Some recall that awareness, empathy, observation, and projection were strongly validated and, in some cases, the only qualities valued and accepted in their families of origin: "I brought the world to my mother through my active social life and my skills as a storyteller" (p. 217). Traits that are directly and indirectly related to psychological-mindedness were apparently early and carefully cultivated in a variety of ways.

Indeed, psychological-mindedness would be the best term to capture the outstanding and overriding commonality across all of Reppen's categories. Reading Reppen, Sussman, or the informal interviews conducted by this writer, the cumulative impression created is of what ordinary, nice, humble, and psychologically minded people most therapists must be.

> Predicting peoples' behavior and possible feeling was a game between my parents and myself.... Introspection, self-awareness, empathy, observation, creating stories, and projection were games that were encouraged. Later in life, I became aware of and grateful for the tremendous intellectual freedom they encouraged and required.
>
> (Reppen, 1998, p. 153)

Psychological-Mindedness

The very term *psychological-mindedness* affects the brain like a trick with mirrors: what attributes of mind contribute to the study of the mind, in self and others? The term tends to be tossed about casually, like an "eye for design," a "head for figures," or a "musical ear." But it is not jargon; this useful concept deserves legitimacy and definition.

Those who consider psychological-mindedness a good thing describe it as an inclination to grasp the emotional meaning of events at the individual, social, cultural, and even political level. It is seen as the moderator of an individual's perception of black and white, and the appreciation of subtle differences. Psychological-mindedness implies some fortuitous attraction and eventual wedding between subjectivity and objectivity.

Psychologically minded people do not think about the world in purely rational terms. They are in touch with emotional nuances in themselves and others; they integrate cognitive and affective components in an adaptive, emotionally rich way. Thus, the term can be seen as a form of curiosity, the desire to understand feelings and behavior.

Applebaum (1973) notes that "connections between affects and insight" and a grasp of "the emotional meaningfulness of events" has increasingly come to inform our understanding of the political, social, and cultural environment. This wholesome view implies that psychological-mindedness is essential not only for the therapist, but it is to be nurtured and developed in patients. It belongs, then, in the human rather than the exclusively professional domain. It is valued as an unconditionally "positive trait, a way of thinking that one should attempt to hone to a maximum degree" (p. 37).

Not everyone agrees. Since Freud's time, critics of psychoanalysis have railed at the promotion of too much introspection among patients and practitioners. By the 1960s, other voices began raising strong arguments disfavoring psychological-mindedness. Outside the field, as Farber (1989) observes, novelists have long preached about the potential ill effects of high levels of psychological-mindedness or self-reflectiveness. In *Notes from Underground*, Dostoevsky's protagonist declares that acute consciousness is a disease that results in the inability to engage in living. Similarly, D. H. Lawrence writes that passion is the ultimate peril of human consciousness, causing the demise of spontaneity and creativity. This is a very provocative view.

If, as Sussman (1992) states, "The psychotherapy setting provides opportunities for a level of human contact and closeness that is rarely achievable in social situations" (p. 115), it consequently attracts individuals with both assets and deficits in regard to the capacity for intimacy. Many studies have examined the therapist's use of the session to gratify neurotic needs at the expense of the patient (Guy, 1987; Henry et al., 1973). Indeed, application of psychological-mindedness in the service of avoiding or undermining intimacy is highly undesirable.

Farber (1989), in an early study, questions whether there can be too much of a good thing. He asks whether psychological-mindedness could undermine the positive, adaptive aspects of denial, and possibly create its own pathology. Applebaum (1973) has already concluded, however, that it "cannot occur 'excessively', nor are there 'optimal levels' beyond which dysfunctional consequences may occur" (p. 40). Here is a reflection of the two-edged argument regarding wounded healers and whether the wound may be central to the ability to heal or inimical to it. The psychologically minded reader will at least agree: there *is* no black and white!

For the purposes of this inquiry, the author posits psychological-mindedness as a capacity to perceive and experience feelings, emotional states, the nuances of these and conflicts between them, both in oneself and in others. This presumes empathy, an ability to adopt another's frame of reference, to feel what others feel. The empathic individual puts on someone else's shoes, but understands that the shoes are *not his*. Beyond this, the psychologically minded person can articulate these perceptions as well as make causal interpretations to another in a way that is emotionally attuned to what he or she can assimilate. Psychological-mindedness can be viewed as a developed capacity to organize and communicate empathic understanding in a meaningful way.

Certainly, psychological-mindedness is associated with a whole constellation of attributes considered desirable in a clinician that only begins with empathy. In addition, there is an intellectual, logical, or "left brain" aspect to the quality of psychological-mindedness that belongs in its definition. Experts at testing clinical hypotheses, establishing diagnoses, and making use of theoretical constructs are psychologically minded too, but in a different way. The term must be understood dimensionally if its study is to contribute significantly to the selection, education, and nurturance of a new generation of psychotherapists.

> *I began my own quest for intellectual satisfaction with the Russian literature beloved by my family, moved on to the French existentialists, then became interested in the work of Vonnegut. I could not pick up a book without being pulled into the inner world within its pages.... I became fascinated with the psychological underpinnings of virtually everything I had contact with... a hunger that could only be sated with further introspection and deeper immersion into the dynamics of human nature.*
>
> (Farber et al., 2005, p. 1021)

Other Gifts: Language and Altruism

Articulateness and a powerful interest in storytelling might be seen as the glue that binds this complex package together. Deep fascination with language and the drama of told experience is a striking commonality among professionals interviewed informally for this chapter, and cited as a desirable trait in psychotherapists by many writers and theorists. Investigation of potential therapists' narrative orientation and capacity to deal with symbolism and extended metaphor would contribute much to the discussion at hand.

Another desirable quality in a therapist, and arguably an aspect of psychological-mindedness, is the motivation to help people. The theme of altruism pervades all the interview material reviewed for this chapter. A concept that transcends mere helping, altruism is observable in animals and emerges early in the development of humans. Research indicates that one of the ways to derive meaning from one's own suffering is to help others (Staub & Vollhardt, 2008). Engaging in altruistic acts helps restore shattered assumptions about the benevolence of the world as well as about the value and worthiness of the self. Helping others increases self-efficacy. It is an effective coping mechanism and a possible pathway to healing.

Psychological-mindedness and associated attributes such as language skills and altruism cannot be viewed as independent of each other, and of course none exists fully realized at birth. The recipe to cook up an astute behaviorist or a sensitive interpersonalist (reverse the adjectives, if you prefer) might read very differently, indeed. Thus, while a tendency toward any specific attribute might be observed as an early indicator, psychological-mindedness must be seen developmentally, as a product of experience. In this dynamic, the specific episodes and conflicts of childhood may be less influential than how one deals with them.

> *After years of reciting permutations of my traumatic upbringing I began losing interest in how hurt I was. The wound that never heals meets the fire that never goes out in never-ending ways. I became less interested in my past than in getting on with my life.*
>
> (Reppen, 1998, p. 84)

The Quality of Resilience

In response to psychic injury, some individuals suffer a lifetime of disability; others develop coping mechanisms and learn to weave traumatic experience into the fabric of their lives in positive ways. Certainly, extremes of abuse might outweigh anyone's capacity for resilience, but a history so sheltered that it fails to test resilience might be seen as a disqualifying factor for the profession. This writer proposes that resilience is a vital component of psychological-mindedness and a critical attribute of the effective therapist.

Trauma literature currently provides the best point of entry to this important topic. White et al. (2008) examine the capacity for resilience in patients disabled by traumatic experience. Acknowledging the difficulty of broad definition, they see resilience as a function of three major variables: psychological and dispositional attitudes, family support and cohesion, and external support systems. The first of these, they suggest, has been over-emphasized. White et al. conclude that while closely linked to personality traits, which they describe as "stable over time," resilience is actually acquired, modifiable, and "learned rather than inborn."

The concept of resilience surfaces frequently in literature related to trauma (Taylor et al., 2000; Tiet et al., 1998; Wyman et al., 1999). There is evidence that resilience can be increased by personal therapy (Taylor & Harvey, 2009). Other research (Foy et al., 2001; Klein & Schermer, 2000) highlights the particular efficacy of group therapy with trauma patients in promoting coping skills and trust, key components of resilience. However, while there is abundant research into the traumatic experience of therapists, little has been done to examine the development of resilience in therapists, whether they have experienced trauma or not.

A case for the importance of resilience as part of the effective therapist's tool set begins, perhaps, with the work of Bonanno (2004), Kobasa (1979), Masten (2001), Rutter (1999), and Werner (1995). These studies suggest that a learned capacity to "roll with" both positive and negative experience promotes optimism, respect for process, empathy, and genuineness. Resilience is critical to confidence, compassion, and the creative use of self, whether it is gained through living or in the course of therapy.

Farber et al.'s (2005) fascinating exploration into "Why did we cross that road?" is based on interviews with clinicians. In a crystalline formulation of resilience, he speculates that "would-be therapists do not differ in the actual extent to which they have been subject to painful situations in childhood, but rather that they construct these experiences in a unique way. This is the notion of therapists as 'sensitizers'—of their holding onto and trying to make sense of their experience in ways that distinguish them from those who tend to minimize or repress these same experiences" (p. 1013).

The acquisition of resilience is closely linked to Erikson's (1993) model of basic trust, but this trust must transcend the idea of the world as a safe place. In the early struggle for trust, a foundation is laid for a worldview that problems can be solved and situations can be improved, and that it is worth the effort to try. Trust defines the individual who seeks satisfaction in the interpersonal realm and sees relationships as the crucible for growth. In this writer's view, the capacity to develop trust and resilience should be a qualifying factor for the profession.

Informal Interviews

This writer felt that a close-up, unstudied snapshot of psychologists conversing among themselves might be revealing in a way that rigorous research cannot achieve. The topic of this chapter was presented to a small group of therapists from the New York City area, including the author, that meets regularly to discuss literary and professional issues. All graduated from a 4-year psychoanalytic program and most are psychologists. Their theoretical orientation is predominately but not exclusively interpersonal. All have practiced for at least 15 years, have published in psychoanalytic journals, and are very accomplished within their discipline. The average age of the six women and two men interviewed is 55. Their names have been rendered anonymous, with the exception of the author's. A single question was posed: "What early experience influenced you to become a psychotherapist?"

The simplicity of the question, the brevity of each vignette (derived from 5 to 10 minutes each, on tape), and the fact that the information was shared in such a close, collegial setting all bear upon the conclusions to be drawn from this mini-survey.

Sally's older brother suffered serious mental illness and was institutionalized for 9 years from the time she was 6. Her parents, in psychoanalysis during this period, "were always having dramatic talks about their transferences with their analysts, and I was fascinated by it." Considered the "normal child," Sally found this "very romantic" and quietly observed slow improvement in her family members. She took college courses with Bruno Bettelheim and became committed to pursuing the psychoanalytic profession when she saw the need for therapists who could work with deaf patients in sign language.

Jeanne's Irish-French mother was "definitely depressed" and her Italian father "emoted all over the place." She worried about her mother and tried to "figure her out," she says, but her father's warmth "saved" her. She became committed to the profession while doing an internship. An isolated and withdrawn patient who was generally ignored by the staff was selected to be interviewed by a respected psychoanalyst at a Grand Rounds. In this public forum, Jeanne heard that for 20 years the fellow had worked as a cook at a resettlement agency for hundreds of Holocaust victims. One day they just closed the place down, and the patient began his decline. "It blew my mind! The analyst brought out the man's humanity. I said to myself, then and there: *I want to be able to do that.*"

Rolf's father returned a beaten man from service as a German officer on the Eastern front. That same year, his sister died, his mother became incredibly depressed, and Rolf became "a listener." Economic woes required a move to Berlin, where he studied medicine to avoid being drafted for "another war." He became intensely interested in patients' complaints that were not associated with their physical ailments, but he found traditional psychiatry "dreadful" until he met a group of psychoanalysts doing casework with patients and was thrilled by their effort to create narratives of peoples' lives, to "make sense out of something senseless." Emigrating on a medical fellowship to the United States, Rolf dealt mostly with psychosomatic illnesses and began to see how angry his patients were. "It whetted my interest in psychoanalysis."

Rachel was 8 years older than her three sisters and largely responsible for raising them: "So, I have this thing about taking care of people." Her father's deafness was seen in the household as "a special gift"; only later did she come to understand it as a disability. She wondered, "What's really going on here in my family?" Rachel had an early passion for stories of all kinds, especially biographies. She recalls reading them at night with a flashlight under the bedcovers, and began academic life as a Russian literature major.

Joan disclosed: "I feel differently than the rest of you. I would not choose to be an analyst if I could do it all over again." Her parents, both general interns, argued all the time and analyzed everything. The well-known psychiatrist who treated them both made their stories public in a book, and described Joan's mother as castrating. "This became a huge thing in my parents' marriage." They labeled every childhood illness she had as psychosomatic. "I could never just be sick. I broke a lot of thermometers! I should have done things differently." But, Joan says, "I never thought of doing anything else."

Lenore's mother had hip dysplasia as a child and remained disabled. This was expected to explain why she had emotional outbursts, and was alcoholic and depressed. The family moved often: "You had to be resilient. I was interested in psychology from the get-go, especially how the body affected the mind." Lenore attended a talk where an analyst touted the profession: "He made it sound so dramatic—but I thought he was full of shit. It completely turned me off." Then, she found a mentor who told Lenore she should study psychoanalysis: "He said to me that analysis is the only theory that has anything to say about depth. And I knew I had to study it."

Rick says he was affected developmentally by his mother's depression and alcoholism. She was literary and smart and made Rick her confidant, "sort of a therapist." His father was married five times and left Rick's mother when the boy was 5 or 6. "As a young man I thought I wanted to be an actor so I could play all the roles I wanted to." He read Freud, Vigotsky, and Stanislavsky while working as a copy editor to cover the shortfall of income from theater work. "One day I just realized that I didn't like what I was doing or any of the people. I had already started therapy, and the only thing I wanted to be was an analyst—not a psychologist—an analyst."

Jessie was thrown into the caretaker role at a tender age. Eldest of six, she also babysat for everyone in her apartment building. "My mother pimped me out to everyone. When I was 7, I had a successful lemonade business. In seventh grade, I won first prize for an ESP project and the next year wrote a paper about a woman who dreamed she was burning up in her sleep while her son was in Vietnam. It also won a prize. I thought this psychology stuff was great." Jessie began therapy, read a great deal, and "detoured" for several years working in the music business. When she applied to graduate school, her mother got the call offering scholarship money and said, "'Yes! She'll go.' So I did." Once immersed in the program she "saw all this wonderful stuff going and I knew I was hooked."

John (the author) had an Irish mother who drank heavily, but he learned not to judge her for this because "she loved me so much." She made Jewish and Italian friends in their poor, multi-ethnic New York neighborhood, but was prejudiced against blacks. John's father's mantra was "stay in school," and he did. Strongly attracted to big ideas, he chose to major in psychology, became politically active during the Civil Rights era, and attempted to distance himself from his parents and their narrow beliefs. John pursued experimental psychology until an important mentor suggested he try a postdoctoral program in psychoanalysis. His current "eclectic" approach is drawn from interpersonal, relational, and dialectical behavioral theories. Besides private practice, he has worked with hospitalized patients from New York City's toughest police precincts. "I used to think black people lived closer to their instincts, whether sexual or aggressive, and saw more pathology in their culture. I came to understand this as unfounded, irrational, and echoing the views of my mother."

Each one of these short profiles illustrates some characteristic deemed important in a good therapist: the determination to understand latent content, the passion for language and storytelling, the fascination with roles, a desire to help and to please, a possibly nobler element of altruism, and, most clearly, resilience. Missing from the group of summaries is a sense of the knowing, sometimes raucous laughter, the silences pregnant with empathy, the "mmmmmmmmm's…" that are heard on the interview tape. It preserves a nearly audible turn of intellectual wheels in a roomful of smart, perceptive, and engaged professionals eager to help a colleague with a writing project. It would be derelict not to include, along with psychological-mindedness, a particular quality this group interview demonstrates: the strong inclination to cooperate and collaborate. A robust appetite for creative interaction and support among peers is critical to becoming a good therapist.

The small group, hardly a study sample, does however reflect the narrow sociocultural bias that, as we have noted, dominates the profession as a whole. What follows is a brief exploration of an issue that will change the face of psychotherapy, whether we are ready for it or not.

> …"to each according to his need, from each according to his ability"… This way of life comes naturally to immigrant families living in poverty, surviving together from month to month and trying individually slowly to raise their standard of living. Add to this a healthy measure of warmth and pleasure in one another's company, stir briskly, and you have the atmosphere in which a future psychotherapist might take root and grow.
>
> (Reppen, 1998, p. 1024)

The Need for Cultural and Ethnic Competence

How bluntly can it be stated: the problem of diversity is the "elephant in the consulting room," on both sides of the couch. The norm in the psychoanalytic profession, since its earliest days, has been that analysts are middle-class, educated, and white. Any serious inquiry into qualities and characteristics that are desirable to seek and to nurture in therapists must address the question of ethnic, racial, and economic diversity, and the limited sphere in which psychotherapy traditionally operates. The group of colleagues interviewed by this writer demonstrates this very bias.

Most therapists outside of a hospital or rehab setting see very few patients of color or of Latino or Asian ethnicity. Few refer such patients to non-white professionals, largely because there are so few of them to recommend, and so few are "in the pipeline." Black and minority candidates are rarities at psychoanalytic and other postdoctoral institutes.

Farber (2005) cites awareness since the 1970s of an "overrepresentation" of Jewish, urban, Eastern European, generally liberal and apostate therapists (p. 1010). It can be inferred that of the participants selected for Sussman's profiles (trainees, practitioners, analysts, men and women), all were white and from relatively middle-class, well-educated families. The only significant demographic shift has been the increased number of women clinical psychologists.

In addition to the narrow demographic range that dominates the profession, a general "tone deafness" to differences of color, ethnicity, culture, religion, and sexual orientation has been sharply criticized recently by writers like Sue and Sue (2007), who charge that racism appears endemic to psychoanalytic theory itself. Their book, *Counseling the Culturally Diverse*, offers a sobering statistic: "The diversity index of the United States stands at 49, indicating that there is nearly a one in two chance that two people selected at random are racially or ethnically different" (p. 48).

In a constructive response to this situation, the APA published, in 2003, extensive "Guidelines for Providers of Psychological Services to Ethnic, Linguistic, and Culturally Diverse Populations." The anonymous authors emphasize their inability to set mandatory standards and the lack of an "enforcement mechanism" to implement suggestions that are "not definitive and … not intended to take precedence over the judgment of psychologists" (p. 378). Even without such teeth, this document shows clear recognition of the profound change that demographics is visiting on our profession, and a grasp of its complexities. For example:

> Guideline 1: Psychologists are encouraged to recognize that, as cultural
> beings, they may hold attitudes and beliefs that can detrimentally influence
> their perceptions of and interactions with individuals who are ethnically and
> racially different from themselves (p. 390).

One of its most interesting contributions is the authors' criticism of a "color-blind" approach to reduce inequity. Instead, they conclude, blindness to difference perpetuates it. This writer strongly supports the argument that culturally sensitive therapy is essential, and eschews the notion that any therapy will do, so long as it is "good."

A relatively uninvestigated "classist bias" among psychologists has also been noted by the APA (Smith, 2005). This writer questions why service to the underclass has fallen short, and acknowledges, "Unconscious distancing from the poor overrides the better intentions that clearly exist among psychologists, with the result that the poor are 'disappeared' from many psychologists' professional and personal worlds" (p. 691). As noted above in the APA Guidelines, we all carry deep biases that are formed early, and are often unacknowledged and unexamined. To question and alter them significantly requires conscious effort that, even if largely successful, may leave emotional residua or perhaps an extreme opposite reaction.

Insufficient attention has been given to this in the selection and training of therapists. In their article "Status of minority curricula and training in clinical psychology," Bernal and Padilla (1982) criticized the nearly nonexistent representation of both minority professionals and minority teachers at the graduate level. They questioned, in their conclusions, whether minority content should be taught in separate courses, or integrated across the curriculum. This author responds decidedly in favor of the latter.

Recently, Tummala-Narra (2009) noted the divide that still exists between multicultural sensitivity in the profession and actual, successful methods for implementation of this critical goal. She sees the problem as a function of emphasis on intellectual rather than emotional insight in regard to social differences. This contributes, perhaps, to superficial solutions. For example, the ability to converse at even an intermediate level with a patient in his or her own language can hardly be considered cultural fluency.

The central question for this discussion is: What kind of person is capable of and inclined to examination of his or her own biases? Who has the motivation and the rigor of mind to undo the results of having been "carefully taught"? Obviously, certain kinds of early experience might predispose one toward tolerance and the embracing of differences: the child of a gay union growing up in a diverse setting where minorities assist one another to survive; the youngster whose parents took leadership roles in dealing with diverse social groups; the member of a peripatetic family that settles for a time in a foreign country. This kind of possibly resilience-building experience should be looked for in conjunction with basic traits and characteristics that synthesize and shape the psychologically minded personality.

Sue and Sue (2007) present a strong argument that in order to engage, appropriately communicate with, and intervene in the best interests of an increasingly diverse clientele, multicultural competence is essential. This capacity encompasses knowledge, skills, and highly developed sensitivities to diversity at the individual level as well as the organizational and political levels. Because psychotherapy focuses primarily on individual dynamics, there is perhaps a built-in avoidance of theory that touches upon issues of a larger societal and cultural nature. Strategies for intervention and advocacy frequently don't take these issues fully into account, resulting in widespread mistrust of the profession, a sense that "this is not for us." At best, the hope would be for a new generation of helping professionals who are culturally fluent and willing to advocate and intervene for patients of diverse cultural, religious, or sexual persuasions in a more open and public way than before. Responsiveness to minority differences may entail some social responsibility. This somewhat radical view will surely cause discomfort. But rather than a call to the street rally, it is an invitation to think differently about issues of diversity. It is out of the box, out of the ivory tower, and away from the generally white, European, middle-class mindset in which the field of psychotherapy has been so firmly entrenched.

> To this day, I continue to believe ... that if psychoanalytic practice and theory are to remain vital and grow, they must be open to developments, thinking and findings in other fields.
>
> (Reppen, 1998, p. 73)

Toward a New Approach

For psychotherapy to flourish and grow in the new century it is essential to understand cultural competence as more than a mere truism. It is also important to de-emphasize pathology or woundedness as the defining factors of suitability for the profession. A new approach would incorporate these needs at the level of research, recruitment, and education. It would address the limitations of using students and neophytes as subjects, the problem of subject/practitioners being too highly attuned to the "meaning" of research questions, and the problems of defining and measuring effectiveness.

Regarding diversity, it is clear from the literature that we need to examine below-the-surface or unconscious prejudicial attitudes. We cannot address them otherwise, or fully comprehend the reasons for choosing our careers, without considering these latent factors. We especially need to examine their influence in the psychotherapeutic dyad. Perhaps we need to re-evaluate the concept of transference and come up with something more inclusive of these issues. The following makes a modest step in this direction, with full understanding that it is not a final answer.

The relational school's here-and-now approach focuses on intersubjectivity and co-construction. This model of transference, with its diminished emphasis on early pathology and oedipal dynamics, is more consonant with non-analytic orientations, such as the cognitive/behavioral, which have rejected many earlier psychoanalytic ideas about transference. The relational model offers a bridge in that the premises of both relational and cognitive theory attach to the constructivist notion that we create our own experience and belief systems. This topic, clearly beyond the scope of this chapter, is in this author's view worthy of serious and thorough exploration in the future.

If we are to liberate our profession from its ivory tower, if we hope to tap a vibrant and diverse pool of younger talent, there is much work to be done. Quite simply, we need to be less elitist, less certain about our theories, more research-focused, more wedded to emotional intelligence, more culturally sensitive, more inclusive in the way we practice, and more willing to be technologically sophisticated in our recruitment efforts so we can appeal to the young. Above all, we need to embrace the reality that the multidisciplinary era has arrived. There are no longer simple, mono-theoretical solutions to the challenges we face; practitioners of every stripe quietly and confidently raid each other's toolboxes already!

Conclusion

Three questions were posed at the beginning of this chapter that the author never expected or promised to answer. Indeed, colleagues shook their heads and said it was an impossible task; it could simply not be done. They argued that given the incredible complexity of life, with its thousands of choice points, how could one ever know what tilts a person toward one career over another? If research does suggest there is a developmental pathway, or manages to pinpoint certain characteristics that make for an effective psychotherapist, might this information narrow and rigidify the selection and training of therapists? Some skeptics felt it might be a really bad idea to try to codify this process.

One cannot dismiss these concerns. Neither, however, can one ignore the need for better quality research. The questions *must* be asked. They may be more important than definitive answers if the result is serious self-evaluation within the profession. At the individual level, as we well know, this deep process is essential to growth, confidence, and creativity.

Writing and thinking about this chapter has helped the author know his colleagues better. It has stimulated compassion for those whose journeys were difficult, and has deepened understanding of the nuances of traits like psychological-mindedness. Most significantly, it has engendered excitement about multicultural competence—in all probability the most important issue facing our profession today across all theories and disciplines. It is hoped that the new generation of therapists will transcend mere political correctness and take on diversity issues with passion.

References

Applebaum, S. A. (1973). Psychological-mindedness: Word, concept, and essence. *International Journal of Psychoanalysis*, 54, 35–46.

Bernal, M., & Padilla, A. M. (1982). Status of minority curricula and training in clinical psychology. *American Psychologist*, 37, 780–787.

Bonanno, G. A. (2004). Loss, trauma, and human resilience: have we underestimated the human capacity to thrive after extremely aversive events? *American Psychologist*, 59, 20–28.

Erikson, E. (1993). *Childhood and Society*. New York: W. W. Norton.

Farber, B. (1989). Psychological mindedness: can there be too much of a good thing? *Psychology and Psychotherapy: Theory Research, Practice*, 26, 210–217.

Farber, B., Manevich, I., Metzger, & Saypol, E. (2005). Choosing psychotherapy as a career: Why did we cross that road? (Special Issue) *Journal of Clinical Psychology*, 61, 1009–1031.

Foy, D. W., Eriksson, C. B., & Trice, G. A. (2001). Introduction to group intervention for trauma survivors. *Group Dynamics: Theory, Research, and Practice*, 5, 246–251.

Fussell, F., & Bonney, W. (1990). A comparative study of childhood experiences of psychotherapists and physicists. *Psychotherapy: Theory, Research, Practice, and Training*, 27, 505–512.

Gabbard, G., & Gabbard K. (1999). *Psychiatry and the Cinema*. Washington, D.C.: American Psychiatric Publishing Inc.

Guidelines on multicultural education, training, research, practice, and organizational change for psychologists (2003). *American Psychologist*, 58, 377–402.

Guy, J. (1987). *The Personal Life of the Psychotherapist*. New York: Wiley-Interscience.

Henry, W., Simms J., & Spray S.L. (1973). *Public and Private Lives of Psychotherapists.* San Francisco: Jossey-Bass.

Holland, J. L. (1997). *Making Vocational Choices: A Theory of Vocational Personalities and Work Environments* (3rd ed.). Odessa, FL: Psychological Assessments Resources.

Klein, R. H., & Schermer, V. L. (2000). *Group Psychotherapy for Psychological Trauma.* New York: Guilford Press.

Kobasa, S. C. (1979). Stressful life events, personality, and health: an inquiry into hardiness. *Journal of Personality and Social Psychology, 37,* 1–11.

Loner, W. J., & Adams, H. L. (1972). Interest patterns of psychologists in nine western nations. *Journal of Applied Psychology, 56,* 146–151.

Masten, A. S. (2001). Ordinary magic: Resilience processes in development. *American Psychologist, 56,* 227–238.

Orchowski, L. (2006). Cinema and the valuing of psychotherapy. *Professional Practice, 37,* 506–514.

Orlinsky, D., & Ronnestad, M. (2004). *How Psychotherapists Develop: A Study of Therapeutic Growth and Professional Growth.* Washington, D.C.: American Psychological Association Press.

Reppen, J. (Ed.). (1998). *Why I Became a Psychotherapist.* New Jersey: Jason Aronson.

Ronnestad, M., & Skovholt, T. (2003). The journey of the counselor and therapist: Research findings and perspectives on professional development. *Journal of Career Development, 30*(1), 5–44.

Rutter, M. (1999). Resilience concepts and findings: Implications for family therapy. *Journal of Family Therapy, 21,* 119–144.

Skovholt, T., & Jennings, L. (2004). *Master Therapists: Exploring Expertise in Therapy and Counseling.* Boston: Pearson.

Smith, L. (2005). Psychotherapy, classicism and the poor: Conspicuous by their absence. *American Psychologist, 60,* 687–696.

Staub, E., & Volhardt, J. (2008). Altruism born of suffering: The roots of caring and helping after victimization and other trauma. *American Journal of Orthopsychiatry, 78,* 267–280.

Sue, D., & Sue, D. (2007). *Counseling the Culturally Diverse: Theory and Practice* (5th ed.). Hoboken, NJ: Wiley.

Sullivan, B., & Hansen, J. C. (2004). Mapping associations between interests and personality: Toward a conceptual understanding of individual differences in vocational counseling. *Journal of Counseling Psychology, 51,* 287–298.

Sussman, M. (1992). *A Curious Calling: Unconscious Motivations for Practicing Psychotherapy.* New Jersey: Jason Aronson.

Sussman, M. (2007). *A Curious Calling: Unconscious Motivations for Practicing Psychotherapy* (2nd ed.). New Jersey: Jason Aronson.

Taylor, J. E., & Harvey, S. T. (2009). Effects of psychotherapy with people who have been sexually assaulted; A meta-analysis. *Aggression and Violent Behavior, 14*(5), 273–285.

Taylor, S. E., Kemeny, M. E., Reed, G. M., Bower, J. E., & Gruenwald, T. L. (2000). Psychological resources, positive illusions, and health. *American Psychologist, 55*(1), 99–109.

Tiet, Q. Q., Bird, H. R., Davies, M., Hoven, C., Cohen, P., Jensen, P.S., & Goodman, S. (1998). Adverse life events and resilience. *Journal of the American Academy of Child and Adolescent Psychiatry, 37,* 1191–1200.

Tummala-Narra, R. (2009). Teaching on diversity: the mutual influence of students and instructors. *Psychoanalytic Psychology*, 26, 322–334.

Werner, E. E. (1995). Resilience in development. *Current Directions in Psychological Science*, 4, 81–85.

White, B., Driver, S., & Warren, A. (2008). Considering resilience in the rehabilitation of people with traumatic disabilities. *Rehabilitation Psychology*, 53, 9–17.

Whitfield, E. A., Feller, R. W., & Wood, C. (eds.) (2009). *A Counselor's Guide to Career Assessment Instruments* (5th ed.). Broken Arrow, OK: National Career Development Association.

Wyman, P. A., Cowen, E. L., Work, W., Hoyt-Meyers, L., Magnus, K. B., & Fagen, D. B. (1999). Cargiving and developmental factors differentiating young at-risk urban children showing resilient vs. stress affected outcomes; A replication and extension. *Child Development*, 70, 645–659.

3

The Mentoring Relationship: Co-creating Personal and Professional Growth

Robin G. Gayle

> *Commitment has kind eyes. (S)he wears sturdy shoes. Everything is very vivid when (s)he is around. It is wonderful to sit and have lunch in the garden around harvest time. You can taste in the vegetables that the soil has been cared for.*
>
> (Gendler, 1984, p. 55)

Along the path of psychotherapist development arise many existential questions: What is personally required? How much self-examination is enough? When, and how much, must one reveal? What kind of commitment is necessary? Questions such as these do not find a simple resolution in texts or lectures, nor are they definitively answered in clinical supervision or professional practica; one person's truth will be only partial for another person. Yet through the kind eyes and sturdy shoes of the mentors beside us, seeds for therapist development are planted and nurtured.

Originating within Greek mythology, the term *mentor* is today defined as a "close, trusted, and experienced counselor or guide" (Gove & Merriam-Webster Inc., 2002, p. 1412). Contemporary mentoring theorists describe mentoring as a "unique relationship form" (Johnson, 2003, p. 129) that is of "vital importance in psychologists' professional development" (Barnett, 2008, p. 3), and it facilitates a "reflective practice" (Ewing et al., 2008, p. 295) that deepens and matures both mentor and mentee. Mentoring relationships that are fluid, voluntary, mutual, co-constructive, and co-creative bring refreshing creativity and possibility to ongoing therapist development before and after licensure. Most importantly, it fosters confidence in a safe and skillful use of self in treatment processes that augments formal therapist training programs.

Some of the most helpful words ever spoken to me for personal and professional development came from a mentor, Dr. Irvin Yalom, during a small gathering of therapists. As I struggled to articulate some wisdom sure to impress this renowned expert, he simply said with a kindness and certainty, "It is the subjective aspect of self-disclosure that is most important" (Dr. Irvin Yalom, personal communication, March 29, 2003). This well-timed insight that emerged from Dr. Yalom's subjective experience of our interchange created an intersubjective field in which my performance anxiety and image worries could subside and an authentic reflection upon my experience could take place. A creative and compelling dialogue emerged that meaningfully shifted my interpersonal style and later helped in my work with clients. I consider this today as one of many important moments of initiation into the practice of effective psychotherapy.

Co-creating Personal and Professional Growth

A culturally diverse and ethically sound environment for growth emerges when an appropriate mentor who is embedded in personal and collective sociocultural contexts intersubjectively interacts with a mentee who brings all of the value systems in which he or she is immersed. The personal emotions, professional assumptions, and cultural influences that underlie the relationship are illuminated thoroughly in the course of this hermeneutical (meaning-making) process, strengthening the mentoring frame. A safe mentoring container matures and supports the examination of experience-near interactions, yielding co-creative growth for both mentor and mentee that cultivates empathy, balances self-disclosure, facilitates transference/countertransference resolution, and fosters a mentee's identification, internalization, and empowerment.

In the example above, Dr. Yalom mentored this type of hermeneutical growth by articulating his experience of my interpersonal style in the here-and-now through process commentary. Rather than engaging the content of my communication, he illuminated the relationship between us. This allowed me to drop below the impression I was trying to make upon him and access a deeper experience of what I was really trying to say and for what purpose. Within this reflective space I had a "corrective emotional experience" (Yalom & Leszcz, 2005, p. 27), a visceral "aha" that helped me to resolve initial transference anxiety and begin to interact more honestly. In return, Dr. Yalom was able to relate to me in a more meaningful way that enriched my personal understanding and professional practice.

This chapter articulates some of the relational/intersubjective dynamics within mentoring relationships and clarifies important hermeneutical processes that foster psychotherapist development. I identify a mentor in terms of ethics, professional expertise, and ideological integrity and a mentee in terms of aspiration, motivation, expectation, and introspective capacity. Assets and liabilities of the mentoring relationship are examined and include personal support, professional identification, and diversified learning (Tentoni, 1995), as well as problematic boundary crossings, power differentials, and triangulation (Barnett, 2008; Scandura, 1998). A mentoring vignette is developed that highlights some of the unique intrapsychic, interpersonal, and sociocultural interplays that co-create personal and professional growth and contribute to psychotherapists' development.

Background Research

Mentoring relationships have been extensively researched and measured within a variety of settings and across many careers. Within classrooms, universities, and workplaces many factors that affect mentoring have been studied: culture (impact of diversity issues upon the process), structure (facilitated vs. non-facilitated, structured vs. non-structured), population (youths, adults, peers, colleagues, and employees), gender (matching vs. diversity), and multidisciplinary task (Allen & Eby, 2007; Blickle et al., 2008; Hu, 2008; Liang et al., 2002b). Common empirical tools for measuring the mentoring relationship include the Mentoring Functions Questionnaire-9 (MFQ-9; Pelligrini & Scandura, 2005), the Mutual Psychological Development Questionnaire (MPDQ; Genero et al., 1992), and the Relational Health Index-Mentor (RHI-M; Liang et al., 2002a).

While there is an abundance of quantitative, correlative, and cross-sectional research designs that use single-source data (from typically the mentee) (Allen et al., 2008), research upon intersubjective and relational dynamics within the mentoring relationship is under-represented in the literature. This chapter, therefore, offers theoretical and qualitative understanding that identifies and characterizes these dynamics within therapist development, augmenting the proliferation of empirical studies reporting on the effectiveness of mentoring skills (Allen & Eby, 2007; Allen et al., 2008; Forehand, 2008; Liang et al., 2002b).

Relational Mentoring

Mentoring relationships offer both career support and personal caregiving, often emphasizing one type of support over another, depending on context or task (Jacobi, 1991; Kram, 1980; Tenenbaum, 2001). Although both functions are important in some measure for effective mentoring, much research indicates that tangible career support is most effective and helpful when embedded in a relational context (Ewing et al., 2008; Johnson, 2003; Liang et al., 2002a; Storrs, Putsche, & Taylor, 2008). A relevant discussion about this is taking place within universities as of late regarding the efficacy of online courses versus classroom learning. Some interesting evidence-based data may be forthcoming from this comparison that identifies elements within the relational (classroom) context that both positively and adversely affect student learning outcomes.

In Jacobi's (1991) review, 15 mentoring functions were identified and divided into either instrumental or psychosocial categories. Instrumental provisions, including offering information, advice, challenge, and role modeling, contribute positively to productivity through unidirectional teaching or advising. This function is characterized within higher education as a relationship where a more experienced, usually older adult acts as a guide, sponsor, role model, or teacher of a less experienced, often younger mentee to facilitate his or her entry into a particular profession (Johnson, 2003). Within therapist development, this type of socialization is well suited to formal mentoring relationships between teachers and students, supervisors and interns, or employers and employees—in other words, settings where tasks and behaviors are well defined and there are high yet achievable expectations.

Psychosocial help, on the other hand, includes mutual exchange that is dynamic and reciprocal, and recognizes a mentee's psychological needs and resources (Mullen, 2007). It includes nurture, emotional support, empathy, authenticity, connectedness, counseling, and friendship. By nature, these mentoring functions best (and most safely) operate in more informal relationships, relatively free of institutional directives and agendas.

Again, career support and psychosocial functions are not mutually exclusive (Kram, 1985); however, the psychosocial and relational context plays a crucial part in therapists' development where growth of a self that is authentic, empathic, subjective, and interactive is central. For example, a traditional model of psychotherapist supervision entails a professional expert who objectively imparts technical knowledge, theoretical ideas, and clinical interventions to the supervisee. This career support role is necessary for psychotherapist training and education, but it may fall short of mentoring a sense of self that will inevitably be a participant in transference–countertransference enactments with patients.

A mentoring relationship that is outside of the hierarchical structures of supervision, higher education, or employment can incorporate psychosocial mentoring functions that encourage shared power and authority. Important intrapsychic, interpersonal, and sociocultural interplays are allowed to emerge that increase self-understanding, authenticity, and confidence. I often notice the qualitative difference in dialogue that occurs once my counseling psychology trainees finish their formalized coursework with me and begin case consultation in our more informal eight-member practicum. Without the pressure of having a letter grade attached, trainees and I can consult as equals, bringing our sociocultural and professional backgrounds, family-of-origin influences, knowledge bases, and affective fields to the discussion with the shared goal of understanding and effectively treating their clients.

It is easy to see why some theorists describe mentoring as the most intense and intimate relationship within the helping professions (Hunt & Michael, 1983; Kram, 1985; Levinson et al., 1978) because it has great potential to be enriched by sociocultural, interpersonal, and intrapsychic domains that are ordinarily well separated from a traditional psychoanalytic dyad or clinical training program. However, these very factors also make the mentoring relationship vulnerable to boundary issues, power imbalances, and special transference–countertransference dynamics (Barnett, 2008; Hunt & Michael, 1983; McAuley, 2003; Scandura, 1998), as will be seen. It is strongly advised that prospective mentors and mentees have some knowledge about the relational/intersubjective dynamics that underlie an effective use of self to avoid some of these potential difficulties.

Relational/Intersubjective Theory

Relational/intersubjective theory offers such guidance to the mentoring relationship by identifying important growth-fostering characteristics within it (Liang et al., 2008; Liang et al., 2002b; Storrs et al., 2008). It attempts to articulate how two subjectivities simultaneously co-inhabit and co-create a unified field of experience and expression that grows and nurtures rather than distorts or destroys. This perspective is particularly important for mentoring psychotherapist development in light of recent research emphasizing the inevitable use of the therapist's self in treatment processes (Arnd-Caddigan & Pozzuto, 2008; Ganzer, 2007; Heffron et al., 2005; Prosky, 1996). Whatever we do or say unavoidably tells another person something about ourselves and the psycho-socio-cultural systems in which we are embedded. Mentoring an understanding of relational and intersubjective dynamics that are involved in voluntary and/or inherent self-disclosure facilitates a skillful and beneficial use of a therapist's subjectivity in this process.

We can best understand some of the relational/intersubjective principles that mentor therapist growth by following the case of Mae, a 26-year-old graduate-level counseling psychology student:

> Mae (a pseudonym) entered her graduate program after taking a vocational test in a career counseling seminar that indicated she had the skills to become a psychotherapist. While many students enter this course of study when life-changing interpersonal, developmental, or existential events call them to help others transform similar pain into growth, Mae reported a relatively healthy upbringing in a functional family and a happy marriage to a man who worked in business marketing.
>
> Mae efficiently and effectively learned the pragmatic skills necessary to become a competent therapist, but problems arose in her second year when she began her supervised practicum and concurrent hours of personal psychotherapy necessary to graduate her program. Consistent feedback from her supervisor indicated Mae's difficulty in understanding "who the client is in the room" and a concomitant inability to formulate an adequate treatment focus, even though her treatment plans were technically correct on paper. This supervisor was trying to help her by analyzing her written case studies and giving feedback about verbal and nonverbal indicators of empathic failures apparent in Mae's videotaped sessions. Transference ensued as Mae enacted in return her relationship with her highly esteemed, protective father (a prestigious university professor) by fervently trying to do everything her supervisor asked, often reporting in frustration and tears, "But I did everything right!" Supervisor countertransference included feeling impotent, redundant, and depleted of methods by which he could point out skill in building therapeutic alliance and therapeutic leverage.

Clearly Mae is at an impasse in her ability to access her internal resources for a use of self that would unfreeze her interactions with clients. But what is this "self" that Mae is trying to ascertain, and how might a mentor's own use of self be helpful to her?

The *self* is defined from a relational/intersubjective perspective as a "process in interaction" (Arnd-Caddigan & Pozzuto, 2008, p. 238) mediated by "discursive and relational influences, dynamic, intersubjective, unconscious processes" (Hollway, 2006, p. 466), and psychosocial characteristics that are "embedded in personal and collective sociocultural and global contexts" (Gayle, 2009, p. 321). Ganzer (2007) describes the use of self within this paradigm as "dialogic, contextualized, decentered, and multiple" (p. 117). This postmodern co-creative use of self is optimal for cultivating responsiveness, collaborative engagement, authenticity, and cultural diversity, but susceptible to distorting alliances, dissipating boundaries, and diluting necessary transference and countertransference enactments (Kirschner, 2003; Meissner, 2002).

In clinical settings, the concept *use of self* indicates a relationship between therapist and patient whereupon personal characteristics of the therapist such as warmth, empathy, concern, and unconditional positive regard enter into the therapeutic relationship to co-create new meaning and ways of being for the client. Mitchell (1998) asserts that this therapeutic encounter for the therapist "is toward a new way of experiencing him- or herself and the patient ... to find an authentic voice in which to speak to the patient, a voice more fully one's own, less shaped by the configurations and limited options of the [patient's] relational matrix, in so doing to offer the [patient] a chance to broaden and expand that matrix" (p. 295).

I believe that Mae found herself in a double bind as she aspired to demonstrate competency in a new profession that by nature has an empathic, interactive, intersubjective self as its main tool. Following professional rules was not helpful to Mae in this dilemma and served to further alienate her from her peers:

> Student peers within Mae's group supervision were earnest in their efforts to be empathic and helpful to Mae. Questions asked centered around what possible diversity, gender, or family-of-origin countertransference might be affectively freezing Mae in the room with her clients. Mae very clearly articulated professional boundaries around self-disclosing personal information to peers who will someday become her colleagues. While technically correct, this injunction had a mild shaming effect on her peers, who had already disclosed a variety of projections, transferences, and diversity issues in the service of becoming better aware of their subjective use of self and therapist development.
>
> When Mae took this issue to her personal psychotherapist, family systems issues were examined in terms of Mae's pattern of repressing emotion during direct experiences of her life in order to engage in stimulating intellectual conversation with her academic father, and of abstracting her immediate experiences into humor and sarcasm in order to banter with her athletic and

witty brothers. She also reported a history of politely resisting attunement and alliance with her mother, who was perceived as dependent and engulfing with histrionic features. Since Mae's therapist was female, their psychotherapy relationship enacted approach–avoidance dynamics as Mae straddled the attempt to please with feelings of engulfment.

It is possible that the pressure to demonstrate comprehensive clinical proficiency in an academic program or supervisory setting can intersubjectively interfere with experiencing new emotions and experimenting with the new behaviors necessary to grow a flexible and authentic self within therapist development. Additionally, increased governmental regulation of community mental health resources and stringent managed care stipulations can intersubjectively constrain development of a mutual, co-creative environment for growth. For these reasons, an informal mentoring relationship that is outside of the hierarchical structures of education, government, or employment can offer important help to developing psychotherapists.

A therapist is called upon to participate in transference and countertransference enactments with both colleagues and patients. Within psychotherapeutic practice, the therapist must temporarily suspend technical expertise and tolerate the ambiguity and uncertainty of the patient's world so that new patterns of interaction emerge and new meanings are co-created. This relational function is operationally defined by Heffron et al. (2005) as learning to inhibit actions in the moment and holding the tension, "the ability to tolerate and hold conflicting ideas, notions, anxieties, or presses felt by a client and work consciously to help the client think about these without pushing for a particular outcome" (p. 330).

Quite by accident, Mae had the good fortune to encounter a mentor who possessed such strengths:

> One day, Mae was talking with a former undergraduate university professor about her seeming inability to turn the technical or interpersonal key to unlock more presence in the room with her clients and form a therapeutic alliance. In the middle of Mae's very articulate and prolific description of her issues, this instructor, playing a mentoring role, simply asked her to pause and describe the "felt sense" (Gendlin, 1978, p. 10) of this issue. In a moment of silence Mae identified a feeling of pressure, if not strangulation, in her throat. The mentor then asked her to describe this felt sense with three adjectives and then come up with a metaphor for the way this whole situation was feeling. Mae came up with stifled, cautious, and fearful as her adjectives. The metaphor she cited was of a racetrack starting gate holding back a stallion from charging. When asked what this charging horse would do if it were let out, Mae said it would first run a precise and powerful lap around the track to show everyone just how exceptionally good it was, then it would hit its stride, relax, and exude balance, well-being, and confidence, resonating with the crowd in meaningful reverie as all kinds of beauty and balance ensued. Finally, having finished the race, the horse would feel

relaxed, whole, and at one with the crowd at the racetrack as they cheered and released their joy.

Indeed, Mae looked relaxed and joyful at the end of this guided imagery. Understandings ensued about the nature of the gate, the horse being held back, and the developmental phases of the race. Mae felt the gate was holding back her astute but over-intellectualized insight into her clients, ostensibly in the service of building empathic resonance, but creating more frustration than potential. On the one hand, she was quite frightened that her intellectual insights would cut and pierce people, as indeed she had experienced doing to her mother and friends many times. On the other hand, empathic immersion felt engulfing and threatening, as if somehow she would be discredited for being too subjective. Mae realized that both insight and empathy needed to operate in balance for her to be an effective therapist.

While these were insights that Mae's supervisor, psychotherapist, and peers had worked hard to convey to her, it was in this freely entered creative space that Mae was able to access the meaning of her experience through the co-creative use of metaphor.

Ethical Considerations

The ability to temporarily suspend technical expertise, open to conscious and unconscious expression, and co-create meaning is best acquired within therapists' development through this type of interpersonal experience. Such experience, for reasons of safety, optimally occurs in non-hierarchical situations where dual relationships and conflicts of interest are minimized (Barnett, 2008; Johnson, 2003). Dual relationships are double or multiple relationships where the roles of student, friend, intern, or employee are merged and create situations where private or personal interests impair objectivity or increase exploitation. Common mentoring examples include professors in counseling psychology training programs who find themselves in a dual relationship when mentoring the psychosocial development of a student to whom they must also deliver an academic grade. This power differential is further amplified if the grade must evaluate personal processes or affect student eligibility for graduation.

A conflict of interest is one where a professional relationship is used to further one's own private interest, hence compromising objectivity. For example, researchers who mentor research assistants may find themselves in a conflict of interest when facing a publishing deadline contingent upon requisite data collection. These situations indicate how important it is to understand the relationship between career support and psychosocial mentoring and to make sure a mentoring relationship is contextualized accordingly with appropriate personal and professional boundaries.

There is a deeper intimacy and intensity involved in psychosocial mentoring that calls upon the mentor-as-person to interact in reciprocal and mutual ways with his or her mentees. Barnett (2008) and Johnson (2003) recommend mentor attention, forethought, and prudence informed by standard professional ethics common to the helping professions (e.g., beneficence, non-malfeasance, fidelity, integrity, and caring) to guide open discussion with mentees about expectations, power differentials, and potential boundary crossings in each context. These boundaries were in place in Mae's situation and, therefore, a safe mentoring container developed:

> Mae reported that interacting through metaphor and narrative enabled her to authentically self-disclose intrapsychic dynamics that were affecting her development without impression management or fear of engulfment. She asked whether she might continue to receive this type of hermeneutical interaction with this instructor-turned-mentor. The mentor also felt enlivened by a sense of creativity and play within this process. She was in a good position to invite Mae to interact freely and safely without a conflict of agendas because she no longer had authority over Mae's education requirements nor had any type of dual relationship (was not part of Mae's peer group, family, or professional practicum). An informal mentoring relationship was clarified whereupon Mae could stop by during office hours as needed and engage in this type of hermeneutical meaning-making process for growth. Mae did so with added benefit as they concomitantly dialogued with the metaphorical horse, the pristine lap, hitting her stride, and allowing audience reverie.

Choosing a Mentor/Mentee

A relational/intersubjective perspective encourages open discussion between mentor and mentee that de-emphasizes judgments, assessments, and interpretations heavily laden with educational or vocational directives and advice. Listening and interacting is mentored without projective anticipation of what the mentee is going to say and without an agenda for mentee experience or productivity. Therapist development is viewed primarily as a process rather than a product, and the mentee enters freely into the mentoring relationship only insofar as there is value seen in the content of the mentor.

By a survey of mentees, the following mentor qualities were identified as important in this regard: interest, support, honesty, dedication, compassion, flexibility, loyalty, humor, knowledge, competence, willingness to share and not be exploitative, and a positive attitude (Cronan-Hillix et al., 1986). Johnson's (2003) research adds that a mentor's emotional facilitation is important to the mentee—for example, the capacity for emotional containment, receptivity, and self-reflection (p. 137).

The mentee must see for himself or herself whether interactions with the mentor bring actual benefit, inspiration, and changes in behavior that are durable and worthwhile, increasing the mentee's faith in the insights gleaned or ideologies conveyed. Steinbock (2001) articulates this growth in his treatment of exemplarity:

> Whereas willing and choosing are directed toward obedience or copying, in the case of the exemplar, one 'freely' devotes oneself to the content of personal value, which must be seen for the person him- or herself. Thus, there is nothing of psychic contagion, identification, obedience, etc., where the exemplar is concerned.
>
> The emulator lives as or becomes in manner of the exemplar in the direction or orientation of the life lived, emulating the sense of the life... (p. 189)

Steinbock asserts that one person can hold someone else as a role model without the person knowing it, and further, that someone can be a role model who has lived years before us (Caesar, Socrates, Jesus, Buddha, Gandhi), or even a literary figure who reveals or expresses a particular value (Goethe's Faust, Shakespeare's Hamlet, Dante's Beatrice, Dostoevsky's Alysha Karamazov) (pp. 188–189). From an object-relations perspective (St. Clair, 2004) this type of mentally represented and introjected mentor provides developmental value. However, a relational/intersubjective perspective calls for a more conscious and dialogic container for the processes involved in self-disclosure and the psycho-socio-cultural interplays that inevitably co-create mutual value.

Relational/Intersubjective Mentoring

Relational/intersubjective mentoring takes into consideration that an individual interacts with and within a complex context of thoughts, values, aspirations, moods, affects, sensations, and structures that concurrently intersect the contexts of other constantly changing lives and environments. This interplay involves interpersonal, intrapsychic, and sociocultural dynamics.

Interpersonal Aspects

Interpersonal aspects of the mentoring relationship include mutual engagement, authenticity, and empowerment (Liang et al., 2008; Liang et al., 2002b; Storrs et al., 2008). Relational theorists at the Wellesley College Stone Center (Liang et al., 2002a) found that an effective mentoring context includes specific mutual qualities: "mutual engagement/empathy (defined by perceived mutual involvement, commitment, and attunement to the relationship), authenticity (the process of acquiring knowledge of self and the other and feeling free to be genuine in the context of the relationship), and empowerment (the experience of feeling personally strengthened, encouraged, and inspired to take action)" (p. 273). These qualities are evident in Mae's relationship with her mentor:

> One day Mae's mentor wondered aloud if Mae would like to experiment here-and-now with empathic use of self by expressing an insight about the mentor's verbal and nonverbal communication. Mae laughed as she recalled that this mentor was an expert in Symbolic Interaction Theory (Sullivan, 1953) and had years ago encouraged students to become aware of feeling a double bind when someone's impression management becomes discrepant with his or her affective or nonverbal displays. After some consideration, Mae felt safe to express her assessment of the mentor as intelligent, articulate, and genuinely concerned for others, except … just as Mae began to move away from the "except" into intellectualization, this mentor said, "Wait … 'except'… what is the felt sense of that 'except'?" Mae was silent for a while, and then said, "You seem sad."
>
> Surprised and touched that nonverbal grief could be seen so clearly, the mentor concurred that there had been some recent and important deaths in her life. Mae visibly relaxed as she was released from the double bind caused by incongruent verbal and nonverbal expression. The mentor's personal and professional understandings expanded in regard to the way inherent existential events express and are perceived by others. Both understood how acknowledging them (without further self-disclosure) could unfreeze and bring more genuine presence into interpersonal interactions. This co-created mutual reverie and resonance, and the mentor wondered if this understanding might be meaningful to Mae's situation with her clients as well. Mae affirmed that allowing both objective and subjective observations into the here-and-now helped her to feel more present, attuned, and connected; she felt excited and empowered to experiment with this relational tool in her client sessions.

In this mentor–mentee interaction, intersubjective processes can be identified as mutuality, perception, attunement, freedom, and inspiration. For example, when Mae freely attuned to her mentor's emotion and expression, her relative perception of sadness emerged partially from observable symbolic data and partially from her own intrapsychic and sociocultural world. This partial truth was expanded through mutual authentic dialogue with her mentor, and understandings emerged that inspired both parties.

The dialectical character of this interaction is examined from a social constructivist viewpoint and applied to the mentoring relationship by Storrs et al. (2008). They find that metaphoric processes enhance the mentoring experience by uncovering the underlying principles, values, and assumptions that produce such metaphors. Metaphors co-construct meaning through reflection and inquiry between social individuals, and Storrs et al. recommend metaphoric exercises that help mentees and mentors co-create meaningful aspirations and goals in the mentoring relationship.

An intersubjective understanding of metaphoric processes is offered by Cohen and Schermer (2004), who articulate that matching or approximate narratives between two individuals "converge in the joint discovery or negotiated construction of a metaphor which links each to the other's subjectivity" (p. 588). This intersubjective "tripod" (Davidson, 2001, p. 220) of subjective, intersubjective, and objective knowledge co-creates meaning that expands and evolves yet again through social interaction, an interaction where "meaning is born of interdependence" (Gergen, 1991, p. 157).

In Mae's case, interacting around concrete observations, symbolic metaphor, and co-creative narratives enabled her to safely navigate the difficult confluences of participant/observer skill, conscious/unconscious disclosure, and transference/countertransference enactment so important to therapists' use of self but so frighteningly subjective for her. It seemed as though metaphor or narrative became an intersubjective third party to the relationship, operationally mediating subjective and objective perceptions and guiding understanding into meaningful expression.

Intrapsychic Dynamics

Intrapsychic dynamics within this triadic interplay of overlapping fields of experience shape the mentoring relationship. The presence of unconscious and preconscious instincts, drives, and internal objects within both mentee and mentor subjectivities re-enact in mutual intersubjective processes creating necessary tensions between self and other that contribute to integration and growth. Theoretical investigations into mentor–mentee psychodynamics identify transference/countertransference (McAuley, 2003), identification/ differentiation (Olds, 2006), neutrality/disclosure (Bosworth et al., 2009), and empathy/containment (Clifford, 1999) as characteristic intrapsychic intersubjective interactions requiring a different treatment in the mentoring relationship than is traditionally assumed in analytic practice.

The mentoring container differs significantly from the analytic container by its informal, multimodal, and psychosocial nature. There may be a wider range of involuntary, nonspecific, self-manifesting, given or "real" (Meissner, 2002, p. 833) characteristics of personhood available (e.g., attire, mannerisms, habits, defenses) that influence a mentee's identification with the mentor and a mentor's discrimination of the circumstances, content, and intent of self-disclosure (Barnett, 2008). A colleague once described to me how challenging it was to attend a conference abroad with two of her mentees when she became very ill and needed help with all of her personal needs. Fortunately, her skill in relational therapy allowed her to intersubjectively enter rather than resist this experience with her mentees and co-create an open, reflective space for expressions and understandings to emerge about our human condition of illness and suffering. The mentor–mentee relationships deepened with existential meaning and the mentor emerged from the experience empowered rather than embarrassed.

There may also be greater intersection of interpersonal and developmental factors (e.g., deaths, births, marriages, milestones) that influence the mentoring relationship from the outside that call for empathic responses ordinarily well contained within an analytic container of anonymity, neutrality, and confidentiality. For example, mentors are likely to go to award dinners and celebrate promotions and milestones with their mentees that will entail meeting family members and friends on both sides. It is recommended that open discussion take place ahead of time between mentor and mentee to mutually co-create an intentional field for navigating through the intrapsychic dynamics underlying such issues as confidentiality and potential dual relationships. Meaningful dialogue must emerge afterwards as well, as the shared experience of another's interpersonal or sociocultural world generates relative perceptions that help to clarify intrapsychic dynamics between mentor and mentee around identification/differentiation, neutrality/disclosure, and transference/countertransference. Through such direct experience and intersubjective dialogue, insights are gained that are greater than either person could access alone with only describing, reporting, or storytelling as his or her method.

While transference and countertransference are considered to be less charged within the mentoring relationship than that within the psychoanalytic encounter, McAuley (2003) asserts that certain themes and situations are likely to replay that facilitate awareness and growth. For instance, transference themes are cited such as respect for the mentor's expertise as idealization (positive transference) or engulfment (negative transference), which might play out in over-dependence (dysfunctional transference) or assertion of independence (functional transference). Common countertransference themes include unconditional positive regard for the mentee as alliance (positive countertransference) or collusion (negative countertransference), which might play out in inflation (dysfunctional countertransference) or empowerment (functional countertransference). A relational/intersubjective perspective views this interplay as one that is shaped by two active subjectivities participating in and reflecting upon conjoint enactments that co-create multiple and shared understandings that guide new behaviors meaningfully.

Sociocultural Aspects

An interesting sociocultural finding that emerged from the Stone Center research that is echoed in other surveys upon mentoring dyads (Hu, 2008; Johnson, 2003; Ragins & Scandura, 1994) is that matching gender and ethnicity in mentor–mentee pairs had limited importance compared to the nature and quality of the mentoring relationship. Inasmuch as this relationship is intersubjectively a "product of presuppositions resultant of interactions between individual subjectivities and sociocultural contexts, which further evolve through socially interacting individuals embedded in personal and collective contexts" (Gayle, 2009, p. 315), gender and ethnic diversity in the mentor–mentee dyad can co-create increasingly meaningful interaction.

Forehand (2008) supports recognizing and addressing challenges, even seizing opportunities, when a mentor and mentee vary on demographic characteristics. A study by Chan (2008) indicates that talking about race, racism, and privilege promotes trust and rapport in cross-cultural relationships. Discussions may encompass the given reality of racial and gender characteristics as well as a diversity of self-disclosed viewpoints that enrich the mentoring relationship. This may be particularly important when power differentiation in mentor–mentee relationships is compounded by power differentials in gender or diversity.

Because mentoring relationships are vulnerable to triangulation with intersecting institutions (e.g., educational institutions, workplaces, fieldwork sites, regulatory boards), attention to the intersubjective interplay between the mentoring relationship and the organizational culture is important. Cultural intentions inherently include the sociocultural assumptions and professional attitudes that presuppose mentoring relationships. For example, counseling psychology training programs must meet certain criteria set by licensing boards who adopt legislation according to sociocultural need. These criteria, often reflected in the curriculum or in continuing education requirements, influence the theoretical orientations and practical applications that presuppose therapist development and formal mentoring relationships.

Awareness of, and discussion about, culture-of-origin influences upon therapist development may mentor empowerment and action. According to cultural psychology, individual and culture "jointly facilitate, express, repress, stabilize, transform, and defend each other" (Shweder, 1991, p. 102). Mentoring an awareness of the cultural domains that intersubjectively affect interpersonal interaction fosters a stronger sense of self and creates a more meaningful mentoring frame.

In Mae's case, oppressive dynamics surrounding her culture of origin were influencing her current relationships:

> Important sociocultural insights emerged when Mae shared that her metaphorical horse was a "champion" groomed by famous horse breeders in Russia. In fact, Mae's parents were Russian immigrants who fled Communist rule in 1958. It took quite some time and many menial jobs before her father could gain citizenship and resume his career in higher education. During that time, Mae remembers that her family was occasionally the subject of prejudice and fear because of international Cold War dynamics. Although Mae identified as second-generation Russian-American, she is embedded in this cultural past and remembers how her family often hid their former heritage, upper socioeconomic class, and rich culture so that they would not stand out. While academia became a safe place to grow and excel for the entire family, Mae's current development as a psychotherapist involved balancing autonomy and self-disclosure in her attempted use

of self with peers and clients. Utilizing metaphor and narrative with her mentor gave her experiences of honoring and integrating her cultural history and social dynamics.

A safe and effective mentoring relationship matures and supports awareness of personal subjectivity, symbolic interaction, and sociocultural embedded intentions. Operationally, this process is an open-ended dialogic interaction that includes immediate experience, allows for free expression, and cultivates understandings that come to rest on a higher level for both participants. Inasmuch as this relationship occurs between relatively situated individuals embedded in personal, historical, social, and cultural contexts, interaction is intersubjectively grounded in a "range of possibility" (Giorgi, 2005, p. 213), which by recognition and open discussion prevents the mentoring relationship from spinning out of control into a boundary-less, frameless, undifferentiated situation or, on the contrary, becoming competitive, vicious, and dysfunctional.

Hermeneutic Model for Mentoring

Questions remain for the practice of psychotherapy generally, and mentoring specifically, about just how two subjectivities simultaneously co-inhabit and co-create a unified field of experience, expression, and understanding. What specific processes keep subjective experiences that often seem indistinguishable from reality from distorting perceptions of self-development, the mentoring relationship, or the external world? Are there methods that *link* (Cohen & Schermer, 2004) or *bridge* (Coelho & Figueiredo, 2003) movements between conscious and unconscious material, subject and object, self and culture safely, reliably, and productively? Can the mentoring relationship retain bifurcations of subject and object, self, relationship, and culture and maintain a reflexive awareness of immediate, shared experience at the same time?

Recently, psychotherapy research has adopted hermeneutical inquiry to understand the simultaneously autonomous, interdependent, and contextualized self. Contributions include conceptions of the self in "process as interaction" (Hoffman et al., 2009, p. 181), co-constructive through discourse and narrative (Freedman & Combs, 1996), co-creative with sociocultural intentional worlds (Gayle, 2009), and co-accommodative of unconscious depth dimensions via "converging metaphoric pathways" (Cohen & Schermer, 2004, p. 580). Identifying such processes involved in meaning-making between two subjectivities participating in immediate and unfolding experience helps to understand mutual growth between individuals situated in personal and collective value systems, contexts, and cultures.

The hermeneutic method is a practice of understanding interior/exterior or part/whole interaction through experience-near immersion, if not direct experience, of immediate or historical events (for a comprehensive historical review, see Grondin, 1994; Packer & Addison, 1989; Ricour, 1981). I have elsewhere articulated a hermeneutic change theory stemming from Dilthey's (1900/1972) articulation of direct experience and Heidegger's (1953/1996) conceptualization of the hermeneutic circle:

> Wilhelm Dilthey (1900/1972) introduced the idea of a reflexive awareness: Through direct experience of either historic or immediate events an implicit kind of understanding occurs, which psychological description can then make explicit. Every understanding and explanation has a beginning root in experience and the immediacy of this experience and understanding continues to unfold within the sociocultural and historical world…. Heidegger (1953/1996) conceptualizes the interactive nature of this experience and understanding into a hermeneutic circle of interior/exterior or part/whole interaction that expresses verbally, non-verbally, and dialogically as individual understanding. Strasser (1985) expands this circle metaphor into a "spiral" (p. 32) representing a process that co-creates meaning as each expression ascends to, and enriches, original understanding.
>
> (Gayle, 2009, pp. 313/316)

From a relational/intersubjective perspective, the notion of "immediate" or "direct" experience is dialectically unresolved. While ontological insight into being itself (Heidegger, 1953/1996) or the givenness of life may contribute important subjective etiology to intersubjective interactions, direct experience of such still takes place in a lived present, and the present is by nature a process captured only by introspection. Therefore, immediate experience in the mentoring relationship is best described as *experience-near* (Kohut, 1959). For example, mutual empathic attunement identifies through emotions and expressions; resonating self-narratives identify through linguistic exchange; and symmetrical depth processes identify through the asymmetrical surface enactments of transference and countertransference.

This understanding meaningfully expands the hermeneutical spiral into one that starts with an *experience-near-experience* of interaction that intersubjectively expresses in understanding and meaning that is integrated again and again, resulting in superior understanding or enriched meaning. This was certainly the case in my experience with Dr. Yalom described at the beginning of this chapter. Articulating experience-near interactions in this way may help individual subjectivities to relinquish or suspend attachment to personal and often cherished ideas in order to engage the insights of another so that mutual understanding may co-create meanings greater than either subjectivity could access alone. While this may be difficult for some mentors and therapists alike, the rewards are worthwhile for *both* mentor and mentee:

> For Mae's mentor, this process provided a refreshing and creative interplay unencumbered by agenda or directives. Entering into the hermeneutic spiral she, too, often emerged with a greater sense of creativity, connection,

empowerment, and sense of possibility. Rather than listening for the clinically significant problem, striving to strike a neutral, autonomous distance, or conversely feeling encumbered by expectations to socialize, this mentor knew that Mae came freely for specific benefit to co-create meaningful personal and professional growth. No money was exchanged, and when Mae graduated her program an informal "let's stay in touch" was initiated.

During her postgraduate internship, Mae would occasionally leave a voicemail or send a card conveying how she continued to draw upon the metaphors and co-creative processes she and the mentor had utilized. A powerful generative effect of this mentoring relationship occurred some years later when the mentor had occasion to call Mae, now a licensed psychotherapist, for collateral information regarding a client they had in common (Mae was counseling the wife in a couple that was engaging in marriage therapy with the mentor). This signified the redefinition of their mentee–mentor relationship as a collegial one that continued to be mutually co-creative in personal and professional ways.

Summary

When a developing therapist appropriately aspires to enter a mentor–mentee relationship with someone possessing the necessary qualifications for safety, trust, fidelity, and ideological integrity, a co-creative environment for growth is available. Temporarily suspending attachment to individual temporal ideas, the mentee opens to and considers insights of the mentor. Immediate experience of the mentor's insight and/or role modeling relatively represents and expresses in words, metaphors, and symbols, which in turn potentiate new insights for the mentor, and intrinsic truths are infused with dynamic meaning-making potential for both participants. This process safely supports flexibility, takes into consideration personal initiative, freedom, creativity, emotions, and value systems, and guards against personal boundary crossings, power imbalances, and transference-countertransference dynamics that arise from intentions disconnected from the social, cultural, and global contexts where mentoring relationships occur.

Understanding and safely experiencing hermeneutical meaning-making within mentoring relationships helps the developing therapist to navigate experience-near interactions that inevitably involve both voluntary and inherent self-disclosures. A mentoring relationship augments insight-oriented psychotherapy by its experiential nature, and supplements formal educational and fieldwork training with a sense of play. Being comfortable and competent in the hermeneutical processes involved in experience-near interactions ensures that therapists will have a method by which to continue their growth and generate healing for others throughout their personal and professional development.

References

Allen, T., & Eby, L. (Eds.). (2007). *The Blackwell Handbook of Mentoring: A Multiple Perspectives Approach*. MA: Blackwell Publishing.

Allen, T., Eby, L., O'Brien, K., & Lentz, E. (2008). The state of mentoring research: A qualitative review of current research methods and future research implications. *Journal of Vocational Behavior*, 73, 343–357.

Arnd-Caddigan, M., & Pozzuto, R. (2008). Use of self in relational clinical social work. *Clinical Social Work Journal*, 36, 235–243.

Barnett, J. (2008). Mentoring boundaries, multiple relationships: Opportunities and challenges. *Mentoring and Tutoring Partnership in Learning*, 16, 3–16.

Blickle, G., Schneider, P., Perrewe, P., Blass, F., & Ferris, G. (2008). The roles of self-disclosure, modesty, and self-monitoring in the mentoring relationship: A longitudinal multi-source investigation. *Career Development International*, 13, 224–240.

Bosworth, H., Aizaga, K., & Cabaniss, D. (2009). The training analyst: Analyst, teacher, mentor. *Journal of the American Psychoanalytic Association*, 57, 663–675.

Chan, A. (2008). Mentoring ethnic minority, pre-doctoral students: an analysis of key mentor practices. *Mentoring and Tutoring: Partnership in Learning*, 16, 263–277.

Clifford, E. (1999). A descriptive study of mentor-protégé relationships, mentors' emotional empathic tendency, and proteges' teacher self-efficacy belief. *Early Child Development and Care*, 156, 143–154.

Coelho, N. E., Jr., & Figueiredo, L. C. (2003). Patterns of intersubjectivity in the constitution of subjectivity: Dimensions of otherness. *Culture & Psychology*, 9, 193–208.

Cohen, B., & Schermer, V. (2004). Self transformation and the unconscious in contemporary psychoanalytic therapy: The problem of "depth" within a relational and intersubjective frame of reference. *Psychoanalytic Psychology*, 21, 580–600.

Cronan-Hillix, T., Gensheimer, L. K., Cronan-Hillix, W. A., & Davidson, W. S. (1986). Students' views of mentors in psychology graduate training. *Teaching of Psychology*, 27, 262–268.

Davidson, D. (2001). *Subjective, Intersubjective, Objective*. New York: Oxford University Press.

Dilthey, W. (1972). The rise of hermeneutics (F. Jameson, trans.). *New Literary History*, 3, 229–244. (Original work published 1900.)

Ewing, R., Freeman, M., Barrie, S., Bell, A., O'Connor, D., Waugh, F., & Sykes, C. (2008). Building community in academic settings: the importance of flexibility in a structured mentoring program. *Mentoring and Tutoring: Partnership in Learning*, 16, 294–310.

Forehand, R. (2008). The art and science of mentoring in psychology: A necessary practice to ensure our future. *American Psychologist*, 63, 744–755.

Freedman, J., & Combs, G. (1996). *Narrative Therapy: The Social Construction of Preferred Realities*. New York: Norton.

Ganzer, C. (2007). The use of self from a relational perspective. *Clinical Social Work Journal*, 35, 117–123.

Gayle, R. (2009). Co-creating meaningful structures within long-term psychotherapy group culture. *International Journal of Group Psychotherapy*, 59, 311–333.

Gendler, J. R. (1984). *The Book of Qualities*. Berkeley, CA: Turquoise Mountain Publications.

Gendlin, E. (1978). *Focusing*. New York: Bantam Dell.

Genero, N., Miller, J., Surrey, J., & Baldwin, L. (1992). Measuring perceived mutuality questionnaire. *Journal of Family Psychology*, 6, 36–48.

Gergen, K. (1991). *The Saturated Self: Dilemmas of Identity in Contemporary Life*. New York: Basic Books.

Giorgi, A. (2005). Remaining challenges for humanistic psychology. *Journal of Humanistic Psychology*, 45, 204–216.

Gove, P. & Merriam-Webster, Inc. (Eds.) (2002). *Webster's Third New International Dictionary of the English Language, unabridged*. MA: Merriam-Webster, Inc.

Grondin, J. (1994). *Introduction to Philosophical Hermeneutics*. New Haven, CT: Yale University Press.

Heffron, M., Ivins, B., & Weston, D. (2005). Finding an authentic voice: Use of self: essential learning processes for relationship-based work. *Infants & Young Children*, 18, 323–336.

Heidegger, M. (1996). *Being and Time* (J. Stambaugh, trans.). New York: State University Press. (Original work published 1953.)

Hoffmann, L., Gleave, R., Burlingame, G., & Jackson, A. (2009). Exploring interactions of improvers and deteriorators in the group therapy process: A qualitative analysis. *International Journal of Group Psychotherapy*, 59, 179–197.

Hollway, W. (2006). Paradox in the pursuit of a critical theorization of the development of self in family relationships. *Theory & Psychology*, 16, 465–482.

Hu, C. (2008). Analyses of measurement equivalence across gender in the Mentoring Functions Questionnaire (MFQ-9). *Personality and Individual Differences*, 45, 199–205.

Hunt, D., & Michael, C. (1983). Mentorship: A career training and development tool. *Academy of Management Review*, 8, 475–485.

Jacobi, M. (1991). Mentoring and undergraduate academic success: A literature review. *Review of Educational Research*, 61, 505–532.

Johnson, B. (2003). A framework for conceptualizing competence to mentor. *Ethics and Behavior*, 13, 127–151.

Kohut, H. (1959). Introspection, empathy, and psychoanalysis: An examination of the relationship between mode of observation and theory. *Journal of the American Psychoanalytic Association*, 7, 459–483.

Kram, K. (1980). Mentoring processes at work: Developmental relationships in managerial careers (Doctoral dissertation). Retrieved from OCLC FirstSearch. (Accession No. AAG8025206).

Kram, K. (1985). *Mentoring at Work: Developmental Relationships in Organizational Life*. Glenview, IL: Scott, Foresman, and Company.

Kirschner, S. (2003). On the varieties of intersubjective experience. *Culture and Psychology*, 9, 277–286.

Levinson, D., Darrow, C., Klein, E., Levinson, M., & McKee, B. (1978). *The Seasons of a Man's Life*. New York: Random House.

Liang, B., Spencer, R., Brogan, D., & Corral, M. (2008). Mentoring relationships from early adolescence through emerging adulthood: A qualitative analysis. *Journal of Vocational Behavior*, 72, 168–182.

Liang, B., Tracy, A., Taylor, C., Williams, L., Jordan, J., & Miller, J. (2002a). The new Relational Health Indices: A study of women's relationships. *Psychology of Women Quarterly*, 26, 25–35.

Liang, B., Tracy, A., Taylor, C., & Williams, L. (2002b). Mentoring college-age women: A relational approach. *American Journal of Community Psychology*, 30, 271–289.

McAuley, M. (2003). Transference, countertransference and mentoring: the ghost in the process. *British Journal of Guidance and Counseling*, 31, 11–23.

Meissner, S. (2002). The problem of self-disclosure in psychoanalysis. *Journal of the American Psychoanalytic Association*, 50, 827–867.

Mitchell, S. (1998). *Relational Concepts in Psychoanalysis: An Integration*. Cambridge, MA: Harvard University Press.

Mullen, C. (2007). Naturally occurring student-faculty mentoring relationships: A literature review. In T. Allen & L. Eby (Eds.), *The Blackwell Handbook of Mentoring: A Multiple Perspective Approach* (pp. 119–138). MA: Blackwell Publishing.

Olds, D. (2006). Identification: Psychoanalytic and biological perspectives. *Journal of the American Psychoanalytic Association*, 54, 17–48.

Packer, M., & Addison, R. (Eds.). (1989). *Entering the Circle: Hermeneutic Investigation in Psychology*. New York: State University Press.

Pellegrini, E., & Scandura, T. (2005). Construct equivalence across groups: an unexplored issue in mentoring research. *Educational and Psychological Measurement*, 65, 323–335.

Prosky, P. (1996). The use of self in family therapy. *Family Therapy*, 23, 159–169.

Ragins, B., & Scandura, T. (1994). Gender differences in expected outcomes of mentoring relationships. *Academy of Management Journal*, 37, 957–971.

Ricoeur, P. (1981). *Hermeneutics and the Human Sciences* (J. Thompson, ed. and trans.). New York: Cambridge University Press.

Scandura, T. (1998). Dysfunctional mentoring relationships and outcomes. *Journal of Management*, 24, 449–467.

Shweder, R. (1991). *Thinking Through Cultures*. Cambridge, MA: Harvard University Press.

St. Clair, M. (2004). *Object Relations and Self Psychology*. Belmont, CA: Brooks/Cole.

Steinbock, A. (2001). Interpersonal attention through exemplarity. In E. Thompson (Ed.), *Between Ourselves: Second-Person Issues in the Study of Consciousness* (pp. 179–196). Charlottesville, VA: Imprint Academic.

Storrs, D., Putsche, L., & Taylor, A. (2008). Mentoring expectations and realities: An analysis of metaphorical thinking among female undergraduate protégés and their mentors in a university mentoring program. *Mentoring and Tutoring: Partnership in Learning*, 16, 175–188.

Strasser, S. (1985). *Understanding and Explanation*. Pittsburgh, PA: Duquesne University Press.

Sullivan, H. (1953). *The Interpersonal Theory of Psychiatry*. New York: Norton.

Tenenbaum, H. (2001). Mentoring relationships in graduate school. *Journal of Vocational Behavior*, 59, 326–341.

Tentoni, S. (1995). The mentoring of counseling students: A concept in search of a paradigm. *Counselor Education and Supervision*, 35, 32–42.

Yalom, I., & Leszcz, M. (2005). *The Theory and Practice of Group Psychotherapy*. New York: Basic Books.

4

The Place of Didactic Preparation in the Therapist's Development

Victor L. Schermer

Thought is action in rehearsal.

Sigmund Freud

Education is not just the filling of a pail; it is the lighting of a fire.

B. F. Skinner

These two quotations, from a Viennese psychiatrist and an American psychologist who inspired opposite poles of 20th-century psychology that informed psychotherapy and lit different fires under it, tell us that the therapist's didactic learning does not exist in isolation. It is fueled by inspiration, and it leads toward therapeutic activity, in turn being transformed by it. Thus, psychotherapy and the careers of the persons who devote themselves to it are driven and informed by a systematic body of acquired knowledge, but such knowledge is intimately intertwined with the craft itself, the persons who practice it, and the patients who ideally will benefit from it.

This interplay is illustrated by the first well-known case of modern psychotherapy, that of Anna O (Ellenberger, 1972). During the years 1880–1882, the Viennese physician Josef Breuer treated a difficult case of hysteria. To further her treatment, the patient disclosed her private memories and emotions to the doctor, suggesting the method that came to be known as the "talking cure." Breuer consulted about the case with Sigmund Freud, a neurologist who would soon expand his knowledge of psychiatry by attending Jean-Martin Charcot's lectures and demonstration sessions at the Salpêtrière Asylum in France for 5 months in 1885 (Gay, 1988, pp. 48–53). Freud told Breuer what he had learned there and, in addition, they discussed defense mechanisms and unconscious dynamics. They co-wrote a series of papers, *Studies on Hysteria* (Breuer & Freud, 1893–1895) that had a controversial and ultimately revolutionary impact on psychiatry. Freud went on to develop a method of treatment called psychoanalysis. Thus, a new era of psychiatric treatment was stimulated partly by Freud's education in psychiatry by Charcot, among others. Taking a cue from the vicissitudes and importance of Freud's educational experience, it is relevant now, more than a century later, to inquire about the changing role of the didactic preparation of therapists in the New Millennium.

The Place of Didactic Education in Developing the Therapist's Approach and Armamentarium in a Time of Change

All schools of psychotherapy, whatever their underlying perspectives, function by transmitting a body of knowledge that informs the treatment process and is subject to proof and revision based on clinical experience and research. Psychotherapy as *praxis* has always been reciprocally embedded in such didactic education, which forms a pivotal component of the therapist's development, informing and inspiring that development and ideally leading toward what the Buddhists call "mindfulness" and "right action" in the consulting room.

Becoming a psychotherapist has always been an adventurous journey, one with twists, turns, and challenges. Freud (1937) gloomily called it "the impossible profession," and while his may have been an overly pessimistic view, the past three decades in particular have seen even greater challenges to the profession than either Freud's or the subsequent generation of therapists could have imagined. In just the past two decades there have occurred monumental shifts in health care practice, finances, and administration; a multiplication of psychotherapy modalities; promising treatment applications from neuroscience and psychopharmacology; and a technologically embedded "information explosion" that has challenged psychotherapy education and practice, while at the same time offering new teaching options such as digital media, manualized treatment protocols, and Internet "distance learning."

Moreover, because of the agendas of managed care, along with the increasing demand for treatment of complex disorders (such as substance abuse, dual diagnoses, comorbidity, borderline personality disorder, complicated grief, and post-traumatic stress), and the ascendance of cognitive and behavioral approaches to therapy, aspiring therapists today must either choose among diverse and sometimes opposing approaches, or juggle multiple frameworks to find what works best in particular situations. Nowadays, the educational requirements for properly treating a given diagnosis with a particular treatment modality may vary considerably. Being educated and trained as a competent generalist or eclectic psychotherapist may pass muster for licensing but is no longer regarded as sufficient to provide an *optimal standard of care* for any number of the DSM disorders (Spitzer et al., 2001).

As technical diversity becomes highlighted and approaches compete with each other for effectiveness and popularity, cognitive therapists may criticize psychoanalysis for lack of empirical validation (Beck et al., 1985). Gestalt therapists may hold cognitive-behavioral therapists culpable of insufficiently addressing "here-and-now" emotions. Substance abuse therapists may advocate treatments derived from 12-step programs rather than professional disciplines

(Flores, 1997, pp. 247–298). There is ongoing debate about the relative effectiveness of medication versus psychotherapy (Antonuccio et al., 1995). Education and training programs, affected by such contrasting and rapidly evolving contemporary influences and points of view, are faced with the quandary of providing a body of commonly accepted knowledge while at the same time offering specialized training in a particular paradigm that an alternative perspective may find difficult to comprehend and accept.

In what follows, taking into account such pressures and complexities of the current health care environment and the ever-increasing pluralism of approaches, we will consider what, for want of a better phrase, can be called "didactic preparation"—that is, the component of therapist training whereby information, guidelines, treatment strategies, ethics, theoretical frameworks, and schools of thought are passed down to the therapist-in-the-making in formal or structured contexts such as graduate programs, internships, residencies, books, online seminars, and other formats in which the primary purpose is to transmit an accumulated body of knowledge. These avenues are distinct from but interface with supervision, mentoring, personal therapy, and other working relationships discussed elsewhere in this book in which the therapist is guided in a process rather than given a body of knowledge as such, although didactic education is often supplemented by them, and integration of knowledge and application is ideally facilitated in all these contexts.

A good deal of what will be discussed here is based on the author's own journey as a psychotherapist, supervisor, consultant, and educator. His training and bias is psychoanalysis, and he emphasizes object relations theory, self-psychology, and relational psychology in his work. However, his graduate work in experimental and social psychology gave him a firm foundation in cognitive and behavioral frameworks as well. He has served as a psychotherapist for more than 35 years, directed several training programs, sponsored conferences, taught numerous college-level and continuing education seminars and workshops, was faculty member and supervisor at a free-standing psychoanalytic institute, and is an active Fellow of the American Group Psychotherapy Association. He has worked in a variety of facilities as well as independent practice, and lived through a time when managed care significantly altered the landscape of the mental health field. During that time and in those contexts, he has witnessed many of the issues and concerns about which he writes, and several of the illustrations of his points are based on his own education and work experience.

The Personal, Humanistic, and Inspirational Elements of Didactic Training

The word "didactic" unfortunately carries the negative connotation of dry, abstruse, and irrelevant teaching, an implication that is certainly not intended here. Rather, we define didactic preparation as that component of training that represents the disciplined acquisition of knowledge for the healing work to be transacted in the consulting room. Didactic education, beginning with a broad liberal arts and sciences exposure, and followed by specialized learning of a discipline, is in fact an honored tradition that has roots in the European university setting. It places a high value on the sources (books, documents, research) and expert transmitters (transcribers, writers, scholars, professors) of knowledge, with an emphasis on the pursuit of truth through disciplined inquiry.

In psychotherapy, "truth" is assessed by a combination of factual, theoretical, pragmatic, and experiential validation. More than a bare-boned statement of facts and theories, the teaching of psychotherapy, like all good education, imparts knowledge in ways that affect both the left and right brain of the student, his or her own personality and experience, and the need to be motivated and inspired, to be shown "how" as well as "what" to learn. Often, it is a combination of the knowledge, experience, and personality of the instructor that carries the day. A reminder to this effect is pertinent during a time when digitalized learning, online courses, and manualized therapy approaches are increasingly available, such that the personal and interpersonal aspects of education are less prominent, especially those features of learning that can occur only in the embodied form of instructor and students present in the same room and having face-to-face contact. As Merleau-Ponty (1976) and other philosophers have argued, it is precisely our embodied mutual presence that makes us alive and human to one another.

The importance of face-to-face "humanized" learning is evident to anyone who has had an inspirational experience with a professor. Freud was literally "dazzled" by Charcot's teaching (Gay, 1988, p. 48). A memorable instance in the author's own education was provided by the late psychoanalyst Gunther Abraham. Dr. Abraham was the nephew of the great psychoanalyst Karl Abraham. He trained at the Berlin Psychoanalytic Institute and moved to England, where he studied with Melanie Klein, Anna Freud, and Donald Winnicott. His background inspired awe. Yet his teaching, far from authority-driven, was relational, compassionate, and vivid. He taught object relations theory, too often expressed in an abstruse manner, in such a way that one could immediately relate it both to oneself and to patients. In addition, Dr. Abraham provided the students with a role model of empathy, highly focused attention, and the "capacity for concern," and he taught theory in such a lively and evocative way that one could readily envision using it in a session with a difficult patient. It has been three decades since the author's classes with him, but recollections of his insights and even some of his unique phraseology continue to be of great value in the author's daily psychotherapy practice. "Make a space for the patient," Dr. Abraham would say. "Find the connections between the thoughts." Or, in an ironic scolding voice, "Don't get married before your father!"—which would make the class chuckle nervously, and by which he seemed to mean, don't be arrogant or draw conclusions too quickly.

Dr. Abraham's teaching was of the highest order, like the "peripatetic" school of Greek philosophy, where the learning resulted from the student–teacher interaction. One could acquire a knowledge of object relations theory from a book, a slide show, or a manual, but, in the words of the main character Lou, played by Bert Lancaster in Louis Malle's film *Atlantic City*, it wouldn't be "the same ocean." The value of didactic learning is ultimately determined by its positive influence on the therapist in working with patients, and this requires a relational element.

Lively, exploratory interaction is essential to a process whereby knowledge is imprinted in a form that can be metabolized and used in a creative, resilient way. Student–teacher bonding plays an important role in achieving this goal. Today, despite the current emphasis on and practical utility of evidence-based treatment protocols that can be conveyed via manuals and digitalized learning, the importance of the student–teacher attachment is irreplaceable and needs to be re-emphasized.

The Basics

Despite the variegated and rapidly changing complexities of the mental health field today, and the elusive quality of elements such as the student–teacher relationship that have an impact upon all learning and application, it is nevertheless possible to articulate the fundamentals of what the student therapist should take away from didactic education that will ultimately be useful in the practice of the art and science of psychotherapy. Among these fundamentals are (1) conceptual and theoretical frameworks for treatment; (2) knowledge of the process of psychotherapeutic change; (3) how to address ethical and legal issues; (4) the use of scientific method; and (5) knowledge and skills to cope with the ambiguity, stress, and personal uncertainty of the work.

Conceptual Frameworks

Training and education should, first and foremost, provide a framework for conceptualizing and organizing clinical data and experience. Such a framework should incorporate, for example, diagnostic knowledge and skills, etiological considerations (knowledge of symptoms and their triggers, childhood origins, and current situational influences), and understanding of the human personality from biological, psychological, and sociocultural vantage points. Such a framework will include both factual elements and theoretical understanding that comes from a general pool of knowledge, inference, and experience, but it will also vary to some extent on whether the teaching emphasizes psychodynamics, interpersonal factors, family dynamics, biological factors, and so forth. Ideally, an awareness of the potential importance of all these factors will be inculcated, whatever the biases that determine which is emphasized and advocated. The patient is a whole person, and no single thread of explanation is sufficient to explain his or her behavior and mentation (Lewis et al., 1976). Moreover, while signs, symptoms, and diagnoses of disorders are a significant component of the craft, psychotherapy, more than other specialties, cannot abstract such entities from the patient who manifests them. Personhood (Rogers, 1995) is a fundamental concept in psychotherapy, and students need to acquire both cognitive and affective understandings of the whole persons whom they will encounter in their work.

In addition to facts and theories, therapist education will include a working knowledge of treatment strategies and techniques and their relationship to the schools of thought and therapy approaches from which they derive. Each psychotherapeutic approach, whether psychoanalytic, gestalt, cognitive, or behavioral, offers a basic set of rules and structures that facilitate desired results and which the therapist-to-be must learn as a preliminary to doing treatment. These may be taught either collectively, in a "compare-and-contrast" manner, or singly, at the point of acquiring a specialized approach.

One subject area that is acquiring increasing importance in the education of therapists is neuroscience. There are now psychotherapy perspectives based on burgeoning brain science (Cozolino, 2002; Siegel, 2007) that did not exist as recently as a decade ago. Further, psychopharmacology is of exponentially increasing importance in the treatment of mental illness, and biofeedback, including the use of electroencephalography and functional magnetic resonance imagery, is finding increasing applicability. Moreover, from the point of view of cognitive, behavioral, and dynamic therapies, findings from neuroscience are now being applied to psychotherapy as such. For example, the functions of so-called "mirror neurons" appear relevant to what transpires in the consulting room (Schermer, 2010). As scientists more clearly articulate the mind–body connection, therapist education is likely to be increasingly based upon biological understanding.

Thus, a broad and comprehensive knowledge base and framework shapes and influences all other aspects of therapist training and development.

The Change Process

In addition to providing a way to understand clinical phenomena, and since therapy is about interventions that lead toward healing, adjustment, and personality integration, therapist education should offer an understanding of the change process and the role of the therapist in that process.

What changes in a patient as a result of successful psychotherapy varies as a function of the duration of treatment, the therapist's approach, the patient's capabilities, and the relationship that develops in the consulting room. At one extreme, symptom alleviation can be a goal of treatment. However, for some patients, especially trauma victims and those with personality disorders, improved social adjustment and resilience is almost mandatory for a successful outcome. In some instances, personality change and transformation (Bion, 1965) may be sought in which the patient undergoes a significant revision of his or her attitudes, perception of self and world, and orientation to life. Some patients come to therapy with a sense of emptiness, internal conflict, and existential ennui that can be alleviated only through in-depth exploration of the self in the context of a deep relationship with the therapist. Therapists need to learn what goals and objectives to set and what is possible under given circumstances and what promotes and interferes with the desired changes.

How change occurs is as much a subject matter of therapist education as what changes are sought. Problematically, there is no universally agreed upon way to conceptualize therapeutic change agents, since constructs of change are a function of schools of thought. A behavioral therapist may use rewards that reinforce desired behaviors. A cognitive therapist offers logical rebuttals to distorted thinking. A psychodynamic therapist formulates an interpretation that recognizes a single meaning of diverse mental associations. In general, we can say that a process of social influence is taking place, but there is little agreement on what makes this influence effective in the healing process.

This conundrum points to two important considerations in didactic education of therapists. First, and paradoxically, given the complexity of change agents, it is probably best that the aspiring therapist undergo extensive specialized training that fosters thorough mastery of at least one approach. This will minimize the trial-and-error "eclecticism" that can confuse both patient and therapist and interfere with assessing the success and failure of ongoing interventions. Second, the student's choice of a training program and school of thought should ideally be congruent with salient aspects of his or her personality. A student who derives satisfaction from observing and measuring the effects of interventions is not likely to function well in the role of a psychoanalytic therapist who needs to listen silently for long periods of time. Or, someone who enjoys creative imagination and play might be best suited for training in psychodrama or art or music therapy, rather than, say, exposure therapy or desensitization protocols. As in other disciplines, the required skill sets should match the person who uses them. It is easily forgotten that "doing therapy" may mean many different things, and, for example, a good transactional analyst may not make a good psychoanalyst. In one training center, a distinguished, high-achieving psychotherapist sought to acquire the skills necessary to move from a more directive, interpersonal form of therapy to a less directive psychodynamic one. The practitioner, despite being bright and accomplished, simply couldn't acquire the necessary non-directive, interpretive attitude, and had to terminate the program. There are thus limits on "transfer of training" between one approach and another, and between working with diverse client populations. Therapist education and selection of candidates can benefit from attention to these contingencies.

The one change agent that is agreed to be helpful in all therapy approaches is *good communication* (Fierman, 1965). There are indeed empirically supported principles (Carkuff, 1969) that facilitate mutual understanding between therapist and patient, such as active listening and paraphrasing, but training programs vary considerably in how much they emphasize such communication skills. Some graduate programs in counseling psychology devote considerable time to the topic, while psychoanalytic programs mention it only in passing with some remarks on "tact" and "timing," although the recent emphasis on empathy and attunement does place increased emphasis on the communication process. Cognitive therapists learn the "Socratic method" (Beck et al., 1985, pp. 167–190), challenging the irrationality of the patient's beliefs, but if this is done without empathy, it may lead to argumentativeness or covert resistance rather than change.

A component of psychotherapy is to motivate the patient via one or another process of social influence. Reinforcement, the therapeutic alliance, "resistance analysis," and hypnotic suggestion are among the more traditional therapeutic "persuaders." More recently, motivational techniques have been imported into psychotherapy, as in W. R Miller's motivational interviewing and motivational enhancement therapy (Miller, 1994). There are potential ethical questions in all persuasive methods, especially when they are manipulative and/or limit the patient's freedom of choice. At any rate, the education of the therapist will include guidelines on how to achieve change and, conversely, what is ineffective, inappropriate, or unethical.

Ethical and Legal Issues

Even though the "medicine" that the therapist uses consists mostly of words, the ethical and legal issues posed by therapy practice can be as daunting as in any other aspect of medical care. As a result, ethics courses and seminars are held with increasing frequency, and many licensing and certifying boards include periodic ethics workshops as part of their continuing education requirements. While a good deal of therapy skill is a result of learning from mistakes, the ability to address ethical and legal matters had better not be learned in that way! Ethics are often best taught through discussions of values and legal issues, along with problem-solving examples of typical dilemmas. Equally important is the oath of Aesculapius: "Physician, do no harm!" If the didactic education of therapists does not lead to a consciousness of how to not harm patients, it will have failed in its mission, no matter how many facts and theories are learned. The Nazi doctors often had considerable medical education and knowledge, but put it to sadistic and malevolent use that was rationalized by a prevailing ideology. In our own culture, sexual relations, inappropriate drug use, so-called "attack therapy," and other unethical practices with patients have similarly been rationalized at one time or another. Moreover, some therapists may exercise power by being doctrinaire about their treatment approaches (Kernberg, 2000). Therapists need to be educated in those values that preserve the rights and dignity of their patients.

Scientific Method

Two additional broad-based components of therapist development are typically addressed only peripherally during didactic education or are expected to be coincidentally absorbed by the student in the learning process. The first is the teaching of the scientific method and its use *in vivo* during assessment, evaluation, and treatment. The author acquired detailed knowledge of the scientific method in undergraduate courses in philosophy of science and in graduate courses in experimental psychology. Paradoxically, he had only two learning experiences emphasizing the scientific method in his subsequent 30-plus years of specialized, postgraduate, and continuing education in psychotherapy! One of these was a segment of a course in psychoanalysis by James Pearson where the class discussed a series of critical readings on the scientific validity of psychoanalysis. The other was in a course in group psychotherapy by Yvonne Agazarian, where she discussed hypothesis formation, inductive-deductive reasoning, and levels of abstraction relative to the leadership of groups. Since what distinguishes professional psychotherapy from informal support with personal problems is its scientific basis, a careful consideration of the scientific method probably deserves a greater place in therapy education than it receives in most quarters. Students do assimilate a degree of scientific-mindedness in studies of case material, consideration of the pros and cons of diverse theories, and so on. But in a field with as many unresolved questions as psychotherapy, the study of the history and philosophy of science and the scientific method deserves more of a place than it usually receives in therapist education.

How to Cope with Ambiguity and Personal Uncertainty

Second, in what is more of a byproduct than a consciously instructed element of didactic education, the aspiring therapist should acquire the ability to deal with the ambiguities and personal uncertainties involved in a psychotherapy career. A question sometimes asked of therapists by both their friends and patients is, "How can you deal with these crazy people all day?" Therapy work is highly stressful because of the sheer amount of listening involved, exposure to the patients' emotional conflicts and trauma, and the uncertainty of therapeutic outcomes. While most of the monitoring and self-management of highly stressful aspects of the treatment process is done in personal therapy, clinical supervision, and informal support systems such as one's colleagues and inner circle of family and friends, didactic education can have a great impact as well. In particular, didactics affords the therapist a cognitive map that provides an avenue for sublimating the intense affects generated in the countertransference. The present author has found that in some phases of his work with borderline patients and substance abusers, an important factor that promoted emotional stability and containment of the patients' projective identifications was an educationally acquired interest in their specific psychodynamics, which acted as ballast in rough seas.

In this respect, it is parenthetically not only the acquisition of theory and technique that provide anchors for the therapist's emotions: it is also the emulation of revered instructors. As part of his group therapy training, the author was fortunate to be taught by the late Ramon Ganzarian, who, among many other accomplishments, co-founded the group therapy training program at the Menninger Clinic. Dr. Ganzarian's (1989) application of object relations theory to group treatment was seminal, but equally instructive was his calm, attentive, containing manner. A similar role modeling of containment was given by Vincent Gioe, former President of the Family Institute of Philadelphia, in his seminars on contextual family therapy, which he conducted with the same detachment, measured words, and unconditional positive regard for the students as he did in sessions with couples and families.

In general, the basics of didactic education can be compared with an artist's sketches for a painting or sculpture. They provide the ideas, form, and structure of what will later be filled in with details, contrast, and color. What the student ultimately does with the education is influenced by circumstances and influences that go beyond it, such as mentoring, personal insight, clinical experience, and life events. Moreover, the education of a therapist has so many dimensions that it must be carried out over an extended period in a series of phases moving from the general to the specific, and systematically incorporating practical hands-on experience that firms up the learning in the therapeutic trenches.

The Four Phases of Didactic Training

Under optimal circumstances, the formal didactic education of the psychotherapist takes place in four distinct phases that follow upon the completion of a general liberal arts education. In the latter preparatory context, the student may major in a discipline related to psychotherapy, such as psychology, sociology, anthropology, or theology. In addition, the broad-based learning during bachelor's-degree programs has other potential benefits to the student who later becomes a therapist. Literature courses may inspire understanding of the human condition. Philosophy may inculcate sound reasoning. The decision to become a therapist may result from a fascinating course in personality theory. But the goal-directed learning process typically begins in what can be called phase I: graduate programs and medical schools, where, even though students may not have yet chosen to pursue a career as a therapist, they begin to acquire the knowledge base of the profession in which they will later function as a psychotherapist. Graduate or medical school is then typically followed by phase II: a residency, internship, and/or fellowship that combines didactics and hands-on experience. Phase III, at the option of the individual, consists of advanced specialized training either in a particular therapy approach or in work with a special populations. Finally, phase IV is a lifetime process of practitioner continuing education, which is especially important given the rapid changes in knowledge and treatment that are occurring today.

Questions can be raised about the necessity of such a phase-specific, costly, and time-consuming process for developing therapist competency.

Indeed, instances abound of excellent clinicians whose training did not follow the usual path. Anna Freud learned psychoanalysis from her father. Ella Freeman Sharpe, one of the finest British analysts, was a professor of literature. Aaron Beck, the founder of cognitive therapy, and Joseph Wolpe, who fathered the systematic desensitization of phobias, were both psychodynamically trained and developed their techniques on their own. Moreover, peer counseling, requiring only a few training sessions, has been shown to be of significant benefit in a variety of contexts (Naylor & Cowie, 1999). So why should there be such an elaborate, long-term educational process, which is becoming increasingly required for licensure?

There are at least two sound reasons for requiring therapists to undergo most or all phases of didactic training. First, at least a core group of practitioners must acquire enough expertise to set and maintain standards of care and practice, much as physicians do in health care, even though nurses, technicians, rehabilitation therapists, and in some cases even family members can carry out a good deal of the work. The long road described is meant for those psychotherapists who wish to be at the leading edge of the profession and set the standard of care. Second, highly trained therapists are frequently called in at points where other interventions and providers have had limited or no success. For example, critical incident stress debriefing (Everly et al., 2000) can be competently carried out by nurses or social workers who have had short-term training in particular techniques for crisis intervention, but only an extensively trained and experienced therapist can provide adequate long-term psychotherapy for complex post-traumatic stress disorder. Thus, despite the fact that some therapists achieve competence without the four-phase process described above, and not all those who provide counseling and therapy need be so extensively educated, an extensive four-phase process of education and training is essential for those at the top of the service-providing pyramid. We will now briefly describe each of the phases and what is derived from each.

Phase I: Graduate or Medical School

The first and formative goal-directed stage of therapist education takes place in *graduate school*, most often within the disciplines of psychology, nursing, social work, or ministry, leading to the PhD, PsyD, EdD, MSN, NP (Nurse Practitioner), MSW, or DMin degree, or *medical school*, offering an MD or DO degree. In these contexts, the student is inducted into his or her profession and acquires a working knowledge of the broad scope of that profession. Occasionally, an ambitious student will acquire two of these degrees, often to pursue dual careers in practice and research.

This phase, which consists of training for a particular profession, incorporates varying amounts of educational emphasis on psychotherapy as such. It typically leads to a working knowledge of the scientific literature of the chosen profession, exposure to academicians and practitioners, and knowledge of linkages between accepted theory and practice. Pragmatically, the student's goal is to obtain the "terminal degree" that serves as the "union card" for licensure in the chosen profession. The extent to which psychotherapy principles and practice are taken up in coursework and rotations varies considerably. In psychiatric nursing, clinical social work, and clinical or counseling psychology programs, there will be a strong emphasis on personality theory, psychiatric disorders, and principles of counseling and therapy. In medicine or administrative social work programs, these subjects typically tend to receive less emphasis and may be covered only peripherally. However, in the latter programs, a good deal will be learned about responsibility for overall patient care, program administration, biochemistry, neuroscience, and/or general biology, which may later prove useful for the psychotherapist. By contrast nowadays, therapists-to-be often enroll in MSW and PsyD programs that specifically emphasize psychotherapy practice. Time will tell whether this focused graduate education produces more effective practitioners than those from programs that seek to develop overall professional competence rather than the craft of psychotherapy as such.

Thus, the value for therapist development of advanced-degree graduate and medical programs lies largely in the formation of a professional identity, knowledge, and values. These are important for all psychotherapy practices, but in certain roles, the professional attitude and mindset may prove especially useful. For example, in an inpatient unit for addictions treatment, while most of the therapists were bachelor's-level certified addictions counselors who themselves were "clean and sober" recovering persons, the value of having a medical director and clinical director was quite apparent. The less-educated therapists were extremely gifted and worked effectively with patients; they had considerable experience and relevant continuing education courses and workshops. But what kept the program well functioning and maintaining high standards was the medical and clinical directors' collective expert knowledge, which provided ongoing in-house education, supervision, and support for the treatment staff and was often required to diagnose and address medical and psychiatric problems among the patient population. The medical director in this instance was a physician who had taken a subspecialty in addictionology, and the clinical director was a doctoral-level counseling psychologist who had logged significant time in addictions treatment.

Graduate and medical education, however, has downsides for aspiring therapists, and for which they sometimes try to compensate. For one thing, the authority role that is inculcated in becoming a full member of a profession may conflict with the interpersonal, dialectical, and empathic role that is called for as a therapist. Medical doctors (and students) are required to make the "right diagnosis" with almost dictatorial certainty, a trait that might be useful in an emergency room but not in interpreting a patient's complexes or having a dialogue with a patient about sensitive aspects of his or her life cycle. Psychologists may rely too heavily on theory and research and not enough on the intuitive judgment that is so important in the consulting room.

Some social workers may too much become "commanding officers" when intervening in a dysfunctional family situation. And so on. It should be said that promising attempts are being made (Schindler, 1995) to humanize training in these disciplines, and therapists are often strongly motivated and personally suited to give up their "uniform" as they encounter actual therapy work.

Another difficulty of graduate and medical education is the type of "pressure cooker" learning it inculcates. The students must learn massive amounts of material, "burn the midnight oil," and prove their mettle to demanding professors. This sets up a high-stress pattern of practice later on. For psychotherapists, a stressful lifestyle can lead to burnout, accepting patients not suited to them, and lack of a full life that refreshes the mind and facilitates the listening process. Emotional balance is important for a psychotherapist, and graduate and medical programs are notorious for the "sheepskin psychosis" (Keats, 1965) that produces a "treadmill" lifestyle unsuitable for someone who must attend well to patients' experiences and reflect contemplatively on them.

Phase II: Internship or Residency

Following graduate or medical degree programs, there usually follows an internship or residency, where the student learns hands-on applications related to mental health and psychiatry within a university and/or treatment facility. In such programs, the student begins to function in the psychotherapist role, ideally surrounded by an experienced multidisciplinary team that provides "in-the-trenches" learning. For example, residents in a psychiatric hospital may co-lead groups with a seasoned co-therapist or observe groups through a one-way mirror, and then reflect on the sessions with an instructor/supervisor. In a psychology internship at a Veteran's Affairs Medical Center, a student took on a case of combat post-traumatic stress disorder and worked closely with a psychiatrist and treatment team to facilitate a positive long-term therapy outcome. Such is the typical format of a residency or internship: hands-on experience combined with ample formal and informal learning experiences with experts and specialists. Frequently, these avenues of learning are supplemented with reading, seminars, workshops, and other didactic learning that leads to mastery of diagnostic, prognostic, and treatment protocols. Because of the somewhat controlled conditions of such programs, and their affiliation with academic institutions, significant research often emerges from them. The resident's or intern's exposure to such research often increases his or her awareness of issues he or she might never encounter otherwise. For example, in a research study testing the effectiveness of several different treatment protocols, the resident or intern may learn to compare several therapeutic regimens with regard to their suitability for a particular patient population.

Because of the combination of didactic learning with hands-on experience and mentoring, therapists and their careers are often strongly shaped by their internships or residencies. Decisions about the type of practice to engage in, which populations to work with, and what "brand" of therapy to emphasize are often made during or upon completion of this phase. Often the therapist will be profoundly inspired by a particular supervisor or mentor in a way that will affect his or her entire career. David Burns, the cognitive therapy "guru," was inspired in his residency by Aaron Beck (Anon., 2006). Graham Gibbard, a group therapy researcher and practitioner, was strongly influenced in his subsequent work during his internship with Robert Bales (Strodtbeck, 1973). The working relationships formed in the internship/residency phase of therapist development can have a lasting and formative impact.

Phase III: Specialty Training

At some point, often subsequent to an internship or residency, an important option becomes available to the therapist, who by this time is usually a licensed and active practitioner. Specialty training typically offers an extended curriculum, often leading to certification, and is provided by free-standing institutes, university departments, and professional organizations. It usually takes one of two forms: (1) training in psychotherapy according to a particular school of thought and (2) training regarding specialized treatment of a particular psychiatric disorder or life dilemma. Examples of the former are the William Alanson White Institute of Psychiatry, Psychoanalysis, and Psychology; the Institute of Group Analysis in London; the Group Psychotherapy program at the Washington Institute of Psychiatry; and the Family Institute of Philadelphia training curricula. Examples of the latter include the Rutgers School of Alcohol and Drug Studies and the Trauma and Bereavement Certificate Program offered by the University of Arizona. Specialized training programs last from 1 to 2 weeks to several years, with more diagnostic-focused or supplemental programs of shorter duration than those that involve mastery of a complex approach to treatment such as psychoanalysis or group psychotherapy. There are many such programs throughout the United States and the world. Although they are not required for licensure, certifying boards will often accept courses taken at accredited schools for part of the continuing education required for license application and renewal.

The educational advantage of such specialized training is that it provides a level of expertise and mastery of a particular subdiscipline that is not possible in the other phases of didactic learning, where the emphasis is often on breadth and diversity rather than concentrated learning of specific treatment modalities and psychiatric disorders. The student is exposed to the multiple perspectives of several instructors, who may understand a technique or disorder in complementary ways. Specific literature can be explored in depth and detail. Didactic education, supervision, mentoring, and sometimes personal psychotherapy can be well coordinated and integrated in such specialized programs.

One problem that may occur in such specialized training is the adoption of a doctrinaire stance or over-alliance with a charismatic faculty member (Kernberg, 2000). Students sometimes emerge from such training with an almost religious zeal for their "brand" of treatment, or they may become "clones" of an admired or innovative teacher. Originality, creativity, and the use of self-experience in the role of the therapist are too often stifled. Difficulties relating to colleagues who do not adopt the same point of view may take on cultish proportions and interfere with the dialogue among viewpoints that is so important in all learning.

The history of the British Psychoanalytic Institute and Society illustrates many of these problems in the context of what otherwise is recognized to be one of the finest training programs in the world. In the 1940s and 1950s, two factions led by the charismatic figures Anna Freud and Melanie Klein fought for hegemony, forcing students to adopt one or the other stance (Grosskurth, 1986, pp. 314–333). Novel theories, such as those of John Bowlby, Ian Suttie, and Ronald Fairbairn, were extruded. Group and family therapy were dismissed as "non-analytic." An "Independent School" emerged to allow students a more flexible curriculum, but itself soon became dominated by charismatic figures such as Donald Winnicott and his disturbed protégé, Masud Khan (Hopkins, 2006). Ordinarily matters do not become as disastrous as they did in the British Institute, but subtle or overt conformity pressures in some specialized training programs are known to adversely affect the educational process (Kernberg, 2000).

Phase IV: Professional Continuing Education

This phase lasts for the remainder of the career. Having arrived at a point of professional competence, experience, and expertise, working therapists update their knowledge and train in areas that are new for them or for the entire field. Continuing education credits toward licensure are often provided for these usually briefer workshops and seminars, as well as "in-service training." Unfortunately, obtaining such credits can become the primary motivation for such education. This pragmatic motive obscures the crucial importance of ongoing learning in a time of information explosion and rapid changes in practice. For example, DBT (dialectical behavior therapy) (Linehan, 1993) and EMDR (eye movement desensitization reprocessing) (Shapiro, 2001), unknown to most practitioners two decades ago, are widely used today. State-of-the-art medications for schizophrenia, bipolar disorder, attention-deficit/hyperactivity disorder, and major depression have changed every few years, and new knowledge about them occurs almost on a daily basis. HIPAA (Health Insurance Portability and Accountability Act of 1996) regulations present confusing problems for recordkeeping and confidentiality that require updating through workshops.

In the past, the psychotherapist was like a traditional craftsman or country doctor, who, once well educated, could practice with great skill for a lifetime with as little as an occasional refresher course. Today, research findings and innovative methods require practitioners to retrain and update their skills on a frequent basis, sometimes even radically altering their clinical understanding and treatment tactics. For example, before 1990, only a few soldiers and accident victims were diagnosed with post-traumatic stress disorder (Herman & Van der Kolk, 1987). Since then, it has been diagnosed far more frequently, trauma studies and related treatments have mushroomed, and only the most complacent practitioner would not want to update his or her knowledge and skills for treating trauma-related disorders. As with rapidly evolving disciplines such as medicine, engineering, and computer technology, contemporary psychotherapy requires frequent refreshing of knowledge and skills.

A fundamental difficulty with continuing education of even the highest quality is that for a variety of reasons, workshops and seminars are usually brief, lasting for as little as 1 or 2 hours and, even when intensive and comprehensive, usually not more than 1 or 2 weeks. Such concentrated learning is often very informative but creates the illusion of a level of competence that in fact would require many months of supervision and courses to acquire. Some advocates of newer therapy approaches are acutely aware of this problem and offer follow-up classes and ongoing supervision as follow-ups, but it is likely that only a minority of those who attend continuing education workshops follow up in this way. It is probably best that the shorter-duration continuing education workshops offer knowledge and skills that can be safely and flexibly applied within the therapist's current approach rather than promising to teach a whole new technique. Those who become inspired and wish to adopt the new approach can then enroll in a more comprehensive training program.

The Impact of Changes in Health Care and the Information Revolution on Didactic Training of Psychotherapists

"Future shock," which not so long ago was a matter of speculation (Toffler, 1970), is with us, here and now. In almost any occupation today, rapid change is the norm ("the only constant is change"), including the information explosion and rapid turnover of ideas and processes. These changes are now operative at critical levels in multidisciplinary fields like psychotherapy, which draws from many knowledge bases and skill sets. The amount of new information has increased exponentially and the half-life for ideas and methods has shortened. While this is not the place for a detailed consideration of the changes in psychotherapy practice that have resulted from such rapid-fire events, it is important in the current context to reflect upon how such changes affect the didactic education of therapists, who, in this "brave new world" are now called "providers," a generic term for those who offer health services. Specific health-care–related agendas, such as managed care, evidence-based therapy, practice-based evidence, and treatment at a distance via e-mail and phone/video conferencing, influence the therapist's didactic education because the latter must be geared to the work to be performed. For example, if the therapist's practice is going to consist primarily of time-limited cognitive-behavioral therapy for an anxiety disorder or clinical depression, the teaching of psychodynamics and group dynamics, while it does have some utility, deserves far less emphasis than if the student is going to conduct long-term intensive psychotherapy. Or, if the practitioner is going to offer phone and e-mail counseling, less emphasis needs to be placed on reading body language and more on how to compensate for the lack of such nonverbal communication, which constitutes about 65% of the message in face-to-face conversation (Birdwhistell, 1970).

In addition to the need to update the subject matter and content of education, teachers need to learn new ways to deliver both traditional and new knowledge to students. As pointed out above, relational, "in-the-room" teaching is qualitatively different from distance learning via e-mail, video classes, and online seminars. "The medium is the message": it is a different experience to carefully read an entire book or article than to read a series of abstracts, blogs, or shorter texts that are readily available on the Internet. The technology-inspired tendency today is to absorb large amounts of information from diverse sources rather than to contemplate a single difficult text, sentence by sentence, and consider its meaning and implications. Digitalization is already having a profound effect on human consciousness, intelligence, and brain function in ways we have barely begun to assess (Jenkins, 2006), and both education and psychotherapy are disciplines that are all about consciousness and the brain.

The dilemmas for psychotherapy educators are more important for graduate/medical education and internship/residency programs than for specialized and continuing education, because the latter can choose content to suit specific purposes and student demand, while the former must adhere to priorities based upon anticipated needs of the future therapist. They must, for instance, maintain a sometimes precarious balance between enduring knowledge versus focused attention on rapidly evolving approaches to treatment that may or may not later prove to have been fads.

Didactic education is subject to the law of supply and demand. Many training programs in psychoanalysis currently receive far fewer applications, and some have been forced to close, because psychoanalysis, while interesting to many, no longer affords most practitioners a livelihood during a time when patients are seeking or covered for short-term cognitive-behavioral therapy and medication. Moreover, psychiatry residencies today emphasize psychotherapy less than before in comparison with psychopharmacology and neuropsychiatry. Clinical psychology graduate programs are likely to emphasize

Axis I disorders and treatment protocols covered by insurance companies, rather than, say, complex personality disorders resulting from dysfunctional family life. These shifts in emphasis resulting from student selection of programs are cultural, political, and economic in origin as much as they are responses to the advancing knowledge of what makes for good clinical care as such. Education and health care are in many ways microcosms of society.

The details and nuances of the shifting educational emphases of the programs aimed at psychotherapists will vary from one facility or institution to another and must evolve in the context of the complex agendas and pressures that are involved in each instance. However, it may be useful here to outline the recurring paradigmatic elements that are nevertheless shifting and changing in this fast-moving New Millennium "future shock" world of psychotherapy education.

A Working Model of Psychotherapy Didactic Education

Modern psychotherapy evolved from the conjunction of three broad disciplines or paradigms of knowledge and care: (1) academic psychology, based upon the natural and social sciences; (2) hermeneutical (interpretive) religion and humanism; and (3) "hands on" medical practice. In the first, the prevailing notion is cause and effect understood through empirical research. In the second, the vehicle for understanding is the interpretation of the "soul," the whole person, and artistic/literary/cultural/symbolic productions. In the third, the central feature is the development of protocols for diagnosis and treatment of disease.

In the last half of the 19th century, psychotherapy emerged within the "medical model" as a form of treatment of mental disorder, but because its focus was on the mind and emotions, it drew heavily upon both empirical psychology and the religious/humanistic tradition.

Freud attempted with mixed results to straddle the three paradigms, using *interpretation* (hermeneutics) based on *empirical data, research, and inference* (psychology) to *treat* (medicine) the diseased personality. His hope was that he could create an empirical psychology based on a religious/humanistic-derived hermeneutics via introspective inquiry that in turn would alleviate psychiatric symptoms. Of course, he only partly succeeded in his mission, leaving it up to others to question and modify or react against his views.

Early divergences from Freudian psychology emphasized the biosocial (Reich), spiritual (Jung), social (Adler), and existential (Jaspers) dimensions of the humanistic/interpretive paradigm. This led to more recent humanistic psychology, experiential, and existential approaches to psychotherapy, which dominated the field during the decades of the 1960s to 1980s.

Independently, some behavioral psychologists (Jones, 1924) began to use classical conditioning to treat phobias and, later, instrumental conditioning using reinforcements for a variety of other conditions (Lindsley et al., 1953). Cognitive psychology, regarding thinking as internal, implicit, mediating behavior, came about as an extension and variation of such methods, all of which emphasized cause and effect, empirical and experimental science as the foundation for psychotherapy.

Such history is taught in basic psychology courses and is common knowledge. The problem for current didactic education in psychotherapy is whether and how to retain aspects of all three paradigms in the "brave new world" of digitalized information, managed care, and evidence-based therapy. If any one of the three paradigms is omitted, one no longer is teaching *psycho*therapy, which is the treatment of the self-in-relation and which has cognitive-behavioral, interpretive, and medical/biological healing components.

We have reached a point in the history and development of psychotherapy where any of the three components can be emphasized and lead to good outcomes (Klerman et al., 1984) as a function of a number of other salient factors such as therapist expectations and attitudes. Cognitive-behavioral and medical-biological approaches are currently dominating the formerly popular interpretive-humanistic therapies because the former are cost-effective (at least in the short run and with particular disorders; long-term follow-up studies of recidivism are scarce). However, deeper empathic understanding of dynamics facilitates healing of all forms, and human development cannot and should not always be cost-effective and time-limited. *A paradigm for human growth and development is as important to successful psychotherapy as are paradigms for cause-and-effect intervention and symptom alleviation.* This suggests that any comprehensive program of education for psychotherapists should include significant exposure to and mastery of elements of all three paradigms.

A Note on Cultural Diversity: The Educational Component

During a century or more, the cultural bandwidth of those who teach, study, practice, and are clients in psychotherapy has increased markedly. In the past, most therapists and patients in Western countries were Caucasian, with European personal and/or family background. In the post-World War II era in America and England, clients and therapists were even more closely matched, with both often of middle-class socioeconomic status and living in the same geographical area. In the past 50 years, the cultural mix in the United States and other countries has become much greater, and many more therapists themselves are now, for example, of Latino, African American, and Asian descent as well as mixed racial and cultural origins. Diversity is a key word in virtually every sphere of our lives today. Moreover, teachers and supervisors are now called upon to provide therapy and disaster relief education to counselors all over the world (Kleinberg, 2009).

Clearly, the didactic education of therapists needs to take this shift toward diversity into account; the question is, how? One obvious way is to expose students to the literature and case examples of various cultural populations, in the same way they now learn about a variety of psychiatric populations. Further, if a therapist knows that he or she will be treating a particular cultural group, specific courses and workshops should be arranged to focus on the issues and cultural norms of that population. Furthermore, therapists need to learn how to cross the communication gap to work well with clients from cultures other than their own. For example, the present author, an urban American of Jewish European extraction, has worked with transplanted Americans who were raised and matured in South America and Africa. Their cultural norms are quite different from his, and they sometimes dream in their native tongue! He has found it helpful in bridging the cultural divide to make reciprocal open communication about culture an explicit, ongoing aspect of the treatment. For example, a female client from Chile noted that the role expectations of women there are somewhat different from in the United States, and an ever-present issue for her as she now resides and works in the United States is how to negotiate her assertive and dramatic femininity in a culture where women are expected to be more passive and receptive in orientation. The therapist initially considered the client's dramatic qualities to be a defense mechanism until an exchange of views clarified that it was partly based upon a cultural difference. Such matters should now occupy a significant place in therapist education.

One of the author's best and most influential educational experiences was a workshop on mourning led by a Native American psychotherapy trainer. Not only did the author learn quite vividly that the grief rituals, ceremonies, and dynamics of grief are markedly different in some cultures, but he also discovered that aspects of his own grief and those of his European-extraction clients had components that are normative in the Seattle tribe, while they are split off, denied, and socially shamed in Caucasian urban society. The workshop helped him to work with those elements of grief in a less shame-based and more sympathetic and empathic way (Schermer, 2010).

In general, cross-cultural education of therapists should not attempt to make the therapist adjust entirely to the culture of the client, but rather to promote a dialogue of diversity in which therapist and client can learn from one another.

The Impact of Didactic Preparation on Subsequent and Ongoing Practice

Since what ultimately matters about therapist education is the effect it has on ongoing practice, a few final points must be made about how didactic education does and does not influence what actually transpires in the consulting room.

The first point is cautionary—namely, that often we don't really know what goes on in the consulting room, since we as a scientific community rarely observe it directly, and even if we did, much of what occurs is in fact implicit, private behavior (thoughts, emotions). Moreover, even in the case material that we do have available, the thoughts and feelings of the therapist are not disclosed to the degree to which the patient does so. Thus, a significant portion of the mutual therapeutic interaction is unknown. The consulting room is comparable to Plato's cave, and those who research, study, and teach psychotherapy see only the shadows of what really takes place. So, in educating therapists, we mostly make "commonsense" guesses about what the therapist internalizes of our teachings and how he or she makes use of it. In the famous case of Dora (Freud, 1905), Freud, in a postscript to the case, disclosed his countertransference problem with the patient but told little of how that affected the patient, except that she aborted treatment prematurely; as Deutsch (1957) later learned, the treatment was a failure that may even have worsened the patient's condition. In Freud's case of the Wolf Man (Gardiner, 1972), Freud, who advocated a surgically detached observing attitude toward patients, did personal favors for the Wolf Man and used behavioral contracting to help him engage in life-enhancing activities in areas where analytic work proved insufficient. Thus the question "Does the therapist practice what he or she learns and what educators preach?" is difficult to answer, and educative efficacy could be considerably aided by more research about what therapists retain from their education, how they internalize it, and how it is expressed or altered in the therapeutic dialogue.

In addition, every therapist has experienced the need to "fly by the seat of the pants" at crucial junctures in treatment. Richard Kluft (1990), a pioneer in the treatment of dissociative identity disorder, tells of the first client whom he diagnosed with the disorder. She was on the couch for many months, and one day surprisingly began to speak in the tongue of an alter ego. Kluft asked her, "Who is that speaking?" She gave a name other than her familiar one. Taken by surprise and wanting for words, Kluft replied, "She needs to be in therapy, too." Didactic education should help prepare a therapist for such unexpected eventualities. One suitable avenue for achieving this objective is to provide the student with problem cases and issues that do not fit the conceptual/theoretical mold and brainstorm on how they might be resolved.

Finally, therapist–client matching, empathy, and bonding have been shown to be important outcome factors (Luborsky et al., 1997). These components may fluctuate during the course of a therapist's career, influenced as they are by countertransference, life stressors, and therapist trauma (see Chapter 8 on the "wounded healer" in this volume). Didactic preparation cannot anticipate or prepare the student fully to address such factors, which may better be dealt with in supervision and personal psychotherapy. However, just as a garden is created both by planting the seeds and tending the shoots with care, so therapist education should attend to the therapist's personhood beyond the transmission of knowledge. This can be done in two ways. Therapist education should include self-study, which may have healing value in addition to being informative. In addition, a supportive relationship should be developed with students. Many faculty members can recall students who came to them in distress, feeling a level of trust they could not find elsewhere. Although the teacher can help only in a very limited way, a compassionate response and useful guidance can help the therapist-in-training and redound to the benefit of his or her clients for years to come. For example, one of the author's students experienced the death of her psychoanalyst during the time she attended the author's course in object relations theory. She shared her profound grief and sense of breakdown with him, and his support played a role in her mourning, recovery, and search for a new analyst. In all aspects of didactic education of therapists, while the emphasis is upon facts and ideas, concern for the personal development of students is especially important in a discipline in which they must give similar concern to those who will eventually seek their help.

Conclusion

The educational road to becoming a psychotherapist is one that negotiates a number of stages, hills, and valleys, and lasts for a lifetime. Today, it is influenced by technological and socioeconomic changes that call for frequent readjustments to "future shock." The student is being didactically prepared for a vocation that is multidisciplinary, multi-paradigmatic, and fast-changing, and that involves responsibility for the well-being of clients. It is naïve to think that the education of psychotherapists is a simple matter of setting up a curriculum and implementing it. Rather, it is a holistic process that requires attention to what is occurring in and around the student and/or practitioner. While in no sense should a teacher-as-such act as a therapist or even a supervisor (although sometimes he or she may play a dual role), the educational process should be informed with mindfulness of the student's life process and personal needs and aspirations, the ideals of the profession, and the context in which learning and practice takes place.

The poet James Wright stated that, "Every poem is a confession in the sense that it is impossible to write a word on the page without revealing some personal feeling" (Graves & Schermer, 1999). Atwood and Stolorow (1993) held that even the most abstract theory of personality is informed by the subjectivity of the theorist. Such is the nature of knowledge about psychotherapy that it always contains subjective and intersubjective aspects, even when soundly based on research and consensually validated facts and concepts. While adhering to the noble tradition of authoritative transmission of an accepted body of knowledge and ideas, and while teaching how to learn as well as what to learn, the didactic preparation of psychotherapists must be additionally alert to the biologist Michael Polanyi's (1974) thesis that all knowledge, even the most scientific, is personal and has an element of faith. Moreover, as Bion (1970) has stated, a considerable amount of psychotherapy occurs "in the absence of memory, desire, and understanding." Acknowledging the unknown is a paradoxical ingredient of therapist education. Without a measure of such humility in the face of the mysteries of nature and the divine and profane in each human being, the education of the psychotherapist is incomplete. The very best education of psychotherapists acknowledges what is unknown and uncertain as much as what is known and understood.

References

Anon. (2006) David Burns. *Wikipedia: The Free Encyclopedia*. Retrieved from http://en.wikipedia.org/wiki/David_D._Burns

Antonuccio, D. O., Danton, W. G., & DeNelsky, G. Y. (1995). Psychotherapy versus medication for depression: Challenging the conventional wisdom with data. *Professional Psychology: Research and Practice*, 26(6), 574–585.

Atwood, G., & Stolorow, R. (1993). *Faces in a Cloud: Intersubjectivity in Personality Theory*, 2nd ed. Northvale, NJ: Aronson.

Beck, A. T., Emery, G., & Greenberg, R.L. (1985). *Anxiety Disorders and Phobias: A Cognitive Approach*. New York: Perseus Books.

Bion, W. R. (1965). *Transformations*. London: William Heinemann.

Bion, W. R. (1970). *Attention and Interpretation*. London: Tavistock.

Birdwhistell, L. (1970). *Kinesics and Context*. Philadelphia: University of Pennsylvania Press.

Breuer, J., & Freud, S. (1893–1895) *Studies on Hysteria*. (transl. James Strachey). New York: Basic Books, 2000.

Carkhuff, R. R. (1969). *Helping and Human Relations. Volume I. Selection and Training; Volume II: Practice and Research*. New York: Holt, Rinehart & Winston.

Cozolino, L. (2002). *The Neuroscience of Psychotherapy: Building and Rebuilding the Human Brain*. New York: Norton.

Deutsch, F. (1957). A footnote to Freud's "Fragment of an Analysis of a Case of Hysteria." *Psychoanalytic Quarterly*, 26(2), 159–167.

Ellenberger, H. F. (1972). The story of Anna O: A critical review with new data. *Journal of the History of Behavioral Sciences*, July, 267–279.

Everly, G. S., Flannery Jr., R. B., & Mitchell, J. T. (2000). Critical incident stress management (CISM): A review of the literature. *Aggression and Violent Behavior*, 5(1), 23–40.

Fierman, L. B., ed. (1965). *Effective Psychotherapy: The Contribution of Hellmuth Kaiser*. New York: The Free Press of Glencoe.

Flores, P. J. (1997). *Group Psychotherapy with Addicted Populations: An Integration of Twelve-Step and Psychodynamic Theory*. New York: Haworth Press.

Freud, S. (1905). *Dora: An Analysis of a Case of Hysteria* (Collected Papers of Sigmund Freud). New York: Touchstone, 1997.

Freud, S. (1937). Analysis terminable and interminable. *Standard Edition of the Complete Psychological Works of Sigmund Freud* (Vol. 23, pp. 216–253). London: Hogarth Press, 1964.

Ganzarain, R. (1989). *Object Relations Group Psychotherapy*. Madison, CT: International Universities Press.

Gardiner, M., ed. (1972). *The Wolf-Man by The Wolf-Man with the Case of the Wolf-Man by Sigmund Freud*. New York: Basic Books.

Gay, P. (1988). *Freud: A Life for Our Time*. New York: Norton.

Graves, M., & Schermer, V.L. (1999). The wounded male persona and the mysterious feminine in the poetry of James Wright: A study in the transformation of the self. *Psychoanalytic Review*, 85(6), 849–870.

Grosskurth, P. (1986). *Melanie Klein: Her World and Her Work*. New York: Knopf.

Herman, J., & van der Kolk, B. (1987). Traumatic antecedents of borderline personality disorder. In Van der Kolk, B. (Ed.), *Psychological Trauma* (pp. 11–126). Washington, D.C.: American Psychiatric Press.

Hopkins, L. (2006). *False Self: The Life of Masud Khan*. New York: Other Press.

Jenkins, H. (2006). *Convergence Culture: Where Old and New Media Collide*. New York: NYU Press.

Jones, M. C. (1924). A laboratory study of fear: The case of Peter. *Pedagogical Seminary*, 31, 308–315.

Keats, J. (1965). *The Sheepskin Psychosis*. Philadelphia: Lippincott.

Kernberg, O. (2000). A concerned critique of psychoanalytic education. *International Journal of Psycho-Analysis*, 81, 97–120.

Kleinberg, J. (2009). From China with love. *Group Circle*, Fall, 1, 6.

Klerman, G. L., Weissman, M. M., Rounsaville, B. J., & Chevron, E. (1984). *Interpersonal Psychotherapy of Depression*. New York: Basic Books.

Kluft, R. (1990) Dissociative identity disorder. Unpublished lecture to the Philadelphia Psychoanalytic Society. Philadelphia: The Institute of Pennsylvania Hospital.

Lewis, J. M., Beavers, W. R., Gossett, J. T., & Phillips, V. A. (1976). *No Single Thread, Psychological Health in Family Systems*. New York: Brunner-Mazel.

Lindsley, O., Skinner, B. F., & Solomon, H. C. (1953). *Studies in Behavior Therapy (Status Report I)*. Waltham, MA.: Metropolitan State Hospital.

Linehan, M. M. (1993). *Cognitive-Behavioral Treatment of Borderline Personality Disorder*. New York: Guilford.

Luborsky, L., McLellan, A. T., Diguer, L., Woody, G., & Seligman, D. A. (1997). The psychotherapist matters: Comparison of outcomes across twenty-two therapists and seven patient samples. *Clinical Psychology: Science and Practice*, 4(1), 53–65.

Merleau-Ponty, M. (1976). *The Phenomenology of Perception*. (Transl. Colin Smith.) London: Routledge and Kegan Paul.

Miller, W. R. (1994). *Motivational Enhancement Therapy Manual: A Clinical Research Guide for Therapists Treating Individuals With Alcohol Abuse and Dependence*. Project MATCH Monograph Series Volume 2. Washington, D.C.: National Institute on Alcohol Abuse and Alcoholism.

Naylor, P., & Cowie, H. (1999). The effectiveness of peer support systems in challenging school bullying: the perspectives and experiences of teachers and pupils. *Journal of Adolescence*, 22(4), 467–479.

Polanyi, M. (1974). *Personal Knowledge: Towards a Post-Critical Philosophy*. Chicago: University of Chicago Press.

Rogers, C. (1995). *On Becoming a Person: A Therapist's View of Psychotherapy*. New York: Mariner Books.

Schermer, V. L. (2010). Between shame, death, and mourning: The predispositional role of early attachments and the sense of self. In J. Kauffman (Ed.), *Shame and Death*. (pp. 34–57). London: Routledge.

Schermer, V. (2010). Mirror neurons: Their relevance for group psychotherapy. *International Journal of Group Psychotherapy,* 60 (4), pp. 487–511.

Schindler, K. (1995). Humanizing medical education. *Emory Medicine,* Spring, 1995.

Shapiro, F. (2001). *Eye Movement Desensitization and Reprocessing: Basic Principles, Protocols and Procedures* (2nd ed.). New York: Guilford Press.

Siegel, D. J. (2007). *The Mindful Brain*. New York: Norton.

Spitzer, R. L., Gibbon, M., Skodol, A. E., Williams, J. B. W., & First, M. B. (Eds.) (2001). *DSM-IV-TR Casebook: A Learning Companion to the Diagnostic and Statistical Manual of Mental Disorders, Fourth Edition, Text Revision*. Washington, D.C.: American Psychiatric Publishing, Inc.

Strodtbeck, F. L. (1973). Review: Bales 20 years later. *American Journal of Sociology,* 79(2), 459–465.

Toffler, A. (1970). *Future Shock*. New York: Random House.

5

The Role of Clinical Experience in the Making of a Psychotherapist

Jerome S. Gans

During my second year of psychiatric residency I was assigned an office in the former nurses' dormitory of an affiliated hospital. Like the dormitory, the offices were threadbare and had clearly seen better days. A new patient, a scion of a famous New England family, a 40-year-old man who had had two previous analyses with prominent Boston analysts and who had failed in several academic and vocational endeavors, entered the office, looked around, and announced, "Not exactly the mainstream of psychiatry, wouldn't you say. I don't see any diplomas on the walls either." His remarks devastated me and I brought my tattered self into supervision, wondering if my core defects could ever be reversed.

Clinical experiences like these, and hundreds of others, contribute to the making of a psychotherapist. The purpose of this chapter is to discuss *exactly how* such experiences help novice psychotherapists become seasoned practitioners of their craft.

Introduction

Beginning therapists undoubtedly have heard lectures and read book chapters that prepare them to deal with the *content* of psychotherapy. Only clinical experience, though, can provide the fledgling therapist with a visceral, emotional, and cognitive understanding of the *process* of psychotherapy (Yalom, 2002). The *process* of psychotherapy refers to all that is involved in the interpersonal relationship between the therapist and the patient. Reading about unpaid bills is one thing; having a patient withhold payment is another. Listening to a lecture on erotic countertransference may provide little guidance to the inexperienced therapist barely in control of his or her sexual feelings. Understanding the concept of a self-object may offer little consolation to the beginning therapist who gradually comes to feel unreal and then obliterated in the presence of her schizoid patient. These experiences alert the neophyte therapist to the fact that there is more to being a psychotherapist than good intentions, sincerity, acting naturally, a very good or very bad upbringing, really caring about the patient, or reading the psychotherapy literature.

This chapter will describe and discuss how, through various clinical experiences, beginning therapists learn about and master concepts that constitute the basis of the practice of psychotherapy. It comprises the following tasks:

1. Monitoring the framework of therapy
2. Evolving a realistic professional ego-ideal
3. Exploring versus acting and/or explaining
4. Containing and metabolizing intense affect
5. Modifying psychological dogma
6. Managing boundaries and dealing with difference

Under these headings, the text will explain how different clinical experiences contribute to the making of a psychotherapist. These clinical experiences include missed and canceled sessions and late and unpaid bills; working with the suicidal patient; patients' requests for immediate therapist action; unilateral termination and erotic transference; the treatment of psychotic patients; and the importance of countertransference (Maroda, 1991) in handling ethical and cultural issues. The ideas and examples presented are based on approximately 70,000 hours of clinical experience in a career that has spanned 40 years. About 2,000 of these hours were devoted to the supervision of beginning psychotherapists.

I urge the reader to notice how often I stress the central role of supervision in assisting the beginning therapist with the many clinical experiences described in this chapter. Supervision is an essential component of psychotherapy practice for experienced as well as beginning psychotherapists. For an in-depth treatment of supervision, I refer the reader to Chapter 6.

The ability and competence of beginning therapists occupy a continuum. If the following examples and discussions of clinical experience that contribute to the making of a psychotherapist seem not to take this reality into account, I hope the reader will appreciate that a pedagogic intent has produced this distortion.

Therapist Traits

While other chapters discuss the many factors that go into the making of a psychotherapist, I wish to emphasize that it is the *interaction* of clinical experience with certain necessary therapist traits that contributes to the making of a psychotherapist. Roth (1987) has noted many of these qualities, which include but are not limited to an ability to tolerate the loneliness and isolation that the profession engenders; the gift of empathic appreciation for another person's experience; the ability and willingness to experience strong affects; a capacity to weather patients' unreasonable (and sometimes reasonable) accusations and rejections; a resonance with expressions of the unconscious; playfulness and benign humor; the capacity to appreciate and even admire individual difference; an interest, even delight in listening to other people's stories; the ability to communicate effectively; and the excitement about learning about oneself through encounters with patients. The ability to profit from examining the interactions between these therapist traits and various clinical experiences can only enhance the neophyte therapist's evolving skills.

Managing the Framework of Therapy

Shortly after beginning the work of psychotherapy, psychotherapists encounter a fundamental necessity of practice: patients who come regularly to their appointments and pay for them in a timely fashion (Krueger, 1986). As obvious and straightforward as this reality may be, therapists practicing for only a short period of time are often surprised when their patients cancel or miss sessions or do not pay their bills. Some of the first concerns that beginning therapists bring into supervision are missed and cancelled sessions and late payment or non-payment.

Therapists seem perplexed when their patients begin missing or canceling sessions or not paying their bills in a timely fashion or at all. After all, they had spelled out for their patients and secured agreement from them about when and where the sessions would take place, how long each session would last, the fee for the service, the missed session and cancellation policy, and problems they would be working on. They had read about the importance of the framework of therapy (Langs, 1976), they were diligent in explaining it, the patient seemed to understand and accept the conditions—so why should there be any problems? It seemed (to the therapists) that if their patients came to their sessions consistently and paid for them in a timely fashion, therapy could focus on the problems for which the patient initially sought help. Instead, they experience discontinuity in the sessions and negatively affected incomes.

The tendency is to address these difficulties in a logical and straightforward manner: vigorous enforcement of the contract with respect to attendance and payment. Other therapists hope that by avoiding these topics entirely, they will resolve themselves. These approaches are usually ineffective: unpaid bills mount up, and premature terminations result in dwindling practices.

It is at this juncture that new learning can occur as therapists begin to understand the *purpose* of the framework of therapy at a deeper level. They begin to appreciate that the items in the therapeutic contract are not meant to be a set of rules to which strict patient obedience is expected. Just the opposite is true: they have secured their patients' willingness to take responsibility for honoring the items in the contract precisely because experience has shown that as therapy unfolds, patients—and sometimes therapists—will violate these very conditions of therapy. Clinical experience is now making real for beginning therapists the phenomenon of resistance (Stark, 1994).

Efforts to alter provisions of the contract often indicate the emergence of dysphoric or unbearably pleasurable feelings that patients (or therapists) wish, often unconsciously, to avoid. The exploration of these thoughts and feelings resides at the very heart of therapy.

Several important verities emerge:

- A basic rule of therapy is to explore requests to change the basic parameters of therapy *before* any action that may be taken.
- Resistance to therapy is an integral part of therapy, and its analysis often constitutes the initial phase of treatment.
- Therapists' feelings and unresolved issues affect the treatment.

Beginning therapists often deal with reality issues on a concrete or practical level. A secretary realizes that she doesn't function well in the early morning and wishes to have a later appointment time. A plumber who is having cash flow problems wishes to defer payment of part of his bill despite the fact that he is heading off for a 10-day Caribbean vacation. The neophyte therapist quickly learns that acting on these requests before exploring the thoughts, feelings, and fantasies associated with them is invariably a mistake. Sometimes a "cigar is just a cigar," but more often than not the request is more complicated than it would appear. The secretary who was given a 5 p.m. appointment without exploring her request now finds that her boss gives her work at the last moment that requires her to be late for or miss her appointment with some regularity. The therapist who accedes to his plumber-patient's request for a partial payment deferral, again without exploring it, finds himself resentful that he is subsidizing his patient's vacation, a feeling that begins to corrode the therapy.

Beginning therapists have difficulty recognizing resistance partly because they are (understandably) preoccupied with concerns about their own competence. Instead of considering that his patient, in canceling several sessions, may be experiencing resistance or at least ambivalence to the therapy, the therapist finds himself preoccupied with the following concerns: Does the patient think I have nothing to offer? Did I make a mistake that I am not even aware of? Is my waiting room too shabby?

Similar self-doubt and unresolved conflicts may interfere with therapists' ability to deal with the fee in a matter-of-fact fashion. Missed and cancelled sessions and unpaid bills alert therapists to their contribution to these distressing signs: they have failed to spell out their missed session and cancellation policies (Gans & Counselman, 1996).

There are several reasons for these omissions. Practicing psychotherapy has not yet become real as a vocation. Doubts about the value of their services make if difficult to announce their fee and their missed session and cancellation policies. Some therapists may be unconsciously uncomfortable with the aggressive elements involved in charging. As they gain more clinical experience, they come to appreciate that charging eases the burden of guilt that patients might feel for bringing destructive feelings into the session. Other therapists may bring to their work a discomfort with financial matters that originated in their families' dysfunctional patterns. Still others, in being nice rather than useful, unconsciously project onto their patients the personal entitlements that they have yet to identify and resolve.

As therapists address their competence concerns and personal issues and are thus freed up to recognize patients' resistance and ambivalence, they react to this resistance in a variety of ways. Some achieve and maintain neutral curiosity, while others have one of two polar reactions.

Consider the following scenario and assume that the therapist has articulated his policy, which the patient agreed to, at the outset of therapy: "You are responsible for payment for all sessions unless I receive 48-hour notice of a cancellation." The session in question involves a 28-year-old female patient who would like to reschedule her appointment. She wishes to have dinner with a close college friend from another state who is visiting and available only that evening. The patient calls her male therapist the day before her appointment with this request. The patient has a history of requesting special treatment in the therapy.

Beginning therapists tend to be overly lax or rigid about such requests. On the lax side of the spectrum, therapists tend to confuse being nice with being useful. As a result, instead of making a *new* appointment and charging the patient for a missed session, they are willing to reschedule. Therapists on the rigid end of the spectrum insist on payment—their pound of flesh—but, in the process, put the therapeutic alliance in jeopardy.

Each of these clinical mistakes provides an opportunity for learning. The therapist who does not distinguish between being nice and being useful begins to feel taken advantage of, resentful, or, if the pattern is pervasive, masochistically submissive. The patient, in turn, senses something inauthentic about the therapist's caring; over time, it becomes clear that in extending such special consideration the therapist is avoiding his own difficulties rather than modeling discussion and resolution of conflict. The casualties here are two-fold: the patient's wishes for special treatment get "acted in" instead of explored and the therapist's conflict avoidance masquerades as caring. More clinical experience, pertinent reading, supervision, and in extreme cases personal therapy can lead to competent boundary maintenance and the ability to explore conflicts within the therapy hour rather than their being acted out.

The rigid therapist exploits, often unconsciously, the power differential intrinsic to the therapy dyad and insists on payment. The patient has reason to feel unsafe for two reasons. First, she—and it is usually a female patient and a male therapist—incurs vulnerability by questioning her therapist's power move in an enterprise that depends on exploration before action. Second, she risks losing faith and trust in her therapist if he resists exploring her feeling of being taken advantage of, even if such feeling flies in the face of the contract to which she agreed. If the therapist "gets" what his patient is pointing out, he has the opportunity to learn that there are no hard-and-fast rules about what to do when therapist and patient have a disagreement about payment. Clinical experience teaches that the best approach is the one that keeps therapeutic space open (Gans & Counselman, 1996). Only through exploration of the issues involved can the therapist determine what that approach should be. Such an exploration will take into account existing transference and countertransference, the state of the alliance, the phase of therapy, past handling of this situation, and the real relationship.

In summary, neophyte therapists learn in their training that the therapeutic contract provides a space in which therapy can take place and offers an agreement that protects their livelihood. Beginning practice disrupts this tranquility and, in the process, disorients neophyte therapists who cannot understand why patients suddenly cancel sessions or do not pay their bills. They initially think they must be doing something wrong or they begin to dislike or indulge the patient, even though the therapy is proceeding on course. Therapists gradually come to appreciate that the therapy is stirring up emotional discomfort and internal conflict that makes its initial appearance as disruption of the framework of therapy. As a result, they are more able to assume a more therapeutic stance that welcomes in for exploration the disruptive and disturbing feelings that the therapy has unearthed.

Evolving a Realistic Professional Ego-Ideal

Edelwich and Brodsky (1980) describe and discuss the potential for "burnout" among "helping professionals." They note that such professionals in particular come to their work with an "idealistic enthusiasm" that breeds a set of "expectations" that cannot be met. Brightman (1984) further defines these expectations as a "grandiose professional ego-ideal" that is composed of the wish to be omnipotent, omniscient, and benevolent.

Working with the suicidal patient, as much as any other clinical experience, can help the beginning therapist gradually replace a grandiose professional ego-ideal with one that is more realistic. How exactly does this transformation take place?

The beginning psychotherapist undertakes the treatment of the suicidal patient with the optimistic belief that a combination of caring, encouragement, hopefulness, good intentions, empathy, and intuition will produce a positive outcome. A "contract for safety," wherein the patient agrees not to act on suicidal impulses and, instead, will call the therapist or seek other help, provides additional assurance. Newly prescribed medication promises to relieve suicidal despair. Hospitalization, if required, will provide needed safety.

Over time though, the suicidal patient does not improve. The despair does not abate. The hopelessness intensifies. The patient can identify no reason to live. Relentless gloom pervades the therapy. Imperceptibly but forcefully, an important realization takes hold of the therapist at a visceral as well as at a cognitive and emotional level: it is impossible for one person to keep another person alive over time. While this insight serves to moderate the pursuit of omnipotence, the realization that even clinical competence does not guarantee that one's patient will not commit suicide is unsettling.

Comforting thoughts begin to give way. Contracts for safety now feel illusory as therapists realize that patients who are in sufficient anguish to want to end their lives will not be compelled to live simply because they have promised (a therapist) they will not kill themselves. Therapists begin to have second thoughts about the unrealistic healing powers they previously attributed to psychotropic medication, although they do appreciate the ability of these medications to sometimes diminish unbearable anguish to the point where patients can address their conflicts and problems. They hear stories of patients who have killed themselves in a hospital.

The responsibility of caring alone for a suicidal patient begins to weigh heavily. The seeming intractability of the patient's despair can affect the therapist in two ways. Burdened by an as-yet-unmodified grandiose professional ego-ideal, therapists begin to feel ashamed of their inability to even modify their patients' condition. The emergence of negative, even hateful feelings toward the patient (Maltsburger & Buie, 1974), including the wish that the patient *would* die, intensifies the shame. Shame leads to professional isolation that intensifies what now feels like the *burden*—as opposed to the responsibility—of caring for the suicidal patient. Supervision is avoided.

Other therapists respond to the almost unbearable pain of sitting with the suicidal patient in what can only be termed the mysterious process of professional and personal growth. This process contains many elements. First, these therapists come to realize that certain well-intentioned approaches have been counterproductive, even harmful. Unable to bear and stay with their patients' anguish, they had tried to provide reasons why the patient *should* carry on. They sensed that this approach left their patient feeling unsafe, wondering for whose benefit such encouragement was being offered. When that approach didn't work, they resorted to guilt induction: "Have you thought of how this will affect your parents, wife (husband), and children?" They watched their patients withdraw into further gloom.

Slowly an obvious fact emerges: If suicidal patients were completely intent on dying, they would have already killed themselves. Some part of the patient wishes to live, and it is with this part that the therapist attempts to connect, no matter how suicidal the patient may be. What emerges from this connection is the therapeutic alliance (Horvath & Luborsky, 1993), the agreement between the therapist and the healthy part of the patient about what to work on in the therapy.

The beginning therapist learns that aligning with the healthy part of the patient is not to be confused with cheerleading for living. Although allied with this healthy part, the therapist maintains neutral curiosity about the parts of the patient that wish to die. The therapist learns to overcome the fear that exploring the patient's wish to die puts such ideas in the patient's mind. Feelings of omnipotence diminish. The therapist comes to see that exploring the patient's inner world with dispassionate, nonjudgmental interest conveys several therapeutic meta-communications: what you are feeling is not unspeakably bad, it is human; I'm interested in whatever you are thinking and feeling; I appreciate the distinction between self-destructive thoughts, feelings, fantasies, and action; your anguish is not as devastating to me as it is to you; my strength will be here for you to borrow if you need to; your therapy is a place where your destructive urges can be understood rather than judged; I will try not to leave you alone with your anguish. A determination to enter the patient's inner world and stay with the associated feelings and thoughts gradually replaces the therapist's quest to be all-knowing.

Treating suicidal patients puts the therapist's quest for benevolence to the test. Perhaps the most difficult task for the beginning therapist treating a suicidal patient is dealing therapeutically with the painful feelings involved. Many of these feeling are the uncivilized ones that the suicidal patient evokes in the therapist, feelings that the neophyte therapist never knew he or she was capable of experiencing. The therapist starts out wanting to help a troubled person, only to feel constantly rejected by the patient's unremitting wishes to die. This dilemma is captured in the following joke.

> A man jumps off a bridge in a suicide attempt. A policeman who happens on the scene witnesses this act and decides to help. He notices a life preserver on the bridge and throws it to the man struggling in the water. Although the life preserver lands only inches from him, the man refuses to take it despite the entreaties of the well-intentioned policeman. After four or five such pleas, the policeman takes out his gun and yells, "Grab on to that life preserver, you son-of-a-bitch, or I'll fill you full of lead!"

The therapist who starts out wanting to help the suicidal patient ends up filled with feelings of frustration, hopelessness, powerlessness, and even murderous rage—just like the policeman in the joke. Such feelings are at odds with the therapist's self-image as a caring professional. Upsetting as these feelings may be, they provide the therapist with the opportunity to modify an unrealistic quest for benevolence. Through the clinical attitude of participant-observation (Havens, 1976), the therapist learns to use countertransference for therapeutic purposes.

Participant-observation denotes a break with the traditional view of the therapist being a mere observer of the strange world of the mentally disturbed by stressing the participation of the observer in the transactional field. The therapist embracing this approach appreciates that therapist and patient affect one another. Thus, the therapist as participant-observer adopts as a major focus the effect on himself or herself of the patient's mental state and behavior as well as his or her effect on the patient. In fact, one of the more profound realizations in a psychotherapist's development is that he or she may be unwittingly impeding the very therapy that he or she has been trying to assist.

Notice the major shift that has occurred in the maturation of therapists who have traveled the path described above. Starting out with the mindset that their good will, encouragement, and hopefulness will constitute a therapeutic matrix for the suicidal patient, they gradually realize that a different approach is required. They slowly acquire the ability to not take their patient's unremitting anguish personally or only as a rejection of their efforts; to contain, metabolize, and detoxify these depressing and self-destructive urges; and, as a result, to stay connected to the patient's pain by sharing it without over-identifying with it or avoiding it. Therapists who stay connected to the anguish inherent in their patients' suicidal state, who are determined not to leave them alone in suffering, provide the most useful antidote to this precarious condition. In arriving at this posture, therapists have modified their grandiose professional ego-ideal and replaced it with a more realistic professional ego-ideal. They now appreciate that their efforts to keep their patients safe are no guarantee that the patients will stay alive, anymore than an oncologist can guarantee to keep a cancer patient alive. Their job is to treat the patient's suicidality with all the skill they possess.

It is important to remember that suicides do occur in competently conducted therapies. Two dangers for the therapist may result from such a regrettable outcome: the failure to keep open for learning the details of the treatment and/or the decision to never again treat sick patients. A cat that sits on a hot stove may never sit on a stove again, hot or cold.

Exploration Versus Action

Patients sometimes ask their therapists to undertake an action on their behalf: "Would you testify at my disability hearing?" "Would you attend my wedding?" "Would you meet for a double session?" "Would you read my term paper?"

Beginning therapists find such requests unsettling for several reasons. They are concerned that in declining to "do something," their patients will be offended, dislike them, or even terminate therapy. More familiar with the institution of friendship than the workings of therapy, therapists feel awkward in declining to do for a patient what they would naturally do for a friend.

A rule so basic to therapy that it is often not explained to patients assists therapists with their dilemma: Requests for action are to be explored before any decision regarding action is made. The two major effects of this rule are so monumental that no textbook discussion can do it justice. First, it helps oppose beginning therapists' tendency to focus on external reality and to act or explain rather than to explore. Second, the emphasis on exploration serves to shift the locus of patients' and therapists' attention from external reality to their respective internal worlds.

> A male patient asked his fledgling female therapist to read his lengthy term paper, which she agreed to do on her own time. Shortly thereafter, she felt upset with herself for having agreed, but didn't know exactly why. Supervision brought several of her concerns to consciousness. She realized

that she felt coerced into agreeing to read the term paper by her fear that if she didn't, her patient, whom she felt attracted to, would leave the therapy. Having agreed to read the paper, what would she do if she thought the paper was poorly done? Could she, would she, actually tell him? And if she did, would he feel criticized or rejected? She also realized that she resented not getting paid for spending her private time gratis—and yet what could she do? After all, *she* had agreed. Or was it permissible for her to broach the possibility of getting paid for her time? And finally, had she unwittingly opened the door to further requests for special attention?

Supervision helped this therapist appreciate that her expertise resided in her ability to explore thoughts, feelings, and fantasies—both her patient's and, silently, her own. She returned to the therapy excited and now equipped with questions that helped her explore her patient's internal world and the therapist–patient relationship: "What would it be like for you if I liked your paper, and what would it be like for you if I didn't?" "How were you hoping I would react?" "What was it like for you to ask me to read your paper?" "Even though I didn't ask, did you think I should be compensated for the time I spent reading it?" And "Could it be that you have other requests that you have not yet shared with me?" Also, as a result of talking in supervision about her attraction to her patient, she no longer felt uncomfortable: her feelings of attraction had lost their sense of urgency.

Exploration produced changes in the therapy hour over time. Her patient seemed less preoccupied with news of the week or other people's psychology. He was more conscious of his longings and began to realize that his therapy consisted of exploring those wishes rather than expecting his therapist to fulfill them. His introspective capacity increased. About herself, the therapist noticed that she was no longer uptight about the consequences of whether or not she liked her patient's paper or not, or whether she would be paid or not. She enjoyed her attraction to her patient rather than being unsettled by it. She gained a clearer appreciation of what patients value the most in therapy: being understood rather than catered to, attaining self-knowledge through heightened introspective capacity, and the therapist's compassionate, curious neutrality.

A therapist's tendency to act before exploring a request can interfere with the evolution and analysis of transference. Beginning therapists often find it difficult not acting on subsequent requests after having acted on the first one—again, usually without exploration.

> Carol, who periodically missed several days from work due to depression, asked her therapist to write a letter excusing her from work for medical reasons. Her therapist initially complied, but as time passed the requests began to feel like demands. In supervision it was suggested that the therapist explore Carol's thoughts, feelings, and associations to the request as well as to the therapist's possible responses. This suggestion led Carol to recall a turbulent period in her early teens precipitated by her mother's affair that

disrupted family life. Although the marriage survived, Carol blamed her mother for ruining her adolescence, which she emerged from with a sense of entitlement: "Mother, I expect you to make up to me the period of my life that you ruined." Carol's sense of entitlement found expression in the transference in her recurrent demands for a letter. The therapist was surprised and gratified to learn that the requests gradually became non-issues in therapy as they were explored.

This clinical experience helped the therapist appreciate that complying with a request before exploring it forfeits the opportunity for personal learning—which is what patients ostensibly enter therapy to gain.

Managing Intense Affect

Most beginning therapists are not prepared to deal effectively with the powerful feelings that inevitably get stirred up in psychotherapy. Despite their avowed intention to use the therapist–patient relationship as the major therapeutic agent, therapists new to the field, more than they realize, prefer their patients to be "good": reasonable, cooperative, committed to the therapy, receptive, appreciative, and verbally expressive. They are unprepared to deal with irrational hatred, intense sexual attraction, sudden unilateral termination, groundless accusation, and provocative distortion. They are especially confused when these reactions occur in a treatment that has seemed stable, useful, and valued. Ironically, what beginning therapists do not yet appreciate is that their skill in establishing safety, trust, and a durable therapeutic framework has made it possible for their patients, often unconsciously, to bring the more unreasonable parts of themselves into the therapy.

When derailed or destroyed therapies are reviewed, it often becomes clear that strong and unaddressed feelings have been involved. Cases involving unilateral termination (Gans, 1994) erotic transference, or the treatment of the psychotic patient illustrate this point.

Unilateral Termination

In unilateral termination, therapists have usually had the opportunity to notice and discuss with patients signs of impending trouble: repeated lateness, cancelled or missed sessions, requests for changes in meeting time or frequency, complaints about traffic, late or unpaid bills, and allusions to more favorable modes of therapy. Rationally, therapists understand that citing these behaviors and discussing the feelings underlying them will often restore the therapeutic relationship. So the obvious question is, why do they sometimes resist such discussions?

At an unconscious or semiconscious level, the specter of rejection or abandonment seems too painful to endure. The result, unfortunately, is even more painful. The announcement of unilateral termination feels like a blow to the therapist's solar plexus. When it finally comes, feelings of surprise in the therapist give way to feelings of anger, deflation, betrayal, ingratitude, abandonment, vengeance, powerlessness, self-doubt, and, occasionally, relief. The aggregate of these feelings has a deskilling and dis-equilibrating effect, sometimes leading to dissociation.

Feeling upset but unable to meaningfully process these feelings, the therapist proceeds with a façade of calm and tries to review the patient's decision-making process. But it is usually too late; the time has passed when discussion can rescue and heal the therapeutic rift. When therapists realize that the emotional pain that results from avoiding impasse or conflict is worse than the discomfort of first talking about them, they gradually learn to welcome in for discussion the danger signs in the therapy.

Erotic Transference

Extreme positive feelings, often sexual in nature, can also derail a therapy. Therapists, especially those new to the field, can feel at greater risk than their patients when sexual desire unexpectedly, forcefully, and persistently strives for completion. The inexperienced therapist's equilibrium may be disrupted by intense sexual feelings that overly stimulate, flatter, and blur boundaries, as the following example illustrates.

> Mary, an attractive married woman in her early 30s, was hospitalized with a major depression. She emerged gradually from her depression with a compelling radiance and began to express her feelings of love for her therapist, a married man about the same age. The patient had rose petals scattered on the driveway of the mental hospital as a sign of her love and urged her therapist to consummate their relationship in a nearby hotel. Her therapist quickly reality-tested his patient's feelings by telling her that he was married and not available, an intervention that he proudly mentioned at the case conference at which the patient was being presented. To the therapist's surprise, the senior psychiatrist chairing the conference questioned the intervention and wondered if the therapist would ever again hear a word about the patient's sexual feelings. (The patient discussed sexual material only once in the following 10 years of therapy.)

Discussion of the case revealed that the therapist was threatened as much or more by *his* sexual attraction to the patient than by her attraction to him. He realized that his intervention was more for his benefit than for his patient's. Although in retrospect he knew that he would neither have violated the patient nor jeopardized his own professional status and reputation, he had lost perspective in the "heat of the erotic transference." Discussions that transpired in the case conference and in subsequent supervisory sessions, combined with exploration of the scenario in his own therapy, provided the therapist with tools to deal competently with subsequent, similar situations. The therapist found two concepts to be especially helpful. The first was to silently screen his interventions with the following question and admonition: "Is what I'm about to say for my benefit or the patient's benefit? If it is primarily for my benefit, I should not say it." Second, the concepts of boundary crossings and boundary violations alerted the therapist to his behaviors that could be treading a "slippery slope," endangering his patient, himself, and the therapy.

Treatment of the Psychotic Patient

Treating psychotic patients provides the beginning therapist with unparalleled opportunities to learn about intense affect. Psychotic conditions involve feeling states and psychic phenomena that evoke disturbing countertransference responses. Periods of massive indecision or unremitting stubbornness, feelings of powerlessness and worthlessness, externalized self-loathing and hatred, delusions of grandeur and persecution, preoccupying hallucinations— to name a few—challenge the therapist's capacity for empathy, concern, and connection. These phenomena require therapists to engage, understand, and accept disturbing parts of themselves in order to empathically connect with their psychotic patients. This self-examination exerts a profound influence on what type of psychotherapist the clinician decides to be. Not every aspiring psychotherapist is cut out to effectively treat people with psychotic disorders. There should be no shame in this discovery: learning what categories of patients one wishes to treat, and is effective in helping, is an important element in the process of becoming a psychotherapist.

Therapists who can manage the intense affect that psychosis elicits and decide to undertake its treatment encounter a host of challenging and potentially enlightening questions: How do I empathize with personal experiences that seem so foreign (Eigen, 1986)? Do I have the temperament to treat a condition in which its sufferer has a limited capacity for personal connection? Can psychosis be understood in simple human terms? How do I talk with a psychotic patient about obtaining his or her family's involvement in the treatment? If given permission, how much should I involve the psychotic patient's family in the treatment? How do I assess the psychotic patient's reliability as a historian?

Modifying What One Has Learned About the Theory and Practice of Psychotherapy

The insecurity of beginning therapists, coupled with the complexity of their task, causes them to hold tight to what they have learned from their teachers and supervisors. These teachings serve as transitional objects until therapists consolidate a more considered and secure clinical foundation. This learning trajectory is both expectable and normal. When these ideas are embraced unquestionably and applied rigidly over time, however, healthy maturation suffers. Fortunately, clinical encounters offer many opportunities to modify such rigidity.

One involves listening to their patients, whose comments indirectly offer them a form of ongoing "supervision." Psychodynamically trained therapists have been taught to follow patients' associations, not lead them. If for weeks, however, a patient sits silently for more than half the session, the therapist has the opportunity to wonder if such abstinence is helping. Therapists do not have to solve this question alone: they can ask their patients if allowing them to speak first is helpful. The ensuing discussion can be a potent learning experience for the therapist.

It can be difficult for beginning therapists to modify their cherished teachings. Taught that interpretation is a therapist's most potent tool, what is the beginning therapist to think when a well-timed, thoroughly considered, and respectfully delivered interpretation is experienced by her patient as a sadistic assault? Beginning therapists tend to wonder what is wrong with the patient rather than what might be unhelpful about their approach. As they say in the research laboratory, "The animal is always right." Through exposure to other ideas and approaches, gathered through reading, supervision, and perhaps their own therapy, beginning therapists have the opportunity to respond effectively to the needs of their patients rather than to feel obligated to a particular theoretical orientation.

Dr. Jones's reaction to his patient, Dorothy, is a case in point. Concerned about "gratifying" Dorothy with answers, Dr. Jones would respond to Dorothy's questions with a question. This approach usually caused Dorothy to shut down. She finally told Dr. Jones that she experienced his not answering her questions to be so disrespectful that she could not imagine ever deriving any benefit from his approach. As Dr. Jones began to answer Dorothy's questions, and *then* asked her why she asked, productive psychotherapeutic work resulted. Dr. Jones began to experience the results of his increased responsiveness: feeling respected and seen, Dorothy began to speak about the deprivation in her early life that left her so sensitive to and hurt by Dr. Jones's former approach.

Through the forbearance, and the feedback, of their patients, psychotherapists have the opportunity to learn an important lesson: while the psychodynamic approach can serve as a foundation for whatever type of psychotherapy is practiced, it is unreasonable to expect that its methods will help everyone. As therapists begin to understand the developmental basis for their patients' negative reactions to their interventions, they have the opportunity to modify their approach.

Managing Boundaries and Dealing with Difference

Managing Boundaries

The intersection—sometimes the collision—of the inner worlds of patient and therapist unleashes powerful emotional currents. The emotions evoked in the therapist by the patient are referred to as countertransference. How therapists deal with these feelings, as the example below illustrates, determines how they will manage the boundaries in the therapy (Gabbard & Lester, 1995).

> Alex, a male therapist 5 years into practice, received a phone message from Susan seeking therapy. From the information that Susan left on the answering machine, Alex determined that not only did Susan live in his town but that she lived across the street from the house directly behind Alex's. Susan, he realized, could literally see into his bedroom from her living room window. When Alex called Susan back he learned that she had gotten his name from two people who spoke very favorably of him: a highly esteemed ex-supervisor and a former patient, who happened to be a close friend of Susan's. Alex noted Susan to have an appealing if not sexy voice. Susan said that she could pay privately but could only make an evening appointment because of her work schedule. Alex did not ordinarily have evening appointments.
>
> Susan's call came at a difficult time in Alex's life. His practice caseload was down significantly. He was temporarily separated from his wife, who had recently moved to another part of town with one of their two teen-age children. He was also feeling burdened by his children's private school tuitions.

How might the competent handling of this clinical scenario, and the countertransference it engendered, contribute to Alex's development as a psychotherapist? As we follow Alex's processing of his feelings, the relationship between countertransference and ethical considerations in psychotherapy will gain clarity.

Overwhelmed by the information he obtained during his brief phone conversation with Susan, Alex told her that he needed time to consider her request. Alex also sought consultation with a respected colleague.

Before calling Susan back, Alex found himself churned up and distracted by many thoughts and feelings. He felt flattered by the high regard in which his ex-supervisor and former patient allegedly held him. He was pleased that his ex-supervisor, a highly esteemed clinician, was referring him a patient and worried that he might jeopardize a potentially excellent referral source in not accepting Susan as a patient. The idea of a patient who could pay his full fee was very appealing.

He began to realize that his state of vulnerability was blinding him to the many hazards posed by taking Susan on as a patient. The proximity of her home to his home office could well compromise his privacy, and perhaps hers. He could come to resent seeing Susan in an evening appointment, a time that he did not usually hold office hours. The fact that his former patient could well return to therapy could compromise the confidentiality of each. Even if Alex could keep the two therapies separate, he might resent the extra effort it took to do so. He recalled his responsiveness to Susan's appealing voice, which got him in touch with his feelings of sexual deprivation. Was he about to go down a slippery slope? Would Susan's ability to pay privately— insurance payments amounted to half his fee— interfere with sound clinical judgment? Thinking clearly, he realized that securing his ex-supervisor as a referral source by taking Susan as a patient was largely an illusion; it was actually a desperate wish to secure imagined love as an antidote to his deprived state.

Alex found taking stock of his countertransference instructive on several levels. He was reminded of basic facts of the patient–therapist relationship. Meaningful psychotherapy depends on a clear, consistent, and sturdy thera- peutic framework. The therapist–patient relationship is unequal: the patient is not there for the therapist in the way the therapist intends to be there for the patient. Comments or decisions that therapists make should be for the patient's benefit, not their own. Boundary maintenance results from counter- transference awareness and monitoring that guards against precipitous, and possibly exploitative, action. Periods of heightened therapist vulnerability increase the chances of pursuing unwitting self-interest. The path to violating patients is paved with successive and seemingly innocuous boundary cross- ings. Ethical behavior goes hand in hand with sound clinical practice. All therapists are well served by seeking periodic supervision.

Occasionally therapists encounter situations that involve two competing ethical values. For example, should a therapist violate a suicidal patient's con- fidentiality by contacting a spouse to arrange for short-term safety? Beginning therapists need to learn that their professional colleagues and societies, as well as society at large, have thought about these boundary considerations in depth and that written guidelines and/or laws exist (American Psychiatric Association, 2001; Pope & Vasquez, 2007). Ethical challenges often require peer and legal consultation. Beginning psychotherapists should be aware of these resources and are encouraged to seek such advice as a normal part of their practice.

Dealing with Difference

This section of the chapter has been the most difficult one for me to write. The first several drafts were sterile, comprising mainly quotes and discussions of cultural competence culled from the literature. Somewhat stymied, I call a Haitian friend, a psychologist and colleague. She pointed out that as a member of "white privilege" it was not surprising that I would have a harder time than a person of color in being in touch with feelings associated with difference. As a white male in America, she said, you probably spend more time with people who are similar to you than different from you. (Theorists differentiate white privilege from racism or prejudice because a person who may benefit from white privilege is not necessarily racist or prejudiced and may be unaware of having any privileges reserved only for whites.) She suggested I think of a situation that alerted me to particulars of my own culture.

I recently was an invited guest conductor at a group therapy conference attended by Caucasians (80%) and people of color (20%). In the course of my three presentations, a relatively young, white participant was offended by two terms that I offhandedly used that she felt were, albeit unintended, racist: "call a spade a spade" and "black sheep." She wondered if it would be appropriate to speak to me about it and if I would be receptive. The conference chair encouraged her to do so. I was surprised, slightly embarrassed, and intrigued by the attendee's reaction as well as impressed by her courage in approaching me. I encouraged her to bring up her concern to the large group. An interesting though intellectual discussion ensued.

Notions of racism and prejudice remained in the air in the demonstration group I conducted that immediately followed the large group discussion just alluded to. The demonstration group consisted of two women of color, a young gay man who worked in an inner-city clinic, a former nun, a divorced Catholic woman whose Jewish ex-husband's family had strongly objected to mixed marriage, and a few others. I began to feel that the group was avoiding dealing with their feelings toward me by settling for an idealization of my Harvard credentials. I said to the group, "How could a fancy, old Harvard psychiatrist in private practice ever connect with a young gay social worker who opted to work in an inner-city clinic?" A debate ensued over whether my extensive education had assisted me in overcoming any prejudice that I might have had. During this discussion I found myself having an association that surprised and concerned me. I recalled being in the Zurich airport on the way to a visit to Israel. A contingent of Orthodox Jews was praying in an adjacent section of the airport. I found myself turned off—even disgusted—by their public display of religion and what I experienced as their clannishness. I was also concerned that my association would offend an Orthodox participant in the conference. I refocused my attention on the proceedings of the demonstration group just in time to hear their verdict that I was not a prejudiced person. I replied, "Actually I am." I recounted my associations to the Orthodox Jews in the airport and spoke of my Jewish self-hate, of which I was not proud. (I silently contented myself with the thought that I am anti-fundamentalist not anti-Semitic, but that is another story.) My revelation had a powerful effect. Members of the demonstration group, and later members of the audience group, began to speak openly of their prejudices. These discussions had a poignant, visceral feel that enlivened the entire conference.

The above example contains many important clinical lessons that contribute to the making of a psychotherapist. We all have prejudice and blind spots. Prejudice can be directed at difference within one's clan as well as without. Proceeding with an awareness of one's prejudice can free up others to recognize and take responsibility for their own. Clinical experiences provide ongoing opportunities to monitor the ways we may be culturally and racially insensitive (Sue, 1998). Dealing openly and honestly with one's blind spots can repair a damaged therapeutic alliance. Sincere apologies (Lazare, 2004) go a long way in leveling the playing field, repairing inflicted hurts, and demonstrating one's common humanity. It is usually not necessary to tell patients about our prejudices—my acknowledgment at the conference was primarily for teaching purposes. Rather, it is our job as therapists to be aware of our prejudices and cultural blind spots in order that they do not harm our patients. And yet, occasional and judicious self-disclosure can be therapeutic for the patient.

After addressing the hurt that one's blind spots or prejudice can inflict, it is good to keep in mind that becoming a psychotherapist involves embracing complexity. For example, if the above scenario took place in a therapy group, the therapist could promote a discussion that encouraged the members of color who did find the remarks racist to explain why, and those who didn't to explain why. Caucasian members could be invited to speak about what sensitized them to the racist overtones. Perhaps the leader's "racist comments" unwittingly reflected racial tensions in the group that had yet to be articulated. The resistance in the group to such a discussion could then be explored. There are always more layers to examine.

Conclusion

Clinical experience can be conceived of as a continuing education gift. The powerful emotional currents unleashed between and within patient and therapist offer a lifelong opportunity for therapists' growth and development. This chapter has provided six basic tasks that, when understood and competently managed, contribute to the making of a psychotherapist:

- Monitoring the framework of therapy
- Evolving a realistic professional ego-ideal
- Exploring versus acting and/or explaining
- Containing and metabolizing intense affect
- Modifying psychological dogma
- Managing boundaries and dealing with difference

These tasks offer the therapist a rich variety of questions for self-reflection. Here are a few:

- Am I clear about my job description?
- Are my interventions conducive to creating safety and fostering connection?
- For whose benefit is what I'm saying to the patient?
- In what ways might I be impeding the very therapy I am trying to facilitate?
- Am I more influenced by the dictates of a particular school of therapy than by what my patient needs from me right now?
- Is my present state of heightened vulnerability leading the therapy down a slippery slope?

- Do I recognize resistance and am I able to work effectively with it?
- Am I sensitive to cultural difference?
- Do I seek out supervision when perplexed or overwhelmed by a patient's effect on me?
- Have I accepted my limits and put my therapeutic aspirations in perspective?

Thankfully, the list of questions is endless. For those therapists who begin and continue their careers by generating and thinking about such questions, their futures as evolving, competent, compassionate, and respectful therapists seem bright.

And finally, for those readers who are still wondering about Alex, he decided not to accept Susan as a patient. He explained to her that he foresaw a number of boundary issues that would compromise the therapy. He offered to provide her the names of competent therapists. She felt rejected and responded angrily, while Alex, who realized that he might have accepted Susan as a patient when he began his practice 5 years earlier, felt relieved and proud of his decision.

Acknowledgments

The author wishes to thank Arnold Cohen, Ph.D., David Fine, Nancy Gans, and Suze Prudent, Ph.D., for their helpful comments.

References

American Psychiatric Association. *Ethics Primer*. Washington, D.C.: American Psychiatric Association, 2001.

Brightman, B. (1984). Narcissistic issues in the training of the psychotherapist. *International Journal of Psychoanalytic Psychotherapy*, 10, 293–317.

Edelwich, J., & Brodsky, A. (1980). *Burn-out: Stages of Disillusionment in the Helping Professions*. New York: Human Sciences Press.

Eigen, M. (1986). *The Psychotic Core*. Northvale, NJ/London: Jason Aronson, Inc.

Gabbard, G. O., & Lester, E. P (1995). *Boundaries and Boundary Violations in Psychoanalysis*. New York: Basic Books.

Gans, J. S. (1994). Indirect communication as a therapeutic technique: a novel use of counter-transference. *American Journal of Psychotherapy*, 48(1), 120–140.

Gans, J. S., & Counselman, E. F. (1996). The missed session: a neglected aspect of psychodynamic psychotherapy. *Psychotherapy*, 33 (1), 43–50.

Havens, L. L. (1976). *Participant-Observation*. New York: Jason Aronson, Inc.

Horvath, A. O., & Luborsky, L. (1993). The role of the therapeutic alliance in psychotherapy. *Journal of Consulting and Clinical Psychology*, 61(4), 561–573.

Krueger, D. W. (ed.) (1986). *The Last Taboo: Money as Symbol and Reality in Psychotherapy and Psycho-analysis*. New York: Brunner/Mazel.

Langs, R. (1976). *The Bipersonal Field*. New York: Jason Aronson, Inc.

Lazare, A. (2004). *On Apology*. New York: Oxford University Press.

Maltsburger, J. T., & Buie, D. H. (1974). Counter-transference hate in the treatment of suicidal patients. *Archives of General Psychiatry*, 30, 625–632.

Maroda, K. J. (1991), *The Power of Countertransference*, 2nd ed. Hillsdale, NJ: The Analytic Press.

Pope, K. S., & Vasquez, M. J. T. (2007). *Ethics in Psychotherapy and Counseling: A Practical Guide*. San Francisco: Jossey-Bass.

Roth, S. (1987). *Psychotherapy: The Art of Wooing Nature*. Northvale, NJ/London: Jason Aronson, Inc.

Stark, M. (1994). *Working with Resistance*. Northvale, NJ/London: Jason Aronson, Inc.

Sue, S. (1998). In search of cultural competence in psychotherapy and counseling. *American Psychologist*, 53(4), 440–448.

Yalom, I. D. (2002). *The Gift of Therapy*. New York: HarperCollins.

6

Psychotherapy Supervision and the Development of the Psychotherapist

Molyn Leszcz

Introduction

Many of the central elements in the development of the mental health practitioner are embedded in the experience trainees have in supervision of their clinical work. This is particularly true with regard to psychotherapy supervision, which is a complex and meaningful learning experience. There is no other aspect of training that focuses more specifically on the trainee's self-awareness, exposure to scrutiny, and opportunity for personal growth and development.

This chapter will describe the challenges and opportunities psychotherapy supervision must engage in order to contribute maximally to the development of the psychotherapy trainee. Guiding this chapter will be perhaps one of the earliest principles articulated regarding education and training. It dates back 2,000 years to *Ethics of our Fathers* (50), in which sages of that time note the following, "The anxious, inhibited student cannot learn; The impatient, critical teacher cannot teach."

This chapter is written from the perspective of an academic psychiatrist who has been involved in the teaching and training of students in psychotherapy over an extended number of years. This supervisory work encompasses approximately 300 supervisees in group and individual psychotherapy and ranges from neophyte psychiatry residents learning group and individual psychodynamic therapy to more experienced practitioners. Supervision has also included responsibility for ensuring therapist competence and adherence in psychotherapy research trials. In addition, I have had recent experience in supervising colleagues in China through the use of modern technology and language translation. This cross-cultural experience has helped to illuminate, shape, and in many instances confirm core concepts related to psychotherapy supervision.

Models of Psychotherapy Supervision

It is well recognized that multiple elements contribute to training in psychotherapy. These include didactic experiences, observational experiences, experiential experiences, clinical training, personal therapy, and, psychotherapy supervision. There is consensus among scholars in the field that psychotherapy supervision plays a pivotal role in the development of the psychotherapist and that training programs must ensure the provision of adequate and meaningful psychotherapy supervision (Watkins, 1998). Ladany (2007) notes that many training programs emphasize the teaching of theory rather than practical skills: the experience of reflection, self-examination, and developing and refining technical skills is insufficiently addressed. The importance of psychotherapy supervision is well underscored in many publications and textbooks regarding psychotherapy supervision (Alonso, 2000; Lambert & Ogles, 1997; Ramos-Sanchez et al., 2002).

Shanfield et al.'s perspective (1993), based upon years of psychotherapy supervision research, is very relevant. They argue that psychotherapy supervision must be shaped by our knowledge of adult development so that it facilitates the trainee synthesizing an identity that balances the professional and personal self, values, and needs. To facilitate this integration we must expect that our trainees talk about their personal reactions to their clinical work as part of their education while maintaining a clear distinction between education and psychotherapy. Alonso captured this well in her statement, "the psychotherapy supervisor in effect must listen with a clinician's ear and speak with a teacher's mouth" (2000, p. 56).

Attention to development no doubt explains why so many developmental models of psychotherapy supervision have been described in the literature. Watkins (1995) cautions against the propagation of competing models of professional development because they are often not replicable and hence fail to advance the field at large. Psychiatry, social work, clinical psychology, and counseling psychology all have developed models to guide the supervisor. However, these different disciplines put forward paradigms that generally are not in communication with one another.

Four general models seem to stand out, notwithstanding little empirical support for them with regard to improving therapist competence or, more importantly, improving patient outcomes: developmental (Stoltenberg et al., 1998), systems (Holloway, 1984), interpersonal (Ladany et al., 2005), and competency-based (Falender & Shafranske, 2004).

The position in this chapter will be to look at these models as linked rather than discrete and to harness contributions of each to help understand and explicate the role of psychotherapy supervision in the growth and development of trainees. In this spirit it is important for the supervisor to have an appreciation of where the trainee is developmentally in order to focus his or her attention and interventions at that level. Without this, supervisory attunement is likely to suffer. It is similarly important to recognize the multiple forces that affect the supervisor/supervisee dyad. Appreciation for a systems perspective that respects the fact that the patient is treated by the therapist in a larger context that is influenced by the environment in which the psychotherapy supervision and clinical care occur, both institutionally and even societally, is also useful. Kilminster and Jolly (2000) underscore how important the clinical setting is through the systems lens of isomorphy. The culture, values, and ethos of the environment provide support and foster commitment to teaching—or it does the opposite. All of these forces will influence what happens between the supervisor and supervisee and in turn between the supervisee and the patient. From an interpersonal perspective, trainees need to gain capacity in how to understand and use themselves relationally as fully as possible. This includes interpersonal skill, reflective capacity, use of self, and recognition of problem behaviors and attitudes that may interfere with the development of the therapeutic alliance. Finally, of course, because psychotherapy supervision also has the responsibility of trainee evaluation and is a gatekeeper to credentialing, attention to therapist competency and effectiveness is also essential. A supervisory model that can integrate these four domains may be particularly useful and will be articulated (Westefeld, 2009).

A simplified model of therapist development and the tasks of psychotherapy supervision was put forward by Inskipp and Proctor (1993). They argue that the tasks of psychotherapy supervision are threefold: normative, formative, and restorative functions. Normative functions include helping to establish the framework for the trainee; determining the administrative structure in which psychotherapy supervision will take place; selection and assessment of suitable patients; recordkeeping; and identification of and responses to the common concerns and questions that trainees have. The formative tasks of psychotherapy supervision relate to learning theory and the application practically of the theory that is being taught and learned. This is the component of psychotherapy supervision that helps shape therapist capacity to intervene effectively and competently, linking theory to practice in ways that are based upon principles that can be replicated over and over again. The third component is the restorative task of psychotherapy supervision, which includes helping with containment and tolerance of intense affects and countertransference reactions that the therapist may experience with the patient; supporting the trainee through periods of doubt; sustaining therapist confidence and helping to re-moralize the trainee in the face of therapeutic challenge, uncertainty, and even failure.

Howard (2008) takes this latter step even further in her emphasis on the important role of psychotherapy supervision encompassing enhancement of wellness and the development of resilience in our trainees. She notes that the work that we do is difficult, demanding, uncertain, and often isolating. She recommends the incorporation of a positive psychology approach emphasizing exploration and discussion of trainee strengths, the meaning of this work, and the development of the capacity to manage and balance work and life.

There are parallels within this framework to the well-known developmental integrated model described by Stoltenberg and colleagues in 1998. They classify trainees according to three levels. In level I the trainee has limited skills and requires a great deal of structure and stability from the supervisor. At this stage the supervisor should focus on building trust and concentrate on establishing an educational alliance, being mindful of the role of the supervisor's relative power and the role of evaluation and its impact on the developing trainee. In level II, the trainee is moving back and forth between autonomy and dependence, and the supervisor needs to have a great range of flexibility to neither infantilize nor neglect the trainee. Finally, at level III, the trainee is functioning at a competent level and seeks now collegial collaboration rather than intense scrutiny.

Principles of Psychotherapy Supervision

How can we do this work as well as possible? The first principle I would put forward is that the work of psychotherapy supervision consists of the transmission of the core values of the field embedded within the supervisory relationship. There are multiple objectives of training, but I argue that transmitting the core values of the field with regard to professionalism and humanism is at the center of these. It is well known that the supervision of psychotherapy is mandated across disciplines and modalities virtually universally (Ogren et al., 2005). Gonsalvez and McLeod (2008) write that the objectives of psychotherapy supervision involve four competencies: knowledge, skills, relationship capacities, and attitudes and values. Other writers argue that self-reflection is the key, and in one study (Coster & Schwebel, 1997), self-reflective capacity was viewed as the number-one priority with regard to the acquisition of skills in training. They view self-reflective capacity as a meta-competence that influences every aspect of the trainee's professional and for that matter personal life, in that it is essential in promoting well-being and reducing therapist burnout.

These principles are ever more prominent in the contemporary practice of psychotherapy as we embrace models that emphasize a two-person psychology and the centrality of the healing context of the therapeutic relationship (Wampold, 2001). Contemporary models of therapy place great emphasis on the therapist's use of self; presence; capacity to use interpersonal processes related to the therapeutic relationship; and capacity to meta-communicate with the patient around these processes (Hill & Knox, 2009; Kiesler, 1996; Wachtel, 2007). Allied with this, of course, is the capacity to identify and utilize countertransference, mindful that therapist hostility is a common contributor to negative outcomes in psychotherapy, and experience alone does not mitigate against this negative effect (von der Lippe et al., 2008). Disciplined personal involvement on the part of the therapist is essential, and psychotherapy supervision is the chief mechanism by which the trainee can mature into a practitioner who is able to engage patients in a way that promotes direct, authentic, meaningful interaction and feedback, respectful of appropriate therapeutic boundaries (Leszcz, 2009).

Psychotherapy supervision is hence also charged with the responsibility to educate the trainee and model how to work within proper boundaries and conduct psychotherapy that respects the fact that psychotherapy is a fiduciary relationship. It is also clear that the effectiveness of psychotherapy supervision is tied to the quality of the supervisory relationship, and the alliance between supervisor and supervisee is as important to the outcome of the training as the therapeutic alliance is to the outcome of the psychotherapy itself (Alonso, 1985).

Trainee Perspectives on Psychotherapy Supervision

A recent training program for supervisors at the University of Toronto (2008) featured a series of presentations by residents at various levels of training. Their comments reflecting their own experience and that of their colleagues are relevant and also echo the literature. With clear unanimity the residents noted that beginning psychotherapy was the most daunting aspect of their work as a psychiatrist. Issues of professional identity and technical competence were primary concerns, and they wished they had been given a handbook of answers to common questions and anxieties as a way of helping to normalize their experience and provide them with essential knowledge. At times they felt so overwhelmed they didn't know even what to ask of their supervisors. Concerns related to basic questions about the time of the session, frequency, and how to manage personal questions that patients asked. Lacking experience, they also lacked confidence and struggled with a feeling of being an imposter in their role as a therapist. They also reported conflict with the medical model of other aspects of their psychiatry training. The pace of work, for example, in other areas is much quicker than the pace in psychotherapy and there was a profound sense that they were not doing this work correctly.

The residents also reported having to manage the different expectations that supervisors had of them with regard to theoretical approaches to the practice of psychotherapy and even the use of integrating pharmacotherapy into psychotherapy. In instances where psychotherapy was viewed as an intrinsic component of general psychiatry the work went better, but in instances where psychotherapy was viewed by their psychiatric supervisors in non-psychotherapy settings as anachronistic and non-evidence-based, the challenges were much greater.

Supervisees also reported how much they disliked the feeling that psychotherapy supervision crossed boundaries into psychotherapy. The imbalance with regard to personal exposure was quite unsettling and led in some instances to shutting down and managing the psychotherapy supervision rather than engaging in it. There was ambivalence expressed about the greater demonstration and access to their clinical work through the use of audiovisual means or direct observation. On the one hand it meant anxiety would rise, but on the other hand it was viewed as incredibly helpful in actually looking at specific techniques and use of interventions.

A key question facing supervisees is the balance between evaluation and training: Is the objective to get a good evaluation, to protect self-esteem, to grow as a therapist, or to benefit the patient? Obviously these questions are not disconnected one from the other, but their relative emphasis in the experience of the trainee can powerfully influence the supervisory experience.

As residents matured and gained competence and effectiveness they reported gaining confidence and feeling less anxious. This was often marked by a greater capacity to use themselves therapeutically, and trusting their reactions and their capacity to find palatable ways of providing unpalatable feedback to patients. They gained the capacity to work within the therapeutic alliance so that it was possible to emphasize the adaptive components of patients' difficulties rather than pathologizing, blaming, or shaming. Trainees also reported a growing capacity to make the shift back and forth between implicit and explicit knowledge—on the one hand being able to know implicitly what to do and proceed in procedural fashion, and on the other hand being able to work backwards to first principles when in therapeutic difficulty.

Our trainees also commented on the impact that the diminishing likelihood that trainees will engage in personal therapy has on their capacity to practice psychotherapy. Although non-medical therapists continue to pursue personal therapy consistently (Bike et al., 2009), there is also clear evidence that fewer psychiatry residents engage in personal therapy now relative to 20 years ago. Historically personal therapy was one of the main avenues for learning about oneself as a therapist, and the loss of that has not yet been replaced in psychiatry training programs (Haak & Kaye, 2008).

Finally, there was unanimity that the opportunity to hear more from their supervisor with regard to supervisory self-disclosure or to observe their supervisor conducting psychotherapy was enormously helpful and normalizing. I myself frequently have taken comfort from the experience I had in observing Irvin Yalom conduct group psychotherapy during my training with him. After a particularly difficult and frustrating session in which little was achieved, Dr. Yalom mentioned in the rehash that there will be days like this in which you may feel you'd be better off selling shoes than being a psychotherapist. Thirty years later that statement still provides comfort in the context of difficult clinical challenges.

Empirical report for this series of concerns raised by trainees is provided by Hess and colleagues (2008) in an examination of what and why supervisees keep things out of psychotherapy supervision. In this study of 14 psychology interns training in a range of models and all near completion of their training, several persistent themes emerged. Trainees commonly withheld information from supervisors that related to their clinical work. There was a clear sense reported by all that this interfered with both patient treatment and therapist learning. In those psychotherapy supervision relationships that were evaluated as being positive, non-disclosure was an isolated event and generally encompassable. Supervisees might conceal information, often about countertransference, both negative and positive feelings that they felt might be shaming if they were articulated. There was a more serious set of non-disclosures reported by trainees in negative supervisory relationships, in which non-disclosure was pervasive. This evasion was correlated with global dissatisfaction with the psychotherapy supervision and concerns about the supervisor's use of power or insensitivities to culture and diversity issues. Trainees would not disclose in these environments because they felt unsafe and that it was futile to protest. Although the fear of a negative evaluation or illumination of incompetence was prominent for all non-disclosures, it was particularly prominent in the context of negative psychotherapy supervision and relationships.

This study, which involved an intensive qualitative exploration and in-depth interviews with trainees, reported that it was quite possible to determine, through the use of a Supervisory Style Inventory (SSI) (Friedlander & Ward, 1984), the quality of psychotherapy supervision on categories of attractiveness, interpersonal sensitivity, and task orientation. Trainees who reported positive supervisory relationships based upon the SSI felt in essence safe, respected, and un-intimidated. Psychotherapy supervision felt supportive and collaborative but was appropriately challenging. Trainees who reported poor supervisory relationships noted that non-disclosure was pervasive and related directly to their fear of being vulnerable, attacked, and shut down. In these negative situations trust was eroded further and the trainee felt further shut down. All trainees reported a loss of confidence and increased insecurity as a result of their avoidance and reported feeling guilty and even embarrassed. It made the work less complete and less authentic, and many of the trainees in the negatively evaluated psychotherapy supervision relationships sought psychotherapy supervision elsewhere.

Trainees felt that in those relationships that were essentially positive, the avoidance of trainee disclosure could have been reduced if the supervisor had pursued more actively those areas that were delicate and difficult to address. Some trainees reported the wish that the supervisor could have modeled and normalized the unease through his or her own self-disclosure about parallel situations. Empirically, self-disclosure on the part of the supervisor contributes to a sense of collegiality and normalizing of difficulties rather than pathologizing the trainee (Knox et al., 2008). Supervisors often lose sight of the perceived power they wield over their trainees and how much this can inhibit open engagement on the part of the trainee. These findings also support earlier findings in a study of neophyte group therapist trainees. That study also showed that there was a direct and complete correlation between unsatisfactory clinical training and unsatisfactory psychotherapy supervision. Murphy and colleagues (1996) reported in this study of 15 neophyte psychotherapy trainees that all reported struggling with intense negative affects at the beginning of treatment, often feeling overwhelmed, insecure, and even frightened by the intensity of the group experience. Trainees who reported positive psychotherapy supervision experiences were able to encompass these difficulties and maintain an effective therapeutic posture and completed their training with a sense of satisfaction and achievement. However, those who experienced psychotherapy supervision as critical, shaming, and blaming all reported that group therapy was something they would never do again. It appears that these therapists felt that the difficulties that were developmentally understandable in the course of group therapy were mislabeled as being pathological and reflective of their own limitations.

Management of Boundaries

If we are to help trainees use themselves fully and effectively as psychotherapists, psychotherapy supervision must be carefully attuned to the role of boundaries, both with regard to the patient/therapist relationship and the therapist/supervisee relationship. Some sobering data inform us about how often this concern is discarded and even violated. Nearly 5% of psychiatry trainees in one study reported that they had been in a sexual relationship with a supervisor over the course of their training (Gatrell et al., 1988). Another study of supervisees across disciplines reported that 6% had had sex with a supervisor (Miller & Larrabee, 1995). An earlier study by Pope and colleagues (1979) reported that 10% of psychologists who completed the survey reported that they had sexual involvement with their supervisors while they were trainees, and 13% of supervisors acknowledged this as well. It is hard to determine how accurate and reflective these findings are, but without a doubt it speaks to the importance of ensuring that one of the core values that does get transmitted in psychotherapy supervision is the importance of establishing, maintaining and respecting boundaries—a central tenet of ethical practice.

An important role of psychotherapy supervision hence is to focus on identifying and managing intense affects experienced by trainees, both positive and negative. A non-shaming environment is essential to create this dialogue. Walker and Clark (1999) noted that supervisors should be proactive, anticipating stressful points for trainees, and should recognize personal situations of their trainees that increase their potential vulnerability. Supervisors are encouraged to engage in a guided exploration of strong feelings experienced by the trainee, any alterations in the treatment frame, giving of gifts, or over-involvement with a patient on any front.

Psychotherapy supervision is essential in helping the trainee transduce into language, rather than enactment, pressures that patients may generate or therapists themselves may generate with regard to inappropriate and unprofessional forms of closeness and intimacy that violate professional boundaries.

Although the extreme end of boundary violations is dramatic, supervisors often have an important role to play in dealing with boundaries at less dramatic levels. More common is the anxiety that trainees feel about psychotherapy supervision morphing into psychotherapy or psychoanalysis. It is as important here to maintain the frame and for psychotherapy supervision to keep the environment safe and secure for the trainee. Psychotherapy supervision is *not* psychotherapy.

A clear articulation and agreement regarding the establishment of an educational alliance is a useful safeguard. In the same fashion that we think about the therapeutic alliance (Bordin, 1979), reflecting patient and therapist agreement regarding the goals of treatment, tasks of treatment, and the nature of the relationship, we as supervisors must also think about establishing an educational or supervisory alliance predicated on the same principles. This educational alliance functions as a contract shaped by the articulated, mutual expectations the trainee and supervisor have regarding supervision. This alliance should note the aims of supervision and how the trainee and supervisor will work together to achieve these objectives. This may productively involve exploration of what the trainee's prior history of supervision has been: what worked well, what was helpful, what interfered with training, and what supervision needs to provide for it to be most useful. Clarity about how the trainee will be evaluated is also helpful.

It is in this context that exploration of countertransference may occur, but within a framework that respects boundaries and the trainee's right to privacy, reducing the risk of pathologizing the trainee or generating a sense of being a *specimen* for examination. Similarly, our attention to parallel process (Arlow, 1963) must be handled with great care so that we do not increase our trainee's identification with the patient at a time when the trainee needs to strengthen his or her identification with the supervisor.

A concept a bit broader than parallel process is isomorphy (Yalom & Leszcz, 2005). Isomorphy acknowledges that whatever gains expression at *any* level of the system will gain expression at *every* level of the system. This affords an examination of themes that occur within the psychotherapy supervision and the therapy as being co-constructed and shaped by multiple forces rather than only being a reflection of the therapist's unconscious identification with the patient and acting this out within the context of psychotherapy supervision. The latter approach frequently places the trainee in a vulnerable and unhelpful position. It serves further to increase the power differential between trainee and therapist and accordingly may undermine the therapist's self-confidence.

Psychotherapy Supervision as a Secure Base

The attachment paradigm has been explored as a model to understand effective psychotherapy supervision. From this perspective, a chief objective of psychotherapy supervision is to create a secure base for the trainee and a safe haven for exploration and growth with little inhibition due to shame or with little undue self-reliance or dismissing of the need for psychotherapy supervision. Secure therapists are able to grow and develop well; insecurely attached therapists become preoccupied by the limits of their abilities and skills (Foster et al., 2007). They both hyperactivate and are distressed and dependent upon supervisors, or they deactivate and become dismissive of the need for psycho-therapy supervision. Dismissively attached trainees overvalue themselves and reduce the role of psychotherapy supervision. They diminish personal vulner-ability, which in turn creates a learning block. Securely attached therapists experience psychotherapy supervision as an environment in which affect is well tolerated and regulated; it is safe to show and ask for help with problem solving, and there is an overall sense of optimism and confidence. Attachment paradigms may be helpful in enabling supervisors to diagnose learning blocks in psychotherapy supervision and to reframe the supervisory alliance more effectively. It may also help protect the supervisor from being pulled into unhelpful positions that increase trainee dependence or engage in a mutually dismissive and critical form of psychotherapy supervision.

Studying 90 trainee/supervisor dyads, Foster and colleagues (2007) determined that trainees' attachment paradigms in life were consistently expressed in the psychotherapy supervision relationship. Hence, the recogni-tion of attachment patterns is of pivotal importance. This can be useful in increasing supervisor self-reflection and flexibility and remind us that a one-size-fits-all approach will not work for all trainees.

In psychotherapy supervisions that were viewed as reflecting a secure attachment, trainees experienced the psychotherapy supervision as supportive and instructional. The psychotherapy supervision was predictable and occurred reliably and with adequate time. The supervisor was also available and accessible in crisis. Feedback was direct and constructive to the trainee and the trainee was able to make use of this directly in training.

A resident who had returned to work after a medical illness began psychotherapy supervision, and in an early supervision session, as we were articulating the educational alliance, it was apparent that the trainee felt emotional. With explicit permission, I inquired about the emotion that was evident and the trainee noted that coming back to work after being ill, she felt vulnerable about her competence and her evaluations. She was concerned that her supervisors would see her as being defective or fragile. She just had a difficult session with a patient that challenged her competence, and she was concerned that in talking about that in psychotherapy supervision would color my sense of her competence and lead to a negative evaluation.

I thanked her for her candor and for raising this with me so directly and suggested that psychotherapy supervision could be very helpful to her in being able to fortify herself against the doubts that could be generated in her as she returns to work, particularly in treating a critical and attacking patient. I underscored that I saw this focus as being an essential part of our work together and that my first objective was to promote her growth and development. I added that I felt confident that if we were able to do that, issues around evaluation would be quite encompassable. At the end of a year of psychotherapy supervision this trainee commented upon completing psychotherapy supervision that the support she received at the beginning was essential in making her feel that she was competent, able, and normal and essential in detoxifying for her sense of being labeled negatively by virtue of her leave of absence.

Applying a developmental approach creates much more working space for trainee and supervisor than a jump toward pathologizing, labeling, or "treating" through the misguided use of psychotherapy supervision as a form of psychotherapy. Underscoring the dual construction of the supervisory relationship in that it is shaped by contributions of both the trainee and the supervisor also models for the trainee the joint construction of the patient/therapist relationship and the joint construction of countertransference. This framing reduces the sense of being faulted and may increase trainee access to feelings of vulnerability and concern that might otherwise get shut down by fear of shame.

Effective and Ineffective Psychotherapy Supervision

The incidence or prevalence of negative supervisory experiences should not be underestimated. A recent survey of APA interns (Ramos-Sanchez et al., 2002) noted that more than 20% of respondents described potent negative supervisory experiences, generally related to the quality of their relationship or to supervisor incompetence with regard to skill level and content expertise. These trainees reported fear of being shamed and that they rejected supervisory input, concealing and distorting what they presented in psychotherapy supervision. Poor psychotherapy supervision contributed to a sense of vulnerability and weakness on the part of trainees and increased their sense of dependence, but without an opportunity to have that need met. Psychotherapy supervision often felt disheartening. Another important feature of unsatisfactory supervision related to ethics. Trainees reported concern with regard to the way in which patients were addressed and referred to, and although frank boundary violations were not prominent, a sense of devaluing the work of therapy was common. These trainees reported a profound lack of satisfaction with their training and felt that their professional development had been negatively affected, speaking to the far-reaching impact of negative supervisory experiences.

Can psychotherapy supervision be too supportive? Perhaps. There is a hazard that if supervisors are too supportive, the trainee will learn less because he or she will be insufficiently challenged. The wish to provide a positive experience in psychotherapy supervision should never lead to the avoidance of formative feedback and the illumination, constructively, of skill deficits. Because supervisees and supervisors can have very divergent experiences of the same psychotherapy supervision, not unlike the differences in therapeutic alliance scores that are provided by patients and therapists, it becomes essential for the supervisor to pay close attention to the process of the supervisory relationship, to illuminate blind spots where possible and issues of avoidance that arise either because of the fear of a negative evaluation or, more subtly, the collusion of a mutual admiration society. If supervisors maintain mindfulness regarding the moment-to-moment transmission of the core values of our profession, through the experience of psychotherapy supervision, these supervisory derailments may be effectively reduced.

As we look at effective psychotherapy supervision, there are two important dimensions to examine. The first has to do with the effectiveness of psychotherapy supervision as experienced by the trainee, and the second has to do with the role of effective psychotherapy supervision in improving patient outcomes. Ultimately we need to achieve more than having a satisfactory training experience: we need to improve clinical outcomes.

Looking at the first issue, Shanfield and colleagues (2001) in a series of studies have described the ingredients of effective psychotherapy supervision. Their work also underscores the discrepancy between subjective scores by trainees and objective ratings of excellence of video tapes of psychotherapy supervision, rated by experts. There is a very strong correlation between satisfaction with psychotherapy supervision and satisfaction with the relationship for both the therapist and supervisor. If the therapist feels understood, both the supervisor and therapist generally report feelings of satisfaction. Shanfield et al.'s research underscored that the effective supervisors were ones who were able to track the immediate experience of the therapist with the patient and, secondly, they allowed the therapist's narrative of the clinical encounter to develop. Residents rated psychotherapy supervision as excellent (1) if they felt supervisors were accepting; (2) if supervisors provided guidance about charged clinical dilemmas, a phenomenon that could be achieved only if the supervisors had an accurate sense of the patient; and (3) if supervisors supported the resident's discussion of the personal experience of the encounter. Allied with this was an opportunity to talk in a collegial way about issues of countertransference.

Trainees also reported a lasting value of supportive supervisors who tuned into their core concerns through the lens of the clinical material. This is an important way of facilitating the development of the trainee and echoes Alonso's dictum of using the ear of a clinician but the mouth of a teacher. Many therapists viewed psychotherapy supervision as one of the most important aspects of their training, echoing the literature.

In contrast, poor supervisors provided little feedback, appeared not to understand the patient, and lacked focus in their comments. As a result, interventions recommended by these supervisors tended to be superficial and irrelevant. Finally, and not unexpectedly, supervisors who were evaluated negatively seemed closed to the resident's personal concerns or emotions about the patient. It appears that supervisors can interfere with their trainee's learning if they are intrusive, hurtful, or not attuned to the supervisee (Nigam et al., 1997).

When trainees describe the effects of successful psychotherapy supervision, themes that emerge relate to a sense of their continued growth and development. In a qualitative study, Worthen and McNeill (1996) noted that trainees who experienced successful psychotherapy supervision, as noted by the hallmark features described in this chapter, reported that psychotherapy supervision contributed to a strengthening of professional confidence. They developed a capacity for meaningful reflection and a non-defensive analysis of their own motivations and effects on their patients. Assumptions about behavior and change were re-examined in a non-defensive fashion as well. The capacity to make sense of experience was similarly enhanced, and therapists reported an improvement in their skill at actual interventions. Importantly, trainees noted that effective psychotherapy supervision promotes healthy professional identification, an important component of the transmission of the core values of our work. Trainees reported improvement in their skills and confidence in their skills coupled with a sense of humility, recognizing their strengths and limitations.

The issue of professional identification is complicated. Where an opportunity for positive identification exists, the opportunity for negative identification also exists, and the weight and pressure of idealization sometimes generates its counterpart, which is devaluation and a sense of ineffectiveness and of never being able to measure up to the standards of the idealized supervisor. Greben (1991) underscored the importance of trainees being exposed to more than one supervisor, feeling that this was the best way to ensure that trainees would see that there is more than one way to think and be as a therapist, and that they could develop their own style rather than feel they needed to adopt that of a supervisor. Multiple supervisors reduce the hazards of idealization, over-identification, and the hostility of dependence on a single supervisor or model. From a more cynical perspective, Boswell and Castonguay (2007) noted that since there is a good likelihood of trainees having a negative experience in psychotherapy supervision, having multiple supervisors increases the likelihood of the trainee having at least one excellent experience.

More empirically, Ogren et al. (2005) reported that positive outcome of psychotherapy supervision was evident in improvements on the trainee self-evaluation scale (Buckley et al., 1982). Trainees demonstrated that as a result of their training and psychotherapy supervision they acquired a capacity for enhanced attention and focus on process, the capacity to make sense of why things are the way they are at this moment in time, opening up the therapist's capacity to think broadly about how the patient experience is overdetermined rather than the result of a single cause and effect. The capacity to understand what is happening psychotherapeutically also increases the therapist's capacity to stay engaged and in fact demonstrate continued positive regard for patients.

One supervisee, an individual with significant clinical experience who sought psychotherapy supervision as a way of improving her capacities, reported that one of the gains acquired through psychotherapy supervision that she had not anticipated related to the concept of mentalization (Fonagy & Bateman, 2006).

She elaborated that having an experience in psychotherapy supervision in which her own reactions, motivations, and emotions could be explored and understood in depth as part of the psychotherapy supervision made her more able to look beyond the manifest with her patients. She could take a deeper, more exploratory approach to understanding the motivations behind her patients' behavior and interactions. She felt significantly more empathic and able to stay in focus without being distracted by content or negative affective reactions to her patients. The psychotherapy supervision also helped to develop the meta-communicative capacities to speak about her understanding about what was happening interactionally and interpersonally. She felt her treatment became more alive and robust as a result.

Psychotherapy is unique in many ways because it involves the integration of both knowledge and techniques mediated by the use of self. Effective supervisors foster the effective use of the therapist's self in the relational matrix of treatment. The therapist's capacity to use himself or herself as a therapeutic instrument is essential and may shape that individual's practice in an enduring fashion. In order for trainees to be able to make the best use of the relational matrix in therapy, they need to have had the experience of psychotherapy supervision making the best use of the relational matrix in psychotherapy supervision. Principles of isomorphy are very relevant with regard to the powerful impact of psychotherapy supervision that provides affirming, thoughtful, direct, alliance-building, and non-shaming feedback and models for the trainee how to provide that for his or her own patients.

The objectives of psychotherapy supervision with regard to countertransference include an emphasis on increasing self-awareness on the part of the trainee and the capacity to modulate anxiety in the face of intense affects. Gelso and Hayes (2007) also note that essential in managing countertransference well are good conceptual skills, the ability to make sense of experience and capacity, and empathy both with regard to receptive abilities in understanding patients and expressive abilities in communicating back to patients in a meaningful, thoughtful, and supportive fashion.

Group psychotherapy supervision is widely practiced in other countries (e.g., Sweden [Ogren & Sundin, 2009]), and they advance this learning objective by providing a non-authoritarian, accepting, and confirming environment for group psychotherapy supervision. Self-disclosure from trainee to trainee may be enhanced in this environment and serves both to model and normalize. It may not be an ideal model for neophyte trainees but may be of use for advanced trainees.

Does Psychotherapy Supervision Improve Clinical Outcomes?

This question has been posited by many in the literature on psychotherapy supervision and training. One of the first studies of this sort, by Ebersole et al. (1969), noted that group therapy trainees who did not receive psycho-therapy supervision in an ongoing fashion lost therapeutic capacity over the course of the treatment that they provided. They became deskilled as they encountered obstacles and challenges that they were not able to understand or address, thereby limiting their therapeutic repertoire.

More recent studies have supported the role of psychotherapy supervision in improving working alliances with patients and improving therapeutic outcomes. Bambling et al. (2006), reporting on brief cognitive-behavioral therapy, noted that psychotherapy supervision improved the working alliance, improved patient satisfaction and retention in treatment, and was also marked by greater falls in Beck Depression Inventory scores. This study compared trainees who received no psychotherapy supervision with those who received psychotherapy supervision based on building the therapeutic alliance, with a third group who received psychotherapy supervision focused on improving interpersonal processes. Both models of psychotherapy supervision were equally effective. The outcomes of psychotherapy supervision in this study were reflected in fewer impasses, stronger working alliances, less anxiety on the part of therapists, and improvement in basic skills.

In psychodynamic psychotherapy, supervision improved the therapist's capacity to track patient affect and the appropriate intensification of emotion in treatment (Diener et al., 2007). Patient outcomes improved with therapist activation, and therapists who were supervised, often with audiovisual record-ings, produced greater positive results.

The literature on patient-centered tracking of outcome and process and the provision of clinical support tools also supports the role of a form of mediated psychotherapy supervision relative to treatment as usual (Harmon et al., 2007). Providing trainees or therapists with skills to redress problems in treatment produces significantly improved clinical outcomes. The clinical support tools described in this work relate to addressing the therapeutic alliance, patient motivation, or social supports available to the patient.

These findings are also demonstrated in the recent research regarding short-term dynamic psychotherapy and the use of training interventions and psychotherapy supervision to improve trainees' capacity to use psycho-dynamic interpersonal techniques. Hilsenroth et al. (2002) showed that psy-chotherapy supervision improved patient outcomes, again evident in the working alliance, and significantly improved depression scores. Tenure of treatment is also improved with supervision, and well-supervised trainees show fewer premature dropouts from therapy (Okiishi et al., 2003).

The Impact of Culture

Culture plays an essential role in understanding attitudes toward power, authority, emotional expressiveness, intimacy, autonomy, and the experience of agency and assertiveness. If we are to be guided by the literature regarding the importance of the supervisor attending to the supervisory relationship and paying particular attention to the processes of communication, interaction, what is said and what is not said, then the contemporary psychotherapy supervisor must also be attuned to the potential impact of culture, ethnocultural diversity, and cultural factors that relate to discipline and sexual orientation. Each of these dimensions may affect the supervisory experience. Trainees come into supervisory relationships with expectations regarding cultural responsiveness and attunement or its absence. The thoughtful and effective psychotherapy supervisor will be alert to potential blind spots that he or she may have in terms of understanding the experience of the trainee as shaped by the dimensions of culture.

Supervisors should aspire to operate with cultural attunement and cultural competence. The definition of cultural competence articulated by Cross et al. (1989) has stood the test of time well and continues to be relevant, never more so in the diverse world in which we work and practice. Cross et al. defined cultural competence as "a set of values, behaviors, attitudes and practices within a system, organization, program or among individuals that enables people to work effectively across cultures. It refers to the ability to honour and respect the beliefs, language, interpersonal styles and behaviours of individuals and families receiving services, as well as staff who are providing such services. Cultural competence is a dynamic, ongoing developmental process that requires a long-term commitment and is achieved over time."

At times our attunement to the cultural contributions to psychotherapy treatment, training, and psychotherapy supervision are easy to recognize. I have recently been involved in developing a group therapy training program for Chinese mental health practitioners. In addition to didactic training and experiential process groups, all provided directly and with moment-to-moment interpretation into Mandarin, I have also been providing regular weekly psychotherapy supervision of ongoing group therapy using the Internet. At the midway point of our supervisory experience I asked the four mental health professionals, representing a range of disciplines in China, to comment on their experience of psychotherapy supervision.

Prominent in their responses were the gains they felt that they had made with regard to self-confidence, agency, and feeling authorized to assert their opinion in the co-leadership of groups. A tendency toward deference to authority and to seniority had initially limited their effectiveness therapeutically. Having understood that the co-therapy models for the members of the group how to deal with issues of assertiveness, agency, and competitiveness, they understood how important it was for them to move beyond their cultural expectations. Allied with this they reported a greater capacity to tolerate feelings of inadequacy in the face of their colleagues by asking questions in the group psychotherapy supervision. They all noted that traditionally self-disclosure and self-exposure was not a norm, yet they realized that if they were to mobilize their patients in this direction they needed to be able to do this between themselves as co-therapists, among the psychotherapy supervision group, and with me as their supervisor. We explored as well the attributions made to me of authority and knowledge and how this could parallel the kinds of transferential experiences members of the group had toward them. They informed me that in their culture there is a tendency to look at relationships as prototypes of families, and in that way female therapists would be viewed as mothers or sisters and I, as a male supervisor, would be viewed as the father. Reflecting on these issues was instrumental in helping them to disengage from what would have otherwise been a rigid adherence to cultural roles. The most senior member of the four supervisees commented about how much of a relief it was for her to not feel that she always had to have the answers and that she could actually share responsibility and authority with her much younger co-leader. She felt liberated from the control exercised by adhering to the maternal transference as a co-therapist. Throughout there was a sense that by tolerating not feeling competent, they set themselves up for greater learning and the capacity to achieve genuine competence and effectiveness. We also examined that our process in psychotherapy supervision was a mirror of the processes within their own treatment environment, and that in order for me to be an effective supervisor I would need for them to feel empowered and authorized as trainees, and in parallel their patients would need to feel authorized as competent patients in a collaborative treatment. Inherent in this summary are elements of psychotherapy supervision that relate to formative, normative, and restorative aspects of psychotherapy supervision.

It is unlikely that a supervisor will be able to help a trainee develop cultural competence in the absence of the supervisor's cultural competence. Attention to cultural factors in formulation, in the etiology of that client's difficulties, and the way in which culture affects the client's engagement with the trainee are important components of the supervisory experience. Again, in some situations the role of culture is obvious, but more prominent is situations in which culture is powerful but unspoken. For example, in the interface between the trainee who is a member of the GLBTT community and a heterosexual supervisor, it is important to ensure that treatment and training are open and do not shut down and block open expression and examination.

Cultural competence is certainly a trainable skill if the trainee is supported in his or her exploration of the role of culture (Ladany & Brittan-Powell, 1997). If not, the therapist will likely encapsulate the role of culture and block it off from examination in psychotherapy supervision (Sue & Sue, 2003). Cultural competence, as a supervisor, is predicated upon the supervisor's awareness of his or her own self-identity with respect to diversity coupled with the supervisor's fundamental worldview. A curious, open, and respectful attitude is also essential, recognizing that in a collaborative model of psychotherapy supervision and treatment the supervisor can be educated about the culture of the trainee and similarly the therapist can be educated about the culture of the patient. The principle of knowledge exchange can supersede that of knowledge transfer. Inman (2006) notes that cultural competence in psychotherapy supervision can be facilitated by the supervisor's openness, the sharing of one's own struggles with the acquisition of this

an introduction to the history of psychotherapy supervision and the opening phase of psychotherapy supervision. This session includes the seven requisite steps for establishing psychotherapy supervision: (1) form an alliance; (2) set frames and goals; (3) discuss evaluation and objectives; (4) provide feedback in a mutual and reciprocal fashion; (5) acknowledge limits of confidentiality in an evaluation framework; (6) encourage self-reflection; and (7) encourage self-knowledge. The other six sessions include an assessment of learning; boundaries in psychotherapy supervision, including responsibilities for the trainee and the patient; the nature of the evaluation process; legal and ethical considerations regarding liability; dealing with intense affect on the part of the trainee; and training about what excellent psychotherapy supervisors do. The feedback on this course has been excellent. It provides an opportunity not only for training but also for peer support.

An important focus in training of supervisors is learning to make psychotherapy supervision meaningful, in particular as it relates to addressing countertransference in a fulsome way, while respecting the fact that psychotherapy supervision is not psychotherapy. Judicious use of supervisor self-disclosure has been cited many times as a way to maintain openness in the training system while respecting the autonomy of the trainee and creating an environment that is non-pathologizing and non-blaming.

Supervisors need to create space for reflection to help maintain an awareness of potential blind spots. A psychotherapy supervision group or even external consultation may be helpful (Frayn, 1991).

Alonso notes that psychotherapy supervision is not benign. Done poorly it can interfere with or stunt therapist development. A poor supervisory experience can transmit negative values to trainees regarding ethics, boundaries, and attitudes toward patients, setting the stage for negative re-enactment. Poor psychotherapy supervision can create a negative ripple effect that compromises clinical care, creating demoralization or withdrawal from the work.

Supervisors are encouraged to be aware of three potential ethical hazards that the supervisory relationship generates (Sherry, 1991): the power differential wielded by the supervisor, particularly in environments where evaluation is a component of the psychotherapy supervision; transforming the educational experience of psychotherapy supervision into a psychotherapeutic exploration; and creating dual relationships, mindful, as noted earlier, of the high percentage of trainees who report sexual harassment and exploitation by supervisors.

Alonso (1985, 2000) states that the core tasks of psychotherapy supervision and training are the provision of didactic teaching about the role of listening; developing an attitude of being able to listen without judgment; developing a capacity to tolerate affects and ambiguity; the capacity to support trainees; and the capacity to work within the frame of the metaphor of transference. Alonso notes that supervisors must have clarity with regard to dealing with the tension that arises at the interface of psychotherapy supervision as teaching or provision of psychotherapy. She is a strong advocate for the maintenance of a clear boundary between these two, but recognizes that both processes are committed to the therapist's growth and development. Both require the supervisor to be respectful at all times, but psychotherapy supervision may emphasize differentially an approach to addressing the trainee's difficulties through the lens of the patient rather than through the lens of the trainee. Allied with this is the capacity to recognize learning difficulties as development challenges rather than as pathology. Supervisory behaviors that undermine psychotherapy supervision arise when a supervisee feels judged, blamed, or pathologized by the supervisor. Supervisors who are competitive and shame-sensitive themselves may have more difficulty in psychotherapy supervision because of the need to externalize difficulties and the need to adhere to a position of authority and superiority, postures that will doom the psychotherapy training experience.

Hence, the capacity to communicate in a non-shaming fashion is critical and also provides the added benefit of modeling for the trainee how to provide feedback to patients. Supervisors must also recognize that they have a duty with regard to evaluation of the trainee and carry responsibility and often liability regarding the care of the patient.

Desired Outcomes of Psychotherapy Supervision

Another way to look at what the objectives of psychotherapy supervision are is to reflect on the literature about effective and ineffective therapists. There is utility in beginning with the end product as a way to shape our thinking about what it is that we actually want to achieve.

Allied with this is an examination of those therapists who are deemed by their colleagues to be master therapists. Certainly, innate ability and intelligence are at least two factors that are not trainable, but it should be an objective of psychotherapy supervision to enhance the capacity of each trainee to be the best version of himself or herself as possible. An essential element of this relates to the capacity to develop relational skills and to engage patients with disciplined personal involvement. Contemporary attention to the importance of the therapeutic relationship underscores the trainee's need to develop the capacity to disclose appropriately and meta-communicate effectively with patients in order to strengthen the working alliance and maximize the patient's ability to understand his or her patterns and their impact on their interpersonal world. Psychotherapy supervision has been demonstrated to improve a trainee's capacity to work within the here-and-now and provide direct feedback to patients (Hill et al., 2008). In this study comparing traditional psychotherapy supervision with self-training and bibliotherapy, all three interventions improved the trainee's self-efficacy, but only the actual psychotherapy supervision facilitated the trainee's capacities to work within the relationship. Psychotherapy supervision must help the therapist develop these relational skills and gain comfort with self-disclosure without fear that it leads to a slippery slope of boundary crossings and violations (Leszcz, 2009).

Psychotherapy supervision can provide a template for this through its modeling of a coherent cognitive and experiential process.

Looking more closely at the characteristics of effective therapists (Hill & Knox, 2009), the following features stand out:

- They are aware of reactions to patients.
- They are able to acknowledge problems within the relationship.
- They are able to empathize and connect to patients.
- They are able to apologize and accept responsibility.
- They demonstrate a commitment to change behaviors that are hurtful or offensive to patients.
- They use immediacy.
- They are able to understand and interpret within the relationship.
- They teach that anger is tolerable within a caring relationship.

In contrast, ineffective therapists tend to be dogmatic, they ignore the patient's concerns, and if difficulties arise, they blame and fault the patient. Disclosures may be tinted with hostile expression or lack authenticity. They are often unsupportive and controlling of patients, exhorting patients to change rather than facilitating a process of working through.

The literature on exemplary therapists echoes these findings. According to their colleagues, exemplary therapists are self-aware; are able to contain anxiety; have good conceptual capacities; are confident; are empathic; are resilient and maintain general well-being; demonstrate a genuine interest and learning and caring about others; develop strong connections to their patients; are able to activate appropriately while maintaining a reflective position themselves; and recognize their own limits and are not adverse to seeking consultation. They value the relationship and recognize the importance of a strong working alliance (Jennings & Skovholt, 1999).

Embedded in this is the recognition that psychotherapy supervision must help trainees identify, utilize, and manage countertransference. It is perhaps in this area that the capacity to work in a non-shaming, non-blaming fashion is most pronounced. Hostile comments from therapists are common and do grave damage to patients and to the therapeutic relationship. Experience doesn't make one less vulnerable to these lapses; experienced therapists are merely more covert in their expressions of hostility (Strupp, 1998). Psychotherapy supervision, accordingly, should foster in trainees the capacity to manage countertransference well. This is one of those tricky areas that sometimes borders on psychotherapy, but if one adheres to the principles noted herein and makes judicious use of supervisory self-disclosure, it is possible to protect the training environment and foster trainee growth.

Supervisor Self-Disclosure

Perhaps one of the most effective ways to teach about disciplined personal involvement and the use of self in therapy is by the supervisor's realization of these same approaches. Self-disclosure, used judiciously and thoughtfully by the supervisor, can strengthen the supervisory relationship and by leveling the hierarchy between trainee and supervisor can also foster trust and increase the trainee's willingness to self-disclose. Knox et al. (2008) define supervisor self-disclosure as those situations "where a supervisor reveals information about her or himself or reveals reactions and responses to the supervisee or supervisee's client as they arise in psychotherapy supervision" (p. 547). As described earlier, it is not uncommon that a supervisee's concern about shame, judgment, and criticism leads to a posture of managing the supervisory relationship rather than engaging with it. The supervisor's use of self-disclosure helps to underscore the co-creation of the supervisory relationship and in so doing becomes perhaps the best model for the trainees using similar principles in treatment.

It appears that as supervisors gain more experience they feel more comfortable in using self-disclosure to model, normalize, and teach. Supervisors report using self-disclosure to promote the development of the trainee when psychotherapy supervision is struggling, always mindful that the impact of this self-disclosure must be aligned with its therapeutic or educational intent, which is generally to reduce shame and increase openness. Typically this kind of self-disclosure involves the supervisor's disclosure regarding reactions to patients both past and present, including reactions to the patient being supervised. Often, self-disclosure is used to demonstrate what professional experience has helped the supervisor to learn. It can reduce shame and increase a sense of similarity, strengthening the bond between trainee and supervisor and fostering greater identification with the supervisor rather than identification with the patient, a hazard that interpreting within the parallel process may generate (Knox et al., 2008). It is of course important that a supervisor be aware of his or her motivation, mindful of the risk of inadvertently shaming the therapist, dismissing the therapist, or competing with the therapist.

Ladany and Lehrman-Waterman (1999) reported that there is a linear correlation between supervisor self-disclosure and the strength of the supervisory working alliance. Judicious self-disclosure on the part of the supervisor fosters greater risk taking on the part of the trainee (Yourman, 2003). It signals the mutuality of the relationship and may diminish trainee anxiety about evaluation, demonstrating that the supervisor is also imperfect and struggles with countertransference. At other times self-disclosure is essential in repairing the damaged educational alliance or strengthening an educational alliance.

When supervisors are questioned about their motivation for self-disclosure, typically they will use self-disclosure to respond to a trainee who is struggling with understanding or self-doubt or lack of confidence. Commonly supervisors regret only that they did not employ self-disclosure earlier in the course of psychotherapy supervision (Knox et al., 2008). Principles to bear in mind relate to respecting boundaries and managing narcissism in the self-disclosure. Self-disclosure should be attuned to the level of the trainee developmentally. Typically it is predicated upon the supervisor's clinical experience, mistakes, or challenges or reactions to the current client being supervised. Self-disclosure may also relate to the here-and-now of the supervisory relationship. The trainee may be surprised by self-disclosure, and as in all instances it warrants processing of the experience and impact of the self-disclosure within the supervisory relationship. It is best not to assume its value or impact.

Four types of supervisory self-disclosure are common: (1) prior clinical experience, personally or professionally; (2) feedback about the here-and-now of the supervisory relationship; (3) training experiences from the past; and (4) relevant biographical data. Supervisor self-disclosure may be helpful in the trainee managing countertransference and being willing to explore countertransference, as the stakes are lower with regard to shame and negative evaluation. It also may be one of the most effective ways of modeling the concept of process, immediacy, and working within the here-and-now of the therapeutic relationship.

Not surprisingly, there are gender and culture differences with regard to the use of self-disclosure in psychotherapy supervision. Heru at al. (2006) reported that male supervisors tend to be more self-disclosing than female supervisors, and this may reflect differences with comfort regarding male/female interaction and boundaries in relationships. We are ever mindful of Freud's comment in 1921, "how easily erotic wishes develop out of emotions of a friendly character based on appreciation and admiration between master and pupil."

How Proximate Should the Supervisor Be to the Trainee's Patient?

The traditional model of psychotherapy supervision rooted in the psychoanalytic tradition always involved an arm's-length process of psychotherapy supervision. The trainee would present detailed process notes and the supervisor would attend to themes and processes that emerged within the trainee's report. As psychotherapy supervision broadens to encompass a range of different therapeutic approaches, there has been similar expansion of models that increase the supervisor's access to the patient. Indeed, recognizing the responsibility that the supervisor has for the clinical care provided by the trainee, in many settings it seems unwise and hard to defend a historic model that kept the treatment behind closed doors, prioritizing confidentiality and privacy at the expense of effective and competent psychotherapy supervision. The *Tarasoff* decision has certainly raised awareness of the vicarious liability of supervisors (Tarasoff, 1976).

Concerns about liability have increased the debate regarding whether supervisors should in fact have direct contact with the patient who is being supervised (Recupero & Rainey, 2007; Schulte et al., 1997). There is less controversy, however, about the importance of the patient knowing that the supervisor is part of the treatment and will have full access to the treatment records as presented by the trainee at the least, or in many situations, as accessed by audio recording, audiovisual recording, and even direct observation. The patient's awareness of the participation of the supervisor in the process may warrant discussion in the therapy itself but rarely in my experience has a negative impact on the treatment.

Direct observation of group therapy provides a unique opportunity to actually examine a trainee's interventions, therapeutic style, and facilitation. I have often had the experience of watching 10 or 15 minutes behind a mirror and coming away with several pages of notes. That same 10- or 15-minute section in psychotherapy supervision might be completely bypassed as not being particularly significant or relevant and hence omitted by the trainee. Closer observation of the treatment by the supervisor enhances psychotherapy supervision even as it makes trainees anxious, and on more than one occasion I have needed to try to understand why the audiovisual setup was not completed before my observation.

A useful way to balance that feeling of trainee exposure and vulnerability is to permit the trainee to observe the supervisor at work as well. This may level the playing field and make the work feel more collaborative. Direct access appears to improve the capacity of psychotherapy supervision to have an impact on trainees' work with their patients (Diener et al., 2007). It has been my experience as well that direct observation enhances the capacity to move between the implicit and the explicit and maximize the building between theory and technique. Therapists are always faced with the choice point analysis of different interventions that might be equally worth considering. Observation of the choices made by therapists enhances the learning through this discussion. Moving psychotherapy out from behind closed doors is likely to benefit both trainees and their patients. There is little question that the trainees value highly watching their supervisor in action (DeGroot et al., 2003). Underscoring that greater access to thoughtful scrutiny provided in the context of a strong educational alliance is a key element in the development of the psychotherapist.

Conclusion

Supervision of psychotherapy is one of the central shaping influences in the development of the therapist. It is a major vehicle for transmitting the core values of the field to our students. Supervision is also charged with the task of evaluating the trainee and ensuring the quality of the care provided by the trainee. Yet supervisors are often expected to fulfill this important pedagogical responsibility without comprehensive training, exposure to the empirical literature, and opportunities for their own professional development. This is an area of great opportunity and challenge for the field at large.

References

Alonso, A. (1985). *The Quiet Profession: Supervisors of Psychotherapy*. New York: Macmillan.

Alonso, A. (2000). On being skilled and deskilled as a psychotherapy supervisor. *Journal of Psychotherapy Practice and Research*, 9, 55–61.

Arlow, J. (1963). The supervisory situation. *Journal of the American Psychoanalytic Association*, 11, 576–594.

Australian Psychological Society (2007). *Code of Ethics*. Melbourne, Victoria, Australia.

Bambling, M., King, R., Raue, P., Schweitzer, R., & Lambert, W. (2006). Clinical psychotherapy supervision: Its influences on client-rated working alliance and client symptom reduction in the brief treatment of major depression. *Psychotherapy Research*, 16, 317–331.

Bike, D. H., Norcross, J. C., & Schatz, D. M. (2009). Processes of outcome of psychotherapists' personal therapy: Replication and extension 20 years later. *Psychotherapy Theory*, Practice and Research, 46(1), 19–31.

Bordin, E. (1979). The generalizability of the psychoanalytic concept of the working alliance. *Psychotherapy: Theory, Research, and Practice*, 16, 252–260.

Boswell, J., & Castonguay, L. (2007). Psychotherapy training: Suggestions for core ingredients and future research. *Psychotherapy: Theory, Research, Practice, Training*, 44, 379–383.

Buckley, P., Conte, H., Plutchik, R., Karasu, T., & Wild, K. (1982). Learning dynamic psychotherapy: A longitudinal study. *American Journal of Psychiatry*, 139, 1607–1611.

Cameron, C. P., Ennis, J., & Deadman, J. (eds.) (1998). *Guidelines and Standards for the Practice of the Psychotherapies*. Toronto: University of Toronto Press

Coster, J. S., & Schwebel, M. (1997). Well-functioning in professional psychologists. *Professional Psychology: Research and Practice*, 28, 5–13.

Cross, T., Dennis, K., Isaacs, M., & Bazron, B. (1989). *Towards a Culturally Competent System of Care*. National Technical Assistance Center for Children's Mental Health; Georgetown University in Washington DC: National Institute of Mental Health.

DeGroot, J., Brunet, A., Kaplan, A. S., & Bagby, M. (2003). A comparison of evaluations of male and female psychiatry supervisors. *Academic Medicine*, 27, 39–43.

Diener, M., Hilsenroth, M., & Weinberger, J. (2007). Therapist affect focus and patient outcomes in psychodynamic psychotherapy: A meta-analysis. *American Journal of Psychiatry*, 164, 936–941.

Ebersole, G. H., Leiderman, P. H., & Yalom, I. D. (1969). Training the nonprofessional group therapist: A controlled study. *Journal of Nervous and Mental Diseases* 149(3), 294–302.

Ennis, J., Cameron, P., Leszcz, M., & Chagoya, L. (1998). Guidelines for psychotherapy psychotherapy supervision. In P. Cameron, J. Ennis, & J. Deadman (Eds.), *Guidelines and Standards for the Practice of the Psychotherapies* (pp. 371–390). Toronto: University of Toronto Press.

Ethics of our Father, 50

Falender, C. A., & Shafranske, E. P. (2004). *Clinical Psychotherapy Supervision: A Competency-Based Approach*. Washington, D.C.: American Psychological Association.

Fonagy, P., & Bateman, A., (2006). Mechanism of change in mentalization based treatment of borderline personality disorder. *Journal of Clinical Psychology*, 62, 411–430.

Foster, J., Lichtenberg, J., & Peyton, V. (2007). The supervisory attachment relationship as a predictor of the professional development of the supervisee. *Psychotherapy Research*, 17, 343–350.

Frayn, D. (1991). Supervising the supervisors: The evolution of a psychotherapy supervisors' group. *American Journal of Psychotherapy*, 45, 31–42.

Freud, S. (1921). *Group Psychology and the Analysis of the Ego* (Standard Edition ed.) (vol. 18). London: Hogarth Press.

Friedlander, M., & Ward, L. (1984). Development and validation of the Supervisory Styles Inventory. *Journal of Counseling Psychology*, 4, 541–557.

Gatrell, N., Herman, J., Olarte, S., Localio, R., & Feldstein, M. (1988). Psychiatric residents' sexual contact with educators and patients: Results of a national survey. *American Journal of Psychiatry*, 145, 690–694.

Gonsalvez, C., & McLeod, H. (2008). Toward the science-informed practice of clinical psychotherapy supervision: The Australian context. *Australian Psychologist*, 43, 79–87.

Greben, S. (1991). Interpersonal aspects of the psychotherapy supervision of individual psychotherapy. *American Journal of Psychotherapy*, 45, 306–316.

Haak, J. L., & Kaye, D., (2008). Personal psychotherapy during residency training: A survey of psychiatric residents. *Academic Psychiatry*, 33, 323–326.

Harmon, S., Lambert, M., Smart, D., Hawkins, E., Nielsen, S., Slade, K., et al. (2007). Enhancing outcome for potential treatment failures: Therapist-client feedback and clinical support tools. *Psychotherapy Research*, 17, 379–392.

Heru, A., Strong, D., Price, M., & Recupero, P. (2006). Self-disclosure in psychotherapy supervisors: Gender differences. *American Journal of Psychotherapy*, 60, 323–334.

Hess, S., Knox, S., Schultz, J., Hill, C., Sloan, L., Brandt, S., et al. (2008). Predoctoral interns' nondisclosure in psychotherapy supervision. *Psychotherapy Research*, 18, 400–411.

Hill, C., & Knox, S. (2009). Processing the therapeutic relationship. *Psychotherapy Research*, 19, 13–29.

Hill, C., Sim, W., Spangler, P., Stahl, J., Sullivan, C., & Teyber, E. (2008). Therapist immediacy in brief psychotherapy therapy: Case study II. *Psychotherapy: Theory, Research, Practice, Training*, 45, 298–315.

Hilsenroth, M., Ackerman, S., Clemence, A., Strassle, C., & Handler, L. (2002). Effects of structured clinician training on patient and therapist perspectives of alliance early in psychotherapy. *Psychotherapy: Theory, Research, Practice, Training*, 39, 309–323.

Holloway, E. L. (1984). Outcome evaluation in psychotherapy supervision research. *Counselling Psychology*, 12, 167–174.

Howard, F. (2008). Managing stress or enhancing wellbeing? Positive psychology's contributions to clinical psychotherapy supervision. *Australian Psychologist*, 43, 105–113.

Inman, A. (2006). Supervisor multicultural competence and its relation to supervisory process and outcome. *Journal of Marital and Family Therapy*, 32, 73–85.

Inskipp, F., & Proctor, B. (1993). *Making the Most of Psychotherapy Supervision, Part 1.* Middlesex, UK: Cascade Publications.

Jennings, L., & Skovholt, T. (1999). The cognitive, emotional and relational characteristics of master therapists. *Journal of Counseling Psychology*, 46, 3–11.

Kavanagh, D., Spence, S., Strong, J., Wilson, J., Sturk, H., & Crow, N. (2003). Psychotherapy supervision practices in allied mental health: Relationships of psychotherapy supervision characteristics to perceived impact and job satisfaction. *Mental Health Services Research*, 5, 187–195.

Kavanagh, D., Spence, S., Sturk, H., Strong, J., Wilson, J., Worrall, L., et al. (2008). Outcomes of training in psychotherapy supervision: Randomised controlled trial. *Australian Psychologist*, 43, 96–104.

Kiesler, D. (1996). *Contemporary Interpersonal Theory and Research: Personality, Psychopathology, and Psychotherapy*. New York: Wiley.

Killian, K. (2001). Differences making a difference: Cross-cultural interactions in supervisory relationships. *Journal of Feminist Family Therapy*, 12, 61–103.

Kilminster, S., & Jolly, B. (2000). Effective supervision in clinical practice settings: A literature review. *Medical Education*, 34, 827–840.

Knox, S., Burkard, A., Edwards, L., Smith, J., & Schlosser, L. (2008). Supervisors' reports of the effects of supervisor self-disclosure on supervisees. *Psychotherapy Research*, 18, 543–559.

Ladany, N. (2007). Does psychotherapy training matter? Maybe not. *Psychotherapy: Theory, Research, Practice, Training*, 44, 392–396.

Ladany, N., & Brittan-Powell, C. (1997). The influence of supervisory racial identity interaction and racial matching on the supervisory working alliance and supervisee multicultural competence. *Counselor Education and Psychotherapy Supervision*, 36, 284–304.

Ladany, N., Friedlander, M., & Nelson, M. (2005). *Critical Events in Psychotherapy Supervision: An Interpersonal Approach*. Washington, D.C.: American Psychological Association.

Ladany, N., Hill, C., Corbett, M., & Nutt, E. (1996). Nature, extent, and importance of what psychotherapy trainees do not disclose to their supervisors. *Journal of Counseling Psychology*, 43, 10–23.

Ladany, N., & Lehrman-Waterman, D. (1999). The content and frequency of supervisor self-disclosures and their relationship to supervisor style and the supervisory working alliance. *Counselor Education and Psychotherapy Supervision*, 38, 143–160.

Lambert, M., & Ogles, B. (1997). The effectiveness of psychotherapy supervision. In C.J.Watkins (Ed.), *Handbook of Psychotherapy Supervision* (pp. 421–446). New York: Wiley.

Leszcz, M. (2009). Therapist transparency and use of self in group psychotherapy. *MIKBATZ, The Israeli Journal of Group Psychotherapy*, 13, 256–272.

Miller, G., & Larrabee, M. (1995). Sexual intimacy in counselor education and psychotherapy supervision. *Counselor Education and Psychotherapy Supervision*, 34, 332–343.

Murphy, L., Leszcz, M., Collings, A., & Salvendy, J. (1996). Some observations on the subjective experience of neophyte group therapy trainees. *International Journal of Group Psychotherapy*, 46, 543–552.

Nigam, T., Cameron, P., & Leverette, J. (1997). Impasses in psychotherapy supervision: A resident's perspective. *American Journal of Psychotherapy*, 51, 252–270.

Ogren, M., Jonsson, C., & Sundin, E. (2005). Group psychotherapy supervision in psychotherapy: The relationship between focus, group climate, and perceived attained skill. *Journal of Clinical Psychology*, 61, 373–388.

Ogren, M., & Sundin, E. (2009). Group psychotherapy supervision in psychotherapy. Main findings from a Swedish research project on psychotherapy supervision in a group format. *British Journal of Guidance & Counselling*, 37, 129–139.

Okiishi, J., Lambert, M., Nielsen, S., & Ogles, B. (2003). Waiting for supershrink: An empirical analysis of therapist effects. *Clinical Psychology and Psychotherapy*, 10, 361–373.

Pope, K., Levenson, H., & Schover, L. (1979). Sexual intimacy in psychology training: Results and implications of a national survey. *American Psychologist*, 348, 682–689.

Ramos-Sanchez, L., Esnil, E., Goodwin, A., Riggs, S., Osachy Touster, L., Wright, L., et al. (2002). Negative supervisory events: Effects on psychotherapy supervision satisfaction and supervisory alliance. *Professional Psychology: Research and Practice*, 33, 197–202.

Recupero, P., & Rainey, S. (2007). Liability and risk management in outpatient psychotherapy supervision. *Journal of the American Academy of Psychiatry and the Law*, 35, 188–195.

Riess, H., & Fishel, A. (2000). The necessity of continuing education for psychotherapy supervisors. *Academic Psychiatry*, 24, 147–155.

Riess, H., & Herman, J. (2008). Teaching the teachers: A model course for psychodynamic psychotherapy supervisors. *Academic Psychiatry*, 32, 259–264.

Schulte, H., Hall, M., & Bienfeld, D. (1997). Liability and accountability in psychotherapy supervision. *Academic Psychiatry*, 21, 133–140.

Shanfield, S., Hetherly, V., & Matthews, K. (2001). Excellent psychotherapy supervision: The residents' perspective. *Journal of Psychotherapy Practice and Research*, 10, 23–27.

Shanfield, S., Matthews, K., & Hetherly, V. (1993). What do excellent psychotherapy supervisors do? *American Journal of Psychiatry*, 150, 1081–1084.

Sherry, P. (1991). Ethical issues in the conduct of psychotherapy supervision. *Journal of Counseling Psychology*, 19, 566–584.

Stoltenberg, C., McNeill, B., & Delworth, U. (1998). *IDM Psychotherapy Supervision: An Integrated Development Model for Supervising Counselors and Therapists*. San Francisco: Jossey-Bass.

Strupp, H. H. (1998). The Vanderbilt Study I revisited. *Psychotherapy Research*, 8, 17–29.

Sue, D., & Sue, D. (2003). *Counseling the Culturally Diverse: Theory and Practice* (4th ed.). New York: Wiley.

Tarasoff v. Regents of the University of California, 13 Cal.3d 177, 529 P.2d 533 (1974), vacated, 17 Cal.3d 425, 551 P.2d 334 (1976).

von der Lippe, A. L., Monson, J. T., Ronnestad, M. H., & Eilertsen, D. E. (2008). Treatment failure in psychotherapy: The pull of hostility. *Psychotherapy Research* 18(4), 420–432.

Wachtel, P. (2007). *Relational Theory and the Practice of Psychotherapy*. New York: Guilford Press.

Walker, R., & Clark, J. (1999). Heading off boundary problems: Clinical psychotherapy supervision as risk management. *Psychiatric Services*, 50, 1435–1439.

Wampold, B. E. (2001). *The Great Psychotherapy Debate: Models, Methods and Findings.* Mahwah, NJ: Mahwah, NJ: Lawrence Erlbaum.

Watkins, C. J. (1995). Psychotherapy supervision in the 1990s: Some observations and reflections. *Journal of Psychotherapy Practice and Research*, 7, 93–101.

Watkins, C. J. (1998). Psychotherapy supervision in the 21st century. *Journal of Psychotherapy Practice and Research*, 7, 93–101.

Westefeld, J. (2009). Psychotherapy supervision of psychotherapy: Models, issues, and recommendations. *Counseling Psychologist*, 37, 296–316.

Worthen, V., & McNeill, B. (1996). A phenomenological investigation of "good" psychotherapy supervision events. *Journal of Counseling Psychology*, 43, 25–34.

Yalom, I., & Leszcz, M. (2005). *The Theory and Practice of Group Psychotherapy* (5th ed.). New York: Basic Books.

Yourman, D. (2003). Trainee disclosure in psychotherapy supervision: The impact of shame. *Journal of Clinical Psychology*, 59, 601–609.

7

Up Close and Personal: A Consideration of the Role of Personal Therapy in the Development of a Psychotherapist

Suzanne B. Phillips

> …Theodor Reik (1948) has said the personality of the therapist is his most important tool… As with any craft, it is vital that the artisan or the scientist know in detail the capabilities and limitation of their tools so they can truly use them as facilitators of creativity rather than stumbling blocks between them and their work.

> (Peebles, 1980, p. 261)

Friedman, in his 2008 *New York Times* article "Have you ever been in psychotherapy, Doctor?" writes, "A therapist should not start exploring a patient's mind without really knowing what is in his own."

Yalom (2002, p. 40) tells us, "To my mind, personal psychotherapy is by far the most important part of psychotherapy training."

This chapter will examine the role of personal therapy in the journey of becoming a psychotherapist. As a clinician practicing for 33 years, with the experience of personal analysis, group therapy, and the privilege of having supervised and been the therapist for many clinicians, I have a clear bias as to the personal and professional benefits of this experience. I do not, however, have to make a case for it. The empirical reality is that an overwhelming majority of therapists of all disciplines across different orientations, both nationally and internationally, seek personal therapy, often more than once, during and after training and for personal reasons (Norcross & Guy 2005; Orlinsky et al., 2005b). Therapists practice what they preach. What can we understand from this? How does it illuminate the role of personal therapy in the developmental journey of therapists? What can we pass on to those who follow us?

In this chapter I attempt to answer these questions. Drawing upon empirical findings, qualitative narrative studies, and personal experience, I recognize the inextricable mix of personal and professional dimensions in the functioning of therapists. I consider personal therapy as integral to a therapist's formative training and ongoing development across disciplines and orientations. I recognize personal therapy as expanding didactic training, clinical experience, supervision, and cultural competence. While no single factor can guarantee the effectiveness of a therapist, I invite practitioners to more openly recommend and model the use of personal therapy as a crucial dimension in a therapist's journey.

This chapter will include a consideration of personal therapy in terms of the mix of personal and professional dimensions; empirical findings, prevalence, differences across orientations, reasons for use, and comparisons with the general population; trauma work, personal and professional benefits, and professional career development; "the person" of the therapist; the therapist's therapist; its value across theoretical perspectives; the interface with supervision; its role in developing cultural competence; the implications of mandated and required therapy; and the legacy of personal therapy.

The Mix of Personal and Professional Dimensions

In a qualitative interview study aimed at identifying learning arenas for professional development, Ronnestad and Skovholt (2001) illuminate the inextricable relationship of personal and professional dimensions in a therapist's development. Drawing upon the retrospective accounts of 12 senior practitioners, ranging in age from 61 to 84, and interviewed twice in a span of 11 years, Ronnestad and Skovholt identify three arenas of learning: (1) awareness of early life experiences, cumulative professional experiences, mentors, colleagues, and adult life experiences as opportunities for professional development; (2) recognition of the significance of processing and reflecting experiences in all domains; and (3) recognition of being a therapist as a rewarding choice that can be maintained despite age.

While a small qualitative study, the broad message offered is that being a therapist is a sustaining identity optimally developed by ongoing reflection and integration of personal and professional life experiences.

Reflected in my own life, I think it is no coincidence that my first professional book, co-authored with Fenster and Rappaport (1986), *The Therapist's Pregnancy: Intrusion in the Analytic Space*, marked the birth of my first son, and that my most recent book, co-authored with Kane (2008), *Healing Together After Trauma: A Couple's Guide to Coping with Trauma and Posttraumatic Stress*, marks the near-death and recovery of my youngest son.

With the first, I had been a therapist for 8 years before having children. The intrusion into the analytic space addressed by me and my co-authors reflected not just the break in the frame and intrusion in the space shared with patients but the intrusion in my definition of self, body, marriage, and my personal and professional life space as I knew it. It would of course result in an expansion of the frame that would be invaluable for me as a person and as a therapist.

In addition to passing on to other couples an understanding of the vulnerability and resiliency shared by a couple facing trauma, my recent book

Healing Together After Trauma represents an integration of personal meanings of loss, professional training, and the gift of experience given by patients, be they runaway girls, rape victims, cancer survivors, widows, or grieving fire-fighters who invited me in to help them face the unthinkable.

Empirical Findings: The Best-Kept Secret

Resonating with this message, a little-known fact is that the majority of mental health practitioners choose to enter personal therapy. Summarizing the prevalence of personal psychotherapy among mental health professionals in the United States from 14 studies, Norcross and Guy (2005) found that with a mean and median of 72% to 75%, the majority of responding professionals have had at least one experience of personal treatment. Bike et al. (2009), in a 2007 replication and extension of a 1987 national survey of psychotherapists, including 219 psychologists, 191 counselors, and 192 social workers, reported that 85% sought therapy, with no differences across gender and professions.

The relevance of personal therapy is further corroborated by the data collected on the prevalence and parameters of personal therapy in Europe and other countries (Orlinsky et al., 2005b; Orlinsky & Ronnestad, 2005a, 2005b, 2005c). Using the Development of Psychotherapists Common Core Questionnaire (DPCCQ), filled out by 5,000 therapists, Orlinsky et al. computed the personal therapy experience of therapists from 14 countries.

The sample included primarily psychologists but also other professions, including social work, counseling, and nursing, primarily in New Zealand and Sweden. Although there was some variation between the countries with the largest samples (Germany, the United States, and Norway), gender was balanced. The orientations of therapists included analytic/dynamic, cognitive-behavioral, humanistic, and broad-spectrum eclectic. Findings reveal that despite many cultural differences, overwhelming majorities of therapists everywhere reported having at least one course of personal psychotherapy, with the sole exception of South Korea. The rates range from 90% in France, Switzerland, Sweden, Israel, and Denmark to a low of 72% in Russia and 66% in Portugal.

Prevalence and Orientation

The question arises as to whether similar value is attributed to personal therapy across orientations. Whereas the relevance of personal therapy for training and effectiveness with different orientations and models will be addressed below, national and international empirical findings suggest that the prevalence of personal therapy varies with theoretical orientation. In considering five representative studies, Norcross and Guy (2005) reveal that 88% to 97%

of self-identified insight-oriented mental health professionals choose personal therapy, compared with 44% to 66% of self-identified behavioral therapists. In between are humanistic, systems, and eclectic practitioners.

Orlinsky et al. (2005b) found similar differences in terms of orientation from their international database. With the exception of South Korea, 92% of analytic/psychodynamic therapists and 92% of humanistic international therapists reported having personal therapy, compared with 60% of behavior therapists. What is perhaps most important to note is that although a greater percentage of therapists with psychodynamic orientations use personal therapy, more than half of the behavioral therapists also seek personal therapy.

In their choice of personal therapy, most therapists choose a therapist with an orientation similar to their own. The exception to this is the choice of behavioral therapists. National and international findings suggest that 44% to 66% of behavioral therapists seeking personal therapy choose non-behavioral therapists, most commonly those from a psychodynamic perspective (Darongkamas et al., 1994; Norcross & Grunebaum, 2005; Norcross & Guy, 2005). This may reflect the changing view held by behaviorists over the past 20 years as to the value of personal therapy, from a training perspective, in terms of the importance of the development of interpersonal skills (Laireiter & Willutzki, 2005). It may also indicate that behavioral therapists, like most therapists, choose therapy for personal reasons. While they are expert in cognitive-behavioral models directed to behavior change and symptom relief, behavioral therapists may choose therapy for less symptom-focused reasons. It is perhaps a testament to their flexibility in terms of a best practice model that they are not held to singularity of orientation as a criterion for choice in personal therapy.

It is worth recognizing that in many cases choice of orientation is not static but rather represents ongoing integration of life experience, clinical practice, personal therapy, and further training. In *The Gift of Therapy*, Yalom (2002) describes the hundreds of hours he spent as a patient at different stages of his life: "I believe there is no better way to learn about a psychotherapy approach than to enter into it as a patient" (p. 42).

Reasons for Personal Therapy

In a national survey of United States psychologists, counselors, and social workers seeking treatment, Bike et al. (2009) asked if therapy was entered for personal reasons, professional reasons, or both. They found that 60% chose personal reasons, 5% chose professional reasons, and 35% chose both. The most common reasons were marital/couple distress (20%), depression (13%), need for self-understanding (12%), and anxiety/stress (19%). In a review of five studies, Norcross and Connor (2005) found that the majority of psychotherapists indicated primarily personal reasons for entering therapy. Norcross and Guy (2005), drawing upon a number of studies, reported that the three most frequent presenting problems were depression, marital/couple conflicts, and anxiety.

Reasons Compared to General Population

The reasons for therapists seeking treatment are no different from those of educated people in the general population seeking treatment. My experience as a therapist's therapist for many years is consistent with this finding. Never has the presenting problem been difficulty with a patient, a practice issue, or a professional problem. Rather, mental health professionals have entered treatment to work on personal issues and, much like other professionals, their work hours and professional demands at times exacerbate personal problems.

Several studies indicate that a larger percentage of married therapists as compared with single therapists seek treatment (Norcross & Guy, 2005). One wonders if the profession exerts a toll on the therapist in terms of personal relationships. While one study suggests an impact on the practitioner in terms of anxiety, depression, and emotional under-involvement with family (Prochaska & Norcross, 1983), there is little evidence of self-reported negative marital consequences. The statistics on divorce for mental health professionals are similar to the general population (Meyers & Gabbard, 2008). There is perhaps a recognition among mental health professionals of the value of therapy in addressing interpersonal struggles, stress, and marital issues.

Prevalence of Use Compared to the General Population

While reasons for seeking therapy are comparable with the general population, the prevalence of use by therapists differs. In a review of 17 studies involving 8,000 participants, the mean and median of mental health professionals having had at least one personal therapy experience clustered between 72% and 75%. This is substantially higher than the general adult population: the estimates from national household surveys and epidemiological studies indicate that 25% to 27% of American adults have received specialized mental health care, and this includes psychoactive medications and psychiatric hospitalization (Norcross & Guy, 2005).

As suggested above, it seems likely that therapists truly believe in the services they provide. While being a therapist is no guarantee of interpersonal strength or capacity for intimacy, it is possible that the nature of the work raises one's consciousness about attachment, emotional pain, conflict, the meaning of symptoms, communication issues, and the possibility of change.

From a professional perspective, it may also be that therapists consciously and unconsciously understand that what they carry personally bears on who they are and how they practice professionally. Accordingly, they take presenting problems like depression, marital/couple conflicts, and anxiety very seriously and seek intervention.

Trauma Work and Personal Therapy

One field of mental health work that has been found to have a more direct emotional impact on therapists is work with traumatized patients. There is increasing evidence that heavy caseloads of severely traumatized patients and lack of training, ongoing supervision, and support in concert with continual exposure to the graphic and shocking details of war, natural disasters, and man-made terror can cause burnout, compassion fatigue, secondary post-traumatic stress, and vicarious traumatization (Cunningham, 2003; McCann & Pearlman, 1990; Palm et al., 2002; Pearlman & Saakvitne, 1995).

The tragedy at Ft. Hood, Texas, on November 5, 2009, illuminates an extreme of the collateral damage of unattended caregiver pain. It underscores the inextricable overlap of person and professional selves. In this case early history, isolation, religious tenets, incompatible ideology, lack of close colleagues, the refusal of personal therapy, and the fear and caution of colleagues collude and erupted with deadly consequences.

One military social worker returning from Iraq made it clear when sharing his experiences that it is not a question of whether caregivers are affected; it is how they are going to deal with the inevitable impact. Reflecting this in his comments about "compassion fatigue," an Army psychologist who planned a career in the military, but burned out after 5 years, reported: "I thought it was a bogus phenomenon, but it's true,…you become detached, you start to feel like you can't connect with your patients, you run out of empathy…" (Carey et al., 2009).

My own work in providing "care of the caregiver" programs nationally and internationally for civilian and uniformed mental health professionals (military, fire, and police) as well as spiritual caregivers sensitized me to the need to train caregivers about the impact of trauma work and to provide a safe venue for them to normalize reactions, share feelings, and bear witness to the imprint of trauma they have been asked to contain.

One of the common countertransference responses to trauma work is to deny helplessness in the face of the horror or loss by not seeking help, support, or consultation. For seasoned professionals there can be an expectation of performance that makes symptoms of anxiety, self-doubt, and burnout something to hide rather than something to address in supervision, group therapy, or individual therapy (Phillips, 2004).

The impact of trauma work on caregivers trumps language, culture, and location. Working at one international meeting, I experienced caregivers from different countries struggling to understand and translate for each other, as well as to corroborate the secondary post-traumatic stress symptoms, feelings of helplessness, horrific images, anger, and isolation felt when working with people who had faced the unspeakable. The intensity, connection, and relief associated with sharing, making meaning, and receiving support in this context were palpable. In trauma work, the caregiver's willingness and capacity to make use of interventions such as group training and group process experiences, supported by group and individual therapy, is a necessity.

Personal Benefits

Regardless of discipline, nature of work, or orientation, another reason for the significant use of personal therapy by therapists may be the reported positive personal outcomes. In national and international studies, over 80% of therapists report positive treatment outcome (Orlinsky et al., 2005a). In their 20-year replication study of 500 psychotherapists, Bike et al. (2009) noted that therapists reported significant improvements in three dimensions: behavioral symptoms, cognitive insight, and emotional relief. In this study, 95% of the sample indicated no harmful effects.

Professional Benefits

What is extremely important about the reported outcomes of therapists' therapy is that although personal reasons are predominately given for seeking treatment, there are consistent and significant findings of positive professional gains. According to Bike et al. (2009), the reported professional benefits include awareness of the importance of a therapist's reliability and commitment; competence and skill; warmth and empathy; patience and tolerance; the value of having the experience of being a patient; and the opportunity to see that therapy can work. Pope and Tabachnick (1994) found that the personal therapy of therapists improved self-awareness, self-understanding, self-esteem, increased openness to and acceptance of feelings, and enhanced the therapists' personal relationships. Linley and Joseph (2007) found that therapists who received personal therapy or were currently in personal therapy reported more personal growth and less burnout.

Professional Career Development

The professional benefits of personal therapy are consistent with the reported findings by Orlinsky and Ronnestad (2005a) in their extensive international study, *How Psychotherapists Develop*. They report that when asked the question, "How important to you is your further development as a psychotherapist?" 80% to 90% of 4,700 therapists of different disciplines, theoretical orientations, career levels, gender, and nationalities rated development as highly important (4 or 5 on a scale of 5). Further differentiating professional development into current development and career development, Orlinsky and Ronnestad (2005b) found that the strongest and most widely endorsed positive influence on current development was "experiences in therapy with patients." The next most widely endorsed positive influence was personal therapy (rated 80% by those having had or in personal therapy).

Matching qualitative analysis with empirical data in terms of career development, Orlinsky and Ronnestad (2005c) found two variables that predicted 40% of the variance of career development. They were breadth and depth of case experience and level of currently experienced growth, which in turn was a function of clinical experience and personal therapy. According to these findings, client experience, supervision, and personal therapy emerge as the major triad of positive influence on therapists' career development. One important conclusion, as suggested by Orlinsky and Ronnestad, is that therapists place much greater emphasis on interpersonal influences than intellectual ones.

The Importance of "The Person of the Therapist"

Hans H. Strupp (1978) considers a therapist's theoretical orientation as an overrated variable, maintaining that "techniques per se are inert unless they form an integral part of the therapist as a person" (p. 314).

At present, we do not have direct corroboration of a cause and effect from the patient's perspective of the personal therapy of the treating clinician as a variable in treatment outcome. We do, however, have consistent findings over time that the "person of the therapist" and the therapy relationship are crucial to therapeutic outcome regardless of theoretical orientation (Engel, 2008; Strupp, 1978; Wilson et al., 1968). Quoting a University of Pennsylvania study, Stossel (2008) reports findings that most successful therapists, regardless of their orientations, are considered to be honest and empathic and able to connect quickly and well with other people. The consistent finding is that the effectiveness of treatment across orientations is not a function of technique but "who the therapist is" (Norcross, 2002).

This recognition of the importance of the "person" of the therapist in therapeutic work bears on the value of personal therapy in the developmental journey of the therapist. It suggests that those very aspects of self (self-awareness, self-esteem, capacity for empathy, and interpersonal skills) reported to be enhanced by personal therapy are intrinsic to therapeutic effectiveness despite orientation.

The Therapist's Therapist

Perhaps the strongest corroboration of the crucial role of the "person of the therapist" comes from a consideration of those factors identified by therapists in their choice of a therapist. In a study of 509 psychologists, Norcross et al. (1988) found that the four top reasons for a therapist's choice of a therapist were perceived competence, clinical experience, professional reputation, and interpersonal warmth. In their review of multiple studies, Norcross and Grunebaum (2005) underscore the consistent finding of interpersonal qualities as openness, flexibility, respect, and caring, in addition to competence and professional reputation. As Grunebaum (1983) concludes, "therapist-patients seek a personal relationship with therapists—one in which they feel affirmed, appreciated and respected by another human being whom they like, appreciate and respect" (p. 1338).

The Value of Personal Therapy from Different Theoretical Perspectives

While the predominant feeling across orientations or perspectives is that personal therapy enhances the personal and professional development of the therapist, there are differences reported when considering personal therapy as necessary and essential to therapeutic effectiveness.

Psychodynamic Perspective

Freud had considered that the unanalyzed analyst could go only as far as her or his own limited experience with the unconscious would let him or her go. As such, the analyst's analysis was an absolute necessity (Freud, 1915/1958). Against this backdrop, the personal therapy or analysis of those therapists working from a psychoanalytic/psychodynamic perspective has always been considered a crucial and integrative component in the development of a psychotherapist (Fromm-Reichman, 1950; Macran et al., 1999).

Historically, the conceptualization of the therapist's feelings in response to the patient was termed *countertransference* and warranted the therapist's own analysis as a way to handle and resolve the emergence of such feelings. As the definition of countertransference has expanded to a totalistic perspective that includes the therapist's conscious and unconscious feelings and verbal and nonverbal responses to the patient based on the therapist's theoretical perspective, training, experience, person, personality, history, and current life events, as well as the impact and transference of the patient, the need for self-understanding is ever more important (Racker, 1968; Roth, 1990). Essentially, evolving psychoanalytic thinking makes psychotherapy for the therapist more important. Whereas the goal of a classical training analysis was to prepare the candidate to become the all-wise and the all-knowing analyst, today, those who subscribe to a relational/psychodynamic perspective no longer presume to "know." Evolving psychoanalytic thinking moves the therapist into a co-participant model that accepts that reality is subjective (Ehrenberg, 1992; Hirsch, 1996). Accordingly, this warrants on the part of the therapist a willingness to know more about self (Aron, 1996; Wachtel, 2008). It demands a tolerance for being affected by the patient's conscious and unconscious.

In concert with this, related issues including the recognition, use, and misuse of countertransference, self-disclosure, enactments, consideration of a dynamic unconscious, and the collaborative use of dreams, make personal therapy a necessary journey of finding and knowing self. To ask whether a therapist from this perspective can be effective without personal therapy is to fail to grasp the use of the therapist's self as necessary in facilitating the patient's self-journey.

It is based on these perspectives that psychoanalytic and psychodynamic training programs view and require analysis and/or psychotherapy of the therapist as central to training and development.

Cognitive-Behavioral Perspective

From a cognitive-behavioral perspective, which sees change as due to learning and the proper application of therapeutic methods, personal therapy has not been seen as crucial to effectiveness (Laireiter & Willutzki, 2005; Norcross, 2005).

In the past 20 years, while not viewed as a standard training element and still considered by most behavioral therapists to be of limited value, personal therapy has been increasingly acknowledged by cognitive behaviorists as helpful in enhancing important training goals (Laireiter & Willutzki, 2005; Geller et al., 2005).

From this perspective, the therapist's personal therapy is not a model of treatment but an opportunity to improve self-reflection, self-knowledge of blind spots, habits, and interpersonal patterns. Personal therapy also offers the therapist the experience of having been in the role of client, which is valuable in terms of empathy for the feelings of the client. Personal therapy also offers incidental learning and modeling of strategies and methods experienced in the relationship with one's own therapist. One cognitive-behavioral therapist shared that it was not until he was the client that he could recognize how difficult it was to change patterns and how much he valued his therapist's patience.

Experiential-Humanistic Perspective

Those coming from an experiential-humanistic perspective, as in person-centered or gestalt therapy, work with the immediate experience of the client and emphasize personal agency. This perspective necessitates attunement to the client, self-awareness, authentic response to the client's reactions, and comfort with complex feelings in self and other. From this perspective personal therapy is seen as valuable but as only one of many possible opportunities for personal growth, which can also be found in training workshops, journaling, growth groups, and other sources of personal expansion (Elliott & Partyka, 2005).

Systems Theory Perspective

While the systems theory (Haley, 1976) perspectives of family and couple therapy have discounted the relevance of personal therapy for the therapist, the more psychodynamic fields of family and couple therapy (Bowen, 1978; Scharff & Scharff, 1987; Whitaker & Keith, 1981) recognize personal therapy as crucial in terms of the therapist's authenticity and handling of counter-transference. In this light, it is interesting to note that they recommend individual therapy, not necessarily family or couple therapy, as a crucial component of training. Whereas family or couple therapy will foster self-understanding in terms of these contexts and may enhance empathy and skill, individual personal therapy is seen as more likely to foster understanding and use of self in the face of family and couple issues.

Group Perspectives

Group interventions can be conducted from many perspectives: psycho-dynamic, cognitive-behavior, self-psychological, psycho-educational, and so forth. Drawing upon my own personal group experience as well as my professional experience conducting groups, and training and supervising group therapists, it is my opinion that the practice of group therapy necessitates the therapist's having had a personal group experience of some kind.

In terms of psychodynamic groups models, for example, the leader's experience as a member of a psychodynamic group dealing with the structure, process, and inevitable interplay of group dynamics, levels of functioning, multiple transferences, group unconscious, and individual and group resistances is integral to his or her development and effectiveness as a group psychotherapist (Ormont, 1980, 1992).

The leader's personal group experience is also crucial for effectiveness in group therapy with other models (e.g., cognitive processing, cognitive-behavioral protocols, time-limited theme-centered, psycho-educational groups). Regardless of the "agent" or model of change for a group, the crucial component in outcome is the leader, through whom all other components of group experience flow. The leader's capacity to utilize the protocol of change, the dynamics of the members, and the structure, frame, and process in a way that facilitates positive outcome results from the leader's training as well as personal group experience (Bieling et al., 2006; Burlingame et al., 2004).

Yalom (2002) tells us, "Only by being a member of a group can one truly appreciate such phenomena as group pressure, the relief of catharsis, the power inherent in the group-leader role, the painful but valuable process of obtaining valid feedback about one's personal presentation" (p. 43).

The Interface of Supervision and Personal Therapy

Regardless of orientation, supervision is intended to expand technique and interpersonal capacities. It invites the supervisee to identify with the supervisor as a mentor as it offers skills that foster autonomy. Reflecting the overlap of personal therapy and supervision, one of the gifts of my analyst was the suggestion that I be in supervision with a brilliant female analyst. Against the backdrop of dreams that was part of my own analysis, this supervisor taught me to step into the unconscious with my patients in a way that was empowering and transforming to them and to me.

Historically, the place where supervision interfaced with personal therapy was in consideration of the supervisee's countertransference—that is, those unconscious reactions to the patient's transference that were viewed as a hindrance or obstacle, something to be analyzed away. The supervisor, from this perspective, would attempt to identify, confront, neutralize, or recommend personal therapy as a way to exclude such feelings and enhance the supervisee's effectiveness.

Evolved psychoanalytic thinking views countertransference in a more totalistic way as a function of the supervisee's person, personality, gender, history, and theoretical orientation. It is seen as inevitable, having both subjective and objective components, and is often a valuable lens for knowing oneself and one's patients (Kernberg, 1984).

While countertransference, seen as the total range of feelings toward a patient, is not automatically a reason to recommend therapy to a supervisee, it is valuable for the supervisor and supervisee to distinguish between those objective and subjective countertransference reactions that can be utilized in the service of the treatment and those that actually disrupt or compromise the care of the patient and the treatment goals. It is at these times that a supervisor who has developed a mutually respectful relationship with the supervisee can identify, clarify, and recommend personal therapy as a way to enhance personal and professional effectiveness. It is of great value for the supervisor to differentiate what personal therapy can offer that supervision cannot.

For example, a supervisee who became extremely negative and dismissive of any sexual issues brought up by a female patient revealed, when asked to consider possible reasons for her reaction, that she had been raped in her first year of college. The supervisor underscored the reality that working as a therapist very often trips the unhealed or unresolved issues in one's own history. The supervisor suggested that when personal triggers provide a reason for us to seek personal therapy, they offer an opportunity to change disruptive countertransference into therapeutic attunement.

In addition to countertransference, supervision interfaces with personal therapy because supervision is an interpersonal experience that occurs in the context of relationships—the supervisor and supervisee, and the supervisee and the patient (group, couple, family). Whatever is imparted or learned is both didactic and emotional and occurs in the context of intersecting relationships. There will be feelings, expectations, conflicts, and realities that will affect supervisor, supervisee, and patient in positive as well as negative ways.

In this regard, as a faculty member and supervisor in doctoral and postdoctoral programs for many years, I have seen students benefit from what

Fleming and Benedek (1966) termed a "learning alliance" with a supervisor—that is, one that parallels the working alliance in terms of the necessary trust, respect, and mutual goals to make the experience viable. As Rock (1997) explains, a supervisory experience is very meaningful when supervisees experience the supervisor as committed, focused, and expert as well as someone with whom they feel respect and mutuality.

On the other hand, I have been aware of students working with authoritative or rigid supervisors with whom they find "no fit" and with whom they become anxious, angry, or frozen. Often they begin to conceal the process, lose confidence, and in some way stop being authentic with self, supervisor, and patient.

Given the reality of differences in supervisors along one's training and career path, personal therapy for the supervisee may serve as a buffer, container, and support system. Whether personally chosen or suggested, personal therapy in concert with supervision offers an invaluable opportunity for integration of conscious and unconscious material, the continual opportunity to examine stirred countertransference and transference issues, and the experience of knowing what it is to be a patient and to have a therapist. What makes personal therapy different from supervision is that it is a reflective space that allows for work on the inevitable overlap of personal and professional issues without fear of judgment or professional evaluation.

As a supervisor, I have been keenly aware of the responsibility as well as the expectations of being the expert as well as the "intruder and the insider" with supervisee and patient (Phillips, 2006). Using a relational style, I have been moved by the mix of passion and humility of new therapists and have told them so. At other times, I have shared my anxiety and confusion on hearing a case and the anxiety or other feelings I may have felt with a former case of my own. Very often supervisees want to know "the right thing to do." It is difficult for them to value their silent presence or empathic listening with a patient. Some supervisees have tried to metaphorically "hand over" their patients, believing I must have all the answers. At those times, I have had to ask myself before I ask them: Did I invite this? Did I need this?

I believe that regardless of orientation, as supervisors we have to consider the value of self-reflection and some form of personal therapy. We have to consider our style and its impact. While there may be mutuality and collaboration, supervision is an asymmetrical relationship in that one is providing a service to the other and is "supposed" to have "super vision." How one uses the power in this relationship is central to what the supervisee will feel, learn, and pass forward. Generally, as supervisors, we may or may not know if we are making a supervisee feel anxious, inadequate, shamed, or blamed. It is crucial that we try to know, as these are feeling states incompatible with learning and growing. The self-reflection that we both overtly and implicitly model becomes the crucial factor of any technique we espouse as curative.

Just as it may be necessary to encourage a supervisee to seek personal therapy, it may be necessary for a supervisor to seek personal therapy because he or she recognizes that his or her functioning as a supervisor is being compromised by personal life events, historical triggers, or the emotional configuration of a particular supervisee or his or her patient. In the interface with supervision, personal therapy should be considered as an important option on a continuum of self-reflection, self-care, and self-development.

Cultural Competence and Personal Therapy

Cultural competence addresses the therapist's worldview and the personal and professional capacity to work effectively with patients from diverse cultural, socioeconomic, and racial populations and sexual orientations. Competence in this regard requires humility, the acquisition of information, and the ability to consider assumptions about self and other, to recognize cognitive and emotional rigidity, and to challenge inherent bias and perspective. To do this, a process of self-reflection, in the form of group process, group therapy, and/or personal therapy, becomes the essential complement to didactic opportunities.

Traditionally, the acquisition of cultural competence involved didactic experience from an "etic" perspective—that is, learning about the aspects of a particular minority group by becoming intellectually aware as an objective outsider of the norms, customs, language, histories, and traditions of the group (Brown, 2009, p. 12). This approach leaves out two essential components of cultural competence: the recognition of the multiple identities owned by anyone identified with any minority group, and the inclusion of the multiple identities of the person of the therapist as an object of self-study relevant to understanding the person, group, couple, or family with whom he or she is working.

An example of the limitations of this perspective is reflected in the situation in one training institute noted for the racial, ethnic, and sexual diversity of its candidates. An unexpected complaint voiced by candidates to faculty was the singularity of definition experienced by members of certain minorities, who felt they were turned to as "the spokesperson" whenever a patient from their minority group was discussed. The surprise and concern on the part of the faculty on hearing this underscored the complexity of cultural understanding and the need for alternative models to address diversity awareness.

Toward this end, Laura Brown (2009) recommends that therapists consider themselves and their clients through Hays' (2008) epistemic model of social identifiers captured in the acronym ADDRESSING, standing for age, disability (acquired and/or developmental), religion, ethnicity, social class, sexual orientation, indigenous heritage, national origin, and gender/sex. This consideration of self and other expands the nature and viability of the therapeutic exchange. To some degree, however, it is only part of the process for developing cultural competence.

Cultural competence requires heightened awareness of what we represent to patients and what they represent to us on a conscious and unconscious basis. To truly facilitate self-consideration of social identifiers, didactic information about another culture, clinical experience, and cross-cultural involvement requires the addition of group process or therapy experience to afford opportunities for both increased feedback and self-reflection.

For example, given the educational and professional background of most therapists, it is likely that they have had "dominant group privilege" as a function of their race, ethnicity, social class, education, and even gender orientation (Brown, 2009). Given that privilege tends to be invisible to those benefiting from it, but very visible to those who do not have it, some opportunity to develop self-awareness is needed to understand what we represent to patients and what they represent to us.

Research has demonstrated the value of multicultural competence programs that include learning through reflection; teams that afford a venue for consistent open dialogues about identities and biases; and group team meetings that include ongoing multicultural supervision (Park-Taylor et al., 2009). Multicultural competency requires an orientation that is didactic, self-reflective, interpersonal, and continuous.

Mandated Personal Therapy

When we think about mandated personal therapy for mental health professionals who have completed their training, we are referring to those cases where professionals are pressured to seek treatment from professional ethics committees, licensing boards, or programs for impaired professionals. According to Norcross and Connor (2005), the most common reasons are sexual misconduct with patients, substance abuse, or nonsexual boundary violations.

Many variables factor into the viability of mandated personal therapy to address personal and professional issues. In her book *Sexual Boundary Violations*, Celenza (2007), for example, makes a crucial distinction between the majority of one-time offenders and the few psychopathic predators, and the amenability of the former to rehabilitation as compared with the latter. Central to the vulnerability associated with professionals who face problems that require mandated treatment is a lack of self-reflection, an inability to recognize warning signs, and discomfort in seeking help in the face of emotional pain and unresolved issues.

In their comparison of multiple studies, Norcross and Connor (2005) report that, regardless of stage of career, those mental health professionals who do not seek personal therapy report similar reasons for their decisions. These include confidentiality concerns, financial expenses, exposure fears, self-sufficiency desires, time constraints, and difficulty finding a good enough therapist outside of their social and professional networks. A number also report using other effective means of dealing with burdens in life.

One wonders if more knowledge about the prevalence of seeking personal therapy by mental health professionals and perhaps more "colleague care" in terms of attention to warning signs and encouragement in seeking help would serve both professionals and those they treat.

While personal therapy is not required in most training programs or graduate programs, the requirement to seek personal therapy is often made by faculty to a student or trainee who demonstrates problem performance or behavior (Huprich & Rudd, 2003). Underscoring this is the program's ethical and legal responsibility to maintain quality assurance in the professional services of trainees seeing clients as well as the professional capacities of their program's graduates.

One of the problems associated with required treatment is the identification of personal therapy with failure, inadequacy, or exposed difficulties. I would suggest that if personal therapy is openly recommended for all candidates as part of professional development, along with didactic training, clinical experience, and supervision, students might avail themselves of personal therapy as a choice that reduces the need for required treatment. In such an atmosphere, the requirement of treatment, if needed, might be experienced differently—that is, with less shame and more effectiveness.

Required treatment often involves treatment progress reporting. For example, the Psychology Code of Ethics states conditions under which a faculty member may require student disclosure of personal information and personal therapy so long as issues of privacy and confidentiality are addressed in advance. In view of these newer regulations designed to protect both the public and practitioners, there must be clear guidelines for confidentiality of material reported to the training committee of an institute or graduate department.

With respect to the issue of communication between the trainee's therapist and the faculty who mandate personal therapy, Elman and Forrest (2004) reviewed the plan of 14 training programs and identified them as using either a "hands-off approach" or an "active involvement" approach. Reporting that the "hands-off approach" was found to be unclear and ineffective, they recommend an active involvement plan with a nuanced and sensitive model of trainee privacy and confidentiality that has real merit.

The plan, which would be spelled out as department policy known by trainees and faculty, includes the trainee's choice of a therapist from an approved list; meeting with the treating therapist and trainee to establish goals of therapy relevant to the professional functioning concerns of the faculty; and agreement by the therapist and trainee that attendance and progress will be reported to the training program. Crucial to this reporting is the clear differentiation between information revealed in therapy like dreams, fears, and personal history, which should remain private and protected, and information pertinent to a trainee's professional competencies and capacity to address issues that might compromise or interfere with treatment, such as boundary violations, excessive use of anger, excessive anxiety, substance abuse, and so forth. It would seem a plan of this type might serve the needs of both trainee and faculty in a professional way.

A crucial aspect of this plan or any required treatment is choice of therapist. Recommended therapists not only need expertise and empathy, but also should have the ability to recognize the needs of the student within the framework and concerns of the department. As with any culture, the therapist also needs to make himself or herself aware of the particular discipline, orientation, and faculty recommending the student. From a systems perspective it is always valid to consider the context of identified problems.

Conclusion: The Legacy of Personal Therapy

An overwhelming majority of therapists of all disciplines across different orientations, both nationally and internationally, seek personal therapy, often more than once, during and after training. They have done so by choice. Licensure in psychology, psychiatry, social work, marriage and family counseling, and psychiatric nursing does not require personal therapy. The reasons that therapists give for seeking therapy are more personal than professional and are consistent with those of the general population. What is different is the prevalence with which they choose therapy and the consistent report by the majority of positive professional gains and career development growth.

Personal therapy is integral to a therapist's formative training and ongoing development across disciplines and orientations because there is an inextricable mix of personal and professional dimensions in the functioning of therapists. Clinical experience, care of the caregiver, supervision, and cultural competence all hinge on the integration of expertise and training with the person of the therapist and the personal qualities and awareness he or she brings to this work.

When asked, most mental health professionals across disciplines and orientations feel that personal therapy in some form should be recommended but not required. As one group therapist working from a cognitive behavioral perspective said, "The model is not critical. It is the act of being in therapy that is significant" (G. Crosby, January 15, 2009).

Personal therapy cannot guarantee the effectiveness of a therapist. This is a rewarding and often stressful profession. It is one that demands and invites a continual awareness of self while one is responsible for another. It is one for which personal and professional dimensions overlap, fostering growth and development or creating stress and disruption. As such, therapists need to do more than recommend personal therapy. As colleagues, faculty, and supervisors, we need to discuss, disclose, and model the personal therapy journey so many of us have taken. Passing on a legacy of personal therapy validates its crucial role in professional development and invites the recognition that our effectiveness as professionals depends on our connection as people.

References

Aron, L. (1996). *A Meeting of Minds: Mutuality in Psychoanalysis.* Hillsdale, NJ: Analytic Press.

Bieling, P., McCabe, R., & Antony, M. (2006). *Cognitive Behavioral Therapy in Groups.* New York: Guildford Press.

Bike, D. S., Norcross, J. C., & Schatz, D. (2009). Processes and outcomes of psychotherapists' personal therapy: Replication and extension 20 years later. *Psychotherapy Theory, Research, Practice, Training, 46*(1), 19–31.

Bowen, M. (1978). *Family Therapy in Clinical Practice.* Northvale, NY: Aronson.

Brown, L. S. (2009). *Cultural Competence in Trauma Therapy.* Washington, D.C.: American Psychological Association.

Burlingame, G. M., MacKenzie, K. R., & Strauss, B. (2004). Small group treatment: Evidence for effectiveness and mechanisms of change. In M. J. Lambert, A. E. Bergin, & S. L. Garfield (Eds.), *Bergin and Garfield's Handbook of Psychotherapy and Behavior Change* (5th ed., pp. 647–696). New York: Wiley.

Carey, B., Cave, D., & Alvarez, L. (2009). For therapists in the military, painful stories. *New York Times,* Nov. 8, A26.

Celenza, A. (2007). *Sexual Boundary Violations.* New Jersey: Jason Aronson.

Crosby, G. Personal communication, 1/15/09.

Cunningham, M. (2003). *Impact of trauma work on social work clinicians: empirical findings. Social Work,* 48, 1–10. Retrieved 11/2/09 http://questia.com/reader/action/open/5002044978

Darongkamas, J., Burton, M. V., & Cushway, D. (1994). The use of personal therapy by clinical psychologists working in the NHS in the United Kingdom. *Clinical Psychology and Psychotherapy,* 18, 299–305.

Ehrenberg, D. (1992). *The Intimate Edge: Extending the Reach of Psychoanalytic Interaction.* New York: W.W. Norton & Co.

Elliott, R., & Partyka, R. (2005). Personal therapy and growth in experiential-humanistic therapies. In J. D. Geller, J. C. Norcross, & D. E. Orlinsky (Eds.), *The Psychotherapist's Own Psychotherapy: Patient and Clinician Perspectives.* New York: Oxford University Press.

Elman, N., & Forrest, L. (2004). Psychotherapy in the remediation of psychology trainees: Exploratory interviews with training directors. *Professional Psychology: Research and Practice, 35*(2), 123–130.

Engel, J. (2008). *American Therapy: The Rise of Psychotherapy in the United States.* New York: Gotham Books.

Fenster, S., Phillips, S. B., & Rappaport, E. (1986). *The Therapist's Pregnancy: Intrusion into the Analytic Space.* Hillsdale, NJ: Analytic Press.

Fleming, J., & Benedek, T. (1966). *Psychoanalytic Supervision.* New York: Grune & Stratton.

Freud, S. (1958). Observations on transference love. In J. Strachey (Ed. and Trans.), *The Standard Edition of the Complete Psychological Works of Sigmund Freud* (Vol. 12, pp. 157–171). London: Hogarth Press. (Original work published 1915)

Friedman, R. A. (2008, February 19). Have you ever been in psychotherapy, doctor? *New York Times.* Retrieved January 1, 2009, from http://www.nytimes.com/2008/02/19/health/19mind.html?pagewanted=print

Fromm-Reichmann, Frieda. (1950). *Principles of intensive psychotherapy.* Chicago: University of Chicago Press.

Geller, J. D., Norcross, J. C., & Orlinsky, D. E. (Eds.) (2005). *The Psychotherapist's Own Psychotherapy: Patient and Clinician Perspectives*. New York: Oxford University Press.

Grunebaum, H. (1983). A study of therapists' choice of therapist. *American Journal of Psychiatry*, 140, 1336–1339.

Haley, J. (1976). *Problem Solving Therapy*. San Francisco: Jossey-Bass.

Hays, P. A. (2008). *Addressing Cultural Complexities in Practice: Assessment, Diagnosis, and Therapy* (2nd ed.) Washington, D.C.: American Psychological Association.

Hirsch, I. (1996). Observing-Participation, mutual enactment, and the new classical models. *Contemporary Psychoanalysis*, 32(3), 359–383.

Huprich, S. K., & Rudd, M. D. (2003). A national survey of trainee impairment in clinical, counseling and school psychology doctoral programs. *Journal of Clinical Psychology*, 60, 43–52.

Kernberg, O. (1984). Countertransfererence, transference, regression and the incapacity to defend. In H. C. Hays (Ed.), *Between Analyst and Patient: New Dimensions in Countertransference*. Hillsdale, NJ: Analytic Press.

Laireiter, A-R., & Willutzki, U. (2005). Personal therapy in cognitive-behavioral therapy: Tradition and current practice. In J. D. Geller, J. C. Norcross, & D. E. Orlinsky (Eds.), *The Psychotherapist's Own Psychotherapy: Patient and Clinician Perspectives*. New York: Oxford University Press.

Linley, P. A., & Joseph, S. (2007). Therapy work and therapists' positive and negative well-being. *Journal of Social & Clinical Psychology*, 26, 385–403.

Macran, S., Smith, J., & Stiles, W. B. (1999). How does personal therapy affect therapists' practice? *Journal of Counseling Psychology*, 46(4), 419–431.

McCann, I. L., & Pearlman, L. A. (1990). Vicarious traumatization: A contextual model of understanding the effects of trauma on helpers. *Journal of Traumatic Stress*, 3(1), 131–149.

Meyers, M. F., & Gabbard, G. O. (2008). *The Physician as Patient: A Clinical Handbook for the Mental Health Professional*. Arlington, VA: American Psychiatric Publishing.

Norcross, J. C. (Ed.) (2002). *Psychotherapy Relationships That Work*. New York: Oxford University Press.

Norcross, J. C. (2005). The psychotherapist's own psychotherapy: Educating and developing psychologists. *American Psychologist*, doi: 10.1037/0003-066X.60.8.840.

Norcross, J. C., & Connor, K. A. (2005). Psychotherapists entering personal therapy. In J. D. Geller, J. C. Norcross, & D. E. Orlinsky (Eds.), *The Psychotherapist's Own Psychotherapy: Patient and Clinician Perspectives*. New York: Oxford University Press.

Norcross, J. C., & Grunebaum, H. (2005). The selection and characteristics of therapists' psychotherapists: A research synthesis. In J. D. Geller, J. C. Norcross, & D. E. Orlinsky (Eds.), *The Psychotherapist's Own Psychotherapy: Patient and Clinician Perspectives*. New York: Oxford University Press.

Norcross, J. C., & Guy, J. D. (2005). The prevalence and parameters of personal therapy in the United States. In J. D. Geller, J. C. Norcross, & D. E. Orlinsky (Eds.), *The Psychotherapist's Own Psychotherapy: Patient and Clinician Perspectives*. New York: Oxford University Press.

Norcross, J. C., Strausser, D. J., & Faltus, F. J. (1988). The therapist's therapist. *American Journal of Psychotherapy*, 42, 53–66.

Orlinsky, D. E., Norcross, J. C., Ronnestad, M. H., & Wiseman, H. (2005a). Outcomes and impacts of the psychotherapist's own psychotherapy: A research review. In J. D. Geller, J. C. Norcross, & D. E. Orlinsky (Eds.), *The Psychotherapist's Own Psychotherapy: Patient and Clinician Perspectives*. New York: Oxford University Press.

Orlinsky, D. E., & Ronnestad, M. H. (2005a). *How Psychotherapists Develop: A Study of Therapeutic Work and Professional Growth*. Washington, D.C.: American Psychological Association.

Orlinsky, D. E., & Ronnestad, M. H. (2005b). Career development: Growth and correlates of evolving expertise. In D. E. Orlinsky & M. H. Ronnestad (Eds.), *How Psychotherapists Develop: A Study of Therapeutic Work and Professional Growth*. Washington, D.C.: American Psychological Association.

Orlinsky, D. E., & Ronnestad, M. H. (2005c). Current development: Growth and depletion. In D. E. Orlinsky & M. H. Ronnestad (Eds.), *How Psychotherapists Develop: A Study of Therapeutic Work and Professional Growth*. Washington, D.C.: American Psychological Association.

Orlinsky, D. E., Ronnestad, M. H., Willutzki, U., Wiseman, H., Botermans, J., & the SPR Collaborative Research Network (2005b). The prevalence and parameters of personal therapy in Europe and elsewhere. In J. D. Geller, J. C. Norcross, & D. E. Orlinsky (Eds.), *The Psychotherapist's Own Psychotherapy: Patient and Clinician Perspectives*. New York: Oxford University Press.

Ormont, L. R. (1980). Training group therapists through the study of countertransferences. *Group*, 4(4), 17–19.

Ormont, L. R. (1992). Subjective countertransference in the group setting: The modern analytic experience. *Modern Psychoanalysis*, 17(1), 3–12.

Palm, K. M., Smith, A. A., & Follette, V. M. (2002). Trauma therapy and therapist self-care. *Behavior Therapist*, 25, 40–42.

Park-Taylor, J., Kim, G., Budianto, L., Pfeifer, G., Laidlaw, P., Sakurai, M., & Pfeifer, J. (2009). Toward reflective practice: A multicultural competence training model from a community mental health center. *Professional Psychology: Research and Practice*, 40, 88–95.

Pearlman, L. A., & Saakvitne, K. (1995). *Trauma and the Therapist: Countertransference and Vicarious Traumatization in Psychotherapy with Incest Survivors*. New York: W.W. Norton & Co.

Peebles, M. J. (1980). Personal therapy and ability to display empathy, warmth and genuineness in psychotherapy. *Psychotherapy: Theory, Research and Practice* 17, 258–262.

Phillips, S. B. (2004). Countertransference: Effects on the group therapist working with trauma. In B. Buchele & H. Spitz (Eds.), *Group Interventions for Treatment of Psychological Trauma*. New York: American Group Psychotherapy Association.

Phillips, S. B. (2006). Intruder and insider: The impact of the supervisor on the supervisee and the process of supervision. *Analytic Insights: The Journal of the Suffolk Society for Psychotherapy & Psychoanalysis*, 4, 5–13.

Phillips, S., & Kane, D. (2008). *Healing Together After Trauma: A Couple's Guide to Coping with Trauma and Post-traumatic Stress*. Oakland, CA: New Harbinger Publications.

Pope, K. S., & Tabachnick, B. G. (1994). Therapists as patients: A national survey of psychologists' experiences, problems, and beliefs. *Professional Psychology: Research and Practice*, doi: 10.1037/0735-7028.25.3.247.

Prochaska, J. O., & Norcross, J. C. (1983). Contemporary psychotherapists: A national survey of characteristics, practices, orientations, and attitudes. *Psychotherapy: Theory, Research and Practice*, 20(2), 161–173.

Racker, H. (1968). *Transference and Countertransference*. New York: International Universities Press.

Rock, M. H. (Ed.) (1997). *Psychodynamic Supervision: Perspectives of the Supervisor and the Supervisee*. Northvale, NJ: Jason Aronson, Inc.

Ronnestad, M. H., & Skovholt, T. M. (2001). Learning arenas for professional development retrospective accounts of senior psychotherapists. *Professional Psychology: Research and Practice*, 32(2), 181–187.

Ronnestad, M. H., & Skovholt, T. M. (2003). The journey of the counselor and therapist: Research findings and perspectives on professional development. *Journal of Career Development*, 30(1), 5–44.

Roth, B. E. (1990). Countertransference and the group therapist's state of mind. In B. Roth, W. Stone, & H. Kibel (Eds.), *The Difficult Patient in Group* (pp. 287–294). New York: International University Press.

Scharff, D., & Scharff, J. S. (1987). *Object Relations Family Therapy*. New York: Aronson.

Stossel, S. (2008, December 21). Still crazy after all these years. *New York Times*. Retrieved February 8, 2009, from http://www.nytimes.com/2008/12/21/books/review/Stossel-t.html?_r=1&sq=Still_Crazy

Strupp, H. (1978). The therapist's theoretical orientation: An overrated variable. *Psychotherapy: Theory, Research & Practice*, 15(4), 314–317.

Wachtel, P. L. (2008). *Relational Theory and the Practice of Psychotherapy*. New York: Guilford Press.

Whitaker, C. A., & Keith, D. V. (1981). Symbolic-experiential family therapy. In A. S. Gurman & D. P. Kniskern (Eds.), *Handbook of Family Therapy*. New York: Brunner-Mazel.

Wilson, G. T., Hannon, A. E., & Evans, W. I. (1968). Behavior therapy and the therapist-patient relationship. *Journal of Consulting and Clinical Psychology*, 32(2), 103–109.

Yalom, I. D. (2002). *The Gift of Therapy*. New York: Harper Perennial.

8

The Psychotherapist as "Wounded Healer": A Modern Expression of an Ancient Tradition

Cecil A. Rice

"Wouldst thou" – So the helmsman answered
"Learn the secret of the sea?
Only those who brave its dangers
comprehend its mysteries!"

Henry Wadsworth Longfellow

Many things contribute to becoming a psychotherapist, including education, training, supervision, family dynamics, and personal therapy, among others, which are examined in more detail in other chapters of the current volume. In what follows, we focus upon the person of the therapist as "wounded healer" and the role of our vulnerabilities in healing others and ourselves. We recognize that therapists, as well as their clients, experience psychological wounds often early in life but also throughout their lives, sometimes traumatically. While those injuries may influence the choice of profession, it is of major importance in therapy itself. To be effective, therapists need some understanding of their vulnerabilities to facilitate their clients' healing and to prevent unrecognized woundedness from blocking that healing. When events touch something about which we are uncomfortable, we say, "Let's not go there." This defensive response on our part can be a loss to the client. Such reactions commonly happen in the transference/countertransference matrix of the co-created intersubjective field (Stolorow et al., 1994; Stolorow & Atwood, 2002).

To explore the impact of therapist woundedness on the treatment process, we will first review the idea of the "wounded healer" as it reaches back into antiquity, followed by a discussion of its more recent expressions, including the close parallels between those ancient roots and our practices today. Then, we will reflect on the role of therapists' woundedness in therapy itself, its capacity to facilitate the client's healing, and on occasion its capacity to prevent healing and the personal and social ramifications of that failure. The author will use personal and clinical examples to illustrate this material.

Early History of the Wounded Healer

The wounded healer is not a new phenomenon, but one that has a long history reaching back to ancient times. Jung called the wounded healer archetypal (Sedgwick, 2001, p. 73), meaning that it is an innate, universal prototype that structures the psyche at its most basic level. Collectively, archetypes are "'primordial ideas of humanity,' 'basic patterns of instinct,' which occur universally" (Dunne, 2000, p. 73)—our psychological DNA, if you will. They are not ordinarily directly available to the psyche, but do find expression in myths and religious symbols. They also find derivative expression in such current forms as the archetype of the "wounded healer-therapist."

Shamans

Shamans are probably the most ancient and most enduring examples of the wounded healer, stretching from antiquity until today in such places as among the Nanai in Russia, China, and Tibet and among Native Americans (Ellenberger, 1970). Shamans acted and act as intermediaries between the world of humans and the world of spirits (Eliade, 1964, pp. 3–7), not unlike the function of modern-day psychotherapists acting as intermediaries between the world of which we are aware and the world of which we are unaware. Some suggest that shamans were originally women, many still are, and sometimes shamans are transvestites or wear women's garb in performing their art, suggesting continuity with the founding women (Stutley, 2002).

The route to becoming a shaman varies. Some may have been people who were more healthy and creative than others, while some also gave evidence of serious mental illness (Silverman, 1967) in which the ritual process of becoming a shaman led to their healing (Stutley, 2002). The initiation processes for the shaman, as Campbell (1968, pp. 98–101) notes, are highly ritualized and often include group dancing during which the hero/shaman collapses into a trance state and acts in ways that look like psychotic states. This process puts the shaman at psychological and even physical risk, but seems to be a necessary step toward becoming a successful shaman, and as suggested above may heal the already wounded shaman. Halifax (1990) puts it more directly, saying that becoming a shaman "involves the experience of a catastrophic encounter with psychological and physical suffering," though she also thinks of the shamans as healed healers. It is a process not unlike the regressive and transformational processes today's psychotherapists may experience in their own therapy.

Shamans have always found support for their activities in the mythologies, traditions, and beliefs of the community they serve. This makes the work of shamans not just an individual activity but also a group activity out of which a particular shaman emerges to serve a particular function for the group. However, unlike priests or their equivalents who support and sustain the community's religious traditions, shamans, while allied to that system, often act outside it. They bear their own truth gained through their direct connection with the world of the spirits (Stutley, 2002).

Chiron and Greek Mythology

Many consider Chiron of Greek mythology to be the archetypal model of the wounded healer (Holmes, 1998). Chiron was a centaur, a mythological beast who was half-human and half-horse and considered by many the offspring of Cronus Saturn and the nymph Philyrra. He never knew his father and his mother abandoned him shortly after his birth: his initial wounding. Arguably, this may have contributed to his later skill as a healer, which was considerable. A later experience added to that skill. Pholos invited the hero god Heracles, Chiron, and others to his cave. After some drinking, a ruckus broke out that Heracles quickly quelled with his arrows. However, one of the arrows accidentally struck the ankle of Chiron. Chiron, the experienced healer, instructed Heracles in the treatment of his ankle. However, on the tip of the arrow was a poison from Hydra whom one could never kill, so that while Chiron's wound eased it would never fully heal, remaining unbearably painful. He later mentored and taught the healing arts to others, among them Asklepios, the god of medicine (whom some speak of as the original wounded healer [Baldwin, 1999, p. 245]), through which lineage Hippocrates later taught the art and science of medicine and whose oath—"first do not harm..."—guides medicine today (Stutley, 2002).

Jacob Wrestles with the Angel

We find a similar mythology to Chiron in the Hebrew tradition, though more closely bound to historical events. In the story of Jacob wrestling with the angel, Jacob was planning to meet with his brother Esau, from whom he had robbed his inheritance many years earlier. He now had to face him, which he assumed meant war, a war in which he, Jacob, might not fare well. Before the meeting with his brother, he had an intense experience that lasted all night in which he wrestled with the angel of God. In that struggle, before releasing him, the angel wounded Jacob's thigh and changed his name from Jacob to Israel. Jacob had struggled with his inner demons, which released him from his shame about his treatment of his brother, prevented a battle, and brought healing instead: healing of his relationship with Esau and healing between two divisions of the tribe that he and Jacob led. Although the wound from wrestling with the angel remained, he also was transformed from a rather selfish and slimy character into a leader and healer of his tribe (Genesis, 32, Hosea, 12).

The Wounded God

Centuries later, one sees similar experiences in the wilderness experiences of Jesus. In the biblical story, Jesus went into the wilderness for 40 days and 40 nights, which we may assume refers to an indefinite time rather than specific days and hours, spent in isolation to struggle with his "calling." Such a struggle reflects a usually very difficult internal turmoil, the successful resolution of which makes future work possible: not unlike those of the shamans. Thereafter, Jesus spent most of his short life healing the ills of others. From our perspective, what is even more relevant than the wilderness experience is the ultimate death and crucifixion of Jesus. The considerable grief experienced by Jesus' closest followers ultimately led to a belief in his resurrection, which from a mythological perspective resolved their grief by seeing Jesus as overcoming his woundedness, enabling them to overcome their woundedness also. This journey also is strikingly similar to the journey of the shamans as they moved from death to rebirth (Halifax, 1990, pp. 54–55). Christians later extrapolated this to the idea of a wounded God, making God closer, less distant and abstract, and part of and hope for human woundedness.

With respect to the current context, these historical legends of wounded healers reveal the archetypal elements that have played out more recently in the evolution of modern psychotherapy. We turn now to the more recent history of wounded healers.

The Recent History of the Wounded Healer: Psychological Roots

The more recent psychological roots of the wounded healer reach back to the late 19th through early 20th century, stimulated in part by the interface of the Enlightenment and the Romantic movement. As is true of all history, these beginnings did not arise *ex machina* but had their own long history as well. However, for our purposes they mark a useful point at which to begin this section.

Sigmund Freud and his student Carl Jung are two key figures in this psychological history, though they too had their precursors (Ellenberger, 1970). Freud believed that just as a patient could have a transference reaction toward the therapist, so the therapist could have a corresponding reaction to the patient, which he called countertransference. In other words, the patient could trigger unresolved issues for the therapist that Freud saw as problematic, and he expected his followers to address those unresolved issues—their woundedness—if they were to work effectively with the patient. He also noted that the transference response itself places the analyst at risk of injury. Throughout his life, Freud worked hard to understand his own woundedness to prevent it from becoming an obstacle to treatment (Freud, 1959, p. 289; Gay, 1988, pp. 252–255).

Freud grew up in a large, complex family, eldest child of Jacob and Amanda Freud, the latter of whose naked body he recalls viewing with pleasure. However, two painful moments stood out for him. The first was when he simultaneously lost his nurse, who left the family permanently, and his mother, who left to deliver a child. Freud found the loss of these two contrasting but dominant figures in his life difficult to cope with, and the experience hung with him most of his life. The second was his major disappointment with his father, Jacob, whom he saw as shiftless and weak and whom he learned was unable to stand up to the Christians who taunted him as a Jew. These injurious moments, among others, colored his thinking and later his clinical practice and writing (Gay, 1988, pp. 3–54).

While much of Freud's approach to countertransference and its related woundedness still holds true, many now also see those countertransference responses and possible expressions of therapist injury as useful data for the therapy and not necessarily an obstacle to it, an important point to which we will return later.

This latter stance is more similar to that of Jung. Jung saw himself as a wounded healer, reflected in the detailed descriptions he gives of his emotional struggles, his dreams and nightmares, his reflections on the shamanic traditions and how in time they found expression in his work with patients (Dunne, 2000). Like Freud, Jung traced his pain to his family of origin, dominated by Protestant pastors and a formal and stifling religiosity. In childhood, he had what he referred to as his "illness," which he believed was likely the result of his separation from his mother because of an illness she herself had. Reflecting on his childhood, Jung wrote that he saw "portraits of a little boy, bewildered and wondering at an incomprehensibly beautiful and hideously profane and deceitful world" (Dunne, 2000, p. 5). This woundedness later led Jung to join Freud in the search for understanding and healing of others. In time, he broke from Freud over differences in their thinking and developed his own way of "healing the soul" (Dunne, 2000, pp. 27–44).

Ellenberger (1970) noted that both Freud and Jung also had emotional difficulties in adulthood that affected their work. Doubts about himself, his work, and his health confounded Freud. He used his physician friend, Wilhelm Fliess, to help him through that struggle. His health concerns included heart symptoms, not specified, but he gave up cigar smoking for a time; later, following his father's death, he went through a similar crisis and his inner sufferings became much worse.

Ellenberger noted that Jung lived through similar crises, including "depression, neurosis, psychosomatic ailments, or even psychosis" (Ellenberger, 1970, p. 447). Ellenberger describes these experiences as creative illnesses that follow upon a period of intense preoccupation with an idea. These experiences Ellenberger (pp. 10–12) views as similar to those experienced by shamans.

We should note in passing that another key figure around this period was Alfred Adler, whose painful struggles with his older brother led to his focus on birth order, among other things (Ellenberger, 1970, pp. 571–656).

In sum, often woundedness or a "creative illness" appears to underlie the "call" to healing or to an elaboration of the call appearing, for instance, for both Freud and Jung, later in life as well as early in life. Fulfilling the call also carries risks. While the woundedness can facilitate therapy, it can also place the practitioner at risk. Jung noted that the patient's illness might infect the practitioner. He wrote, "and the psychotherapist in particular should clearly understand that psychic infections … are in fact the predestined concomitants of his work" (Jung, 1946, p. 172). In the current psychodynamic framework, we would see the client as transferring the infection to the therapist through the mechanism of projective identification (Ogden, 1982), to be discussed later.

Reflections on the Contemporary Practitioners as Wounded Healer

The thinking about the wounded healer continues, but in recent years it has taken more focused forms that reflect the relationship between the therapist and the patient or the therapy group. In other words, sometimes a healer who provides the healing has the same wounds as the client. For instance, Alcoholics Anonymous believes in the healing value of being with others who have the same difficulties, at least in one area. In addition, some therapists and clients argue that it is important that the healer and client have the same injuries. For instance, people with physical illnesses often find it especially helpful to have a therapist who has been through similar experiences (McDaniel et al., 1997).

In the field of group therapy, it has become common practice to design groups, especially short-term groups, for people with shared woundedness, such as groups for people who have been bereaved, addicted, traumatized, divorced, and sexually abused, or groups for men, women, and gays and lesbians, and so on. Not uncommonly, leaders of such groups have the same conflicts as the members, giving them an "inside track" to the clients' struggles; the clients in turn may feel understood because of a shared specific kind of injury (Frost, 1998).

However, others have observed that while indeed it is valuable to promote healing around shared difficulties, such an approach has limitations. This is particularly true of groups with shared difficulties. Such groups often cohere very rapidly and the experience of healing follows, usually around the members' sense of not being alone with their particular difficulties. The downside of such groups is that the members often have difficulty addressing deeper layers of conflict, which are often attenuated by the nevertheless important value of support. The members of such groups are also at risk of co-creating a victim identity. Thus, we often recommend that such groups be time-limited and that in the future or as a next step, the members consider entering a more general therapy group where there is a variety of woundedness to facilitate a more rounded identity. Sometimes one recommends that they do both—for example, join both AA and a therapy group (Bernard et al., 2008; van der Kolk, 1993).

Early in the 20th century, the literature on the wounded healer focused on analytical (Jungian) psychologists and pastoral counselors. Now it has enlarged to include physicians and most of the healing professions, including nurses, social workers, addiction counselors, abuse counselors, pastors, and so on (Acker, 1999; Conti-O'Hare, 2002; Jackson, 2001). With this widening use of the term, interest has increased in considering how to help psychiatrists and others become aware of their woundedness and how to train them in its use in therapy (Kirmayer, 2003).

The Wounded Healer-Therapist and the Universality of Woundedness

Given that few, if any, escape psychic wounding, it seems unlikely that psychotherapists are the only professionals who experience woundedness. For instance, we know that many political and national leaders, among others, suffer wounds and that woundedness has affected their leadership, such as was the case for Napoleon, Hitler, and Nixon (Volkan, 2009). Great artists have also experienced woundedness and expressed their injuries in their work—for instance, Van Gogh, Dostoevsky, and Gustav Mahler, among others (Andreasen, 1987).

However, granting that universality, do therapists have particular forms of woundedness? Or does their uniqueness lie in the role that those wounds play in the healing art? Or do particular wounds play a role in the choice to be a healer? For instance, one piece of research (Henry et al., 1971) suggests that many therapists were individuals who grew up in marginalized groups. The authors write, referring to psychiatrists, psychoanalysts, psychologists, and social workers who practice psychotherapy (the so-called Fifth Profession), that their roots were disproportionately from Eastern Europe: "In an important sense these professionals are a culturally homogeneous group, but also a culturally marginalized one" (Henry et al., 1971, p. 8). The present author has also observed in his work in Northern Ireland that mental health workers and psychotherapists in that country are largely Catholic, which in that context is also a marginalized group—an observation requiring more rigorous investigation. The use of the term "alienists" to describe psychiatrists in the past further suggests marginalization (125th Anniversary of the American Neurology Association History Exhibit, 2000). It also suggests a particular set of emotional experiences generated by living in that position. Henry et al. (1973), in a later study of 4,000 mental health professionals, suggested that they have difficulty in interpersonal relations and may seek such intimacy in the setting of the consulting room.

A similar idea is reflected in more detail in the work of Sussman (1992), who studied a smaller number of mental health students and professionals (14 in all, 9 of whom are reported in his book), and did so by in-depth interviews of each subject rather than through questionnaires (as Henry et al. did). Sussman made his observations through several lenses representing the major psychoanalytic schools: namely classical drive theory, object relations, and self-psychology. Among his conclusions, Sussman observed that, having acknowledged the limitations of his study, "The interview material provides additional support for the general hypothesis that an important determinant of the desire to practice psychotherapy involves the attempt to come to terms with one's own psychological conflicts" (p. 235). The specifics of this general hypothesis include characteristics highlighted in the psychology schools noted above, such as voyeuristic tendencies, dullness in their intimate relations, indirect sexual gratification in therapy, masochistic and sadistic tendencies, narcissism, need for power and control, and so on. He also notes the significantly higher rates of suicide among mental health professionals than in the general population. Others have supported this observation for physicians and health care professionals (Adams, 2001; Coombs et al., 1986; Daneault, 2008; Noonan, 2008; Schernhammer, 2005), though a few have cast doubt on the accuracy of those statistics (Foxhall, 2001; Phillips, 1999). Sussman also notes, however, that focusing on the pathology risks overlooking the equally positive motives for being a therapist.

In two volumes, Goldberg takes the reader on the personal journeys of psychotherapists relatively early in their professional lives (1986) and later in their professional lives (1992). He sees a direct line from shamans to psychotherapists, as we do in this chapter. Quoting from Longfellow's *The Secret of the Sea*, he summarizes the importance of healers' wounds to their capacity to heal. "Wouldst thou" – So the helmsman answered "Learn the secret of the sea? / Only those who brave its dangers/ Comprehend its mysteries!" (1986, p. 11). Goldberg addresses a wide variety of issues related to becoming a therapist, noting that therapists' family experiences and their willingness to bear and explore them and to remain vulnerable are key ingredients to being an effective therapist. In his second volume, the theme continues addressing how, as the years advance, healers may easily lose the desire and richness of the profession they have joined/been "called to." He invites the wounded healers to confront the disillusionment that many senior clinicians face. Facing the challenge and braving its dangers restores the power to heal.

It seems, then, that psychotherapists have often experienced certain emotional "illnesses" while growing up that influenced their choice of a profession. However, such trauma and conflict are probably not the only influences: teachers, mentors, friends, and family members, among others, may also play a role. The personal and interpersonal forces may come together to affect the choice to become a therapist. For example, on a personal level, the author recalls a crisis in adolescence. His father seemed to be more aware of or more puzzled by the crisis than the author: he was just miserable, though with little other awareness. His father took him to see the president of a theological seminary who also was a pastoral counselor, one of the originals. After a brief conversation, he felt heard and left feeling much better.

The pastor had noted that as the only member of his extended family to win acceptance into a scholarship-based pre-university school, his space to do the subsequent required work became eroded by the activities of a large rambunctious family—nowhere to study, nor any understanding of the need for it, resulting in dropping grades. He recommended that his father create a personal workspace for him: a small event that made a huge difference and relieved his father as well. Later, the author found himself identifying with the pastor, following a similar educational and career route that combined theology and psychology.

As we noted earlier, the beliefs, symbols, and rites of the local tribe supported the activities of shamans. Likewise, the environs in which we find ourselves: our culture, society's demands and values, and our ethnic backgrounds, influence our choice to be healers and the kind of healers we become. For instance, the work of Freud grew in parallel with an increasing public interest in and exploration of sexuality, and his personal woundedness related closely with what became known as the oedipal complex, inspired by the Greek myth. Furthermore, his woundedness as an Austrian Jew excluded from mainstream medicine led to his turning that injury into pioneer work in healing outside medical academia. If Freud had remained within medical academia, he would most likely have been a neurologist and less likely have become the founder of psychoanalysis. Furthermore, the Romantic movement of the time, with its emphasis on the importance of feelings and of experience, in contrast to the rational and reasoned stance of the Enlightenment, greatly influenced the work of Freud and Jung and others of the time (Ellenberger, 1970).

Likewise, many of the pioneers of group therapy found themselves drawn into that area of work because of a lack of resources to meet the mental health demands of the armed forces during World War II (Rice & Rutan, 1987). Other, still earlier pioneers found themselves in similar compelling situations. For instance, for Pratt (Rice & Rutan, 1987) it was the demands of a growing number of tuberculosis patients in the early 20th century and his observation of how those patients helped each other in their conversations in his waiting room that led him to make the groups formal.

Thus, much contributes to becoming a therapist, and while that role and vocation has the makings of Jung's archetype of the wounded healer-therapist, such wounds are of course not unique to therapists. While some literature noted earlier suggests that suicide, depression, and difficulty with intimacy may be more common among healers than the general population, what appears to be more common to those who become therapists is the desire to acknowledge those scars. They may even have had initial or early life sensitivity to them (true of Jung [Dunne, 2000]) but show a willingness to wrestle with them, as did Jacob, to live knowingly with them, at some risk as Longfellow suggests, and to use the experience to help others. In brief, the awareness of and the relationship to that awareness may be more central to a wounded healer's effectiveness than the actual woundedness itself. After all, the "illnesses" of Jung and Freud, while painful to them, were not especially different from those suffered by their patients or many others who never became therapists.

The Relationship of Wounded Healers to their Wounds

Freud addressed this issue in his ideas of transference and countertransference, where transference described how a patient over time comes to see the therapist as representing important figures and related experiences from the past and responds to the therapist as though he or she were those persons. Countertransference describes the therapist's emotional response to the patient's transference, often triggered by unresolved issues from the therapist's past: the therapist's woundedness, if you will. Freud believed that when such countertransference arose, the therapist needed to return to analysis to resolve the emotional issues that the countertransference represented, as the latter interfered with effective healing for the patient. In the language of this chapter, we can say, perhaps stating the obvious, that unattended therapist woundedness can get in the way of healing the patient's woundedness.

An Illustrative Example: The Therapist's Self-Reflection on Feelings of Woundedness

Some time ago, the author worked as chief psychologist and primary group therapist at a private psychiatric hospital. As group therapist and leader of community meetings—a large group of 50 or more patients and staff—he was in contact with most of the patients and hospital staff at any given time. It was an exciting if at times challenging task. Some months after his arrival at the hospital, he had a dream, a dream that seemed startlingly real. In the dream, he was sitting in the nurses' station with some psychologists, psychiatrists, nurses, and other staff. As the dream progressed, he realized that in the dream, he was a patient, not a staff person, and that he liked being a patient. As he noted in an earlier essay (Rice, 2008) it was a turning point in his work at the hospital. He had been aware of walking along the hospital driveway each morning before beginning work feeling as though he was walking forward while simultaneously leaning backwards. He felt stiff and uncomfortable. Reflections on this dream led him to realize again his own struggles with dependency wishes. Being, as he referred to himself in that earlier essay, the godfather successor to his father in his very large extended family, he was used to solving problems for others and denying his own needs and uncertainties. In the dream, he had allowed his yearnings for nurturance and his wish to have others take care of him find their rightful place. He could relax. Further reflection also led him to an acceptance of how terrifying psychosis can be and his limited influence over it, whether in others or himself.

Such revisiting of his old scars and associated fears, as with Chiron, did not "remove" the wounds, but it did allow him to find a place for them in his conscious psychic field, making his work more comfortable and creating less interference in his work with others.

Therapist reflection can take many forms. In the above instance the primary form was thinking about a dream and as a consequence considering the author's way of entering the hospital as well as contemplating the continuing yearnings he had not been acknowledging or been aware of at the time. Reflection can also mean wondering aloud with others, such as colleagues, friends, or a therapist or analyst. It can mean becoming attuned to the state of one's body: its tensions, relaxation, pains, aches, postures, and so on. It can mean becoming attuned to passing feelings that one would normally not attend to and fantasies that arise during therapy that one might prefer to ignore. They are ways of becoming more aware of one's woundedness and one's relationship to it in the context of therapy. To the therapy or analysis noted above as ways to become more aware of one's injuries, it is important to add group therapy, which is the *sine qua non* for seeing and understanding how one's injuredness affects others and how others affect it. Group therapy also connects with the original wounded healers, the shamans, whose woundedness found voice and endorsement in a group.

In brief, the reflection process increases awareness and facilitates the healer's movement between the world we know and the world of which we are unaware, the conscious and unconscious worlds, or as the shamans might say, the world of humans and the world of the spirits.

A Further Example: Therapist Woundedness Negatively Affecting Milieu Treatment

The following clinical illustration acts as a bridge to the next section. Bob was a very competent aide at the above psychiatric hospital. Routinely, the author supervised his group work in a supervisory group at the hospital. However, on this occasion, because of the critical nature of his and the staff's concerns, he met with him individually. When working on the night shift Bob got into trouble with the patients and them with him. He also found himself at odds with fellow staff members and managers as a result. It was routine for the staff to check in informally with the patients who were relaxing in groups or individually in the various lounges in the evenings. If the patients began to get very loud, especially when other patients were sleeping, the staff person would ask them to tone it down. Usually, this process went very smoothly. However, when Bob was on duty the noise increased and the patients became very angry with him. This meant additional work for the other staff. Bob was very concerned about this behavior and about his image with the staff and talked with the author about it, which other staff also encouraged him to do. The following story emerged during their conversation.

Bob was a child of Holocaust survivors from World War II. His parents never talked about it but it hung around as a dreadful silence of which Bob was very aware. He wanted to talk about it but knew he never could. Breaking the silence was taboo. He did not recall any threats; he just knew that one could not speak about it. The pain of this circumstance reappeared in the evenings when the patients "broke the silence" with their loud talking. This caused considerable anxiety for Bob that pressed him to silence the patients at all cost. Unlike other staff members, he could not be relaxed about asking the patients to tone it down. Emotionally for him they had to be silent, "no if, ands or buts." The patients, triggered by his behavior, became louder and louder. This further angered and frustrated Bob and his colleagues. As the patients continued to "disrespect" the silence, Bob became more anxious and angrier, and the patients broke the silence even more—and so it went.

This was a horrendous experience for Bob, reflecting not just his own internal struggles but also a transgenerational trauma that felt beyond words. Paradoxically in a small way he found himself behaving toward the patients as others had behaved toward his parents, a not uncommon feature that Volkan et al. noted in *The Third Reich in the Unconscious* (2002). What is important for us, and leads into the next section of the chapter, is how the interactions between the internal and external, the unconscious and conscious worlds—the shamans' worlds of the spirits and humans—co-created a chaotic field in which none of the parties could work or live effectively. They had co-created a toxic intersubjective field, which could be addressed only when the therapist's self-reflection began to shift.

The Relationship Between the Wounded Healer and Wounded Clients

As the last illustration makes clear, the relationship between therapists and clients, between wounded healers and wounded clients, is complex, which for heuristic purposes we can divide into two broad categories: the real relationship and the preconscious/unconscious or transference/countertransference relationship (Greenson, 1978). These two sets of relationships, while easily categorized, also overlap considerably.

The real relationship refers to the conscious aspects of the relationship, such as words spoken, agreements made, and conscious ways of relating. In the last illustration, the conscious aspects between Bob, his colleagues, and the patients included such things as rules about behavior and expectations in the evenings in the hospital. These included behaving respectfully toward others and not letting the behavior or pleasures of one group infringe upon those of others, namely the need of others for quiet or for sleep. It often also had the salutary effect of keeping agitation or anxiety in individual members within reasonable parameters. There were also similar parameters for the staff about how they would treat their clients—namely firmly, with kindness and respect.

The author has illustrated aspects of Bob's pre/unconscious world that significantly affected the behavior of the patients and staff in this hospital. Before our conversation, Bob had little understanding of what was going on.

For him it seemed the patients were simply behaving unreasonably, and he felt greatly unsupported by the staff. In brief, he felt very alone, much as he had felt at home, at least in some areas—as with the "silence"—growing up. While we are unable to illustrate it here, it is fair to assume that in addition to the annoying things that he may have done, Bob's behavior triggered similar old wounds, often unconscious, among the patients, to which they responded with anger and misbehavior, further magnifying Bob's aggressive responses. One can make a similar assumption about unconscious struggles— as well as the real ones—among the staff that further magnified the situation, co-creating an unhelpful intersubjective field.

According to psychodynamic theory, often the unconscious mechanisms that help birth these intersubjective relations and the resultant intersubjective field include such phenomena as transference, countertransference, and projective and introjective identification. Due to his countertransference reactions, Bob saw his patients, or at least the mandate that they be quiet, as a repetition of his childhood experience, including his possible rage at the unspoken mandate from his parents not to break the "silence" and his own wish to act against it. While transference and countertransference color and shape how we may perceive others and act toward them, projective and introjective identification invite others to behave as we and our countertransference reactions expect them to behave. For the sake of argument, we may assume that Bob longed to break the silence in his home; maybe he wanted to scream out against it, but never did.

However, Bob's behavior, verbal and nonverbal (his manner, his stances, his body movements), toward the patients conveyed and stimulated this yearning in them—that is, he projected his yearning to scream into them, identifying with their response. The patients took in the projection (i.e., introjected it), identified with it, and acted it out in a disconcerting way. When the infant screams from hunger or other discomforts, the mothering person feels the scream or other behavior viscerally as well as through sound, tuning into the infant's projected need. Typically, she responds to this visceral message by accepting the projection and containing it with physically nurturing hugs, embraces, and, if needed, food. This contains the infant's distress, and normal development can proceed. Similarly, as adults, we take in a troubling or frustrating experience and in time become increasingly able to comfort ourselves, and, then too, the comforting other(s) becomes an essential part of all human life. In Bob's case, the needed mothering function was absent, so that neither the staff, the patients, nor Bob could move on. After the author's conversation with him, Bob began to relax and the collective relations between Bob and the community eased as he became aware the role of his woundedness in this context. Fortunately, Bob was a sensitive and insightful clinician, which meant that the author's consultation largely involved listening, with occasional comments or questions. He invited Bob to wonder about the importance of maintaining silence, and slowly his story emerged. The author's knowledge, gained from the supervision about Bob's Jewish ancestry, also informed his reflections. In addition, the author had some prior knowledge of the effects of the Holocaust on the next generation, which attuned him further to Bob's concerns.

The Healing Intersubjective Field: An Emerging Crisis in the Therapist's Life Affects the Therapy Group

We argue, in this chapter, that the healing role of the wounded healer with the wounded client takes place within a largely pre/unconscious co-created intersubjective field, and further that the nature of the intersubjective field has the capacity to heal or harm. This is true whether the co-created field takes place in individual, couple, family, or group therapy. Clearly, the larger the client group, the more complex the intersubjective field. We will now provide an example of a problematic intersubjective field in group psychotherapy, and then discuss how a subsequent severe wound to the therapist and his family impinged on the group and was gradually resolved with the help of his colleagues.

For 3 months one of the author's therapy groups was at impasse. During each session, he felt burdened and interventions he made were ineffective. After unsuccessfully trying to figure it out, he obtained a consultation from several colleagues. One colleague suggested that he had a sympathetic countertransference toward the members triggered by the horrendous histories of a number of them. This comment struck home (interesting word to leave out!). At the following session, he found the group in the stuck position with which he had become familiar. However, following the consultation he observed himself more closely and noted the following. As he listened to the group, he had the sensation of his brain slowly shutting down. It seemed to start at the top of his head and move slowly downward toward the base of his skull. As he observed this happening, he heard the voice of Hercule Poirot, Agatha Christie's famous fictional detective, say, "Remember the little grey cells." He realized that he had been absenting himself emotionally from the group for some time—turning off his brain—and began to wonder what he was avoiding. It slowly dawned on him that he was unable to face or give voice to the despair these group members felt, not just in the group but also in most of their lives. He slowly realized that he himself did have experience with hopelessness and despair in life, whether resulting from an incurable brain illness in one of his extended family members, or his own experience of the air raids on Northern Ireland during World War II, from which there seemed to be no escape. The therapist's family coped with these by an optimism that said, "We can deal with these, we can survive," and they did. It was important to keep on plugging. The belief that the author could cope stayed with him, but the despair of this group challenged that belief, and he did not want to deal with it. Some things do not change no matter how hard we try. The group triggered the uncertainty behind his ability to cope, and he found it difficult to tolerate the fact that he could do nothing about the members' despair.

After the author had gone through this reflective process, which he did not disclose to the group, he finally said words to this effect: "I am struck by the sense of despair and hopelessness with which we are struggling." After a very brief pause, the group erupted. Several asked him "where the hell" he had been for the past few months. "Of course we feel hopeless," they added. The author guessed that the unspoken word was "dummy!" The group remained difficult—despair is hard to tolerate—but a significant shift had taken place, and his resistance and the groups' resistance to the helplessness and despair modified. Earlier the therapist had joined the group in establishing a co-created intersubjective field where we could not acknowledge the despair nor address it. Now the therapist and group were beginning to establish an intersubjective field where we could acknowledge the despair and possibly heal from it or at least live with it.

In the above illustration, the author did not need to share his thoughts and experience—his barely conscious conflicts and fears—with the members. His primary task was to address his fears first so that the members could address theirs in the intersubjective field he was no longer blocking. However, is there a time when therapists should share their woundedness or aspects thereof? What if the client learns about the therapist's woundedness from another person, or through some public event? While this is no longer an unconscious event, the therapist's knowledge and acceptance or lack of acceptance or unacknowledged pleasure/shame about and injuries from that event will affect the real (conscious) and unconscious intersubjective field. In other words, it may help or prevent adequate discussion about and healing from the effect of the discovered information. It will also create an intersubjective field that will make it difficult for the members to address similar events or experiences in their own lives.

The Impact of a Personal Tragedy of the Therapist on the Life of the Group

Given that the author's office was in the lower level of his home, several relatively minor events took place there of which the members were aware, as were individual patients and couples. Much of the time, the therapist and clients dealt with them as part of the treatment process. However, a major life-shattering event in the therapist's life profoundly affected his groups and other clients.

Several years ago, the therapist was stunned and aggrieved to learn that his daughter and two grandsons were murdered, which coincidentally led to headline news for several weeks. The therapist and his wife were devastated. Before he returned to practice, numbers of colleagues came to his aid, leading the groups in his office and giving them an opportunity to begin processing the news. Other colleagues telephoned individual and couple clients, letting them know what had happened and making services available to them while the therapist was unable to be present.

When, finally, he returned to his practice, the first concern the groups addressed was whether he was in fact able to conduct treatment with them. They had many questions about how he was faring, which he answered directly. It seemed very important to deal with the "world of humans" (the real situation) first before looking at the "world of the spirits" (the unconscious dynamics). The author was direct about the nature of his loss and its impact. Like Chiron, he had a new injury that would never fully heal. Likewise, this injury has also remained with the groups. It is part of their histories and reappears some months after each new member joins a group. However, at this particular time in the groups' histories, it seemed important to support and be reassured of the leader's well-being.

Upon reflection, the group members and the author had co-created several intersubjective fields that permitted the groups to take care of the leader. Acknowledging his trauma was important in building these intersubjective fields and in time enabled the members to garner some reassurance that he could be available to them. He made an agreement with them that if he felt unable to be present and emotionally available he would let them know. In addition, as one member noted, she could not have continued in the group had the members not met during the interim. Only one member, a new member, of one of the groups did not return.

Nevertheless, the author did ask himself if his own self-care would predominate and deprive the members of their right to healing and exploration. As it turned out, somewhat ironically, he need not have worried. After a few weeks, and while the members were still concerned about the author, they became more concerned about themselves. One woman, Sara, became very angry about the possibility that those who covered for him during his absence were not paid. If they were not to be paid, she wanted her money back. The therapist and the group members learned that money became her focus because she felt the crisis had ripped her off. Her anger at the therapist also left her feeling very alone in the group—she was the only angry one. The therapist wondered about this aloud and suggested that Sara may not be alone in this. Soon Bill asked how the therapist could possibility protect them if he could not protect his daughter, and why had he permitted his daughter to live the life she lived that brought this about, perhaps referring to some comments in the newspapers by the defense attorney. Whatever the source, it gave voice to the members' concerns and anger at the therapist for bringing this whole situation upon them. This theme reappeared later in all the groups: the leader had brought an unwanted assault upon the groups. The concern about the therapist re-emerged when Mel said he thought the therapist had coped remarkably well.

The author/therapist's task as the wounded healer became managing his own feelings. He angrily experienced unspoken thoughts such as, "You feel you have been gypped! Give me a break!" Yet, strangely, that sense of having been gypped gave us a common bond. They knew the therapist was furious with the murderer. They had asked earlier how he felt and he told them. For a few, knowing about the therapist's rage and injury was more troubling than relieving. The therapist believed at the time that to turn the question back on the members would have been what in the 1960s we called "mind fucking": it would have been a way of projecting his stuff into the members and individually or collectively burdening them with it, without an easy way to address it in the groups.

It is important to note that there are few guidelines by which to manage this kind of wounding and transform it into effective healing experiences for the patients. Thus, a few additional comments and observations are in order, and readers can judge their value for themselves. The therapist did share some other thoughts with the groups, such as noting that there were few things that the members wondered about, sometimes critically, regarding his behavior toward his family that he did not wonder about himself. A few years later, another group member used that information to call him to task for injuring her. When one is seriously injured, it is difficult not to injure someone somewhere along the line and threaten a healing intersubjective field. Amy had said with certainty that there was no way that what happened to his daughter could have happened unless there was a problem between her and him. Another member called Amy cruel, and the therapist instantly agreed, which devastated Amy, especially because in her mind being thought cruel was the worse thing anyone could say about her. Her father was especially cruel to her. The following week the therapist apologized, which gave them both a chance to begin healing. The fact that there were other people in the room to evaluate the situation addressing both the therapist and Amy made this process easier. One of the advantages of a therapy group is that on occasion it can protect the members from the leader.

The issue is not that in therapy the co-created intersubjective field must always be pleasant or good—it never is—but that the field allows space for the errors, for the bad and the good, for wounding and healing, where all parties can acknowledge and own them: creation and destruction are two sides of the same coin.

Self-Disclosure of Therapist Wounds

This illustration raises a question concerning how much therapists should share their experiences, thoughts, and feelings about their woundedness and when they should do it. At one time, within the psychodynamic perspective, therapist sharing was taboo (Wachtel, 1986), whereas currently some consider it useful (Billow, 2009). In this last illustration, the therapist had no choice but to share his woundedness, since others had already done it for him. He also learned that transference and countertransference are themselves resilient and can withstand considerable intrusion. However, as he reflected on his own woundedness, he often felt conflicted between being the therapist on the one hand, and on the other hand wanting to join the group for his own healing, especially when the members were sometimes offering it, albeit for their own needs as well. It is also clear that the therapist's and the group members' healing went hand in hand, so that it was difficult to walk the lines between revealing and not revealing, and when to reveal or not reveal. Additionally, one can also injure the members by not allowing them to take care of the leader when an occasion may call for it.

Knowing there is no easy answer to this question, the author will nevertheless make several suggestions about it. As already noted, one reveals and shares experience around public knowledge of the therapist's woundedness, although even then one often has to draw a line—hence the next two guidelines. First of all, one shares personal material with the individual client, couple, or group when the therapist judges that it is beneficial to the clients. However, how does one know when and what sharing of one's woundedness or other experience is beneficial to the client? The second suggestion is that, as Langs (1979, p. 327) said, if we listen to the clients' derivative material, they will give us information that will confirm the value or lack of value of the shared knowledge for the clients.

One advantage of leading therapy groups is that in addition to the information gathered from derivative material, it is highly likely that someone in the group will tell the therapist that sharing his or her woundedness is not helpful.

Some sharing and its related behaviors are definitely harmful to clients and to the intersubjective field where the potential for healing lies. We will now explore when and how such countertherapeutic harm from therapist wounds can occur.

When Woundedness Results in Damage to Clients

As we noted and demonstrated earlier, therapist woundedness can lead to some disruption in any therapy, but it is usually such that one can correct it readily, usually to the client's benefit. However, if the author had not found a way to address and acknowledge the severe harm noted above, he could have caused serious damage to the intersubjective healing field. The therapy group described earlier, which was aided by the therapist's introspection about Hercule Poirot, was at serious risk of such harm, because the impasse was in danger of becoming chronic. Had it continued, leaving the group might have been a wise self-preservative act because the author felt unable to face his despair and could readily create a damaged and damaging group.

The ways in which our woundedness can generate a damaging intersubjective field are legion. However, the particular nature of our own woundedness, as the above illustrations make clear, while often a creative stimulus for healing, can also generate particular kinds of harm (Maniar, 1995). Of the many tasks the therapist must address, the maintenance of boundaries is one of the areas where our woundedness can readily generate damaging inter-subjective fields. For instance, our need to please and our fear of not being loved can invite us to be unnecessarily flexible about therapy boundaries, such as when to agree to spend time with patients or group members outside the office to meet special needs. The author consulted with one therapist who spent time with a client to help her choose a new home. Except in rare instances, such "kindness" risks the safety of the therapy relationship. By contrast, if we have a very strong need to control events to contain or manage our own fears, as we saw in our illustration of Bob in the hospital, we hold boundaries too rigidly, with the outcome of a very unsafe group that makes moving beyond anger and the group's lack of safety hard to do. It also prevents the therapist from modifying boundaries when it might be helpful to the client to do so. Our grandiosity can invite clients or therapy groups to become highly dependent on us—as if, quite erroneously, we alone are the source of healing. In a therapy group, it invites the members to idealize the leader and remain in a dependency phase, unable to differentiate and move on. The group and its members become an extension of the leader. The boundaries do not seem as rigid as with the fearful leader, but the members may find them excessive. For the therapist such rigidity leaves little space for not knowing (Kurtz, 1983). In brief, while in general there are numerous possibilities for harm, the particular nature of therapist woundedness presages particular vulnerabilities that require attention.

As implied in the earlier illustrations, therapists can significantly reduce the possibility of doing serious harm when they have supervision and/or a community in which the latter can give voice to those moments when they perceive that therapists are at risk to injure their clients. Like the shamans of old and their successors, support communities are essential to effective outcomes. It was largely as a result of support from a local community of friends and colleagues that the author was able to address the murder crisis with his groups.

Supervision is an important aspect of the community of colleagues. While supervision is not the primary subject of this chapter, it is important to note the role of supervision in issues regarding the wounded healer. For example, it is highly likely that the supervisor is also a wounded healer. Thus, an important task for supervisors, as for fellow therapists, is to be aware of their vulnerabilities, to reflect on them, and to a reasonable degree to have mastery over them so that at a minimum they do not get in the way of building a co-constructed learning field with supervisees. This is a psychic space that encourages and allows reflection by supervisees of their own dynamics vis-à-vis their own patients, bolstered by the knowledge of psychotherapy those supervisors can pass on to the supervisees. That co-created learning field can support and help sustain the intersubjective healing field of which the supervisee is a part.

A brief reflection on situations of grievous harm is in order here and will act as a bridge to a discussion on the broader context in which psychotherapy and the work of the wounded healer must situate themselves. While the attention here is limited and at risk of being overly simplistic, it will connect us with the paper's beginning and with the roots of the wounded healer.

Sexual abuse of the client by the therapist is one of the more obvious kinds of serious abuse, though not the only one Brodsky (1989) (Gartrell et al (1986). The emotional response to such abuse is understandably very strong such that we can erroneously see all abuse as the same. In practice, there are many nuances to sexual abuse; for our purposes we can think of two broad categories.

"Falling in love" is a situation where the therapist becomes very attracted to the patient—and sometimes vice versa—that leads to inappropriate intimacy. Sometimes, such a therapist may seek help, or if challenged will reveal considerable shame and guilt about the behavior. Frequently, such overly intimate behavior takes place when therapists seek to salve their own difficulties in an intimate relationship. The couple co-creates an intersubjective field that provides some momentary ease at the expense of healing, understanding, and change. While such situations are co-created, the primary responsibility lies with the therapists because their role and authority creates an unbalanced power relationship, and because of their mandate to do no harm.

The second broad category of sexual abuse with clients is that of predatory behavior. Predatory abuse in therapy represents an abhorrent situation where a clinician repeatedly engages in sexual behavior, often with several clients, while rarely acknowledging any sense of guilt or shame.

Sexual Acting-In and Abuse in Psychotherapy: Two Case Illustrations

Steve was greatly loved by the members of the group to which he belonged. He worked hard in the group and in individual therapy, first with the author and later with another therapist. Steve happened to be a mental health professional, and had been very quiet in the group for some weeks. During this quiet period, he called the therapist, asking for an individual session because he had something he wanted to talk about in the group but was afraid to do so and wondered if he should continue in the group because of it. In the individual session, he told of a female patient with whom he had fallen in love and who gave every indication of having fallen in love with him and behaved seductively. In time, this led to an actual sexual relationship. His individual therapist recommended against talking about it in the group. The group therapist took a different stand, saying that while he knew it would be very difficult to talk about it, in the end, it could be very helpful.

At the next session, he began to talk about it. Initially, very slowly and somewhat indirectly, he then read a prepared statement without looking at the members. He was surprised that no one was surprised. As one member reminded him, "I had told you to be careful with her, because I felt you were in danger of crossing the line." Thus began a long series of sessions in which the members also talked about their feelings about the event and about the roots of their feelings. In this group, a number of members had experienced incest in varying degrees. One of the members, who had had a particularly long struggle with her incest, was also very helpful. She shared her rage and disappointment with Steve, but also recognized the struggle he had with his mother, who frequently used him as a surrogate husband and lover, though no actual sexual contact took place. His mother's behavior conveyed the expectation that he should rescue her from the pain left by an abandoning husband—a major wound. Thus, Steve was vulnerable to the neediness and seductive behavior of his female patient.

Over the weeks, as the group worked with him, Steve spoke of his terrible shame, and by mutual agreement he stopped the relationship with the patient, obtained supervision with a senior colleague, and continued his own therapy. He closed his private practice and instead worked in the prison system, where much of his expertise lay.

Therapists of good will like Steve are much less likely to repeat such malevolent enactments than those in the second broad category, the predator type of molester. As noted earlier, the predatory therapist is likely to deny the activity or otherwise obfuscate events and is unlikely to change his or her behavior. One such professional with whom the author had a relatively close association had been rumored to have slept with or made significant boundary crossings with numbers of patients. Some suspected him for years, but there was never any hard evidence. When the facts finally came to the fore following a patient going public, colleagues and the court confronted him but he denied it all, often responding in a confusing manner but without ever acknowledging it or revealing any guilt or shame about that situation or any other, at least not directly, though one could argue that the behavior was a defense against the shame. However, as with any wounded healer, acknowledging and understanding the wound is essential to effective cure for all parties; instead it was a tragedy for the therapist, his patients, and his colleagues, whose behavior cast a shadow over all involved.

There are many gradations between these two forms of grievous behavior. The latter is an extreme pathological form of the wounded healer, a circumstance that suggests that careful reflection by therapists, while very important, may not in itself be enough, and begs the question about the need for a larger context in which wounded healers must work. Indeed, predatory behavior usually precludes the possibility of self-reflection and requires a larger context in which to address it.

The Need for a "Containing" Community of Healers and Society

Therapy is a private and isolating process, making it important for therapists to find nurturance, collegiality, and friendship outside the consulting room. Professional groups are very important in this respect, although involvement with other non-professional groups is also important. Without such external supports, therapists may turn to their clients for the healing of their wounds, further complicating and threatening the therapy and co-creating a destructive intersubjective field. Professional groups have the added advantage of providing ethical frameworks and offering some objectivity to a very subjective and intimate process (Bernard et al., 2008). In addition, belonging to professional and other groups can protect therapists working in isolation from the risk of being "infected" by the patients with whom they work that Jung noted earlier. Research can provide a similar function: it can evaluate what works, what does not, and what helps or does not help therapists address their woundedness (Langs, 1979). In this context, it is worth noting that shamans—as well as spiritual leaders like Jacob and Jesus—were part of a group, emerged out of it, and were beholden to it.

Society adds an important aspect to the above. It provides a legal framework of accountability beyond even what professional organizations can provide. It acts as a protector of the citizenry against therapist woundedness should it become destructive. It can protect particular clients from seriously damaging behavior by particular therapists and hold them accountable. However, this system is by no means failure-proof. Society can itself get caught up in hysteria and distort the law to the detriment of all concerned. Society is made up of wounded citizens, who when fear is strong enough can wound those trained to heal the wounds of others. However, it is the best we have, and through an interdigitation between social and professional groups, as well as societal oversight, we may reduce egregious errors in each area.

One such interdigitation in the author's home state of Massachusetts is the Physicians Health Services, which requires oversight of an impaired therapist under the subsection of Physician Substance Abuse Monitoring. Initially while under this umbrella the state itself is not required to intervene legally, but it would intervene subsequently if the substance abuse monitoring failed. Many states have one version or other of such divisions that address the problem of the impaired physician or other practitioner.

Summary

The wounded healer has a long history, beginning with the early shamans of antiquity, through the Greek myth of Chiron, through Jewish and Christian stories and mythologies of Jacob and Jesus, through the work of Freud, Jung, and Adler and the psychotherapist practitioners of today. It is also worthy of note that shamanism itself is still practiced today in different parts of the world, very likely making shamans the longest line of wounded healers.

Woundedness is universal no matter what one's work or career. The author argues that therapists seem to be people who acknowledge and understand their woundedness, may even have been very sensitive to it early in life, and have been willing to wrestle with it and continue to do so. Clearly, other features contribute to the decision to be a therapist, as therapists are not the only ones who struggle with their complexes. However, it is that very awareness and the willingness to accept it and wrestle with it that can contribute significantly to the effectiveness of their work and redound to their clients' benefit. Such willingness operating in the background during sessions allows the therapist, in conjunction with clients, to co-create an intersubjective field within which healing can take place. Arguably, without an understanding of their woundedness and some mastery over it, the effectiveness of therapy will be limited no matter what the therapy approach is. Even with the use of cognitive-behavioral therapy protocols guided by a treatment manual, therapists' vulnerabilities and their relationship with the client will shape how they use the manual and how the client responds to it (Summers & Barber, 2009).

Wounded healers must also operate in a broader social system above and beyond their reflective and exploratory processes. These processes alone do not always guarantee effective psychotherapy, as the injuries of particular therapists may be such as to lead to harm for clients. For instance, some therapists' vulnerabilities may lead them to such harmful practices as excessive intimacy with their clients. Thus, it is important that psychotherapists also operate in collegial, professional, and civic contexts that can support their work, enabling them to be effective and preventing them from acting destructively.

References

125th Anniversary of the American Neurology Association History Exhibit 2000. 125th Anniversary of the American Neurology Association History Exhibit 2000. http://www.aneuroa.org/html/c19html/010-NandP.htm; downloaded 06/16/09

Acker, G. M. (1999). The impact of clients' mental illness on social workers job satisfaction and burnout. *Health and Social Work*, 24(2), 112–119.

Adams, C. (2001) Do dentists have the highest suicide rate? *The Straight Dope* http://www.straightdope.com/columns/read/2301/do-dentists-have-the-highest-suicide-rate downloaded 02/10/2009

Andreasen, N. C. (1987). Creativity and mental illness: prevalence rates in writers and their first-degree relatives. *American Journal of Psychiatry*, 144, 1288–1292.

Baldwin, M. (1999). Implication of the wounded-healer paradigm. In M. Baldwin (Ed.), *The Use of Self in Therapy*. Philadelphia, PA: Haworth Press.

Bernard, H., Burlingame, G., Flores, P., et al. (2008). Clinical practice guidelines for group psychotherapy. *International Journal for Group Psychotherapy*, 58(4), 441–542.

Billow, R. M. (2009). Modes of leadership: Diplomacy, integrity, sincerity and authenticity. In R. H. Klein, C. A. Rice, & V. Schermer (Eds.), *Leadership in a Changing World: Dynamic Perspectives on Groups and their Leaders* (pp. 29–48). Lanham, MD Lexington Books.

Brodsky, A. M. (1989). Sex between patient and therapist: Psychology's data and response. In G. O. Gabbard (Ed.), *Sexual Exploitation in Professional Relationships* (pp. 35–37). Washington, D.C.: American Psychiatric Press.

Campbell, J. (1968). *The Hero with a Thousand Faces* (2nd ed.), Bollingen Series XVII. Princeton, NJ: Princeton University Press.

Conti-O'Hare, M. (2002). *The Nurse as Wounded Healer: From Trauma to Transcendence.* London, England & Sudbury Massachusetts: Jones and Bartlett Publishers International.

Coombs, R. H. D., May, S., & Small, G. W. (1986). *Inside Doctoring: Stages and Outcomes in the Professional Development of Physicians.* New York: Praeger.

Daneault, S. (2008). The wounded healer: Can this idea be of use to family physicians? Canadian Family Physician 54(9): 1218–1219.

Dunne, C. (2000). *Carl Jung: Wounded Healer of the Soul.* New York: Parabola Books.

Eliade, M. (1964). *Shamanism, Archaic Techniques of Ecstasy,* Bollingen Series LXXVI. New York: Pantheon Books.

Ellenberger, H. F. (1970). *The Discovery of the Unconscious: The History and Evolution of Dynamic Psychiatry* (second printing). New York: Basic Books.

Foxhall, K. (2001). Suicide by profession: lots of confusion, inconclusive data. *Monitor on Psychology,* http://www.apa.org/monitor/jan01/suicide.html

Freud, S. (1959). *Collected Papers* (vol. 2, translated by Joan Riviere). London: Basic Books.

Frost, J. C., Kranzberg, M. B., & Hawkins, D. M. (1998). Countertransference considerations for the gay male when leading psychotherapy groups for gay men. *International Journal of Group Psychotherapy,* 48(1), 3–38.

Gartrell, N., Herman, J., Olarte, J., et al. (1986). Psychiatrist-patient sexual contact: results of a national survey. *American Journal of Psychiatry,* 138, 51–55.

Gay, P. (1988). *Freud: A Life for Our Time.* New York: Norton.

Genesis, 32 & Hosea, 12. Christian Bible, Revised Standard Version.

Goldberg, C. (1986). *On Being a Psychotherapist: The Journey of the Healer.* New York: Gardner.

Goldberg, C. (1992). *The Seasoned Psychotherapist: Triumph Over Adversity.* New York: Norton.

Greenson, R. R. (1978). The real relationship between the patient and the psychoanalyst. In R. R. Greenson (Ed.), *Explorations in Psychoanalysis* (pp. 425–440). New York: International Universities Press.

Halifax, J. (1990). The shaman's initiation. *Re-vision,* 13(2), 53–58.

Henry, W. E., Sims, J. H., & Spray, S. L. (1971). *The Fifth Profession: Becoming a Psychotherapist.* San Francisco: Jossey-Bass.

Henry, W. E., Sims, J. H., & Spray, S. L. (1973). *The Public and Private Lives of Psychotherapists.* San Francisco: Jossey-Bass.

Holmes, C. A. V. (1998). *The Wounded Healer.* London: Karnac Books.

Jackson, S. W. (2001). The wounded healer. *Bulletin of the History of Medicine,* 75(1), 1–36.

Jung, C. G. (1946). The psychology of the transference. In *Collected* Works (vol. 16, pp 163–323). Princeton, NJ: Princeton University Press.

Kirmayer, L. J. (2003). Asklepian dreams: The ethos of the wounded-healer in the clinical encounter. *Transcultural Psychiatry,* 40(2), 248–277.

Kurtz, S. (1983). *The Art of Unknowing.* Northvale, NJ: Jason Aronson.

Langs, R. (1979). *The Supervisory Experience.* New York: Jason Aronson.

Longfellow, H. W. (1850). "The Secret of the Sea." *The Seaside and the Fireside.* Cambridge.

Maniar, S. (1995). *Personality Characteristics of Psychotherapists and their Effect on Therapeutic Outcome*, Ph.D. Thesis, Institute of Clinical Psychology, University of Karachi, Karachi, Pakistan.

McDaniel, S. H., Hepworth, J. W.m & Doherty J. (1997). *The Shared Experience of Illness: Stories of Patients, Families, and Their Therapists*. New York: Basic Books.

Noonan, D. (2008). Doctors who kill themselves. *Newsweek*, April 28.

Ogden, T. H. (1982). *Projective Identification & Psychotherapeutic Technique*. New York: Jason Aronson.

Phillips, S. (1999). U.S. psychologists suicide rates have declined since 1960s. *Archives of Suicide Research*, 5, 11–26.

Rice, C. A, & Rutan, J. S. (1987). *Inpatient Group Psychotherapy*. New York: Macmillan.

Rice, C. A. (2008). Arriving where I started. *Group*, 32(2), 137–144.

Schernhammer, E. (2005). Taking their own lives—high rate of physician suicide. *New England Journal of Medicine*, 352, 2473–2476.

Sedgwick, D. (1994). *The Wounded Healer: Countertransference from a Jungian Perspective*. New York: Routledge.

Sedgwick, D. (2001). *An Introduction to Jungian Psychotherapy: The Therapeutic Relationship*. New York: Brunner-Routledge.

Silverman, J. (1967). Shamanism and schizophrenia. *American Anthropologist*, 69(2): 21–31.

Stolorow, R. D., & Atwood, G. D. (2002). *Contexts of Being: The Intersubjective Foundations of Psychological Life* (Psychoanalytic Inquiry Book Series, Vol. 12). New York: The Analytic Press.

Stolorow, R. D., Atwood, G. E., & Brandchaft, B. (1994). *The Intersubjective Perspective*. Northvale, NJ: Jason Aronson.

Stutley, M. (2002). *Shamanism: A Concise Introduction*, Routledge.

Summers, R. F., & Barber, J. P. (2009). *Psychodynamic Therapy: A Guide to Evidence-Based Practice*. New York: Guilford Press.

Sussman, M. B. (1992). *A Curious Calling: Unconscious Motivations for Practicing Psychotherapy*. Northvale, NJ: Aronson.

Van der Kolk, B. (1993). Groups for patients with histories of catastrophic trauma. In A. Alonso & H. I. Swiller (Eds.), *Group Therapy in Clinical Practice*. (pp. 289–305). Washington, D.C.: American Psychiatric Press.

Volkan, V. D. (2009). Some psychoanalytic views on leaders with narcissistic personality organization and their roles in large-group processes. In R. H. Klein, C. A. Rice, & V. E. Schermer (Eds.), *Leadership in a Changing World: Dynamic Perspectives on Groups and their Leaders* (93–118). New York: Lexington Books.

Volkan, V. D., Ast, G., & Greer, Jr., W. F. (2002). *The Third Reich in the Unconscious: Transgenerational Transmission and its Consequences*. New York: Brunner-Routledge.

Wachtel, P. L. (1986). From Neutrality to Personal Revelation: Patterns of Influence in the Analytic Relationship (A Symposium)—On the Limits of Therapeutic Neutrality. *Contemporary Psychoanalysis*, 22, 60–70, Psychoanalytic Electronic Publishing.

9

Has the Magic of Psychotherapy Disappeared? Integrating Evidence-Based Practice into Therapist Awareness and Development

Debra Theobald McClendon and Gary M. Burlingame

There is an *essential tension* (Kuhn, 1979) within the therapy process that requires clinicians to negotiate two dimensions of psychotherapy practice that on the surface appear contrary. The first is the creative interconnectedness between clinician and client that is difficult to objectively measure and study—we will call this the magic of psychotherapy (Bandler & Grinder, 1975). The second are technical features of treatment that are quantifiable and assessed by standardized outcome or process measures.

In this chapter we examine the tension in relation to its effect on therapist awareness and development. We propose a method for navigating the tension, practice-based evidence (PBE), in which clinicians use real-time data of their client's current functioning from a standardized measure to assist them in their clinical decision-making processes. Using PBE, we introduce case studies and discussion that illustrate how current requirements for accountability may lead to greater therapist anxiety and/or therapist awareness and growth. Cases in which clinicians used PBE for greater awareness and development illustrate the magic of psychotherapy.

As a note, this discussion is heavily laden with a variety of acronyms that may be unfamiliar. These acronyms, used regularly in the literature and in practice settings, are summarized in Table 9.1. Levant and Hasan (2008) recommended that graduate students and early career professionals become familiar with these terms and acronyms associated with evidence-based practice (EBP).

The Magic of Psychotherapy

Magic tends to be a taboo subject in Western culture, particularly within the field of psychology. Nevertheless, Bandler and Grinder produced two volumes called the *Structure of Magic* (Bandler & Grinder, 1975; Grinder & Bandler, 1976). These texts focus on the underlying structure of psychotherapy,

Table 9.1. Frequently Used Acronyms

Acronym	Meaning
EBP	Evidence-based practice
EBT	Evidence-based treatment
EST	Empirically supported treatment
HMO	Health maintenance organization
PBE	Practice-based evidence
PBT	Practice-based treatment
RCT	Randomized controlled trial
RST	Research-supported treatment

equating psychotherapy with magic. They began the first volume with this narrative:

> Down through the ages the power and wonder of practitioners of magic have been recorded…these people of power, wrapped in a cloak of secrecy, presented a striking contradiction to the common ways of dealing in the world…Whenever these people of power publicly performed their wonders, they would both shatter the concepts of reality of that time and place and present themselves as having something that was beyond learning. In modern time, the mantle of the wizard is most often placed upon those dynamic practitioners of psychotherapy who exceed the skill of other therapists by leaps and bounds, and whose work is so amazing to watch that it moves us with powerful emotions, disbelief, and utter confusion. (p. xiii)

Clark (2002) more recently offered this definition of *magic* relative to his work on group analysis: magic is an "experience of connectedness which is numinous, beautiful and profound…This interconnectedness allows for an exchange of influence which we might nowadays regard as magical" (pp. 74–76). He continued to explain that this interconnectedness allows room for "the blending of minds, of internal and external, which could be described as magical" (p. 85). As we speak herein of the magic of psychotherapy, our use of magic is consistent with Clark's. We do not speak of magic outside of practical or rational explanation, but of the creative connectedness that allows for a meaningful and enriching experience for clinician and client alike.

We want to directly challenge the belief that clinicians are unable to draw upon magical, creative, or intuitive processes with validated treatments, mandates of managed care companies or other administrative policies, and/or EBP. We do not believe that the magic of psychotherapy has disappeared, and we intend to integrate both herein.

Evidence-Based Practice

The movement toward EBP has become a key feature in health care systems and policies (APA, 2006). EBP is defined as "the integration of the best available research with clinical expertise in the context of patient characteristics, culture, and preferences" (p. 273). EBP provides a more comprehensive view of client treatment relative to empirically supported treatments (ESTs, formerly known as *empirically validated treatments*; Kazdin, 2008; Levant & Hasan, 2008; Wampold et al., 2007). In other words, the concepts of EBP and EST are not synonymous (Bauer, 2007; Leffingwell & Collins, 2008; Levant & Hasan, 2008; Luebbe et al., 2007; Spring, 2007).

ESTs are specific treatments that have shown efficacy in controlled clinical trials and take a nomothetic or general laws approach (i.e., diagnostic classification; Spring, 2007). In treating a specific client, a clinician using an EST identifies a particular treatment that has been shown to be empirically supported for the predominant disorder with which the client is struggling. ESTs include treatment manuals that outline how therapy is to be conducted, which often seem to leave out the magical aspects of psychotherapy. Schwartz and Flowers (2008) commented on the process of therapy undertaken from a manualized approach:

> Unfortunately, the topic of therapeutic creativity is largely missing from clinical training programs. More and more the field resembles that of medicine and at its worst—automobile repair. We learn to diagnose, assess, and to implement predetermined manualized treatment plans. Could it be that much of what we call therapist burnout relates to the lack of room for the creative act in doing therapy? (p. 48)

In contrast to using manualized treatments and EST approaches, the clinician using the *creative act* (Schwartz & Flowers, 2008) of psychotherapy looks not to a particular treatment initially, but to the client—a complex and textured person. The client's unique constellation of attributes guides the therapist to consider what research evidence may be most helpful to achieve the best outcome for the client (APA, 2006; Kazdin, 2008). EBP is an idiographic approach (i.e., pertaining to the study of individual cases) that "promotes lifelong learning" (Spring, 2007, p. 611). EBP encompasses a broader range of clinical activities than just the treatment intervention, and cannot be reduced to an EST (Spring, 2007). The function of EBP is to "promote effective psychological practice and enhance public health by applying empirically supported principles of psychological assessment, case formulation, therapeutic relationship, and intervention" (APA, 2005, p. 1).

EBP is a standard model across other professions, such as nursing, social work, and library science (Walker & London, 2007), providing opportunities for better interdisciplinary collaboration (Spring, 2007). The general process of EBP includes the following steps as outlined by Walker and London (2007):

1. Ask a clinically relevant question based on information needs.
2. Search for the best research evidence.

3. Evaluate the evidence that you discover.
4. Integrate the best evidence with clinical judgment and the client's circumstances. (Hunsley [2007] noted that to operate in the context of patient characteristics, culture, and preferences, as EBP proscribes, a clinician must inform the client of viable treatment options, such as assessment, prevention, or intervention services.)
5. Evaluate the outcome.

This movement toward EBP highlights the importance of clinical expertise in the psychotherapy process. Kazdin (2008) stated:

Those coming from a strict research perspective often lament the term EBP because there is…not much in the way of evidence that draws on and modifies the application of these treatments in light of clinical judgment, expertise, and contextual considerations in practice. Therapy will invariably involve judgment and experience. We may always want evidence seasoned by experience and clinical judgment; when the evidence is unusually weak or barely existent, we want experience seasoned by evidence. (p. 155)

EBP supports the development of clinical expertise as it promotes life-long learning for the clinician. Varra et al. (2008) indicated that learning new treatments and treatment processes is challenging in and of itself; experienced clinicians may find themselves as they felt as new therapists—anxious about lacking in such areas of confidence, clinical certainty, and skill. Clinicians will need to negotiate those reactions as they arise throughout the EBP process. For example, Hunsley (2007) indicated that the simplest part of EBP may be gathering the evidence, but for some this may be a daunting expectation that requires the development of new skills. A new literature called *systematic reviews* has emerged to assist clinicians in this information-gathering process. These articles gather, evaluate, and synthesize primary studies in a systematic fashion with higher scientific rigor than a standard literature review (Walker & London, 2007). Web sites for accessing these systematic reviews or other resources (such as setting up alerts to receive updated information) are provided by Walker and London (2007); interested readers are referred to their text. Gathering evidence in this manner is one way that promotes lifelong learning for clinicians.

Gathering evidence does not ensure the practice of EBP; indeed, that is only the beginning of the process. Clinical expertise is required to know how to use the evidence in the treatment of a specific client (Hunsley, 2007). It can be challenging when the client's characteristics and presenting problems are complex and the research does not appear relevant, or there is little or no research available. In this situation, the clinician is encouraged to gather the most pertinent research and then develop a treatment that addresses the client's concerns, modifying when needed.

Some have begun to use the term "evidence-based treatment" (EBT) as a synonym for EBP (c.f., Hunsley, 2007). This term has become confused with ESTs and practice guidelines that present strategies for client care (Burlingame

& Beecher, 2008). To clarify the confusion, some researchers have now adopted the term "research-supported treatment" (RST) to discuss ESTs, referring to specific treatments that have been shown to be efficacious for specific disorders in randomized controlled trials (RCTs; see Johnson, 2008). This allows EBT to remain on a synonymous level with EBP. Thus, EBP/EBT is a decision-making *process* that integrates a variety of evidence into treatment, rather than simply a noun representing a particular RST treatment (APA, 2006; Johnson, 2008; Leffingwell & Collins, 2008).

Impact of EBP in Areas of Diversity and Training

Practicing in culturally competent ways with clients from diverse backgrounds constitutes ethical practice, yet RSTs are generally not sensitive to multicultural differences. Burlingame and Beecher (2008) outlined difficulties in using standard RST protocols with multicultural populations. There is an absence of theory for culturally relevant treatments that are found to be effective. There is a lack of data regarding how combinations of cultural factors (gender, ethnicity, or sexual orientation), psychopathology, and context (rural, urban, academic, or psychiatric) affect how a specific client may relate to a treatment. Also, establishing culturally relevant definitions of what constitutes change is problematic. Furthermore, there are few assessment measures normed for multicultural populations.

With these limitations, it becomes clear that clinicians attempting to work from an EBP framework with clients from diverse populations will encounter significant difficulty, since these challenges are each relevant to the EBP operational step of gathering relevant evidence. Chen et al. (2008) indicated that therapists have to adapt and modify existing evidence and/or EBP models. This may include adjusting the manner in which treatment and/or specific interventions are delivered; making changes in the nature of the therapeutic relationship; or changing specific treatment components in order to accommodate the beliefs, behaviors, or culture of diverse clients. Thus, clinical judgment, as explicated in the EBP definition, becomes paramount in creating an EBP with multicultural clients.

Current training programs do not appear to fully prepare clinicians for consistent practice from an evidence-based perspective. Researchers examining graduate programs' instruction of EBP found that many students could not define EBP and commonly, yet mistakenly, equated EBP with ESTs (Luebbe et al., 2007; Spring, 2007). Graduate training programs appear strong in teaching the use of evidence through research methodology, statistics, and the study of RSTs. However, Spring (2007) recommended teaching additional skill sets for becoming research evidence creators, evidence synthesizers, and evidence consumers. In like manner, Bauer (2007) suggested new content, such as epidemiology, clinical trials methodology, qualitative research methods, measurement, performing and evaluating systematic reviews and meta-analyses, and skill sets involved with database searching and information gathering. These changes would more fully prepare trainees to practice EBP consistently, ethically, and with a variety of diverse populations.

Practice-Based Evidence Approach to RST

Burlingame and Beecher (2008) discussed three models for defining *evidence-based*: RSTs, practice guidelines, and practice-based evidence (PBE). RSTs and practice guidelines have been briefly introduced. PBE is a newer term that describes "real-time patient outcomes being delivered to clinicians immediately before treatment sessions so that they can make decisions about effective interventions based on current patient status" (p. 1200). This particular definition is the focus herein in the context of integrating EBP into therapist awareness and development.

Wampold et al. (2007) stated that the EBP policy is "remarkably inclusive of various perspectives while remaining unambiguous about the need to use evidence in a way that leads to effective services" (p. 618). Although therapists will continue to practice from a variety of theoretical orientations, they can integrate evidence into their practice by the use of systematic, pan-theoretical measures to evaluate client progress. Wampold et al. stated that "monitoring patient progress should be informed by state-of-the-art methodological, theoretical, and empirical considerations" (p. 617). When clinicians gather PBE and apply the data to their treatment, the process may be called *practice-based treatment* (PBT).

Some clinicians may object to the use of this type of monitoring evidence. They may view this process as intrusive or disruptive to their practice. They may also be mandated to do so by administrative policies or managed care companies, which may prompt clinician frustration or resistance. With managed care's significant influence in this area, we turn now to a brief discussion of its influence on the field. This discussion provides context for later discussion on how PBE, even when its use may be mandated, can be used by clinicians seeking professional growth and development to enhance their practice.

Managed Care

Managed care represents an effort to provide quality health care while containing the spiraling costs of treatment (Broskowski, 1991; DeLeon et al., 1991; Kiesler & Morton, 1988). Managed care may be defined as any form of peer review, case management, or other such activities that assist in meeting those two goals. An organization that uses several means to manage care is a health maintenance organization (HMO; Broskowski, 1991). PBE is one resource these companies use in setting administrative policy and making decisions (Brown et al., 2001, 2005; Lambert & Burlingame, 2007; Wampold & Brown, 2005).

Although managed care offers the advantage of a referral base for clientele to practicing clinicians, the presence and influence of managed care produces some areas of concern important to clinicians. Managed care strategies seem to represent variations on a single theme—that therapists conduct "externally mandated brief therapy" (Stern, 1993, p. 162). Some have been concerned that there has been less attention from managed care companies at improving quality and access to health care than there has been on containing costs (Broskowski, 1991; DeLeon et al., 1991; Stern, 1993). Buie (1989) argued that HMOs do not provide psychotherapy, but instead provide only a few hours of *crisis intervention*.

Bukloh and Roberts (2001) found that psychologists endorsed fairly negative attitudes in regards to managed care, with private practice clinicians reporting significantly more negative attitudes than did those working in hospital settings. Dissatisfaction was present in areas of ethics and finances, quality of clinical treatment, and general work conditions. Surveyed psychologists largely believed communication with the managed care company violates confidentiality and that managed care limited treatment length or promoted client abandonment. Also, psychologists believed managed care policies promote misdiagnosis, since treatment is excluded or limited from managed care payment for some diagnoses. Yet Bukloh and Roberts (2001) found that negative attitudes about managed care did not affect the ethical decision-making process of their surveyed clinicians.

Training programs appear to be adequately preparing new psychologists to work with managed care by teaching students to competently provide brief therapeutic interventions, and offering study in areas of ethics, diversity issues, and outcome assessment (Cantor & Fuentes, 2008). Outcome assessment is particularly important for preparing trainees to navigate work with managed care.

Local Clinical Scientist Use of PBE

The burden of proof regarding the quality of treatment continues to rest upon the clinicians as treatment providers (DeLeon et al., 1991). Nevertheless, the use of evidence by a creative clinician creates an opportunity for growth and development. PBE is intended to complement clinical judgment for improving client care (Burlingame et al., 2006; Schwartz & Flowers, 2008). Kazdin (2008) commented that the "best practice will continue to be based on the best science" (p. 157) and maintained that the use of systematic measures does not replace clinical judgment. Indeed, the work of integrating evidence into practice uses the clinician-as-instrument:

> Even the most research-informed therapist is constantly forced to rely on existing theory, personal clinical experience, and the cumulative clinical

wisdom in the field when making specific therapeutic judgments and decisions. Indeed, the capacity to make such judgments is at the heart of what it means to be a professional in a scientifically based discipline.

(Stern, 1993, p. 163)

Commentators have noted that researchers have yet to help clinicians learn to integrate evidence with their clinical expertise to inform their decision-making process (Hoagwood, 2002; Kazdin, 2008). Indeed, although informed by research, EBP continues to leave much of the treatment process to the clinical judgment of the therapist. Yet if EBP is examined from the perspective of PBE, the work of researchers to offer real-time data to clinicians over the past two decades shows that researchers have been working to assist clinicians in this integration process (c.f., Burlingame et al., 1995; Lambert, 2007).

The Youth Outcome Questionnaire (Y-OQ) is one example of a standardized, brief measure that can provide clinicians with evidence to inform their practice. It is one of a family of measures that has been developed by researchers at Brigham Young University in collaboration with several managed care organizations that oversee health care throughout the western United States (Burlingame et al., 2001). Although the Y-OQ may not be familiar to some, it was highlighted by Kazdin (2005) in his commentary on evidence-based assessment as an illustration of a child and adolescent measurement option.

The Y-OQ is completed by a child's parent or caregiver, and also by self-report if the child is an adolescent. The measure is scored via a computer scoring program; results provide both descriptive and inferential information to clinicians about their client's current functioning. Figure 9.1 is an example of a Y-OQ clinician report. The descriptive data specify the content and severity of the client's level of distress. The inferential information indicates whether the client's progress is or is not following the expected trajectory for improvement based on previous research studies, making the science behind the measure immediately available to clinicians and helping them bypass some of the lag-time from research to clinical incorporation of results. This information is provided to clinicians in a feedback paragraph beneath the report.

Using PBE, such as data from the Y-OQ, to develop an EBP provides several advantages for clinicians, as outlined by McClendon (2009). First, this evidence provides an intake measure of current functioning, initial severity, and an index of risk factors. These data support the therapist in conceptualization, developing treatment plans, and assessing prognosis. Second, observing the data over repeated administrations allows a clinician to track client change. Third, a standardized measure can provide outside validation of clinical judgment, which can aid practitioners in providing better services for their clients. For example, if the data show deterioration in client functioning, the clinician can assess and perhaps alter the current course of treatment;

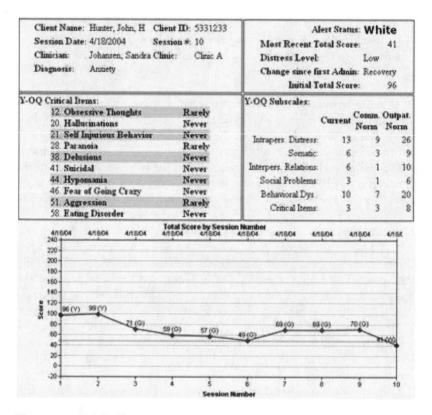

Figure 9.1. Y-OQ Clinician Report.

the data alert the clinician to things he or she may have missed. Fourth, by analyzing data from their own clients, clinicians can make decisions about the effectiveness of their own delivery of psychotherapeutic services. And, finally, gathering PBE by the use of outcome or other such measures represents a more ethical practice. These opportunities afforded to clinicians by PBE allow them to become *local clinical scientists* (Stricker & Trierweiler, 1995), clinicians who use their own attitudes, knowledge base, and observations to address the clinical problems of their clients. These clinicians are constantly learning and improving.

The selection of a measure for use in a PBE approach requires careful consideration, as also reviewed by McClendon (2009). A measure should have excellent reliability and validity. It should be normed so clinicians can assess the clinical significance of treatment effects and allow for frequent use to track progress or monitor treatment. It should be brief, easily scored and interpreted, and inexpensive. The items should be sensitive to client symptomatic and behavioral changes that occur with treatment and provide relevant information so they are practical and helpful to the clinician. Clinicians should obtain adequate training for their selected measure through manuals, seminars, or peer consultation to increase ethical and competent practice.

Therapist Awareness and Development

As seen, PBE allows clinicians to satisfy administrative, managed care, and EBP mandates while also promoting lifelong learning. Lifelong learning contributes to therapist awareness and development. Awareness that leads to development requires therapists to continue a mindful and intentional approach to their practice. Awareness in this sense is a keen understanding of oneself as a clinician and of the work of psychotherapy. It is a broad concept that includes understanding of interventions, client issues, and personal and professional stages of development. Clinicians are then able to use the insights gained from their awareness to improve their clinical intuition and skills with their clients.

Vinton (2008) interviewed seasoned psychoanalysts about their development as therapists. The most consistent theme that emerged was that of the importance of integration—integration of ideas, experiences, therapy styles, and theories. Vinton emphasized that one's ability to conduct critical self-reflection is crucial to this integration process. Nuttall (2008) also advocated the importance of integration in therapist awareness and development. He encouraged clinicians to question, invent, research, and even *interrogate* the psychology discipline in their own personal journey and development as a therapist. Integrating personal experience into one's learning as a clinician also provides a vibrant resource. For example, such experiences as participating in formal and informal groups (Nicholas, 2008), personal therapy (Daw & Joseph, 2007), parenting a child in crisis (Slattery & Park, 2007), debilitating illness (Stratton, 2007), and death of a child (Callahan & Dittloff, 2007) have been recently reported as having a significant influence on the development of clinicians.

Vinton (2008) identified three additional themes in the development of psychoanalytic therapists. First, she found that receptivity to new ideas created vulnerability in the therapists' developmental process. Clinicians were influenced by others in the training process and often felt hesitant or doubtful of their abilities in the process. Second, organizing ideas and experience, such as with a theory or concept, was important to provide structure through the development process. Third, the prevalence of the clinicians' use of creativity (writing, teaching, composing music or playing musical instruments, singing, dancing, painting, and acting) was an important theme in the development of clinicians. These creative endeavors became extended metaphors in their psychoanalytic work, in addition to helping them create a more balanced sense of self.

PBE as a Tool for Therapist Awareness and Development

Therapist-as-tool is an important principle that could easily be lost in discussions of managed care, where the therapist may feel that he or she is little more than a technician applying RSTs. However, EBP requires more personal involvement of the therapist, involvement that requires a great deal of insight and self-examination. It may be said that it sets a higher standard for practice. EBP promotes lifelong learning and is entirely consistent with perspectives that place a greater emphasis on the role of the therapist in the psychotherapy process.

Schwartz and Flowers (2008) stated that therapy is a process of delayed gratification, with the therapist always waiting for reinforcement or feedback. To expedite the process they recommended: "Use client satisfaction surveys and short assessment tools. Brief scales...can provide direct positive feedback (and useful negative feedback as well) on the progress of therapy and the quality of the client-therapist relationship" (p. 71). This recommendation captures the essence of PBE as a tool for therapist awareness and development.

A cardinal consideration in the scientific method is designing a method for testing and falsifying one's theory. In short, a scientist asks: "How would I know if I am wrong?" PBE, or the use of ongoing monitoring of treatment, offers the same benefit for the clinician as he or she works with clients. PBE is a method for knowing when one is right and when one is wrong by exposing to view another source of information in at least three illustrative ways. First, the measure monitors symptoms a clinician may not inquire about regularly in session. Second, it may be easier for some clients to endorse an item on a measure than to share with the clinician critical information such as, "I've been having more thoughts of suicide" or "I've been drinking more." In essence, PBE functions as a co-therapist, gathering information about the client from a different perspective and through a different modality. Third, the data may also corroborate information the clinician has gathered, underscoring the importance of that issue for the client and encouraging mindful attention from the clinician. With data in hand, the clinician then uses his or her expertise to utilize it within the therapy process. PBE does not supplant clinician awareness and wisdom; rather, it supplements it.

A poem written by Greening (2006) highlights one therapist's desire for assistance in his work with his clients:

Empirically Validated Psychotherapy
What works in psychotherapy?
That's far beyond the likes of me.
I've only practiced fifty years,
and still am plagued by doubts and fears.
I muddle on and try my best
to aid my clients in their quest

for ways of being more alive,
somehow in spite of all to thrive.
I wish I knew the right technique
to give them more of what they seek.
The mystery of change persists
unsolved by dogged scientists.
I hope that they will soon impart
quick ways to heal a broken heart.
My efforts stagger, balk, and lurch
unguided by precise research
to tell me how to ease life's pains,
and thus flawed intuition reigns.
Pray science soon will guarantee
sure cures for human misery,
but meanwhile I'll do what I can
without a validated plan.

PBE is the tool, the *validated plan* (Greening, 2006), that researchers
have to offer such clinicians. PBE is applicable to the four clinician development themes from the Vinton (2008) study. First, it provides a source of
information for the process of integration. Second, it creates an opportunity
for personal knowledge and insight that may create feelings of vulnerability
yet enhance learning. Third, the data provide a structure or a framework for
aiding clinicians in organizing their ideas. Fourth, the use of PBE represents
a creative endeavor when seeking to utilize and integrate data within real-
time clinical work (Vinton, 2008).

An illustration of the second theme may be instructive. PBE aggregate
data can show a clinician that he or she tends to produce good outcomes with
certain clients (anxiety) but poorer outcomes with others (eating disorders).
Armed with this information, a therapist can maximize his or her strengths
and address weakness through continued education. Awareness may also
serve to alert clinicians to the need for personal healing: perhaps their difficulty with eating-disordered clients reflects a countertransference issue that
needs to be explored.

Uses of PBE

There may be uncertainty or even resistance to the use of PBE in establishing
an EBP. According to Kivlighan (2008), the process of creative discussion
allows any resistance to EBP to be addressed. What follows is a glimpse into
a series of discussions that were held with clinicians, administrators, and Gary
Burlingame, developer of the Y-OQ. These discussions followed a statewide
mandate to use outcome measures in a community mental health system.
Clinicians were required to administer an instrument to clients at every session.

The portions of discussion presented here illustrate how resistance was reduced and clinicians integrated the magic of psychotherapy while using a mandated evidence-based procedure.

This first discussion illustrates how one fairly resistant clinician began to get interested in using data from his clients after hearing other therapists talk about their cases. It then shows how he also worked with others to help them become more receptive to using PBE even when they felt compelled (and frustrated) by administrative policies to implement its usage.

From "What's the Use" to Usefulness

Clinic administrator: I'm curious, and this is kind of a process question to you, but you're kind of fairly new to using [outcome measures to guide your practice]. What's your experience so far? Is it useful for you?

Resistant clinician: After sitting in here, honestly, and truly honest, it was like, "What are we doing this for? What's the utility?" And after our first meeting I said, "OK. Let's give it a shot." So I've been trying to collect more often with them and get into the habit of doing it on a regular basis.

Clinic administrator: And now that you're giving it a shot?

Resistant clinician: I'm thinking that it can be useful to gauge what's going on with [my client], you know if you use it on a regular basis and you learn how to interpret the data. So, that's what I'm trying to do.

Clinic administrator: I really appreciate you sharing this. I know you're not an easy buy, is that fair to say?

Resistant clinician: You know, I'm not into doing things for the sake of doing things.

Clinic administrator: And I mean that as a positive, you're asking questions, but what excites me is with the administrative push, we get kind of the resisted compliance, you know it's, "Yeah we have to do this or…"

Resistant clinician: "Well, what's the purpose of it?" That is the whole thing.

Clinic administrator: But when you started talking about it and saying maybe we should try it, you weren't convinced yourself of the purpose for it. But all of a sudden the therapists, knowing that you're a tough customer in a lot of ways, said, "Let's get with it and give it another shot."…

Test developer: I learned something from you today… There were two or three of us last time that went through some cases… and what I learned was you listening and watching what other people were doing was…

Resistant clinician: It made some sense.

Test developer: Yeah, it was sufficient. It had nothing to do with research, it had to do with, "Well, [the Creative Clinician] is making sense of this." So that's, I think, an important message.…

Clinic administrator: If I may ask another question, how did the other therapists that you kind of basically enticed, if you will, to use the instrument…respond to using it?

Resistant clinician: Well, I think they're trying to learn how to use it too. They're trying to look at what is useful…I took in some of the graphs here and showed one of the other school-based therapists…I think, they're going, "Oh, OK. So there is something I can discern from this. We just have to learn how." And I haven't gone through the manuals yet either, but I think if we go through the manuals and distribute those to everybody and teach them how to use them, then it will be even more useful.

After initial resistance to using PBE, this clinician was able to begin to see the usefulness of the data as he heard other clinicians talk about their experiences. As he began to work more intentionally with the data for his own clients, he then began to share the process with other clinicians as well. This discussion also underscores the importance of gaining competence in *how* to use the evidence through study of manuals and collaboration.

Once a clinician has worked through any resistance to using evidence in practice, as the resistant clinician demonstrated, the benefits of PBE are easily observed. For example, although repeated administrations are desirable, a clinician who administers a measure only one time may still derive benefit. The following dialogue shows how a clinician who worked in a short-term clinical setting benefitted from viewing data from a single administration.

Helpfulness of Only One Score

One-score clinician: He got a score of 79, and then it was "what problems were 'frequent' and 'always' and stuff?"…and they were basically his diagnoses. They were substance abuse, that's what he does, hypomania and he has ADHD, and they were aggression and he's always getting into fights. So the score he got that one time was exactly what his issues are.
Test developer:… A single administration is descriptive information, right?
One-score clinician: And he got "frequent" on delusions, and he has tons of thick hairs in how he sees them.
One-score clinician: Yeah, he is totally honest. He'll say, "I smoke every other day. I do this, and I don't think there's any point to…"
Test developer:… a single assessment that can be useful to get a glimpse into whether someone really has insight?
One-score clinician: Yeah, even if it's just the number, 79, somebody's having some problems. Most people wouldn't be there if it were low. It's a crisis going on.
Test developer:… So it's almost a measure of the mental health vital sign distress.

Being willing to consider the client's score and review answers to specific questions from one assessment, the therapist was able to increase awareness of the client's level of insight into his own symptoms and behaviors. Understanding a client's level of insight may significantly influence the approach a clinician takes to treatment.

The next dialogue illustrates how the use of evidence from repeated measures allows clinicians many of the benefits of PBE already discussed. Clinicians versed in the use of such instruments often do *not* feel the use of the measures to be intrusive or disruptive, but an integral part of their treatment process. This creative clinician was trained in a graduate program that regularly used standardized measures. Her comfort with using data, and even relying on the data as a co-therapist, assisted her with a client with whom she discussed the questionnaire at the beginning of each treatment session.

Repeated Measures Creativity

Creative clinician: This client came in—severe depression, teenage girl, and just you know kind of classic depression, tells herself negative things about herself all the time…

Clinic administrator:… And I thought that was fascinating, number one, in terms of getting some concrete feedback for both of you. It's like, "Here's the data." The client got really excited seeing the results as an accurate reflection of where she is…

Creative clinician: Yes, the results are part of the dialogue throughout the session.

Clinic administrator: Actually it's part of the intervention. You structured your intervention around it. "Let's talk about it when you're at a 50." So part of her is kind of… like, "Boy, I want to talk about it, but I'm also not quite sure when, so [my therapist] is going to play part in it by telling me when I'm below [a critical point], and that's when I'll be ready." So the [data] became a vital part of the actual treatment plan…Do you think you could have been therapeutically as far with her without that instrument?

Creative clinician: Oh, no. I don't think so because… she's not a good reporter…it gave me a lot to talk about that I wouldn't have known at all if I hadn't been using the [measure]. Or at least you know at this point, I might not have known things were better, it might have felt like everything was flat-line and nothing was getting better, and I wouldn't have had that conversation, "Why aren't you getting better?"…

This dialogue reveals more of the magic of psychotherapy. This creative clinician used the data in a way not conceived by researchers—as a therapeutic intervention! She integrated the data into her therapy style and relied on it to assist both her and her client in knowing when to take certain therapeutic steps. She ascertained that she was able to make greater therapeutic progress with her client than she would have been able to achieve with her clinical skills alone.

There are some challenges afforded by PBE that give rise to therapist ingenuity. For example, PBE may not always appear to give valid information. However, even in such scenarios, discovering this challenge still enhances therapist awareness. In the following scenario, the very act of administering a questionnaire helped a mindful clinician to understand and conceptualize the true abilities of her lower-functioning client.

When the Data Are Not Trusted

Mindful clinician:… this is an example of someone who scores are either "almost always" or "never." And I see him when he does it, scroll right down the sides. And I've taken him aside and talked about how to fill it out. I've tried to explain it to him, and he doesn't get it…But it's really not valid; it's completely invalid.

Administering the measure became a way for this clinician to observe and become mindful of her client's abilities. She then evaluated the value of the data appropriately.

Furthermore, if valid data are obtained, it is not always accurate; it is limited by the perspectives and personal issues of the informant. A clinician who is operating with little critical examination or intentionality may be misled by PBE if he or she observes a score yet does not verify its accuracy with the client or the informant. Nonetheless, it is not uncommon for a clinician to distrust the data based on clinical expertise, yet still, with some creative artistry, be able to glean valuable information that influences case conceptualization and treatment planning. For example, in the following dialogue the data provided by a mother were not accurate representations of her daughter's symptoms, but they did provide the therapist information about the mother's inability to deal with the problems she had created for her daughter.

When the Data Teach Something Else

Creative clinician:…a mom that came in with a little girl, probably about 5, that the girl had witnessed a lot of domestic violence, Mom used drugs. So Mom had major guilt about everything she had exposed her daughter to—Mom using meth, Mom being in a domestically violent relationship—severe domestic violence, like bad stuff this little girl witnessed. Mom completed the Y-OQ for her daughter, giving her a 21 [a score below average for untreated community normals]. It was not accurate. What I saw as progress was that Mom's score went up. For Mom to get to a point where she could be less guilt-ridden and report a more realistic and accurate set of symptoms for her daughter, that's when I knew we were in business.
Test developer:…would you say anything to Mom about the low scores…?
Creative clinician: I said, here's what that means. Usually kids that we see come in here for the first time are more like 70. So that's kind of low. I don't think I checked in with her as much as I do with other clients, because it was so low. I noticed when it was going up and said…, "I think you're doing a lot better. I think you're answering more realistically now and you're less afraid to say that there's problems and more willing to be open."

Test developer:... there may be times when a low score is just something that we note and don't make a deal about.

Creative clinician:..... . I think it was guilt for what she'd put her daughter through. If she comes in and says, "My daughter's at an 80—I did that to her." She was just unable to own up to this. And so for her [scores] to go up, showed Mom could be more realistic, meaning she could respond appropriately when her daughter says, "I had a nightmare that Dad was trying to kill you."

In this example, the creative clinician invited the mother into the therapy process. Although the score for the client was not accurate, it was correct as an indicator of the mother's reality testing. This seemed to prove helpful in the clinician's case conceptualization and work with the mother–daughter relationship. For other cases in which the informant is the client, evidence that does not appear accurate can heighten a clinician's awareness regarding client resistance, lack of insight, or the need to seek additional information from another source, such as a parent, teacher, or spouse.

Potential Problems with the Use of PBE

PBE may create some challenges to clinician awareness and development by increasing anxiety over performance and outcomes. Okiishi et al. (2003) suggested that examining therapist effects and searching for empirically supported therapists was more important than identifying RSTs. They rank-ordered clinicians relative to the outcomes of their clients and called top-performing therapists *supershrinks* and poorly performing therapists *pseudoshrinks* (p. 371). They advocated providing this type of performance data to individual clinicians to promote discussion and training. For clinicians who are willing to lean into the vulnerability, this could be an opportunity to increase awareness and further their development as a clinician. However, there seem to be some potential problems to using the evidence in this manner: for example, licensing boards could sanction poorly performing therapists, managed care organizations could pay clinicians based on outcomes, or administrators could limit clinical opportunities for clinicians (Okiishi et al., 2003; Wampold & Brown, 2005).

PBE could also be used by organizations to justify excluding clients from continuing therapy who do not seem to be making therapeutic gains, as defined by their selected measurement tool (Haas & Cummings, 1991). Though it does not appear that managed care currently uses PBE in this manner, the possibility concerns clinicians and was expressed by the resistant clinician.

Recognizing Potential Problems

Resistant clinician: The danger would be if they score below a certain level for six sessions in a row, "why are you continuing treatment,"...If they come up, if they use this to determine who's going to get treatment and who's not, that could become a real problem...

This use of PBE could undermine the role of the therapist. If a client is not progressing based on scores from an assessment instrument, the therapist's helpfulness to the client may be misrepresented. Indeed, the therapist may be competent and insightful and the client making significant personal gains, yet the scores may not reflect the degree of psychological work occurring in the therapy process due to limitations in the assessment instrument.

Beecher (2008) described "... feeling many of the doubts and concerns common among practitioners who believe that evidence-based practice means more hassle, imposition of researcher-driven 'lists,' limited utility, and threat to one's self as a competent (if not 'above average') therapist" (p. 1279). However, he further commented that his fears about PBE have not been validated as he has used standardized questionnaires in his own practice. He also stated that the data have helped inform his practice and contributed to his awareness of client needs. We propose that PBE is a tool that largely influences clinician awareness and development positively, despite the aforementioned challenges or potential problems, because therapists are moved to negotiate and overcome the challenges in creative, magical ways.

The Magic of Psychotherapy Revisited

Bandler and Grinder (1975) quoted *The Magus* by John Fowles, which presented a discussion between a prince and his king father. In this dialogue, the prince declared: "I must know the truth, the truth beyond the magic." To this, the king replied: "There is no truth beyond the magic" (p. xv). We disagree: the truth beyond the magic is present and thriving. As seen in the case examples, clinicians using PBE, even when constrained by mandate, use data in creative ways to enhance interconnectedness between themselves and their clients. They are finding a way to negotiate the *essential tension* as described by Kuhn (1979):

> [O]nly investigations firmly rooted in contemporary scientific tradition are likely to break that tradition and give rise to a new one. That is why I speak of an "essential tension" implicit in scientific research. To do his job the scientist must undertake a complex set of intellectual and manipulative commitments. Yet his claim to fame, if he has the talent and good luck to gain one, may finally rest upon his ability to abandon this net of commitments in favor of another of his own invention. Very often the successful scientist must simultaneously display the characteristics of the traditionalist and of the iconoclast. (p. 227)

As we have shown, clinicians have the burden of integrating research and clinical practice. This integration is crucial and lies at the heart of what may be termed *expertise*. The clinical expert is called upon to negotiate the world of magical artistry and rigorous scientific evidence to maximize treatment outcomes, enhance awareness of personal issues that may need examination, increase awareness of the need for consultation or professional training, and facilitate the development of an ethical and evidence-based practice in psychology. This is not a technical, mundane process, but a vibrant creative undertaking by local clinical scientists (Stricker & Trierweiler, 1995) who are seeking to improve client welfare and grow professionally.

This magical undertaking, supported by the use of PBE, encourages therapist awareness and development and allows for greater depths of interconnectedness with clients. These principles are important for all clinicians, regardless of professional status. For trainees or early career professionals, PBE becomes an important guidepost as skills are obtained and mastered. For more seasoned clinicians, PBE offers tremendous value without requiring therapists to change the way they conceptualize or execute their treatment approach. It is like having an independent, pan-theoretical co-therapist who does not have personal needs that must be recognized and negotiated! PBE provides a wealth of data, the meaning of which is only beginning to be explored. To undertake a full exploration of what the evidence has to offer, clinicians are encouraged and invited to be inquisitive, creative, and playful. As clinicians courageously look at the data and take a stance of wonder, they can examine the message about their clinical practice: "I wonder what this says about me? I wonder what it reveals about my preconceived ideas of the therapy process? I wonder how I might be wrong?" This type of questioning, supported by data from PBE and other evidence in EBP, provides fertile ground for insight, awareness, and growth for students, early career professionals, and seasoned clinicians alike.

References

American Psychological Association (APA). (2005). *Policy Statement on Evidence-Based Practice in Psychology*. Retrieved June 6, 2008, from http://www2.apa.org/practice/ebpstatement.pdf.

American Psychological Association (APA). Presidential Task Force on Evidence-Based Practice. (2006). Evidence-based practice in psychology. *American Psychologist*, 61, 271–285.

Bandler, R., & Grinder, J. (1975). *The Structure of Magic* (Vol. 1). Palo Alto, CA: Science and Behavior Books.

Bauer, R. M. (2007). Evidence-based practice in psychology: Implications for research and research training. *Journal of Clinical Psychology*, 63, 685–694.

Beecher, M. E. (2008). A clinician's take on evidence-based group psychotherapy: A commentary. *Journal of Clinical Psychology: In Session*, 64, 1279–1283.

Broskowski, A. (1991). Current mental health care environments: Why managed care is necessary. *Professional Psychology: Research and Practice*, 22, 6–14.

Brown, G. S., Burlingame, G. M., Lambert, M. J., Jones, E., & Vaccaro, J. (2001). Pushing the quality envelope: A new outcomes management system. *Psychiatric Services*, 52, 925–934.

Brown, G. S., Lambert, M. J., Jones, E. R., & Minami, T. (2005). Identifying highly effective psychotherapists in a managed care environment. *American Journal of Managed Care*, 11, 513–520.

Bukloh, L. M., & Roberts, M. C. (2001). Managed mental health care: Attitudes and ethical beliefs of child and pediatric psychologists. *Journal of Pediatric Psychology*, 26, 193–202.

Burlingame, G., & Beecher, M. (2008). New directions and resources in group psychotherapy: Introduction to the issue. *Journal of Clinical Psychology: In Session*, 64, 1197–1205.

Burlingame, G. M., Lambert, M. J., Reisinger, C. W., Neff, W. L., & Mosier, J. I. (1995). Pragmatics of tracking mental health outcomes in a managed care setting. *Journal of Mental Health Administration*, 22, 226–236.

Burlingame, G. M., Mosier, J. I., Wells, M. G., Atkin, Q. G., Lambert, M. J., Whoolery, M., et al. (2001). Tracking the influence of mental health treatment: The development of the Youth Outcome Questionnaire. *Clinical Psychology and Psychotherapy*, 8, 361–379.

Burlingame, G.M., Strauss, B., Joyce, A., MacNair-Semands, R., MacKenzie, K.R., Ogrodniczuk, J., et al. (2006). *CORE Battery-Revised: An Assessment Tool Kit for Promoting Optimal Group Selection, Process, and Outcome*. New York: American Group Psychotherapy Association.

Buie, J. (1989, November). Managed care debate covers pros and cons. *APA Monitor*, 20, p. 21.

Callahan, J. L., & Dittloff, M. (2007). Through a glass darkly: Reflections on therapist transformations. *Professional Psychology: Research and Practice*, 38, 547–553.

Cantor, D. W., & Fuentes, M. A. (2008). Psychology's response to managed care. *Professional Psychology: Research and Practice*, 39, 638–645.

Chen, E. C., Kakkad, D., & Balzano, J. (2008). Multicultural competence and evidence-based practice in group therapy. *Journal of Clinical Psychology: In Session*, 64, 1261–1278.

Clark, A. (2002). Interconnectedness and the magic of group analysis. *Group Analysis*, 35, 73–88.

Daw, B., & Joseph, S. (2007). Qualified therapists' experience of personal therapy. *Counselling and Psychotherapy Research*, 7, 227–232.

DeLeon, P. H., VandenBos, G. R., & Bulatao, E. Q. (1991). Managed mental health care: A history of the federal policy initiative. *Professional Psychology: Research and Practice*, 22, 15–25.

Grinder, J., & Bandler, R. (1976). *The Structure of Magic* (Vol. 2). Palo Alto, CA: Science and Behavior Books.

Greening, T. (2006). *Empirically Validated Psychotherapy: A Poem*. Retrieved August 4, 2009, from http://www.psychotherapy.net/article/Existential_Poems.

Haas, L. J., & Cummings, N. A. (1991). Managed outpatient mental health plans: Clinical, ethical, and practical guidelines for participation. *Professional Psychology: Research and Practice*, 22, 45–51.

Hoagwood, K. (2002). Making the translation from research application: The *je ne sais pas* of evidence-based practices. *Clinical Psychology: Science and Practice*, 9, 210–213.

Hunsley, J. (2007). Addressing key challenges in evidence-based practice in psychology. *Professional Psychology: Research and Practice*, 38, 113–121.

Johnson, J. (2008). Using research-supported group treatments. *Journal of Clinical Psychology*, 64, 1206–1224.

Kazdin, A. E. (2005). Evidence-based assessment for children and adolescents: Issues in measurement development and clinical application. *Journal of Clinical Child and Adolescent Psychology*, 34, 548–558.

Kazdin, A. E. (2008). Evidence-based treatment and practice: New opportunities to bridge clinical research and practice, enhance knowledge base, and improve patient care. *American Psychologist*, 63, 146–159.

Kiesler, C. A., & Morton, T. L. (1988). Psychology and public policy in the health care revolution. *American Psychologist*, 43, 993–1003.

Kivlighan, D. M. Jr. (2008). Overcoming our resistances to "doing" evidence-based group practice: A commentary. *Journal of Clinical Psychology: In Session*, 64, 1284–1291.

Kuhn, T. S. (1979). *Essential Tension: Selected Studies in Scientific Tradition and Change.* Chicago: University of Chicago Press.

Lambert, M. J., & Burlingame, G. M. (2007). Uniting practice-based evidence with evidence-based practice. *Behavioral Health Care*, 27, 16–20.

Lambert, M. J. (2007). Presidential address: What we have learned from a decade of research aimed at improving psychotherapy outcome in routine care. *Psychotherapy Research*, 17, 1–14.

Leffingwell, T. R., & Collins, F. L. Jr. (2008). Graduate training in evidence-based practice in psychology. In R. G. Steele, T. D. Elkin, & M. C. Roberts (Eds.), *Handbook of Evidence-Based Therapies for Children and Adolescents: Bridging Science and Practice.* New York: Spring Science+Business Media.

Levant, R. F., & Hasan, N. T. (2008). Evidence-based practice in psychology. *Professional Psychology*, 39, 658–662.

Luebbe, A. M., Radcliffe, A. M., Callands, T. A., Green, D., & Thorn, B. E. (2007). Evidence-based practice in psychology: Perceptions of graduate students in scientist-practitioner programs. *Journal of Clinical Psychology*, 63, 643–655.

McClendon, D. T. (2009). *Relative Sensitivity to Change of Psychotherapy Outcome Measures for Child and Adolescent Populations: A Comparison Using Parent- and Self-Report Versions of the CBCL/6–18, BASC-2, and Y-OQ-2.01.* Brigham Young University, Provo.

Nicholas, M. (2008). The groups in my life and my development as a group therapist. *Group*, 32, 129–136.

Nuttall, J. (2008). The integrative attitude—A personal journey. *European Journal of Psychotherapy and Counselling*, 10, 19–38.

Okiishi, J., Lambert, M. J., Nielsen, S. L., & Ogles, B. M. (2003). Waiting for supershrink: An empirical analysis of therapist effects. *Clinical Psychology and Psychotherapy*, 10, 361–373.

Schwartz, B., & Flowers, J. V. (2008). *Thoughts for Therapists: Reflections on the Art of Healing.* Atascadero, CA: Impact Publishers.

Slattery, J. M., & Park, C. L. (2007). Developing as a therapist: Stress-related growth through parenting a child in crisis. *Professional Psychology: Research and Practice*, 38, 554–560.

Spring, B. (2007). Evidence-based practice in clinical psychology: What it is, why it matters; what you need to know. *Journal of Clinical Psychology: In Session*, 63, 611–631.

Stern, S. (1993). Managed care, brief therapy, and therapeutic integrity. *Psychotherapy*, 30, 162–175.

Stratton, J. S. (2007). Retrospectives from three counseling psychology predoctoral interns: How navigating the challenges of graduate school in the face of death and debilitating illness influenced the development of clinical practice. *Professional Psychology: Research and Practice*, 38, 589–595.

Stricker, G., & Trierweiler, S. J. (1995). The local clinical scientist: A bridge between science and practice. *American Psychologist*, 50, 995–1002.

Varra, A. A., Hayes, S. C., Roget, N., & Fisher, G. (2008). A randomized control trial examining the effect of Acceptance and Commitment training on clinician willingness to use evidence-based pharmacotherapy. *Journal of Consulting and Clinical Psychology*, 76, 449–458.

Vinton, E. A. (2008). Finding a voice of one's own: The development of a unique, authentic manner as retrospectively reported by highly experienced relational psychoanalysts. *Dissertation Abstracts International: Section B: The Sciences and Engineering*, 69, 1349.

Walker, B. B., & London, S. (2007). Novel tools and resources for evidence-based practice in psychology. *Journal of Clinical Psychology*, 63, 633–642.

Wampold, B. E., & Brown, G. S. (2005). Estimating variability in outcomes attributable to therapists: A naturalistic study of outcomes in managed care. *Journal of Consulting and Clinical Psychology*, 73, 914–923.

Wampold, B. E., Goodheart, C. D., & Levant, R. F. (2007). Clarification and elaboration on evidence-based practice in psychology. *American Psychologist*, 62, 616–618.

10

Becoming a Cognitive-Behavioral Therapist: Striving to Integrate Professional and Personal Development

Edmund C. Neuhaus

Introduction

Cognitive-behavioral therapy (CBT) represents a broad spectrum of theory, research, and practice. A core value of the field is that practice should be evidence-based whenever possible.[1] Treatment objectives across the spectrum share the essential elements of diminishing a patient's suffering, improving mood, and increasing functioning, which in turn lead to enhancing one's quality of life. A cognitive-behavioral therapist's role is to be an active agent to facilitate change in collaboration with the patient, with skills training and psychoeducation as the primary means by which treatment objectives are achieved. For the professional development of a cognitive-behavioral therapist, clearly defined paths exist to attain competency, and while there may be variation among paths as they lead to different ways of practicing, all of them require rigorous understanding of theory, research, and case formulation, as well as facility in applying the core interventions of skills training and psychoeducation with patients.

The personal development of a cognitive-behavioral therapist, in contrast, has no clearly established path for training because the *personal* role of the therapist has been controversial for years. While a good therapeutic relationship is viewed as a necessary component for good outcomes in CBT (Wright et al., 2006), there is no consensus in the field that the cognitive-behavioral therapist *as a person*, with unique characteristics and personal experience (e.g., personal reactions, be they emotions, thoughts, or behaviors), is a deciding factor for effective treatment. My view, supported by a faction of leaders in the cognitive-behavioral field (Freeman & McCloskey, 2003; Goldfried & Davilla, 2005; Leahy, 2003b; Linehan, 1993; Persons, 2008), is that the therapist is an active participant in the therapeutic relationship whose influence contributes to treatment outcome. By extension, I subscribe to the position that personal development and personal experience must be incorporated into the training of cognitive-behavioral therapists. This will make more effective therapists as it prepares them for working in the context of complex interpersonal relationships with patients who can be at times intense, unpredictable, frustrating, satisfying, scary, enlivening, or all of the above.

Readers from other psychotherapeutic perspectives may view the importance of personal development and the personal role of the therapist as obvious; however, CBT subscribes to a different set of basic assumptions. Historically, CBT treatment approaches have been studied empirically through the lens of diagnosis, case formulation, and the therapist's application of clearly defined interventions to effect change leading to good outcomes; the therapist's personal role has been classified in the realm of nonspecific factors contributing to change.

My aim is to make cognitive-behavioral therapists more effective. Accordingly, this chapter will identify ways to integrate personal development with professional development in the training of cognitive-behavioral therapists. I define personal development to include present and past. *Present* refers to the developmental[2] process of learning how to become a therapist who reacts as a person with emotions, thoughts, and behaviors both inside and outside the therapy hour. *Past* refers to one's personal history (e.g., lifespan development, identity development, family relationships) that may have a significant influence on the ways in which the therapist reacts in the therapeutic relationship and performs as a therapist. In short, I propose that cognitive-behavioral therapists will be most effective with their patients when they strive to integrate personal and professional development over the course of their training and career.

CBT in Context

This is the only chapter of this volume that addresses the process of becoming a cognitive-behavioral therapist, and some readers may not be familiar with this important branch of psychotherapy. Therefore, I believe it is essential to define CBT in terms of the model and its strong research base, to discuss how it is practiced, and to address some stereotypical perceptions and misperceptions.

For many years it has been familiar for me to hear a colleague who practices from another perspective to refer to CBT as if it were one thing; typically that one thing is characterized as a therapeutic approach comprising techniques and lacking substantial depth. CBT is anything but lacking in depth; however, I can understand why this perception is so prevalent. The basics of CBT are intuitive and straightforward. There is in fact a large toolbox of techniques and methods that address problems and symptoms. And one phrase can capture a fundamental premise for treatment: change thoughts and behaviors to improve mood and reduce symptoms (Beck et al., 1979). While this all appeals to common sense and on the surface is very easy to understand, the irony is that the development of effective CBT treatment approaches has required substantial research efforts over many years, and learning how to do this work effectively as a therapist requires rigorous training. It is not as easy as it looks.

Author Context

Participant-Observer

I write this chapter as both a participant and an observer.[3] I am a participant in CBT with a career-long pursuit of how best to translate research to practice: as a clinician; as a teacher and supervisor in formal training programs in hospital psychiatry and outpatient settings; as an administrator responsible for designing and directing clinical training programs; as an author (Neuhaus, 2006, 2008a) and researcher of CBT in naturalistic settings (Christopher et al., 2009; Neuhaus et al., 2007); and as a teacher of professionals, both within the United States and internationally (Neuhaus, 2008b, 2009). I am an observer as well of trainees and graduate students, clinical supervisors who work with trainees, colleagues, and professionals who come to my workshops to learn CBT for the purpose of enhancing their existing competencies as a therapist in a variety of settings. Thus, as both a participant and an observer, I hope to provide a fair and balanced view of the field, and then I will offer my own perspective about how to improve on the process of becoming an effective cognitive-behavioral therapist.

Objectives

The basic assumption for this chapter is that attention to personal development is essential for cognitive-behavioral therapists. My aim is to identify ways in which to integrate professional and personal development in training. Four objectives serve this aim, with a dedicated section for each: (1) define the broad field of CBT with reference to theory, research, and practice; (2) review the current thinking and controversies about the therapeutic relationship and the personal role of the therapist in therapy; (3) describe the various paths to becoming a cognitive-behavioral therapist and the specifics of training for each path, with consideration of how personal development and the therapeutic relationship are addressed; and (4) offer my own model that strives to integrate professional and personal development with the hope that it will result in improving a cognitive-behavioral therapist's effectiveness to treat a wide range of patients under various circumstances.

CBT: The Big Picture

The Broad Field

CBT is a heterogeneous treatment perspective with many subdivisions and approaches, including, but not limited to, behavior therapy, cognitive therapy, cognitive-behavioral therapy, dialectical behavior therapy (DBT), acceptance commitment therapy (ACT), and mindfulness-based cognitive therapy (MBCT). The heterogeneity of approaches is commensurately reflected in how therapists are trained. These distinctions within CBT are analogous to the breadth of psychodynamic and psychoanalytic perspectives, which include classic Freudian psychoanalysis, object relations, self-psychology, transference-focused psychotherapy (TFP), mentalization-based treatment (MBT), and intersubjective and relational models. These schools of thought have common origins but are quite different in their approaches to treatment. To be consistent with terminology, I will use "CBT" to refer to the broad field of cognitive-behavioral therapy and the basic assumptions that are shared across the various approaches. I will refer to a specific approach, particularly when necessary to clarify some aspect of training, practice, or research.

Practice and Basic Assumptions

General CBT Practice

CBT is a structured treatment approach focused on changing thoughts and behaviors to improve mood, decrease distress, and improve functioning (A. T. Beck et al., 1979; Wright et al., 2006). Figure 10.1 illustrates the CBT Triangle, showing mutual influences of thoughts, feelings, and behaviors on

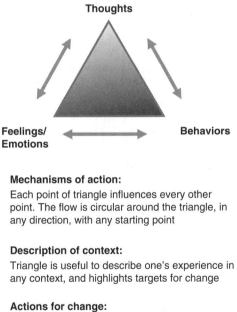

Thoughts

**Feelings/
Emotions**   **Behaviors**

Mechanisms of action:
Each point of triangle influences every other point. The flow is circular around the triangle, in any direction, with any starting point

Description of context:
Triangle is useful to describe one's experience in any context, and highlights targets for change

Actions for change:
Feelings cannot be changed directly. Direct changes are made with behaviors and thoughts, which in turn influence changes in how one feels.

Figure 10.1. The CBT Triangle: Core principles of cognitive behavior therapy.

symptomatic and functional changes. The therapist and patient have an active working relationship and engage in a collaborative process that utilizes evidence-based skills training to achieve mutually agreed upon treatment goals. Therapists directly challenge patients' beliefs and choices, educate patients about their condition, teach skills to cope and improve functioning, and support patients through the difficult and bumpy process of change (Heinssen et al., 1995; Wright et al., 2006). It is best for a therapist to provide a structure within therapy sessions (e.g., set an agenda, review homework, assess levels of distress, review treatment goals) as well as structures outside the sessions (e.g., homework or home practice) to increase the likelihood that patients will practice skills in everyday life. Whether patients actually do their homework or not is quite variable (Tompkins, 2003). As CBT is problem-oriented and present-focused, a focus on a patient's developmental history becomes a means-ends issue. Accordingly, the primary point of reference is the present, with a patient's developmental history serving as a means to illuminate presenting problems and functional difficulties. The therapist works collaboratively to guide the patient in identifying behavioral patterns, core beliefs, emotions, and interpersonal patterns that may have evolved over the course of his or her life, all of which contribute to the case formulation. Case formulation is a necessary component for effective treatment as it underlies the treatment plan, and it guides clinical decision making as it changes and develops over the course of treatment (Neuhaus, 2008a; Nezu et al., 2004; Persons, 2008).

Theory Informing Practice

CBT has deep philosophical and theoretical roots regarding the processes of behavioral and cognitive change. Beck et al. (1979) traced the origins of the assumptions for cognitive therapy back to the Stoic philosophers of ancient Greece, who emphasized that one's perspective directly influences how one reacts and feels in daily life. Knowledge of the broad range of learning theory is essential in order to appreciate why CBT is what it is, and why it can be effective. Simply put, CBT emphasizes an overt process of learning how to overcome psychological difficulties through the use of skills and education about one's problems, in addition to learning through lived experience. How the learning occurs is open to debate, but various types of learning include, but are not limited to, operant conditioning (e.g., behavior modification and behavioral activation), classical conditioning (e.g., systematic desensitization), social learning theory (e.g., self-efficacy), and skills practice to achieve competency.

Research and Evidence-Based Treatments

Classifying People for Treatment

The proliferation of evidence-based treatments has been mainly oriented to specific diagnoses, which provide the main criterion for classifying patients in randomized controlled trials (RCTs); hence some tension exists between focusing on the whole person versus the diagnostic problems to be treated. For example, some patients present with straightforward diagnostic profiles, while for many others the diagnosis is murky, or there are multiple diagnoses. The challenge is to use what is known about treating a particular diagnosis, develop a rigorous case formulation, and use clinical judgment to develop a treatment plan that matches treatment to the patient and his or her unique characteristics and life circumstances (Barlow et al., 2004; Friedberg, Gorman, & Beidel, 2009; Neuhaus, 2008a; Persons, 2008; Wright et al., 2006). From a research perspective, Barlow et al. (2004) have developed a "unified treatment approach" through their research to address problems of emotional dysregulation that are manifested across a wide range of diagnoses, including anxiety disorders, mood disorders, personality disorders, and eating disorders. To date this is the most sophisticated and elegant approach to reconciling the tension between diagnosis and functional problems that are not limited to one diagnosis.

Evidence-Based Treatment Approaches

CBT evidence-based treatment approaches are available for a wide range of diagnoses. Depression includes treatments grounded more cognitively (Beck et al., 1979; Beck, 1995), behaviorally (Dimidjian et al., 2006; Jacobson et al., 1996; Martell et al., 2001), the "equal opportunity" CBT combination (Neuhaus, 2008a; Padesky & Greenberger, 1995; Persons, 2008; Wright et al., 2006), and in mindfulness (Segal et al., 2002). Anxiety disorders have highly refined interventions designed to address specific disorders such as panic disorder (Barlow, 1988; Craske & Barlow, 2001) and social anxiety (Turk et al., 2001). For borderline personality disorder, DBT (Linehan, 1993) has a comprehensive approach and in recent years more breadth as it has been applied to other patient populations, such as substance abusers and adolescents. Psychotic disorders have a strong evidence base in CBT (Wright et al., 2009) but are typically much longer in treatment duration than treatment for non-psychotic disorders.

Protocols and Principles

The most common type of evidence-based treatment is a protocol-based approach. "Protocol-based" implies that a specific method of treatment interventions is essentially predetermined. Protocols tend to be rigid such that adherence is consistent with the ways in which it was tested in clinical trials, and effective for those patients whose diagnosis and constellation of problems fit the protocol. In clinical trials, variations of the protocol are typically not part of the protocol for obvious reasons. In clinical practice, if therapists do vary the protocol, it is based on their clinical judgment; guidance for such variation is typically not included in the protocol.

Principle-based evidence-based approaches are more flexible than protocol-based approaches. Knowledge of the principles prepares a clinician to make decisions according to the contingencies a patient presents. In effect, the principle informs the clinicians' choice of intervention, or protocol, that is most appropriate for an individual patient; the sequence and timing of interventions have greater flexibility than treatments with strict protocols. The best-known principle-based approach is DBT, originally developed by Marsha Linehan (1993) for borderline personality disorder. More generalist principle-based approaches include Persons' case formulation approach (2008), which she has refined over three decades, and more recently the flexible CBT approach (Neuhaus, 2008a) for patients suffering from depression, anxiety, and one or more personality disorders. In short, principle-based approaches use principles to decide on the protocol that meets an individual patient's needs rather than trying to fit a patient to a protocol.

Summary

CBT represents a broad spectrum of theory, research, and practice. Much variation exists within this perspective for psychotherapy, but at its core CBT is practiced as a structured treatment approach whose values rest on evidence-based knowledge and methods to effect positive outcomes. The primary focus is on present problems and patients learning how to cope and change their thoughts and behaviors in the service of improving mood and functional capacity. Within the therapeutic relationship, the therapist is an active collaborator who is required to have refined skills in the technical proficiency of applying treatment interventions.

The Therapeutic Relationship and the Person of the Therapist

Framing the Questions

A tension in the CBT field has been emerging over the past decade that is forcing a reassessment of how to translate research into practice. In CBT, the importance of empirical study is without question, and any factor introduced into a model for change is open to the challenge of empirical support. The values of CBT demand that treatment be evidence-based; however, a major problem exists "on the ground," or as some describe it the "real world" (Neuhaus, 2006, 2008a) or the "raw world" (Friedberg et al., 2009) of clinical practice, that is quite unlike the highly controlled world of clinical trials.

One main area of tension centers on the therapeutic relationship and how to view the cognitive-behavioral therapist's role. Is the therapist essentially a facilitator of change whose role is subservient to the methods applied in treatment? Likewise, to what extent should the therapeutic relationship be viewed as a separate source of variance from the methods applied, commonly referred to as nonspecific factors? Or is there something more fundamental in the therapeutic relationship that has a direct bearing on how the therapist applies the methods leading to a particular treatment outcome? With the assumption that the therapeutic relationship is more central to good treatment outcomes than what has been typically considered in CBT, it points to the importance of viewing the therapist as a person in the relationship whose personal experience enters into the therapy. And by extension, if one takes this more enhanced view of the personal role of the therapist in the treatment, how should personal development and personal experience be incorporated into training without losing focus on the importance of evidence-based methods that are the foundation of CBT?

In this section on the therapeutic relationship and the person of the therapist, I review the current thinking and controversies. This will set the framework for the last section, which will describe my recommendations about how to integrate personal and professional development in the training of cognitive-behavioral therapists, both early and throughout their careers.

How Did We Get Here?

Over several decades of psychotherapy research, the contributions of the therapist have been demonstrated to be important for treatment outcome for CBT, psychodynamic, and interpersonal approaches (Luborsky et al., 1986, 1997; Norcross, 2002; Persons, 2008; Raue et al., 1997; Roth & Fonagy, 2005), but the specifics of what therapists actually contribute are difficult to sort out (Roth & Fonagy, 2005). Historically in the CBT literature, the role of the therapist, as a *person* in a therapeutic relationship, has been addressed (Freeman, 1990; Kendall et al., 1998; Raue et al., 1997), yet arguably as a second-tier issue. The trend of evidence-based practice to validate highly refined treatment methods has been most prominent and has overshadowed attention to the personal aspects of the therapist. The conventional view has held that a productive therapeutic relationship is essential but less important for good outcomes than the specific skills-based interventions of CBT applied competently and adherent to the CBT model (Beck et al., 1979). Here, the personal role of the therapist is mainly to use self-practice as part of training to learn the skills first-hand as well as to go through the process of experiential learning, which in turn will improve the therapist's effectiveness with patients (Beck, 1995; Wright et al., 2006).

What Now?

Evidence-based treatments have become a lightning-rod issue, as the direct applicability of a protocol is seen to have many obstacles (Addis, 2002; Friedberg et al., 2009; Neuhaus, 2006, 2008a; Tellides et al., 2007). Moreover, in a recent position paper, Friedberg et al. (2009) argue that the perceptions of many practitioners in the community, with no connection to the academic field of CBT, lead them to be unwilling to embrace evidence-based protocols because they do not meet the practitioner's need to treat patients who are very different than the homogeneous samples found in clinical trials. Moreover, psychodynamic voices are loudly questioning the validity of evidence-based treatments. Concerns include the limitations of applying them in real-world practice, and skepticism about the notion that the contributions of therapists in the relationship are secondary to the technical aspects of providing such treatments (see Chapter 1 and the conclusion to this volume). While the limitations of evidence-based treatment are clear, the argument goes astray when it becomes polarized around whether evidence-based treatments are either valid or not. In fact, psychotherapy is not an all-or-nothing endeavor. In my view, we can channel the conflicting energy generated by this controversy in a productive fashion because, regardless of theoretical perspective, we all want our patients to benefit from treatment.

The CBT field is now actively re-evaluating itself with a particular focus on the therapist role, including but not limited to clinical judgment to use evidence-based approaches more flexibly to meet the individual needs of patients, utilizing the combination of the therapeutic relationship and technique to effect change, and viewing the therapist as a person with personal reactions who is actively participating in the process of change (Freeman & McCloskey, 2003; Friedberg et al., 2009; Goldfried & Davilla, 2005; Laireiter & Willutzki, 2003; Leahy, 2003b; Neuhaus, 2006, 2008a; Persons, 2008). Within the CBT literature, and on the ground in conversations among CBT clinicians, are loud calls to find more effective ways for therapists to adapt evidence-based knowledge and methods to real-world practice. It is not that evidence-based treatments are effective or not effective; the challenge for us is to figure out how to use the strength of evidence-based knowledge and make it as accessible and practical as possible so that patients may reap the benefits. To accomplish this, I believe the therapist as a person is where we need to focus our energies.

Foundation for Moving Forward

The Dialectic of Technical Interventions and the Therapeutic Relationship

Persons (2008) frames the challenge as a dialectic. On one side of the dialectic, the relationship in CBT is viewed as necessary but not sufficient. This captures the conventional thinking of CBT in general, and evidence-based protocols in particular (Beck et al., 1979); that is, it is assumed that the therapist is warm and compassionate and works collaboratively with the patient, although this is not sufficient for real change to occur. On the other side, the "relationship as treatment view" (Persons, 2008, p. 168) brings the therapeutic relationship to the fore, as what occurs in the relationship becomes a primary focus for the treatment.

For the "necessary but not sufficient" viewpoint, change occurs because of the technical interventions made (p. 167), with the relationship serving in a supportive role, literally and figuratively, and relegated to a nonspecific factor contributing to treatment outcome. When the relationship is good and the therapist and patient are working collaboratively, the treatment will most likely be effective. The limitations of the "necessary but not sufficient" view are seen with patients who have difficulty forming relationships and who present resistance to the technical interventions called for in protocols. In effect, the technical treatment may be correct for the technical problem, but the relationship creates obstacles to success.

The "relationship as treatment" perspective directly addresses the obstacles that the "necessary but not sufficient" view does not (Goldfried & Davilla, 2005; Persons, 2008). The interpersonal process between therapist and patient provides data for assessment, case formulation, and eventually focus for change. This view is controversial in some factions of CBT because on an individual-by-individual basis, a therapist must use more clinical judgment than strictly adhere to a protocol.

The next step is to synthesize the technical and the interpersonal aspects of the relationship for CBT. Persons (2008) describes this as the therapist utilizing the relationship to bolster the technical interventions, and the relationship itself, with its trials and tribulations, providing opportunities for the therapist to address the patient's problematic behavior in the therapy. A focus on the nuances of the relationship and specific interactions between therapist and patient also requires the cognitive-behavioral therapist to look at his or her role in the process. It is of utmost importance that the therapist is aware of his or her reactions that are played out in the therapy, either to the betterment or detriment of the treatment (Freeman & McCloskey, 2003; Goldfried & Davilla, 2005; Laireiter & Willutzki, 2003; Leahy, 2003b; Needleman, 2003).

The Treatment of Difficult Patients: The Relationship Front and Center

When things go well with the right patient, the conventional view (i.e., "necessary but not sufficient") of the relationship in CBT has been proven quite effective. In contrast, a focus on the relationship in CBT does not have the strong empirical support of the conventional view. Nevertheless, the relationship is being viewed by some as prominent in determining treatment outcome (Bennett-Levy et al., 2001; Laireiter & Willutzki, 2003; Persons, 2008), even though we do not have the robust data to support this view that we would like. Observation and common sense tell us that it is of critical importance. Some of the most senior leaders in CBT are questioning the conventional view. Goldfried has been at the forefront for years in discussing the therapeutic relationship, and claims that the relationship and technique are part and parcel of one another in an effective treatment (Goldfried & Davilla, 2005).

Leahy (2003a, 2003b) talks about how after years of practice he has much greater appreciation for the complexities of the relationship, and describes how he has learned to adjust his style, particularly with resistant patients. Freeman and McCloskey (2003) discuss "impediments to effective psychotherapy," which is a reframe of countertransference into the language of behavioral treatment. These impediments divert the therapist from being most effective. Others agree that all the refined techniques are rendered ineffective if the therapist cannot manage the relationship and himself or herself adequately in the face of challenging patients (Friedberg et al., 2009; Needleman, 2003).

The Therapist's Personal Development

The premise here is that cognitive-behavioral therapists must have training to prepare them to survive and thrive in the complexities of the therapeutic relationship with a myriad of patients, although it is not a "one-size-fits-all" world of training. I will touch on some pertinent issues here regarding personal development as a preface for the next section on the actual training contexts and approaches for cognitive-behavioral therapists. It is a complex developmental process for therapists to learn how to comport themselves, manage patients who may be unpredictable and frustrating, as well as manage the responses within them evoked by their patients. With these nuances to be addressed in the relationship, it begs the question of how therapists actually get to the point of being able to do so, and what type of training will best achieve those goals. How these issues are addressed is directly influenced by one's theoretical perspective.

Theoretical Perspective and Personal Development

Theoretical perspective influences one's personal development as the training of the therapist reflects the type of treatment being provided. A psychodynamic perspective, most broadly, addresses the personal history of a patient in order to reveal unconscious processes that must become conscious in order for real change to occur; moreover, examining the relationship itself takes precedence over any technical interventions of the treatment. In contrast, a cognitive-behavioral perspective is based on a different set of assumptions. CBT is present-oriented and problem-focused. There is not a presupposition of an unconscious, though some will acknowledge that unconscious processes may carry importance in treatment (Alford & Beck, 1997).[4] CBT is about developing an awareness of one's life patterns—behavioral, cognitive, emotional, interpersonal—that can be known through directed self-observation. And progress is considered to be observable as it is directly reflected in changes in thoughts and behaviors. For the cognitive-behavioral therapist, personal development as a therapist has much to do with actions and thoughts in the context of the therapeutic relationship. At the same time, no clear standards or paths are prescribed to become a compassionate therapist, nor for integrating one's personal history into training to become a cognitive-behavioral therapist. No requirements exist pertaining to personal therapy in order to achieve competency as a cognitive-behavioral therapist, and the literature lacks consensus on this, although some have suggested ways to incorporate these issues in training (Friedberg et al., 2009; Laireiter & Willutzki, 2003).

Summary

The fundamental aspects of CBT are to help people overcome their psychological suffering and improve their functioning, with a clear emphasis on addressing problems and developing strengths through evidence-based approaches. The research that forms the foundation of evidence-based CBT looks at the application of treatment approaches and specific methods, with an assumption that the therapist has an effect on treatment by being warm, supportive, and compassionate, but this is not viewed as the primary determinant of outcome. The priority is for the therapist to practice his or her craft in a competent way by adhering to the dictates of the treatment.

For CBT, a sea change is under way in which more and more practitioners are looking to use the best of evidence-based treatment methods, while at the same time going beyond them to meet individual patients where they are instead of trying to fit a patient into a protocol. A substantial change in thinking has emerged, as the empirical evidence and attitudes among academics and practitioners are slowly building to support the claim that the therapist, as a person in the therapeutic relationship, contributes significantly to treatment outcome.

This section on the therapeutic relationship and the therapist as a person has attempted to cover a disparate landscape. Some paths are forming that give increased weight to the relevance of the therapeutic relationship as it pertains to treatment effectiveness in CBT. The next section reviews what exists now in training of cognitive-behavioral therapists, and the final section focuses more on what is possible and necessary for our next steps in striving to integrate the professional and personal development of the therapist.

Training to Become a Cognitive-Behavioral Therapist and the Role of Personal Development

Overview

I begin this section by reiterating my statement in the introduction about striving to integrate personal development with professional development in the training of cognitive-behavioral therapists. I define personal development to include present and past. *Present* refers to the developmental process of learning how to become a therapist who reacts as a person with emotions, thoughts, and behaviors both inside and outside the therapy hour. *Past* refers to one's personal history (e.g., lifespan development, identity development, family relationships) that may have a significant influence on the ways in which the therapist reacts in the therapeutic relationship and performs as a therapist.

CBT has a set of core tenets that, more or less, most professionals could agree are necessary for the general practice of CBT, as outlined earlier in this chapter. It is also assumed that therapists will engage in self-practice of CBT skills as part of their training, both to learn experientially and to become more competent in their work with patients (Beck, 1995; Wright et al., 2006). It is not assumed or expected that personal therapy is a component of training. No standard is in place requiring a trainee to trace his or her personal development through graduate school, clinical placements, internships, and postdoctoral work. Nor is the exploration of the personal history of a therapist in training viewed as a necessary component of training for a cognitive-behavioral therapist. But are any of these necessary? Of course in particular instances, trainees are advised by supervisors or other training faculty to enter therapy, or address personal issues when the personal appears to encroach into the professional realm, adversely affecting the work. Historically in the field of CBT training, personal issues have been more typically subsumed under professional development—namely, an issue is evoked in therapy with a patient and is addressed in clinical supervision. Maybe the personal development aspect is addressed and maybe it is not.

These generally accepted practices do not imply, however, that there is a single path to become a cognitive-behavioral therapist. Efforts have been made to standardize general competencies in CBT using the framework of knowledge, skills, and attitudes set forth in psychiatry residency training standards (Beck, 1995; Wright et al., 2006), yet it is still not formalized. Similar to other theoretical perspectives, training paths in CBT have a variety of starting points and end points. Some paths converge, resulting in personal development being incorporated, while other paths do not.

A Growing Trend Toward the Personal

A change of direction is evidently gaining momentum regarding the role of the personal aspects of a therapist. Most recently a position paper (Friedberg et al., 2009) proposes more mainstream acknowledgement of the personal and interpersonal experiences that cognitive-behavioral therapists have, and contends that if they are left unaddressed, treatment effectiveness is undermined. Friedberg et al. propose a clinical supervision model to address the personal aspects of being a clinician. Wright et al. (1993, 2006) highlight countertransference as important for cognitive-behavioral therapists to acknowledge and address as needed, and Freeman and McCloskey (2003) discuss the importance of a therapist's monitoring and overcoming impediments that pertain to what he or she brings to the therapeutic relationship. A therapist's emotional responses in therapy inform case formulation and treatment, which can be operationalized into specific interventions (Leahy, 2003a; Persons, 2008). Lareiter and Willutzki (2003) offer a model for personal reflection that should be a necessary component of CBT training. Their work is noteworthy as they represent a European perspective about CBT (Germany in particular), which is further along than is the United States in moving toward requiring therapists to address personal issues in their training.

Three Factors on the Path

I take the position that the relative emphasis on personal development varies according to three factors on the path to become a cognitive-behavioral therapist: (1) training environment, (2) opportunities offered by specific training environments to broaden training, and (3) self-selection: a decision by a therapist in training that determines the extent to which personal development is a priority.

To address these three factors, training environments are the points of reference to describe the paths taken. I will describe what would be considered typical for training environments, including graduate programs, clinical placements (e.g., practicum, externship) during graduate school, psychology internships, and postdoctoral clinical fellowships, formal specialty training leading to certification, and self-driven continuing education as a licensed professional.[5]

Academic-Clinical Path

Training Environment

I begin my discussion with the clinical psychology graduate program oriented primarily to clinical research. It is the prototype of the clinical scientist training model where research on evidence-based treatment protocols is conducted, with graduate students (i.e., therapists in training) learning these methods. The environment places relatively more emphasis on being a scientist than a clinician; it prioritizes the pursuit of clinical knowledge using the most rigorous research methods. Most generally, clinical training experiences are oriented to the approaches of RCTs, whether they are through sanctioned clinics or actual research studies; namely, the training requires students to become skillful in the protocol being delivered to a specific clinical population (e.g., depression, panic, social anxiety). Exhaustive training is necessary and clinical supervision for an RCT protocol is largely about ways to maximize adherence. The therapists in training must become technically proficient and go through a painstaking evaluation of their performance (i.e., level of adherence).[6]

Opportunities

Standards for a student to address personal development are not hard-wired into academic-clinical training, and personal therapy is typically not in the conversation in an academic training environment. The main determinant, in my view, rests with clinical supervisors. If they are orientated and open to address personal matters of development and identity, then trainees will more likely have this incorporated into their training.

The academic-clinical training environment is obviously broadened with practicum experiences. Once again, the ways in which personal development are addressed really depend on clinical supervisors assigned and the student's willingness to address these issues. One student may go to a placement with a supervisor whose supervision is oriented to the personal issues of the therapist in training, whereas another supervisor may not.

Self-Selection

Students in academic-clinical programs generally pursue one of two paths after graduate school: one is a path oriented toward the clinical scientist research; the other is to use the training in clinical research as a foundation for a broader type of clinical practice that will evolve with more training and clinical experience. From my experience with trainees from these programs, those wanting to identify themselves as clinicians in their career are more interested in looking at their personal development and personal experiences. They are responsive to clinical supervision that addresses these issues, and they are known to form "under-the-radar" peer supervision groups for support as they all go through the trials and tribulations of being a therapist in training, faced with many emotional challenges.

While it is evident that the academic-clinical path beginning in graduate school is not typically designed to incorporate the personal development of the cognitive-behavioral therapist in training, it is still only the first leg of the journey

Psychology Internships and Clinical Postdoctoral Training

Internship begins with a major life transition: from graduate student to clinical intern with new roles and responsibilities. This transition is a huge opportunity for personal and professional development if an intern is open to it and has the proper guidance and support.

Training Environment

By definition, clinical internship training for psychologists and clinical postdoctoral training are clinical immersions that are fundamentally different than graduate school and facilitate greater depth and breadth of clinical experience.

Having reviewed thousands of internship applications and interviewed hundreds of applicants for a teaching hospital-based training program, I have found that one common thread is the stated desire of countless applicants to work with "severe psychopathology" because this was not available in graduate school, and they believe it is important for their training. However, the shock is compelling for many interns as they treat patients with severe psychopathology (e.g., multiple diagnoses, severe personality disorders, psychosis, dissociative disorders, severe post-traumatic stress disorder, substance abuse) for the first time. Their expectations do not match the reality of their experience. The protocol-based methods they learned in graduate school are not effective with their patients. The emotional stress is substantial as they are quickly out of their comfort zone.

The transition from graduate school to internship offers many challenges. The above vignette illustrates an important point for CBT, namely that technical proficiency in certain areas does not directly generalize to other areas. Thus, interns with high technical proficiency with depressed or anxious patients find themselves lacking the skills to work with patients with multiple diagnoses who fit in no particular category. A main reason for the intern's emotional stress is the experience of being incompetent after having attained a high level of mastery in graduate school. Supervisory support is necessary for development on both fronts, technical and emotional.

Another vignette provides a concrete example of this theme of transition from an academic environment to an ambiguous clinical environment. The example pertains specifically to CBT group therapy and highlights the challenges for professional and personal development in this environment, which I have seen many times.

Trainees (e.g., psychology or psychiatry) will begin their training rotation by observing CBT groups before taking on the group leadership themselves. They observe an experienced leader run the group with what seems like a clear protocol for skills training. Typical responses to the observation include "Oh, I understand it…this material about the skills isn't that complicated" or "I'm worried because I haven't done this type of group before with these types of patients" or "What is the specific protocol for this group?" Later, when leading the group, the responses include "The protocol I was given to lead this group was not adequate preparation" or "The patients are not cooperative enough" or "Wow, this is more complicated than I thought to lead a group and teach the skills."

This second vignette highlights comparison of expectations with actual experience and the challenge for trainees to be open to their weaknesses. Trainees who enter the situation believing that their experience must match their expectations are, on the face of it, prioritizing the technical aspects of CBT (e.g., the protocol, predefined goals, necessity of patient compliance) over the more ambiguous interpersonal factor of leading a group effectively. Yes, the skills training material is fairly straightforward, but being effective requires a level of composure and personal comportment that technical proficiency does not ensure. When trainees can be open about their struggle, manage their anxiety about this unfamiliar situation, and accept their temporary state of incompetence, then professional and personal development will occur. In my experience, the most technically proficient CBT group leaders are also the most flexible and interpersonally skilled and do not maintain rigid adherence to a protocol, yet they still meet the goals of the group for it to be effective for the patients.

Opportunities

Once again, clinical supervision is the primary anchor throughout training, but in my view it also provides the cognitive-behavioral therapist in training with opportunities to go more deeply into the work and to be more reflective about oneself. The two vignettes illustrate the opportunities for trainees to look more closely at how they react to patients and to their own struggle to become competent therapists. Because this environment is so raw, it is likely that many patients will evoke strong reactions that have historical significance to the intern. The quality of the supervisory relationship is important as trust and a sense of safety are necessary for trainees to work with supervisors about their defensiveness, fears, narcissism, connections to their family, and their overall struggle. Without supervisory support, a trainee's professional and personal development will be undermined.

Self-Selection

Interns who began in the academic clinical environment typically select one of two career paths after internship (or postdoctoral fellowship): primarily academic with little or no interest in clinical work with patients, or a career path that has a significant element of clinical work. For interns on their way to an academic career, it is more likely that the intent is to gain exposure to the messiness of clinical work in an internship setting, but the real prize is to get back to research to pursue their passion as a scientist. When clinical work is not on the horizon for one's career, I have seen a tendency to focus more on the technical aspects of the clinical work and less on the personal.[7] This situation typically requires a supervisor to push an intern to incorporate personal experiences into his or her discussions; if the supervisor doesn't initiate such discussion, it is often never explored. In contrast, interns with strong academic-clinical training who embrace this environment and intend to pursue clinical work as a substantial part of their career will most likely be open to exploring personal experience and be mindful of their personal development.

Summary

The common factors for addressing personal development are clinical supervisors and self-selection of trainees. While important, these factors are not determined on the level of curriculum standards; rather, they are manifested downstream and are contingent upon the right supervisors working with the right trainees for personal development to be adequately addressed. If the match of supervisor and trainee does not exist, optimal personal development goes by the wayside.

Formal Specialty Training Leading to Certification

The two most prominent specialty training programs are the Academy of Cognitive Therapy in Philadelphia (www.academyofct.org) and DBT training, offered under the auspices of Marsha Linehan, the founder of DBT, and Behavioral Tech, LLC (www.behavioraltech.com).[8] They both offer the highest-level, intensive training for certification. Cognitive therapy certification has rigorous standards to assess the extent to which therapists are adherent to the model with whatever patient they treat, and requires engaging in substantial self-practice. This training is typically for already devoted cognitive-behavioral therapists who are looking for the highest level of certification. Personal development is not a focus of the training *per se*, but it is addressed as needed in supervision as therapists have their reactions to patients and have difficulties because of their own personal issues. The solution is typically seen as the necessity to contain one's reactions in order to provide proper treatment, rather than exploring personal history.

DBT training has different levels, with the top tier having two essential components: intensive didactics during workshops and home study, and consultation teams. Participants are required to form consultation teams with the stipulation that members of the team will meet regularly for case discussion, peer supervision, and support. Guidelines of the team have been established through DBT clinical research. A fundamental principle of DBT is the dialectic between acceptance and change; this holds for patients as well as for therapists providing the treatment. The structure of the training provides a forum for therapists who may choose to address personal issues that are relevant to becoming an effective therapist with patients who typically evoke strong personal reactions; however, a focus on personal development is not a requirement.

Self-Driven Continuing Education in CBT

Therapists who seek CBT training after licensure are the most diverse group in their training background, and there is no statement I can make about a typical training environment. Training is typically not formalized or certified. CBT training typically begins after the formative years of graduate school. The training environments include workshops, books and journals, treatment manuals, and online training, which is now gaining in popularity. My impression from having observed many professionals who attended my workshops, and colleagues, is that CBT offers something concrete and practical that has been missing in a therapist's skill set. I infer the motivation to be largely professional development to get training in evidence-based CBT practices. Because of the clinical experience of these therapists, they are by and large more open to acknowledge that personal issues can encroach on their work, and are responsive if and when this is raised in CBT training; however, by no means is personal development a primary component of the training. Consistent with earlier statements, one's personal development is relevant as it arises in the course of therapy, and it will depend on the type of CBT practice one is pursuing, the orientation of one's supervisors to personal issues, and the trainee's willingness and interest in addressing the personal in his or her training.

Because this training environment is not formalized, the onus is on the therapist to be diligent and professionally responsible in his or her pursuit of learning CBT and practicing it effectively. Didactic training in CBT can go just so far; becoming competent requires at the minimum clinical supervision by an experienced cognitive-behavioral therapist to complement the didactic training.

Summary of Training

CBT focuses primarily on the present: the emphasis is on problems that affect a patient's current functioning. Personal development is not the primary focus of the therapy, nor is it overtly relevant for the therapist. Personal therapy is not typically a requirement for cognitive-behavioral therapists, although self-application of CBT skills is expected for therapists in training. The therapeutic relationship is a central concern for cognitive-behavioral therapists *only* as it relates to positive treatment outcomes. By virtue of the interpersonal nature of therapy, the ways in which therapists respond to patients in their behavior, thoughts, or emotional experience all are relevant to treatment outcome, but no consistent standard exists for addressing these reactions, nor the personal development that may influence these reactions.

Without curriculum-level standards for incorporating personal development in training, two factors determine whether and how it is addressed: clinical supervisors and trainees who have a self-selected interest. If both are open to it, then it will be addressed; if one or the other, it may be addressed but probably insufficiently; if neither, then personal development is not going to be in the conversation.

An additional factor to highlight is the types of patients a therapist treats in various training environments. Patients who present the greatest challenges, including those with complex diagnostic profiles, personality disorders, resistance to treatment, and anger directed at the therapist, are likely to evoke the strongest reactions in their therapists. Thus, the mutually contributing interpersonal aspects of the therapy relationship will point to how relevant personal development is for the therapist in training to address, but of course it is contingent on the aforementioned supervisor–trainee match of interest.

Striving to Integrate Professional and Personal Development

The Big Picture

My view is that psychotherapy must be performance-based. To evaluate performance, a therapist and patient must have some mutual agreement about *realistic* treatment goals to decrease symptoms and improve functioning[9] with observable criteria to measure progress, all of which are consistent with how CBT is practiced. The premise of this volume is that reflection on personal development, in itself, is important for any therapist in training, but I do not subscribe to this premise. In my view, it is a means-ends issue: the relevance of a cognitive-behavioral therapist's personal development is important insofar as it contributes to the therapist's providing effective treatment because he or she is better prepared to engage in and withstand complex therapeutic relationships with a wide range of patients.

My approach to training cognitive-behavioral therapists is pragmatic with respect to integrating professional and personal development. The organizing principle of my approach is to link training with treatment context. A fundamental objective of CBT is to improve a patient's functioning. Likewise, a therapist must function optimally in order to provide the most effective treatment possible. CBT covers a broad spectrum of contexts (e.g., settings, types of patients, methods) with a correspondingly wide range of requirements for therapists. Thus, my approach is pragmatic as it evaluates how personal development is relevant in helping a therapist function optimally in a particular treatment context. When successful, a therapist uses sound judgment in making clinical decisions, and sound judgment to determine the extent to which his or her own personal reflection is necessary for effective treatment to be achieved.

Ideal Course of Training

The Foundation

Whether through self-directed reflection or through personal therapy, it is wise at the outset of training for a cognitive-behavioral therapist in training to take the broad view of his or her life. To enter this stage of life is a critical life transition (Wapner, 1981) that predictably causes some disruption and disorientation regarding one's sense of identity, role, environment, and interpersonal relationships. With the proper concentrated effort, this transition should result in substantial personal and professional development. At a minimum, it is useful to reflect on one's life and look at the path that brought one to this point in time. It is desirable for a developing therapist to consider significant life events, difficulties, traumatic events, and family relationships to address now, or to note them for consideration later. Moreover, such self-reflection can be integrated with the self-practice aspect of CBT training, and it can become a pragmatic task: to take an honest look at oneself and one's history, and apply the skills that are being learned as a cognitive-behavioral therapist to help organize how one understands oneself.

For therapists in training, or experienced therapists, one of the greatest challenges is to be confronted by personal issues seemingly coming out of left field. In effect, the therapist, as a basic requirement, goes through a self-assessment process to identify life patterns, strengths, and vulnerabilities. The objective is for therapists to identify life patterns by taking an honest look at themselves and maintain a personal ethic that values openness to such reflection. The onus is on the training program (e.g., graduate program, internship) to highlight the importance of therapists in training being open to look at themselves, and seeking support, through therapy or other means, if and when personal issues become problematic.

Preparing for What Happens in Session

Before entering graduate school, my sense of therapy was based on what I read. The recurring question for me was, what does a therapist actually do in therapy? There's much talk about therapy, but little about what the therapist actually says. The only way to really learn it is through direct experience. For protocol-driven treatments, the training tilts toward adherence to the protocol in the face of whatever the patient may present. Conversely, to be a well-rounded and versatile clinician requires being skillful at your craft in applying skill training and psychoeducation, in addition to clinical judgment, composure, maturity, courage, and the capacity to tolerate the ambiguity of the therapeutic relationship. Friedberg et al. (2009) describe a supervision model that incorporates the didactics for technical proficiency with a focus on being actively present with one's patient moment to moment in session (what they refer to as achieving "immediacy" in the session). Moreover, a therapist's sensitivity to his or her own emotional arousal, positive or negative, also requires an emotional openness that benefits both the patient and the therapist. Unchecked emotional reactions will obstruct the therapeutic effectiveness of CBT (Freeman & McCloskey, 2003; Friedberg et al., 2009; Leahy, 2003a; Needleman, 2003) regardless of one's technical proficiency.

Going further, a training program can offer a more structured approach to self-reflection and self-practice, as outlined by Laireiter and Willutzki (2003). They describe self-practice as a first level on the way to greater depth in self-reflection. They present a European perspective that has advanced significantly further than the United States has with respect to formal standards for the personal aspect of training. They identify goals such as managing personal involvement and boundaries in therapy and improvement in insight, empathy, and sensitivity to the nuances of the interactions in the therapeutic relationship. These goals are in addition to experiential learning through self-practice and skillful competence in applying evidence-based methods in therapy. I am impressed with this perspective as it formalizes much of what I believe to be true for training effective cognitive-behavioral therapists; namely, a holistic view of the therapist as a person who must be trained on many levels, the result of which is greater integration of professional and personal development.

The Treatment Context

The requirements of how a therapist must function in the therapy correspond to the treatment context and treatment objectives. On one end of the spectrum is when a therapist is providing treatment through a clinical trial (i.e., RCT) or its equivalent.[10] The overt need to focus on personal development and personal experience is low when using an established protocol for the choices one must make and the sequence of interventions offered. Supervision is focused on being adherent with the treatment; the therapist's personal history, by definition, is not incorporated. This is not to say that a therapist will not have strong reactions connected to personal development. If this occurs, he or she will have some preparation for finding a course of action to manage it.

The other end of the spectrum is a cognitive-behavioral therapist in training working in a hospital-based setting treating complex patients with severe psychopathology. This is an area with which I am most familiar, and my experience influences my perspective (Christopher et al., 2009; Gunderson et al., 2005, 2009; Neuhaus, 2006; Neuhaus et al., 2007). The universal assumption is that cognitive-behavioral therapists must be human, supportive, and generally empathic to achieve a good therapeutic relationship. We know that it does not always go according to plan, however. When a patient becomes enraged at the therapist, maligns the treatment and the therapist, or is resistant to treatment, the therapist's composure is obviously challenged. And for therapists oriented to using protocols, they can feel particularly lost because the roadmap they have does not reflect the path they are on. The therapist's ability to function is challenged not only by the patient, but also by his or her own thoughts and feelings. If not adequately addressed, the therapist's behaviors (e.g., statements, judgments and decisions) will be compromised. Thus, this treatment context requires an infrastructure of support for trainees, with clinical supervisors trained themselves to address these issues. A trainee in collaboration with a supervisor must determine the extent to which supervision needs to focus on managing the personal aspects of the situation, and exploring one's personal history in order for the trainee to function optimally as a therapist.

The treatment of patients suffering from personality disorders illustrates the personal challenges for cognitive-behavioral therapists, or any therapist for that matter. In my own career, I have been particularly oriented to treating borderline and narcissistic personality disorders and have designed training curricula and provided clinical supervision for trainees and professional therapists to treat these patients from a cognitive-behavioral perspective.

The interpersonal intensity of doing such treatment can make it difficult for therapists to find their way. I see the effectiveness of evidence-based treatments for Axis I disorders (e.g., depression, panic, eating disorders, social anxiety) breaking down with patients whose comorbid personality disorder is prominent (Neuhaus, 2006, 2008a; Tellides et al., 2007).

The prototypical example for the relevance of looking closely at one's personal development, personal experience, and emotional reactions is when cognitive-behavioral therapists treat patients with borderline personality disorder, or at least some borderline traits. These patients demand much from therapists, overtly and/or covertly. They are frequently suicidal, self-harming, angry, hopeless, and desperate. And they are compelling, either by drawing a therapist in or by pushing a therapist away. Where cognitive-behavioral therapists often get caught is in not seeing that they are being drawn in or pushed away more as a function of their dynamics than those of the patient. This brings us to personal development. The therapist might feel inclined to run and hide, or enter the fray headfirst without looking. It is important for the therapist to see this in real time during the therapy, and gain perspective by viewing these reactions in terms of his or her life patterns. DBT consultation teams were designed exactly for these purposes and help therapists to stay grounded through their bumpy rides. Clinical supervision, or personal psychotherapy, can address a therapist's painful experiences and difficulties. The priority is to manage oneself to optimize the effectiveness of the therapy, and to determine what is necessary to achieve this.

Vignette About Treatment Adherence and Homework in CBT

CBT uses homework as a cornerstone for skills training. Patients learn skills through practice, and it follows that doing homework outside the therapy hour is necessary. One of the biggest issues I have encountered in working with patients, and in supervising trainees, is how to respond when patients fail to do the homework that was assigned. The scenario is as follows: A trainee reports that a patient is not doing homework, which leads to the conclusion that patient is not adhering to treatment. Questions arise that the patient is not making progress and treatment efficacy requires completed homework. If the patient continues on this path, perhaps treatment should end.

In this vignette, the trainee raises valid points, but the conclusions must be reassessed in light of who the patient is, who the therapist is, and the effectiveness of their working relationship. The basic premise is that failure to do homework reflects a lack of adherence to the treatment. Further lack of adherence is sometimes thought of as grounds for ending the treatment. While I agree that homework is an essential component of treatment, how it is incorporated into treatment is not so straightforward, particularly with borderline patients. When a trainee reports that a patient did not do the homework, my first response is, "Was it the right homework for this patient, under these circumstances?" In effect, a protocol may dictate an assignment that is a mismatch for the treatment at this time. It could be that the patient is oppositional, and this must be addressed, or the patient is confused, or the patient needs more support, or the expectations are too high for what is reasonable to expect of the patient at this point. Frustration and judgment will reign if the therapist views it simply as the patient not adhering to treatment, and it often results in the therapist attempting to exert more control. If the therapist's personal reactions are not addressed, the treatment will most likely not be effective. This can be seen as an opportunity to discuss the therapeutic relationship openly with the patient and find a way that patient and therapist can work more effectively, be it with homework or in their sessions. Such an open discussion may create anxiety for a therapist, and an open discussion in supervision about this emotional response will help the therapist be more effective.

Countertransference and Transference

My view of how to incorporate these important issues in CBT training is as follows. The discussion of the treatment context leads directly to the issues of countertransference and transference, which at a minimum are important for cognitive-behavioral therapists to acknowledge, even if they are not interpreted directly to patients. Patients who tend to form emotionally charged relationships challenge therapists interpersonally and personally. Transference and countertransference are thus important processes about which cognitive-behavioral therapists must be aware. Unfortunately these are concepts that have not been embraced across the CBT field, particularly by those in an academic setting. Some have acknowledged the importance of the transference/countertransference processes in CBT directly (Neuhaus, 2006, 2008a; Persons, 2008; Wright et al., 1993, 2006), and others have done so indirectly (Freeman & McCloskey, 2003; Friedberg et al., 2009; Laireiter & Willutzki, 2003; Persons, 2008). All emphasize the importance of acknowledging that patients will develop strong feelings for a therapist no matter what approach they use, and therapists have emotional reactions to their patients as well.

Acknowledgement of transference/countertransference may take several forms for the cognitive-behavioral therapist: (1) therapists being internally aware of the issues and acting accordingly without directly naming it for the patient; (2) therapists naming it for the patient, followed by an overt discussion between therapist and patient; and (3) therapists deciding it is necessary to offer an interpretation as to why it is occurring because otherwise the therapy cannot move forward. These acknowledgements are all in the service of moving the therapy forward toward achieving the mutually agreed upon goals for functional improvement.

Clinical supervision offers CBT trainees the opportunity to clarify the transference and countertransference, and then to make decisions about the extent to which they are discussed overtly in the therapy. Trainees who are exclusively focused on the technical aspects of the treatment more than the relational aspects will have more difficulty in acknowledging the importance of this. Prescriptive guidance from a supervisor is necessary, although adoption by the trainee is by no means guaranteed. Thus, supervision becomes a process whereby CBT trainees confront their interest and comfort levels in addressing their countertransference reactions. It is safe to assume that the relationship between therapist and supervisor will be a determining factor in how successfully these issues are addressed. Trainees not comfortable displaying their weaknesses to a particular supervisor because of fear of being evaluated and judged negatively will be less likely to effectively address these issues than will trainees who feel validated, safe, and comfortable in exposing their personal weaknesses, fears, and worries.

In short, proper acknowledgement of transference and countertransference will help cognitive-behavioral therapists be more effective with their patients. Cognitive-behavioral therapists must take the responsibility to monitor themselves and their relationships with their patients, especially when the therapy is not going as planned, or if patients are resistant, or if the therapist is having a strong reaction to a patient for whatever reason (feeling stressed about the suicidal intent of a patient, feeling hated by a patient, liking a patient and feeling uncomfortable about it, or disliking a patient).

Case Example of Treatment Adherence and Working Through Resistance

A patient, Linda, presented many challenges in how we worked together to diminish her self-harm behaviors, including cutting and drinking. Her diagnoses included borderline personality disorder with avoidant features, major depression, and alcohol abuse. In session she stated her commitment to reach out and get help before she drank or cut herself. Nonetheless, a pattern quickly developed in which she would call me a day or two *after* she drank or cut, which clearly was not in line with the expectation (that she would reach out to me before she harmed herself). After several times, I had an open discussion with her about my frustration and I told her the treatment would not be effective if she continued this pattern. I framed this as an issue in our relationship and indicated that we needed to stay connected and work together even if she felt scared and ashamed. Had I not spoken openly with her, I probably would have gotten more frustrated than I already was, and pulled away emotionally. It still took some time for her to get more control of her behavior and contact me proactively; however, my repeated focus on the relationship was instrumental to help her change. This redirected the focus from the self-harm behaviors exclusively to how her behavior affected our relationship; eventually her self-harm behaviors decreased.

Had I maintained a focus only on her self-harm behaviors, without consideration of our relationship, the treatment would have failed. It highlights the importance of a cognitive-behavioral therapist being open to look at a problem in treatment reflective of the therapeutic relationship. If personal expectations are focused only on patients adhering to treatment, the therapy will stall, if not end. Therefore, cognitive-behavioral therapists must be open to looking at what they may be contributing to the situation. Higher levels of personal development are evidenced by a therapist willing to question his or her role and be authentic with patients, all of which is in the service of improving treatment effectiveness.

Striving to Integrate Professional and Personal Development

While the treatment context is an important factor determining the extent to which the personal and professional are integrated, we must have some basic standards that all cognitive-behavioral therapists are required to meet. Once those standards are met, the impact of context and self-selection is much more of a choice by the therapist. Adopting these enhanced standards would be, in my view, the next developmental step in the field of CBT training. It is value-driven in that the hard data are lacking; but through my own experience, and observing the experiences of trainees, clinical supervisors, and patients, I believe we need to embrace these standards so that the whole person of the cognitive-behavioral therapist in training is addressed.

Table 10.1 describes three levels of standards to consider for the training of cognitive-behavioral therapists: (1) existing standards for the training of cognitive-behavioral therapists, (2) enhanced standards for personal development and self-reflection, and (3) contextual standards for cognitive-behavioral therapists practicing in diverse treatment environments.

The enhanced standards level is the logical next step for improving the curriculum training standards for all CBT trainees. Therapy, by definition, is personal in nature, however technical it may be. Thus, the clinical training curriculum needs a structure for incorporating personal development into training, regardless of specialty, clinical context, or career path. Even for students whose career path is academia and research, their clinical training should include these enhanced standards. Once in place, this addition to the curriculum can be a point of reference for the field, and a healthy debate can ensue about its validity. Without it, the field will continue to address personal development in idiosyncratic and haphazard ways.

The contextual standards take the enhanced standards to a level of greater depth and intensity. The decision to invoke these standards is contingent upon the treatment environments in which therapists practice. Therefore, it is not necessary for all cognitive-behavioral therapists to meet these standards if the clinical environment does not warrant it (e.g., specialty clinics offering protocol-based treatments for homogeneous patient populations).

Table 10.1. Standards for Integrating Professional and Personal Development

Existing Standards for Training: These typically begin in graduate school but may start at any point in one's career when one begins CBT training:

- Didactics in theory, research, and practice
- Emphasis on case formulation to guide treatment
- Technical training in application of skills training and psychoeducation
- Self-practice of skills
- Learn collaborative relationship skills and practice being compassionate, warm, and supportive
- Clinical supervision to monitor and teach application of interventions and to address personal issues as needed

Enhanced Standards for Personal Development and Self-Reflection in CBT Training

- Introduce framework for CBT therapists in training to look at personal factors that led to choice of entering graduate study
- Didactics about personal development and what to expect on the journey to becoming a CBT therapist—the trials and tribulations, emotional reactions
- Identify aspirations, strengths, fears, worries about being a therapist— emphasize the developmental process of incompetence to competency and the challenge of tolerating feeling incompetent
- Trainees learn to assess their own needs to look at personal development, which is a marker of developing personal maturity.
- Learn how treatment context can influence the extent to which therapist must address personal issues
- View the therapeutic relationship as an agent of change, requiring the trainee to learn how to integrate technique and the therapeutic relationship
- Clinical supervision oriented to personal development and attention to immediacy in session and emotional reactions of therapist in training; empathy, validation, and support by supervisors are essential
- Clinical supervision to address the limitations of protocols and how trainees can work with resistant and challenging patients, with particular emphasis on trainees' personal reactions
- Create structure to facilitate peer supervision groups to address integration of personal and professional development
- Periodic review of personal development with supervisors
- More open attitudes toward personal psychotherapy for students

Table 10.1. *Continued*

Contextual Standards for CBT Therapists Practicing in Diverse Treatment Environments

- Work with severe psychopathology requires more focus on personal development to manage oneself and one's patients compared to in a more controlled clinical environment treating less severe and more homogeneous patients.
- If the therapist is working with these patient populations and unwilling to look at his or her personal reactions, this is a red flag.
- Concentrated attention to the integration of technical proficiency with the interpersonal aspects of the therapeutic relationship
- Develop therapeutic techniques and comfort level to be open with patients about the process of change, and the trials and tribulations of the therapeutic relationship
- Learn how to stay connected with patients while confronting them about problematic issues in therapeutic relationship
- Clinical supervision more closely focused on emotional reactions and effects of personal experience
- Personal psychotherapy to explore issues evoked through clinical work, including blind spots, difficulties with certain types of patients, etc.
- Ongoing monitoring of therapists feeling inadequate or lacking in competence through supervision and/or peer supervision
- Peer supervision and consultation

Conclusion

The question remains: why should cognitive-behavioral therapists focus on personal development as a priority of training when the issue of personal development is not necessarily a priority when treating patients? The short answer is that it is a matter of values and pragmatism. I believe cognitive-behavioral therapists should prepare themselves to enter into a wide variety of interpersonal relationships with patients. A solid awareness of oneself is an essential factor that allows cognitive-behavioral therapists to know where they are emotionally, cognitively, and behaviorally, and therefore what they are bringing to their relationships with many kinds of patients, some of whom are extremely challenging. Moreover, I believe this awareness is pragmatic in that it helps therapists be more effective with the complexities of these challenging therapeutic relationships with patients who are often hopeless, traumatized, suicidal, attractive, sexually arousing, and confusing. Attempting to relate to such patients often leads to varying degrees of frustration, emotional closeness (or lack of it), and satisfaction or dissatisfaction with the work.

Psychodynamic therapists may view these assertions as obvious because the therapeutic relationship is considered to be the primary causative agent of change. The attachment between the therapist and patient is seen as facilitative of a patient achieving a transformative outcome. These goals are all important, but they are less concrete than what CBT typically identifies as treatment goals. For CBT, in contrast, both technical interventions (e.g., skills training) and the therapeutic relationship are the causative agents of change; the relative importance of the technical and the relationship depends on the context (e.g., the patient's active and cooperative involvement vs. the patient manifesting a high degree of resistance; the patient's severity of psychopathology; and the extent to which the therapist identifies with the patient). The therapeutic relationship in CBT is of utmost importance; if the relationship becomes less than collaborative and open, the onus is on the therapist to notice this and to bring it overtly into the therapeutic process. If unaddressed, we can expect that therapist and patient will become more disconnected and isolated from one another, thereby undermining the treatment. When addressed properly, we can expect the treatment to achieve its goals of symptom relief as well as facilitating functional changes in daily life, work, school, play, self-care, and relationships, all of which will lead to an enhanced quality of life.

The bottom line is that the cognitive-behavioral therapist in training and those of us providing training all have responsibilities to acknowledge the importance of addressing the trainee's personal development, and to strive to integrate this exploration with the professional development of becoming an effective psychotherapist. This is by no means "one size fits all"; there is no single way to address these issues, but it is essential to have a foundation established in one's training that will prepare therapists to meet the challenges of providing psychotherapy to a wide variety of individuals over the course of one's career. Speaking as both a participant and as an observer of the CBT field, I believe the integration of the professional and the personal must be pragmatically connected to treatment effectiveness. It is to be hoped that more and more therapists will employ evidence-based treatment approaches in the future; I believe that an added focus on the therapist as a person will make these approaches more relevant to real-world practice and therefore likely to be more widely used.

Notes

[1] "Evidence-based practice" is the broad term for clinical practice informed by research. In the CBT literature, the term used most often is empirically supported treatments (ESTs). ESTs are established through research using randomized controlled trials (RCTs) to test the efficacy of a specific treatment approach, usually with a protocol, adherence to which is also measured as part of the research. A growing trend in the field is to adapt ESTs to real-world practice, which can also be considered evidence-based

practice without the use of a strict protocol. Thus, to minimize confusion of terms, "evidence-based practice" will be used in this chapter because it most broadly covers practice informed by research, strictly or otherwise, and this term is more commonly seen in the professional vernacular across theoretical perspectives and disciplines.

2 Development is not limited to lifespan development. Rather, development is defined here in terms of organizational principles that view development as beginning from a global, undifferentiated state that progresses toward greater differentiation of parts to eventual integration into a complex whole (Wapner, 1981; Werner, 1948). Thus, the developmental process of a therapist begins with no knowledge; as knowledge is acquired, it gradually becomes more differentiated and organized, eventually becoming integrated into a complex whole of competency and emotional maturity.

3 This is in the spirit of Harry Stack Sullivan (Sullivan, 1954), who paved the way for an active interpersonal approach in psychotherapy.

4 In my experience, many CBT practitioners do operate under the assumption that unconscious processes exist and are important to consider.

5 Individual differences certainly exist within each type of training environment and there are exceptions to what I present.

6 If the graduate student does not actually participate in the clinical trial, it is most likely that the work with patients is oriented to the adherence standards of RCTs.

7 In my experience there have been notable exceptions, with academically oriented interns who are very open to self-reflection about personal issues and personal history.

8 The Beck Institute (which is related to the Academy of Cognitive Therapy) and Behavioral Tech, LLC, offer workshops and other educational offerings that are considered to be continuing education in CBT for purposes of this chapter.

9 Symptom change and functional change are related but not synonymous; when symptoms are stabilized, it paves the way for functional changes in capacities for healthy relationships, work, school, and play.

10 A treatment context equivalent to an RCT is a clinic that uses strict criteria to screen patients and match them to the treatment being offered.

References

Addis, M. (2002). Methods for disseminating research products and increasing evidence-based practice: Promises, obstacles, and future directions. *Clinical Psychology: Science and Practice*, 9, 367–378.

Alford, B. A., & Beck, A. T. (1997). *The Integrative Power of Cognitive Therapy*. New York: Guilford Press.

Barlow, D. H. (1988). *Anxiety and Its Disorders*. New York: Guilford Press.

Barlow, D. H., Allen, L. B., & Choate, M. L. (2004). Toward a unified treatment for emotional disorders. *Behavior Therapy*, 35(2), 205–230.

Beck, A. T., Rush, J. A., Shaw, B. F., & Emery, G. (1979). *Cognitive Therapy of Depression*. New York: Guilford Press.

Beck, J. S. (1995). *Cognitive Therapy: Basics and Beyond*. New York: Guilford Press.

Bennett-Levy, J., Turner, F., Beaty, T., Smith, M., Paterson, B., & Farmer, S. (2001). The value of self-practice of cognitive therapy techniques and self-reflection in the training of cognitive therapists. *Behavioural and Cognitive Psychotherapy*, 29, 203–220.

Christopher, M., Jacob, K., Neuhaus, E., Neary, T., & Fiola, L. (2009). Cognitive and behavioral changes related to symptom improvement among patients with a mood disorder receiving intensive cognitive-behavioral therapy. *Journal of Psychiatric Practice*, 15(2), 95–102.

Craske, M. G., & Barlow, D. H. (2001). Panic disorder and agoraphobia. In D. H. Barlow (Ed.), *Clinical Handbook of Psychological Disorders* (3rd ed., pp. 1–59). New York: The Guilford Press.

Dimidjian, S., Hollon, S. D., Dobson, K. S., Schmaling, K., Kohlenberg, R., Addis, M. E., et al. (2006). Randomized trial of behavioral activation, cognitive therapy, and antidepressant medication in the acute treatment of adults with major depression. *Journal of Consulting and Clinical Psychology*, 74(4), 658–670.

Freeman, A. (1990). Technicians, magicians, and clinicians. *Behavior Therapist*, 13, 169–170.

Freeman, A., & McCloskey, R. D. (2003). Impediments to effective psychotherapy. In R. Leahy (Ed.), *Roadblocks to Cognitive-Behavioral Therapy: Transforming Challenges Into Opportunities for Change*. New York: Guilford Press.

Friedberg, R. D., Gorman, A. A., & Beidel, D. C. (2009). Training psychologists for cognitive-behavioral therapy in the raw world: a rubric for supervisors. *Behavior Modification*, 33(1), 104–123.

Goldfried, M. R., & Davilla, J. (2005). The role of relationship and technique in therapeutic change. *Psychotherapy: Theory, Research, Practice, Training*, 42(4), 421–430.

Gunderson, J., Gratz, K., Neuhaus, E., & Smith, G. (2005). Levels of care in treatment in the treatment of personality disorders. In J. M. Oldham, A. E. Skodol, & D. S. Bender (Eds.), *Textbook of Personality Disorders*. Washington, D.C.: American Psychiatric Publishing, Inc.

Gunderson, J., Gratz, K., Neuhaus, E., & Smith, G. (2009). Levels of care in treatment. In J. M. Oldham, A. E. Skodol, & D. S. Bender (Eds.), *Essentials of Personality Disorders*. Washington, D.C.: American Psychiatric Publishing, Inc.

Heinssen, R. K., Levendusky, P. G., & Hunter, R. (1995). Client as colleague: therapeutic contracting with the seriously mentally ill. *American Psychologist*, 50(7), 522–532.

Jacobson, N., Dobson, K., Truax, P., Addis, M., Koerner, K., Gollan, J., et al. (1996). A component analysis of cognitive behavioral treatment for depression. *Journal of Consulting and Clinical Psychology*, 64(2), 295–304.

Kendall, P., Chu, B., Gifford, A., Hayes, C., & Nauta, M. (1998). Breathing life into a manual. *Cognitive and Behavioral Practice*, 5, 89–104.

Laireiter, A.-R., & Willutzki, U. (2003). Self-reflection and self-practice in training of cognitive behaviour therapy: an overview. *Clinical Psychology and Psychotherapy*, 10, 19–30.

Leahy, R. (2003a). Emotional schemas and resistance. In R. Leahy (Ed.), *Roadblocks in Cognitive Behavioral Therapy*. New York: Guilford Press.

Leahy, R. (2003b). Preface. In R. Leahy (Ed.), *Roadblocks in Cognitive-Behavioral Therapy*. New York: Guilford Press.

Linehan, M. (1993). *Cognitive Behavioral Treatment for Borderline Personality Disorder*. New York: Guilford.

Luborsky, L., Crits-Christoph, P., McLellan, A. T., Woody, G., Piper, W., Liberman, B., et al. (1986). Do therapists vary much in their success? Findings from four outcome studies. *American Journal of Orthopsychiatry*, 51, 501–512.

Luborsky, L., McLellan, A. T., Diguer, L., Woody, G., & Seligman, D. (1997). The psychotherapist matters: Comparison of outcome across twenty-two therapists and seven patient samples. *Clinical Psychology: Science and Practice, 6*, 95–106.

Martell, C. R., Addis, M., & Jacobson, N. (2001). *Depression in Context: Strategies for Guided Action*. New York: Norton.

Needleman, L. D. (2003). Case conceptualization in preventing and responding to therapeutic difficulties. In R. Leahy (Ed.), *Roadblocks in Cognitive-Behavioral Therapy*. New York: Guilford Press.

Neuhaus, E. C. (2006). Fixed values and a flexible partial hospital program model. *Harvard Review of Psychiatry, 14*(1), 1–14.

Neuhaus, E. C. (2008a). The flexible CBT approach. *An Online Textbook and Training Program*: Atheneum Learning /TRi Behavioral, LLC www.atheneumlearning. com.

Neuhaus, E. C. (2008b). *The Flexible CBT Approach: Foundational Knowledge, Assessment, Case Formulation, and Treatment*. Paper presented at the 1st Chinese CBT Conference, Nanjing Brain Hospital, Nanjing, China.

Neuhaus, E. C. (2009). *The Flexible CBT Approach for Depression and Anxiety Disorders*. Paper presented at the Cognitive Behavioral Therapy for Mood, Anxiety, and Personality Disorders, Shanghai Mental Health Center, Shanghai, China.

Neuhaus, E. C., Christopher, M., Jacob, K., Guillaumot, J., & Burns, J. (2007). Short-term cognitive behavioral partial hospital treatment: a pilot study. *Journal of Psychiatric Practice, 13*(5), 298–307.

Nezu, A. M., Nezu, C. M., & Lombardo, E. (2004). *Cognitive Behavioral Case Formulation and Treatment Design: A Problem Solving Approach*. New York: Springer Publishing Company.

Norcross, J. (2002). Empirically supported relationships. In J. Norcross (Ed.), *Psychotherapy Relationships that Work; Therapist Contribution and Responsiveness to Patients*. Oxford, England: Oxford University Press.

Padesky, C., & Greenberger, D. (1995). *The Clinician's Guide to Mind Over Mood*. New York: Guilford Press.

Persons, J. B. (2008). *The Case Formulation Approach to Cognitive-Behavior Therapy*. New York: Guilford Press.

Raue, P., Goldfried, M. R., & Barkham, M. (1997). The therapeutic alliance in psychodynamic-interpersonal and cognitive behavioral therapy. *Journal of Consulting and Clinical Psychology, 65*(4), 582–587.

Roth, A., & Fonagy, P. (2005). *What Works For Whom? A Critical Review of Psychotherapy Research*. New York: Guilford Press.

Segal, Z. V., Williams, J. M., & Teasdale, J. D. (2002). *Mindfulness-Based Cognitive Therapy for Depression: A New Approach to Preventing Relapse*. New York: Guilford Press.

Sullivan, H. S. (1954). *The Psychiatric Interview*. New York: Norton & Co.

Tellides, C., Harrington, A., Neuhaus, E. C., & Shapiro, E. (2007). Strategic choices in the psychotherapy of a "fragile" patient. *Harvard Review of Psychiatry, 15*(1), 18–29.

Tompkins, M. (2003). Effective homework. In R. Leahy (Ed.), *Roadblocks in Cognitive-Behavioral Therapy: Transforming Challenges Into Opportunities for Change*. New York: Guilford Press.

Turk, C. L., Heimberg, R. G., & Hope, D. A. (2001). Social anxiety disorder. In D. H. Barlow (Ed.), *Clinical Handbook of Psychological Disorders* (3rd ed.). New York: Guilford Press.

Wapner, S. (1981). Transactions of persons-in-environments: Some critical transitions. *Journal of Environmental Psychology*, 1, 223–239.

Werner, H. (1948). *Comparative Psychology and Mental Development*. New York: International Universities Press, Inc.

Wright, J. H., Basco, M. R., & Thase, M. E. (2006). *Learning Cognitive Behavior Therapy: An Illustrated Guide*. Washington, D.C.: American Psychiatric Publishing.

Wright, J. H., Kingdon, D., Turkington, D., & Ramirez Basco, M. (2009). *Cognitive Behavior Therapy for Severe Mental Disorders*. Arlington, VA: American Psychiatric Publishing, Inc.

Wright, J. H., Thase, M. E., Ludgate, J. W., & Beck, A. T. (1993). The cognitive milieu: structure and process. In J. H. Wright, M. E. Thase, A. T. Beck, & J. W. Ludgate (Eds.), *Cognitive Therapy with Inpatients* (pp. 61–87). New York: Guilford Press.

11

Psychotherapy Research: Implications for Optimal Therapist Personality, Training, and Development

Shannon Wiltsey Stirman and Paul Crits-Christoph

What makes a good therapist? Are therapists with particular personality traits, backgrounds, or characteristics more likely to have successful therapeutic outcomes? Are psychotherapists more successful when they work with patients who are similar to them in particular ways? What types of interventions and techniques should psychotherapists learn and use? How do we train them to do so? These questions have inspired a great deal of research over the years. Although some of the findings to date have raised more questions than they have answered, others have generated results that have important implications for therapist development. In this chapter, we will highlight some of the research that is relevant to these important questions, and discuss their implications for established psychotherapists, trainees, and supervisors.

Therapist Characteristics as Predictors of Outcome

Since Ricks (1974) first described a psychotherapist, dubbed "supershrink," whose severely disturbed patients fared well for years after treatment, researchers have produced evidence that psychotherapists vary in terms of their therapeutic efficacy. Findings of individual studies have indicated that therapist differences account for anywhere from 0% to 40% of the variance in outcomes (Crits-Christoph & Mintz, 1991; Luborsky et al., 1997; Lutz et al., 2007; Orlinsky & Howard, 1976). Based on findings from many of the studies that have examined therapist differences, it appears that patients of some therapists can indeed expect better outcomes than others.

What drives such differences is less clear, despite research using a variety of methods. Researchers have examined numerous factors in efforts to understand the contribution of specific therapist attributes to treatment outcomes. Some of the factors that have been considered include therapist personality, background training and experience, theoretical orientation, attitudes, and participation in personal psychotherapy.

Early psychotherapy research (conducted from about 1950 to 1985) on the relation between therapist characteristics and outcomes in group and individual therapies was summarized by Luborsky et al. (1988). This review concluded:

1. There was a trend for "healthier" therapist personality qualities to be associated with better patient outcome (four of seven studies that tested such relationships reported a significant finding).
2. The amount of therapist personal therapy was unrelated to patient outcome (zero of five studies).
3. Greater therapist level of experience was related to better outcome (7 of 16 studies).
4. Greater therapist skill was related to outcome (three of four studies).
5. There is some evidence that "type A" therapists (personality characterized as more active, personality-oriented, problem-solving, and expressive; Yalom & Lieberman, 1971) were somewhat more effective than other therapists (6 of 12 studies).
6. More favorable therapist attitudes toward treatment were related to better outcome (two of three studies).
7. There are not enough studies of specific therapist demographic characteristics in relation to outcome to draw any conclusions.

While the findings from these early reports should not be dismissed, these studies predate the advent of several major changes in how psychotherapy research is conducted. In early research the methodologies used and means of assessing outcomes varied widely. Beginning in the 1980s, psychotherapy research began to study specific psychotherapies for specific types of patient problems and disorders, and typically used the randomized clinical trial methodology. In addition, primarily short-term treatments have been investigated since the 1980s. In these studies, treatment interventions and methods are held relatively constant within study condition through the use of therapy manuals. When naturalistic studies have been conducted, large sample sizes are employed. In contrast to earlier research, outcomes in this more recent research have been examined using structured diagnostic procedures and established symptom measurements, administered by independent diagnosticians. In contrast, the earlier studies reviewed by Luborsky et al. (1988) focused primarily on open-ended, naturalistic psychotherapies using relatively small and heterogeneous patient samples.

Using data from the landmark Treatment of Depression Collaborative Research Program (TDCRP; Elkin et al., 1989a, 1989b), Blatt et al. (1996) studied the outcomes of 28 therapists who conducted interpersonal psychotherapy (Klerman et al., 1984) or cognitive therapy (Beck et al., 1979). They examined a number of therapist factors, including demographic variables, professional history, and attitudes and expectations regarding the treatment of depression. Theoretical orientation, years of experience, and demographic variables were not found to relate to therapist effectiveness. Therapists found to be more effective reported that they treated significantly more of their non-study patients with psychotherapy alone. Compared to moderately effective therapists, both the less and the more effective therapists considered life and environmental stressors and psychological factors to be central to the etiology of depression These findings suggest that more effective therapists may have been more able to convey an expectation that psychotherapy would be effective in helping their patients to change psychological factors and manage stressors than less and moderately effective therapists. Less effective therapists, on the other hand, may have conveyed doubts that treatment could be effective in changing factors such as environmental stressors. Further study is necessary to understand the relationship between therapist attitudes and clinical outcomes.

Huppert et al. (2001) conducted a study on the outcomes of 14 experienced therapists who provided a cognitive-behavioral intervention for panic disorder in a large clinical trial (Barlow et al., 2000). Patients of all clinicians experienced marked improvement, although there was variability between clinicians in terms of the size of the improvement. Although clinician experience in practicing psychotherapy did not predict overall outcomes, patients who were seen by more experienced therapists (defined as number of years practicing any form of psychotherapy) showed greater improvement than did patients seen by less experienced therapists on measures that are important for cognitive-behavioral therapy (CBT) conceptualizations of panic. These findings suggest that more experienced clinicians may have been more successful at targeting symptoms that are central to a CBT conceptualization of panic. Theoretical orientation, therapist gender, and age were not related to outcomes.

More recent studies have been conducted in the context of training clinics and practice settings as well. In a study of 30 trainee therapists, Lafferty et al. (1989) examined the contribution of personality and other therapist attributes to outcomes. These authors examined personal values, theoretical orientation, therapist emotional adjustment (neuroticism), relationship attitudes, perceptions of patient involvement, credibility, and directiveness/support. Neuroticism did not discriminate between more and less effective therapists. However, more effective therapists placed significantly less importance on having a prosperous and stimulating life and placed significantly more importance on being intellectual and reflective than did less effective therapists. The authors speculated that such values may affect clinicians' ability to provide empathic understanding and limit the extent to which they refine skills that could affect the process of psychotherapy.

Other studies have examined characteristics related to training background and experience. For example, Okiishi et al. (2003) examined the association between outcomes, gender, and three training-related variables: type of training (counseling psychology, clinical psychology, social work), years of training (pre-internship, internship, post-internship), and theoretical orientation (cognitive, behavioral, humanistic, psychodynamic). They conducted a large-scale naturalistic study of outcomes for 1,841 university clinic students and 91 therapists. Despite significant variability in individual clinician outcomes, none of these factors appeared to affect patient outcomes.

In another study, Wogan (1970) used the MMPI to examine the relationship between therapist personality and outcomes in 82 inpatients, each of whom received therapy two or three times per week from one of 12 psychiatric residents. After the subscales were grouped into six factor scales, two factors, anxiety and repression, were found to be associated with outcomes. These findings suggested that patients liked their therapist and showed more progress in therapy when they had therapists who were able to acknowledge some forms of unpleasant experience in themselves and tended not to deny symptoms in themselves.

A recent study (Leon et al., 2005) examined the effect of experience with particular types of patients on clinical outcomes. Using administrative data, patients were matched within 92 individual therapist caseloads on a number of clinical and demographic variables. The findings indicated that therapists can make use of prior experience with future similar patients as long as the subsequent patients enter treatment shortly after the initial patient. This research suggests that when training clinicians, allowing them to strengthen their skills with particular types of patients by working with multiple similar patients may be effective in terms of helping them improve outcomes.

The impact of group leadership style on process and outcomes has also been a focus of research. In early research focusing on encounter groups with 210 student participants, five leadership styles were identified: emotional stimulation (e.g., challenging), caring, meaning attribution (e.g., explaining, clarifying), executive management (e.g., directiveness, setting limits), and use of self (e.g., self-disclosure, participation as a member) (Lieberman et al., 1973). In this study, therapists who were moderate in stimulation and high in caring, used meaning attribution, and used a moderate amount of executive management behaviors were found to be most effective. In more recent research, in a study with 205 students, Shechtman and Toren (2009) found that support, meaning attribution, executive management, and emotional stimulation related to process variables, but only the group leader's use of self and emotional stimulation affected outcomes. Specifically, these variables were positively related to gains in interpersonal relationships. In contrast, in a study with a medical population, executive management and meaning attribution appeared to have the greatest impact on outcomes (Lieberman & Golant, 2002). From this body of research, it appears possible that group leader behaviors may need to vary depending on the focus of the group and the participants (Shechtman & Toren, 2009).

As the above summary indicates, despite decades of research, few factors have been consistently associated with variations in efficacy between therapists. Although there is some evidence that outcomes may improve with therapist experience, to our knowledge there has not been research to characterize what aspects of experience are important. Based on the research conducted to date, there is little indication that a therapist's personality necessarily relates to his or her therapeutic efficacy. However, some aspects of the clinician's personality, experience, and behaviors have not been fully explored.

For example, although there has been research to examine the relation between the therapist's flexibility and work stress (c.f., Hellman, Morrison, & Abromowitz, 1986), the relationship between factors such as therapist boundary setting, burnout, or stress and psychotherapy outcomes has not been fully characterized. Given the demands of full-time clinical practice, such an inquiry may have important implications for therapist development and self-care.

Taken together, findings regarding particular therapist characteristics are not strong enough to suggest that trainees in graduate programs should be selected based on particular attributes. Nor is there sufficient evidence that therapists with particular traits will reliably have more successful outcomes. Still, variability between therapists in terms of outcomes cannot be denied. Additional inquiry, using different measures and examining previously unstudied attributes or behaviors, will be necessary to determine what accounts for such compelling differences.

Matching

Although researchers have not found that the gender, race, personality, or ethnic background of clinicians is associated with differential outcomes, many have argued that a more important factor to consider is the fit, or match, between psychotherapists and patients. It may be that patients feel more comfortable and understood working with therapists who are similar to them in terms of characteristics that are central to their identity. Thus, researchers have attempted to determine whether patients are more likely to stay in therapy and benefit from it if they are matched on such characteristics. Few studies have experimentally manipulated match; instead, most have examined the association between match and outcomes by examining match *post hoc*. Findings regarding match on a variety of characteristics and outcomes have not been consistent across studies or diagnoses.

Several studies have examined the association between gender match and outcomes (Huppert et al., 2001; Sterling et al., 1998, 2001; Zlotnick et al., 1998). In a study with 976 patients in an intensive treatment program for cocaine dependence, partial support was found for an association with gender matching. Although match was not associated with overall substance abuse outcomes, female patients who were matched with female clinicians were more likely to continue with outpatient treatment after discharge from an intensive program, and gender-matched patients remained in the program for approximately 5 days more than mismatched patients (Sterling et al., 1998). However, in a study of depressed patients who participated in the TDCRP, no relationship was found between gender matching and outcomes (Zlotnick et al., 1998). Similarly, Huppert et al. (2001) did not find an association between gender match and outcomes for patients with panic disorder. In one of the few studies with lesbian, gay, bisexual, and transgendered individuals who received psychotherapy, 2,000 patients completed a survey about their experience and outcomes. The gender of the therapist was a significant predictor of self-reported benefit only for female respondents, and the sexual orientation of the therapist was a significant predictor only for the male respondents (Jones et al., 2003).

In a review of the findings on race and ethnic matching, Karlsson (2005) found that overall, outcomes did not appear to be associated with match. However, in some studies reviewed, patients in mismatched therapy dyads were more likely to terminate therapy prematurely. Matching did not appear to affect outcomes or dropout in some large retrospective studies with African American patients in substance abuse programs (Sterling et al., 1998, 2001). One study examined the impact of unmet preference for ethnic matching among 31 African American veterans (Rosen & Proctor, 1981). Patients were not randomized into met or unmet preferences, but findings indicated that unmet preferences for ethnic matching did not affect the dropout rate or post-treatment satisfaction. Studies that examined matching among other ethnic groups have not yielded consistent findings. Sue et al. (1991) found that ethnic and language match was a predictor of treatment lengths for African Americans, Mexican Americans, Asian Americans, and Caucasians in a community mental health setting. Ethnic and language match also predicted outcomes for Mexican Americans and for those for whom English is not a first language. In a large study with samples from college mental health clinics, ethnic mismatch was associated with the completion of fewer sessions (Erdur et al., 2003), except among Latin American patients, who completed fewer sessions when they were matched with therapists of the same ethnicity.

Some considerations regarding the interpretation of findings regarding ethnic matching are important. Many studies are archival, and few have involved experimental manipulation of match. In addition, little attention has been paid to the role of acculturation, cultural sensitivity, and stage of identity development in these studies. Such factors may moderate the relationship between matching and outcomes (Karlsson, 2005).

Sensitivity to patients' backgrounds and needs may be more important than match. For example, Yamamoto et al. (1984) compared groups of psychotherapists treating ethnically diverse patients from the working class. One group received an orientation about the patient's cultural background, expectations, and needs. In the follow-up interview after the termination of the treatments, it was found that the patients who worked with a therapist who received the orientation were more satisfied, independent of ethnic match and the length of the therapist's experience. It is also important to note that findings of several studies have suggested that socioeconomic (SES) status may be more strongly associated with dropout rates than ethnicity or match (Karlsson, 2005). Similarly, different therapist behaviors may be indicated depending on the patient's SES. In a study of clinician behaviors in couples therapy with couples of differing income levels, therapist directiveness was related positively to a number of outcome measures for lower-SES women but negatively related to a number of outcome measures, including social behavior and marital satisfaction, for middle-SES couples (Cline et al., 1984).

Matching in terms of personal characteristics and values has been examined somewhat less frequently in the literature. One study examined self-reported fit between therapists and patients in terms of sense of humor, political and personal values, activity level, and cognitive style. Therapist- and patient-rated positive matches correlated with self-reported assessments of therapy progress (Dolinsky et al., 1998). Other studies have examined the match between therapist and patient personality characteristics and alliance and found positive associations, suggesting that fit may be more strongly related to alliance than outcomes (Coleman, 2006; Hersoug et al., 2001).

Findings regarding matching suggest that psychotherapists can provide effective treatment even for patients with whom they have less in common. However, more research is necessary in some areas. To our knowledge, the relative importance of fit between patient and therapists in terms of outcomes for different types of therapy has not been studied extensively and still warrants investigation. In addition, adequate research has not been conducted to determine whether matching can affect outcomes in treatments for individuals who have experienced a trauma. It is possible that survivors of sexual trauma may indeed be more comfortable working with therapists of the same gender. This has been assumed in many studies, which have matched trauma survivors and therapist gender by design. Sensitivity to such factors in conducting therapy and choosing interventions is important regardless of the match, and in some cases, research suggests matching may affect factors such as dropout and alliance.

Technique

In addition to the exploration of clinician attributes that may contribute to psychotherapy outcomes, the impact of technique in psychotherapy has been investigated extensively. Researchers have generally focused on general psychotherapy techniques (also known as common factors or nonspecifics), techniques specific to a particular intervention, and the relative contribution of the two to clinical outcomes. We will summarize findings in each of these areas and then will discuss implications for therapist development.

General Techniques

General techniques include the facilitation of the therapeutic relationship, therapist warmth, empathy, and understanding, a rationale for treatment, and encouraging positive expectations for improvement. The impact of these factors on outcome has been studied extensively, through a variety of strategies. Some of the evidence that suggests that common factors contribute to psychotherapy outcomes include meta-analyses that find few differences in outcomes of specific models of psychotherapies (e.g., Luborsky et al., 2002;

Smith & Glass, 1977; Wampold et al., 1997). The methods used for identifying studies and conducting the comparisons in some of these studies have been questioned (Crits-Christoph et al., 1997), as has the use of such findings as evidence for the causal role of common factors in treatment outcomes (Chambless, 2002; DeRubeis et al., 2005). Relevant to the current chapter, these comparative studies do not directly address the therapist's, as opposed to the patient's, contribution to common factors.

Numerous studies, however, have directly assessed the relation of therapist general techniques in relation to treatment outcome. These studies typically conduct ratings of therapist techniques using tape recordings of therapy sessions. Summarizing the early period of psychotherapy research, Luborsky et al. (1988) conclude that therapist empathy (8 of 13 studies), therapist warmth and positive regard (9 of 14 studies), and therapist genuineness (3 of 5 studies) all are related to treatment outcome.

In more recent research, there is some indication that the contribution of common factors to outcome may vary by therapeutic model, with less of an influence found in most studies of more structured therapies. In an examination of psychodynamic therapies, therapist warmth, understanding, and affirmation was found to be positively associated with therapy outcome, whereas behaviors including belittling, blaming, neglecting, attacking, and rejecting were found to be negatively related to outcome (Najavits & Strupp, 1994). In their study of therapist trainees in a counseling program, Lafferty et al. (1989) found that in addition to particular therapist values described previously in this chapter, therapist empathy and therapist directiveness distinguished more effective therapists from less effective therapists. In contrast, when examined in two studies of cognitive therapy for depression, therapist-offered facilitative conditions such as warmth and empathy did not predict outcomes (DeRubeis & Feeley, 1990; Feeley et al., 1999). However, in a recent study of inpatient interpersonal psychotherapy or CBT for social anxiety, therapists' early alliance and empathy ratings did predict improvement during the course of therapy. Changes in these ongoing processes often affected subsequent outcomes (Hoffart et al., 2009).

Therapeutic Alliance

The therapeutic alliance is a common factor that has been defined by Bordin (1979) as composed of three elements: the emotional bond between patient and therapist, agreement on therapeutic tasks, and agreement on therapy goals. Thus, the alliance is not a pure therapist variable *per se* but involves both patient and therapist components as they interact during therapy. The alliance is believed to play a central role in almost all forms of psychotherapy. For many psychotherapies (e.g., Beck et al., 1979), a positive alliance is seen as "setting the stage" for technical factors to have an impact on outcome and thus is viewed as a necessary but not sufficient cause of therapeutic change. Other forms of psychotherapy, such as patient-centered therapy (Rogers, 1951), supportive-expressive psychotherapy (Luborsky, 1984) and Safran and Muran's (2000) relational approach to resolving ruptures in the alliance, view the alliance as a curative factor in its own right.

Across numerous empirical investigations, the therapeutic alliance has repeatedly been found to be a consistent predictor of treatment outcome. The first meta-analysis of this literature involved 24 studies and found an average effect size (correlation coefficient) of 0.26 between the alliance and psychotherapy outcome (Horvath & Symonds, 1991). A subsequent meta-analysis found an average correlation of 0.22 between the alliance and treatment outcome across 68 studies (Martin et al., 2000). The association of the alliance to outcome is generally found across a wide range of types of therapies, durations of treatment, and patient populations.

One of the difficult issues to sort out in studies of the alliance in relation to outcome is the direction of causality (Crits-Christoph et al., 2006b). Because the alliance is typically assessed after three or four sessions of therapy, it is possible that positive improvements occurring before the alliance is assessed in therapy might be associated with both the alliance and eventual outcome, producing a spurious correlation between alliance and eventual outcome. Thus, it may simply be that patients who have already benefited from therapy will tend to bond to their therapist and agree with the therapist on the tasks and goals of therapy. However, at least four studies have now statistically controlled for the impact of early improvement on the alliance–outcome relationship, with each providing evidence that the alliance continues to be associated with positive treatment outcome even after controlling for early improvement (Barber et al., 2000; Crits-Christoph et al., 2009; Gaston et al., 1991; Klein et al., 2003).

A recent development has been efforts to separate the therapist's and the patient's contributions to the alliance–outcome relationship. This separation is done using modern statistical methods of multilevel modeling. To evaluate the therapist component, the analysis examines the relation of therapist average alliances (i.e., the mean alliance for each therapist across all patients treated by that therapist) to outcome, and separately tests the patient component by examining the average relation of the alliance to outcome within therapists' caseloads.

Two studies have taken this approach. Using naturalistic psychotherapy outcome data from university counseling centers, Baldwin et al. (2007) found that therapist variability in the alliance, but not patient variability in the alliance, predicted outcome. In a substance abuse sample treated with motivational enhancement therapy (Miller & Rollnick, 2002) or treatment as usual (standard drug and alcohol counseling and AA facilitation), Crits-Christoph et al. (2009) also found that therapist variability, but not patient variability, in the alliance was related to outcome. Moreover, it was found that either relatively poor or very strong alliances were associated with worse outcomes. This finding of very high scores on alliance measures being associated with poor outcomes had been reported previously (Saunders et al., 1989), but the reasons for this effect are not clear. Crits-Christoph et al. (2009) speculate that very high therapist average alliances with patients may be a marker for a therapist who relies excessively on supportive techniques to the exclusion of other therapy techniques. Thus, while the alliance is an important aspect of successful therapy, other components of therapy are also likely to be necessary for optimal patient change.

The above studies documenting that therapists' variability in their average alliances predicts treatment outcome raise the question of which therapist factors and techniques might be most effective to establish and maintain a positive alliance. Ackerman and Hilsenroth (2003) have reviewed correlational studies of therapist factors in relation to the alliance and conclude that therapists who are more flexible, experienced, honest, respectful, trustworthy, confident, interested, alert, friendly, warm, and open have better alliances. In addition, the following therapist techniques are associated with better alliances: being reflective, being supportive, noting past therapy success, providing accurate interpretations, facilitating emotional expression, being active, and being affirming. The implication of these findings for the training of therapists is considered later in this chapter.

Specific Techniques

In addition to aspects of psychotherapy that are common across models and interventions, the role of techniques that are specific to a particular intervention has been explored in psychotherapy research. Evidence of the relationship between specific techniques and outcomes includes research findings that particular psychotherapies result in superior outcomes when compared to other *bona fide* treatments. Research on treatments for disorders including obsessive-compulsive disorder, social anxiety disorder, panic disorder, and post-traumatic stress disorder have yielded evidence that one active treatment produces greater therapeutic change than another (c.f., DeRubeis et al., 2005). Such findings suggest that at least for these disorders, specific techniques contribute to clinical outcomes.

Research on the association between clinical change and adherence to particular models, or competence in delivering specific interventions, has been suggested as further support of the argument that specific techniques and interventions are more likely to produce therapeutic change. Competence in implementing interventions has been shown to relate to clinical outcomes in several studies, but findings are inconsistent across different psychotherapies, methodologies, competence measures, and outcome measures (Barber 2009; Webb, DeRubeis, & Barber, 2010). Competence in cognitive therapy predicted improvements in studies of depression and anxiety (Kingdon et al., 1996; Shaw et al., 1999; Trepka et al., 2004; Webb, DeRubeis, & Barber., 2010), suicide prevention (Davidson et al., 2004), and personality disorders (Hoffart, Sexton, Nordahl, & Stiles, 2009). Huppert et al. (2001) found a curvilinear relationship between competence and outcomes for panic disorder: moderate competence was more predictive of symptom improvement than high or low competence. Strunk et al (2010) found that competence in cognitive therapy predicted end-of-treatment depressive symptoms, particularly for patients with high anxiety and early onset depression. Findings for dynamic therapies and other therapies have indicated a more mixed relationship between competence and outcomes. Competence predicted improvements in depression (Barber et al., 1996), but in a study of short-term anxiety-provoking therapy, competence did not predict global symptom improvement (Svartberg & Stiles, 1994). Fewer studies on competence have been conducted on other psychotherapies. O'Malley et al. (1988) found that competence in interpersonal psychotherapy predicted patient-rated improvements in depression symptoms. A measure of competence in emotion-focused therapy did not predict outcomes (Paivio et al., 2004); neither did competence in individual drug counseling (Barber et al., 2006).

Further refinement of methods of assessing competence is necessary for many treatments. However, some tentative generalizations can be made. The research to date indicates that competence in interpersonal psychotherapy, cognitive therapy, and supportive-expressive therapy for depression have all been shown to predict outcome. Thus, in working with depressed patients, developing competence in a particular method or intervention appears to be advisable. Less research has been conducted for other disorders and interventions.

In addition, the interaction between alliance and specific techniques warrants further exploration (Webb, DeRubeis, & Barber, 2010). Studies of the contributions of factors such as therapeutic alliance and specific techniques have become increasingly common. DeRubeis and Feeley (1990) examined the relations of both techniques specific to cognitive therapy and general therapy process variables to outcome in a sample of depressed outpatients. The use of concrete methods of cognitive therapy in the second session correlated significantly with subsequent symptom change. Other variables, including the therapeutic alliance, were not significantly correlated with outcomes. In a subsequent studies, concrete methods of cognitive therapy, measured early in treatment, predicted subsequent change in depression over and above the therapeutic alliance (Feeley et al., 1999). In a study of the relationship between adherence, competence, and alliance in supportive-expressive therapy for cocaine dependence, moderate adherence and competent delivery were associated with poorer outcome, while a strong alliance combined with low levels of adherence was associated with a better outcome than moderate or high levels of adherence (Barber et al., 2008).

The relative impact of common and specific factors to outcomes has been the subject of considerable debate (c.f., DeRubeis et al., 2005; Messer & Wampold, 2002). Citing findings that common factors account for a large proportion of variance in outcomes (Wampold al., 1997), some have suggested that rather than solely focusing on empirically supported treatments, clinicians should focus on empirically supported relationships (Messer & Wampold, 2002; Norcross, 2002). In one of the more recent meta-analyses examining the issue of common and specific factors, Stevens et al. (2000) examined 80 studies to compare the impact of specific techniques and common factors. Similar to the findings of Lambert and Bergin (1994), they found that the mean effectiveness of specific treatments surpassed the mean effectiveness of common factors, which in turn proved superior to no treatment. Findings differed according to severity: for research participants with less severe disorders, the magnitude of common factor and specific treatment effects was nearly identical, while for those with more severe disorders, only the specific treatment component was beneficial. These findings suggest that when treating severe disorders, the use of specific techniques is indicated (Crits-Christoph, 1997).

Based on the above research on the alliance and on techniques, several tentative conclusions can be offered. Both general therapy skills (common factors) and specific skills appear important. While both may be necessary for therapeutic change, it may be that neither is sufficient by itself. In implementing manual-based psychotherapies, adherence to the manual is a priority, but excessive adherence appears to have a negative impact in some studies. Thus, psychotherapists need to balance their attention to alliance and techniques. The extent to which these issues vary depending on the type of patient, modality, presenting problem, or specific treatment has been largely unexplored in research. Furthermore, recent studies of the relationship between adherence and alliance indicate that the relationship between common and specific factors may be somewhat complex for some treatments. Additional investigations that include measures of both will be necessary to understand the nature of the interaction between common and specific factors in different psychotherapeutic models, and in different modalities. However, both general and specific factors appear to be important in the development of a well-rounded and effective therapist.

Therapists' Attitudes Toward Evidence-Based Treatments and Training Considerations

The past several decades have produced an enormous amount of research regarding treatments for a variety of clinical issues and diagnoses. Psychotherapists have a variety of decisions to make regarding the models of psychotherapy they will practice generally, and the methods they will use in working with particular patients. Perhaps due in part to the size of the literature on psychotherapy outcomes, implementation of many of these treatments has not kept pace with the research. Thus, clinicians' attitudes toward new treatments, and factors that determine the decision to adopt new treatments, have been the focus of a significant body of research. Cohen et al. (1986) reviewed studies of clinicians' attitudes and conducted interviews to determine factors that had the greatest influence on clinicians' decisions to adopt treatments with demonstrated efficacy. Fairly consistently, discussions with colleagues are weighted more heavily than research articles or books. Subsequent research confirmed these findings and confirmed that therapists are more inclined to try a new treatment if they are provided with a clear description of the tested treatment, can receive training in that treatment, and view the treatment as compatible with their own usual intervention strategies (Aarons, 2004; Cohen et al., 1986; Najavits et al., 2004; Stewart & Chambless, 2007).

Research on attitudes toward psychotherapy manuals has found wide variation among practicing psychotherapists. Many clinicians have generally positive beliefs and attitudes about the manualized psychotherapies that are tested in psychotherapy outcome research. For example, recent surveys of therapists showed that the majority of respondents had positive attitudes toward evidence-based psychotherapies (Gray et al., 2007; Stewart & Chambless, 2007). However, in several studies, some clinicians have also expressed the view that manual-based therapies are overly structured, potentially damaging to the therapeutic relationship, and unlikely to allow them to treat their patients as individuals or use clinical judgment (Addis & Krasnow, 2000; Barry et al., 2008; Cahill et al., 2006; Gray et al., 2007). Clinicians may also weigh findings on specific and general factors differently in their clinical decision making and choose to focus more on the therapeutic relationship than on specific interventions (Messer & Wampold, 2002). Others may doubt that the interventions have been used and tested with more complex or challenging patients, such as those they see in their everyday practice (Goldfried & Wolfe, 1998). Such concerns can limit psychotherapists' willingness to learn and use evidence-based treatments.

A number of practical considerations can influence clinicians' ability to receive further training or change the way that they practice as well. First, many barriers to training exist. Not only are the costs of workshops substantial, but they also require therapists to give up billable hours to read training materials and receive training. In addition, there is increasing evidence that workshops and manuals do not provide sufficient training for clinicians to confidently and competently implement the intervention (Miller & Mount, 2001; Miller et al., 2004; Sholomskas et al., 2005). Supervision and consultation requires more time away from psychotherapy practice and is often limited by the availability of supervisors with adequate experience and training in the intervention. Thus, after graduate training and internship, it may be difficult for therapists to pursue adequate training and supervision in new skills (Crits-Christoph et al., 1995). Innovative training programs that remove some of the barriers to post-professional training may be necessary before practicing clinicians can be expected to pursue training in new areas.

Not surprisingly, a number of models of training and supervision have emerged over the years. Researchers have examined the impact of training on basic therapy skills and on the implementation of specific psychotherapy models. While the majority of the research on basic therapy skills has focused on pre-professional training, the movement toward evidence-based practices has generated an interest in examining models of training for practicing psychotherapists in specific models of psychotherapy.

Three methods that have been used to train clinicians in developing basic helping skills are Truax and Carkhuff's (1967) human relations training (HRT), Ivey's (1971) microcounseling model, and Kagan's (1984) interpersonal process recall (IPR). Both HRT and microcounseling consist of didactic training, while IPR involves more experiential training. A meta-analysis that compared the three methods found that trainees benefit more from HRT than microcounseling or IPR, and more from microcounseling than IPR (Baker et al., 1990). Although length of training may be confounded with efficacy in this study, the differences in outcomes may also reflect the utility of a more structured, instructor-directed focus on learning specific helping skills, which may be particularly important at earlier stages of training (Hill & Lent, 2006). Hill et al. developed a training program that integrates aspects of HRT, microcounseling, and IPR as well as research on the effects of helping skills in the therapy process (Hill, 2004; Hill & O'Brien, 1999). In this program, students learn about the skills using a three-stage framework: exploration (e.g., open questions, restatements, and reflections of feelings), insight (e.g., challenges, interpretations, self-disclosures of insight, and immediacy), and action (e.g., information and direct guidance). The model was associated with changes across the course of training in trainees' use of the helping skills, ability to establish a therapeutic relationship, and ability to conduct a good session, as assessed by volunteer patients (Hill & Kellems, 2002).

Another line of research relevant to training has examined therapists' "conceptual level" (CL; Hunt, 1977–1978) as it affects the acquisition of psychotherapy skills. Those assessed to be concrete (low CL) types, exhibit conceptual simplicity and external, dependent orientations to interpersonal affairs. Abstract types (high CL) exhibit greater conceptual complexity and more internal, interdependent orientations to the interpersonal. Holloway and Wampold (1986) used a meta-analytic strategy to study the impact of CL on clinicians' learning and performance. The majority of the 24 studies they reviewed examined CL in undergraduates or counseling trainees. They found that counselors who were matched with a compatible environment (i.e., low-CL individuals with high structure and high-CL individuals with low structure) demonstrated better acquisition and application of counseling-related skills such as problem definition or facilitative conditions than those who were mismatched. In addition, low-CL individuals performed significantly better in highly structured environments, while the level of improvement among high-CL individuals improved only slightly in low-CL environments.

Holloway and Wampold's findings suggest that structuring education and training environments to fit the trainee's CL may result in greater improvement or skill acquisition. Further, such findings imply that counselors may benefit from selecting training and work environments based on their CL. However, a later study (McLennan et al., 1993) suggested that counselors' cognitive complexity may be more of a dynamic quality that is modified according to the nature of the counseling interview. Citing these results, as well as methodological limitations of many of the earlier CL studies,

McLennan (1995) called some conclusions about CL into question, suggesting that additional research be conducted before it should be used as a basis for selecting trainees.

Empirical findings (reviewed earlier) on three topics bear on the training of therapists to develop a strong therapeutic alliance: (1) the alliance is a consistent predictor of outcome, (2) therapist variability in the alliance is associated with outcome, and (3) correlational studies suggest that therapist behaviors and techniques can improve the alliance. Putting these findings together, the empirical literature suggests that to improve treatment outcomes, one approach would be to train therapists to use interventions that foster and maintain the alliance.

Two studies have directly evaluated the impact of specific therapist training on the therapeutic alliance. Hilsenroth et al. (2002) found that graduate student therapists (n = 13) who received structured training in a therapeutic model of assessment and short-term psychodynamic psychotherapy had better alliances than graduate student therapists (n = 15) who received unstructured training in assessment and therapy. A study by Crits-Christoph et al. (2006a) directly examined the extent to which therapists could be trained to improve their average patient alliances. In this study, therapists were trained in alliance-fostering therapy, a 16-session treatment for major depressive disorder that combined interpersonal-psychodynamic interventions with techniques for enhancing the alliance based on Bordin's (1979) model of the alliance. Five psychotherapists who had less than 3 years of postdoctoral clinical experience treated three patients in each of three study phases: before, during, and after training in alliance-fostering therapy. From before to after training, moderate to large increases in the alliance were apparent, although these effects were not statistically significant because of the small sample size. Of note was that some therapists improved their alliances considerably, while others did not. The training resulted in improvements in depressive symptoms but even larger improvements in quality of life, particularly at follow-up (6 and 12 months after termination).

Researchers have also studied methods of training in specific interventions at both pre- and post-professional levels. Such studies have ranged from investigations of didactic training and continuing education workshops to studies of more intensive training programs. Intensive workshops and Internet-based training programs for clinicians have been shown to increase knowledge about evidence-based psychotherapies (Cucciare et al., 2008). However, studies have shown that participants in such programs did not typically reach adequate skill levels without additional consultation (Martino et al., 2008; Miller et al., 2004; Schoener et al., 2006; Sholomskas et al., 2005).

More intensive training in manual-based psychotherapies has generally been shown to increase adherence and competence in delivering interventions. For example, a 40-day training program in cognitive therapy appeared to have a significant impact on competence after training (Milne et al., 1999).

Similarly, training in manual-based time-limited dynamic psychotherapy was associated with greater levels of adherence across four supervised training sessions (Multon et al., 1996). Henry et al. (1993) studied the effects of weekly didactic–supervisory group meetings for a manual-guided time-limited dynamic therapy. After 1 year, with each therapist having one training case, therapists showed increased use of specific techniques (e.g., exploration of the therapeutic relationship) and improvement in interviewing style and general therapeutic techniques. Crits-Christoph et al. (1998) also studied manual-based training in supportive-expressive psychotherapy, drug counseling, and CBT. A large effect across cases was detected for training in CBT. Supportive-expressive therapists and individual drug counselors demonstrated statistically significant learning trends over sessions but not over training cases. These findings indicate that while the number of cases optimal for training may vary according to the specific therapeutic model, supervision is an important component of clinical training.

In another approach, Reese et al. (2009) have studied the impact of patient feedback on outcomes in which the therapists are clinical trainees. All participants received regular supervision with session reviews. The trainees in the feedback condition also discussed patient scores to determine if the patients were progressing as expected. The feedback was used to guide discussion of new strategies as well as to allow the supervisor to prioritize case discussions in supervision. The patients of trainees who received feedback experienced better outcomes than those in the no-feedback condition. Thus, it appears that teaching clinicians to regularly seek feedback regarding patients' progress through the use of symptom inventories or other instruments during therapy is another potentially important element of training.

Taken together, the evidence to date suggests that training programs designed to impart basic skills or competence in particular interventions must be fairly intensive, even when designed for more experienced psychotherapists. Such findings suggest that the use of brief continuing education activities alone may not be sufficient for practicing clinicians to build new skills. Ongoing study and supervision appear to be necessary for the development of new skills for clinicians at any stage of career development.

Summary and Recommendations

Despite decades of research on the attributes of more versus less successful therapists, few psychotherapist characteristics have consistently been associated with clinical outcomes. In some ways, this is a puzzling finding, as therapist effects have been found in a number of clinical studies, including those that include the use of a manual to minimize variations in in-session behaviors. The lack of consistent findings suggests that while it is possible to train students to be efficacious therapists, trainees do not necessarily need to be selected based on particular attributes. However, further research, in individual, group, couples, and family contexts, will be necessary to determine the behaviors or attributes that account for the intriguing differences in therapeutic efficacy that have been found in psychotherapy research.

Rather than selecting trainees based on particular characteristics, it appears to be more advisable for supervisors to focus on the development of solid basic clinical, case conceptualization, and intervention skills and emphasize the importance of cultural sensitivity. Furthermore, supervisors must provide training in the critical review and appropriate use of the psychotherapy outcome literature. An important aspect of both the scientist-practitioner training model and the more practice-oriented practitioner-scholar training model is the integration of the most relevant and high-quality research findings into a case formulation and treatment strategy for individual patients. Without the ability to evaluate the methods used in both original research and meta-analysis, clinicians are limited in their ability to distill research findings and integrate research as appropriate into their practice.

In providing clinical training, research also suggests that didactics alone are not sufficient. Studies of training methods suggest the importance of direct observation and review of work samples. Clinicians have been shown to overestimate their skill levels (Brosan et al., 2008), and verbal reports about sessions from clinicians may omit important process variables or misrepresent what occurred in session (Martino, Ball, Nich, Frankforter, & Carroll, 2008; Perepletchikova et al., 2007). Thus, we recommend that supervisors regularly supplement discussion of case materials with review of audio or video recordings of sessions. Furthermore, supervisors who provide post-professional training should be aware of the challenges associated with training established clinicians and should develop training programs accordingly.

Our recommendations for therapists are similar to those we provide for supervisors. Therapists must review the current psychotherapy literature and develop the ability to review research and appraise the methods used in research critically and thoughtfully. Continued openness to new developments in the field, skill development, consultation, and feedback are essential for psychotherapists at any stage of development. Attention should be paid to both general clinical skills and competence in delivering specific interventions. For a number of common diagnoses, research indicates that specific therapies are more effective than others, and clinicians and researchers continue to develop and test new interventions. In addition, the relationship between the therapeutic alliance and the use of specific clinical interventions appears to be more complex than early research has suggested, and we expect that researchers will continue to examine these elements of psychotherapy. Thus, as new methods are developed and research is done, it will be important for therapists to remain aware of new findings, consider their implications for practice, and adjust their clinical practice accordingly.

References

Aarons, G. A. (2004). Mental health provider attitudes toward adoption of evidence-based practice: The Evidence-Based Practice Attitude Scale (EBPAS). *Mental Health Services Research*, 6(2), 61–74.

Ackerman, S. J., & Hilsenroth, M. J. (2003). A review of therapist characteristics and techniques positively impacting the therapeutic alliance. *Clinical Psychology Review*, 23, 1–33.

Addis, M. E., & Krasnow, A. D. (2000). A national survey of practicing psychologists' attitudes toward psychotherapy treatment manuals. *Journal of Consulting and Clinical Psychology*, 68(2), 331–339.

Baker, S. B., Daniels, T. G., & Greeley, A. T. (1990). Systematic training of graduate-level counselors: Narrative and meta-analytic reviews of three major programs. *The Counseling Psychologist*, 1 8(3), 355–421.

Baldwin, S. A., Wampold, B. E., & Imel, Z. E. (2007). Untangling the alliance-outcome correlation: Exploring the relative importance of therapist and patient variability in the alliance. *Journal of Consulting and Clinical Psychology*, 75, 842–852.

Barber, J. P. (2009). Toward a working through of some core conflicts in psychotherapy research. *Psychotherapy Research*, 19, 1–12.

Barber, J. P., Connolly, M. B., Crits-Christoph, P., Gladis, M., & Siqueland, L. (2000). Alliance predicts patients' outcome beyond in-treatment change in symptoms. *Journal of Consulting and Clinical Psychology*, 68, 1027–1032.

Barber, J. P., Crits-Christoph, P., & Luborsky, L. (1996). Effects of therapist adherence and competence on patient outcome in brief dynamic therapy. *Journal of Consulting and Clinical Psychology*, 64(3), 619–622.

Barber, J. P., Gallop, R., Crits-Christoph, P., Barrett, M. S., Klostermann, S., McCarthy, K. S., & Sharpless, B. A. (2008). The role of the alliance and techniques in predicting outcome of supportive-expressive dynamic therapy for cocaine dependence. *Psychoanalytic Psychology*, 25(3), 461–482. doi:10.1037/0736-9735.25.3.461

Barber, J. P., Gallop, R., Crits-Christoph, P., Frank, A., Thase, M. E., Weiss, R. D., & Gibbons, M. B. C. (2006). The role of therapist adherence, therapist competence, and alliance in predicting outcome of individual drug counseling: Results from the National Institute on Drug Abuse collaborative cocaine treatment study. *Psychotherapy Research*, 16(2), 229–240.

Barlow, D. H., Gorman, J. M., Shear, M. K., & Woods, S. W. (2000). Cognitive-behavioral therapy, imipramine, or their combination for panic disorder: A randomized controlled trial. *JAMA: Journal of the American Medical Association*, 283(19), 2529–2536.

Barry, D. T., Fulgieri, M. D., Lavery, M. E., Chawarski, M. C., Najavits, L. M., Schottenfeld, R. S., & Pantalon, M. V. (2008). Research- and community-based clinicians' attitudes on treatment manuals. *American Journal on Addictions*, 17(2), 145–148.

Beck, A.T., Rush, A.J., Shaw, B.F., & Emery, G. (1979). *Cognitive Therapy of Depression*. New York: Guilford.

Blatt, S. J., Sanislow, C. A., Zuroff, D. C., & Pilkonis, P. A. (1996). Characteristics of effective therapists: Further analyses of data from the National Institute of Mental Health treatment of depression collaborative research program. *Journal of Consulting and Clinical Psychology*, 64(6), 1276–1284.

Bordin, E. S. (1979). The generalizability of the psycho-analytic concept of the working alliance. *Psychotherapy: Theory, Research, and Practice*, 16, 252–260.

Brosan, L., Reynolds, S., & Moore, R. G. (2008). Self-evaluation of cognitive therapy performance: Do therapists know how competent they are? *Behavioural and Cognitive Psychotherapy*, 36(5), 581–587.

Cahill, S. P., Foa, E. B., Hembree, E. A., Marshall, R. D., & Nacash, N. (2006). Dissemination of exposure therapy in the treatment of posttraumatic stress disorder. *Journal of Traumatic Stress. Special Issue: Dissemination: Transforming Lives through Transforming Care*, 19(5), 597–610.

Chambless, D. L. (2002). Beware the dodo bird: The dangers of overgeneralization. *Clinical Psychology: Science and Practice*, 9(1), 13–16.

Cline, V. B., Mejia, J., Coles, J., Klein, N., & Cline, R. A. (1984). The relationship between therapist behaviors and outcome for middle- and lower-class couples in marital therapy. *Journal of Clinical Psychology*, 40(3), 691–704.

Coleman, D. (2006). Therapist–client five-factor personality similarity: A brief report. *Bulletin of the Menninger Clinic*, 70, 232–241.

Crits-Christoph, P. (1997). Limitations of the dodo bird verdict and the role of clinical trials in psychotherapy research: Comment on Wampold et al. (1997). *Psychological Bulletin*, 122(3), 216–220.

Crits-Christoph, P., Connolly Gibbons, M.B, Crits-Christoph, K., Narducci, J., Schamberger, M., & Gallop, R. (2006a). Can therapists be trained to improve their alliances? A pilot study of alliance-fostering therapy. *Psychotherapy Research*, 13, 268–281.

Crits-Christoph, P., Connolly Gibbons, M. B., & Hearon, B. (2006b). Does the alliance cause good outcome? *Psychotherapy: Theory, Research, Practice, Training*, 43, 280–285.

Crits-Christoph, P., Frank, E., Chambless, D. L., Brody, C., & Karp, J. F. (1995). Training in empirically validated treatments: What are clinical psychology students learning? *Professional Psychology: Research and Practice*, 26(5), 514–522.

Crits-Christoph, P., Gallop, R., Temes, C. M., Woody, G., Ball, S. A., Martino, S., & Carroll, K. M. (2009). The alliance in motivational enhancement therapy and counseling as usual for substance use problems. *Journal of Consulting and Clinical Psychology*, 77(6), 1125–1135.

Crits-Christoph, P., & Mintz, J. (1991). Implications of therapist effects for the design and analysis of comparative studies of psychotherapies. *Journal of Consulting and Clinical Psychology*, 59(1), 20–26.

Crits-Christoph, P. (1997). Limitations of the dodo bird verdict and the role of clinical trials in psychotherapy research: Comment on Wampold et al. (1997). *Psychological Bulletin*, 122(3), 216–220.

Crits-Christoph, P., Siqueland, L., Chittams, J., Barber, J. P., Beck, A. T., Frank, A., Liese, B., Luborsky, L., Mark, D., Mercer, D., Onken, L. S., Najavits, L. M., Thase, M. E., & Woody, G. (1998). Training in cognitive, supportive-expressive, and drug counseling therapies for cocaine dependence. *Journal of Consulting and Clinical Psychology*, 66(3), 484–492.

Cohen, L. H., Sargent, M. M., & Sechrest, L. B. (1986). Use of psychotherapy research by professional psychologists. *American Psychologist. Special Issue: Psychotherapy Research*, 41(2), 198–206.

Cucciare, M. A., Weingardt, K. R., & Villafranca, S. (2008). Using blended learning to implement evidence-based psychotherapies. *Clinical Psychology: Science and Practice*, 15, 299–307.

Davidson, K., Scott, J., Schmidt, U., Tata, P., Thornton, S., & Tyrer, P. (2004). Therapist competence and clinical outcome in the prevention of parasuicide by manual assisted cognitive behaviour therapy trial: The POPMACT study. *Psychological Medicine*, 34(5), 855–863.

DeRubeis, R. J., Brotman, M. A., & Gibbons, C. J. (2005). A conceptual and methodological analysis of the nonspecifics argument. *Clinical Psychology: Science and Practice*, 12(2), 174–183.

DeRubeis, R. J., & Feeley, M. (1990). Determinants of change in cognitive therapy for depression. *Cognitive Therapy and Research*, 14, 469–482.

Dolinsky, A., Vaughan, S. C., Luber, B., Mellman, L., & Roose, S. (1998). A match made in heaven? A pilot study of patient–therapist match. *Journal of Psychotherapy Practice & Research*, 7(2), 119–125.

Elkin, I., Shea, M. T., Watkins, J. T., Imber, S. D., Sotsky, S. M., Collins, J. F., et al. (1989a). NIMH Treatment of Depression Collaborative Research Program: General effectiveness of treatments. *Archives of General Psychiatry*, 46, 971–982.

Elkin, I., Shea, M. T., Watkins, J. T., & Imber, S. D. (1989b). National Institute of Mental Health treatment of depression collaborative research program: General effectiveness of treatments. *Archives of General Psychiatry*, 46(11), 971–982.

Erdur, O., Rude, S. S., & Baron, A. (2003). Symptom improvement and length of treatment in ethnically similar and dissimilar client-therapist pairings. *Journal of Counseling Psychology*, 50(1), 52–58.

Feeley, M., DeRubeis, R. J., & Gelfand, L. A. (1999). The temporal relation of adherence and alliance to symptom change in cognitive therapy for depression. *Journal of Consulting and Clinical Psychology*, 67(4), 578–582.

Gaston, L., Marmar, C. R., Gallagher, D., & Thompson, L. W. (1991). Alliance prediction of outcome beyond in-treatment symptomatic change as psychotherapy processes. *Psychotherapy Research*, 1, 104–113.

Goldfried, M. R., & Wolfe, B. E. (1998). Toward a more clinically valid approach to therapy research. *Journal of Consulting and Clinical Psychology*, 66(1), 143–150.

Gray, M. J., Elhai, J. D., & Schmidt, L. O. (2007). Trauma professionals' attitudes toward and utilization of evidence-based practices. *Behavior Modification*, 31(6), 732–748.

Hellman, I. D., Morrison, T. L., & Abramowitz, S. I. (1986). The stresses of psychotherapeutic work: a replication and extension. *Journal of Clinical Psychology*, 42(1), 197–205.

Henry, W. P., Strupp, H. H., Butler, S. F., Schacht, T. E., & Binder, J. L. (1993). Effects of training in time-limited dynamic psychotherapy: Changes in therapist behavior. *Journal of Consulting and Clinical Psychology*, 61(3), 434–440.

Hersoug, A. G., Høglend, P., Monsen, J. T., & Havik, O. E. (2001). Quality of working alliance in psychotherapy: Therapist variables and patient/therapist similarity as predictors. *Journal of Psychotherapy Practice & Research*, 10(4), 205–216.

Hill, C. E. (2004). *Theoretical Foundation of the Three-Stage Model of Helping*. Washington, D.C.: American Psychological Association.

Hill, C. E., & Kellems, I. S. (2002). Development and use of the helping skills measure to assess client perceptions of the effects of training and of helping skills in sessions. *Journal of Counseling Psychology*, 49(2), 264–272.

Hill, C. E., & Lent, R. W. (2006). A narrative and meta-analytic review of helping skills training: Time to revive a dormant area of inquiry. *Psychotherapy: Theory, Research, Practice, Training*, 43(2), 154–172.

Hill, C. E., & O'Brien, K. M. (1999). *Becoming an Effective Helper*. Washington, D.C.: American Psychological Association.

Hilsenroth, M. J., Ackerman, S. J., Clemence, A. J., Strassle, C. G., & Handler, L. (2002). Effects of structured clinician training on patient and therapist perspectives of alliance early in psychotherapy. *Psychotherapy*, 39, 309–323.

Hoffart, A., Borge, F., Sexton, H., & Clark, D. M. (2009). The role of common factors in residential cognitive and interpersonal therapy for social phobia: A process-outcome study. *Psychotherapy Research*, 19(1), 54–67.

Holloway, E. L., & Wampold, B. E. (1986). Relation between conceptual level and counseling-related tasks: A meta-analysis. *Journal of Counseling Psychology*, 33(3), 310–319.

Horvath, A. O., & Symonds, B. D. (1991). Relation between working alliance and outcome in psychotherapy: A meta-analysis. *Journal of Counseling Psychology*, 38, 139–149.

Hunt, D. E. (1977–1978). Conceptual level theory and research as guides to educational practice. *Interchange*, 8(4), 78–90.

Huppert, J. D., Bufka, L. F., Barlow, D. H., Gorman, J. M., Shear, M. K., & Woods, S. W. (2001). Therapists, therapist variables, and cognitive-behavioral therapy outcome in a multicenter trial for panic disorder. *Journal of Consulting and Clinical Psychology*, 69(5), 747–755.

Ivey, A. E. (1971). *Microcounseling: Innovations in Interviewing Training*. Oxford, England: Charles C. Thomas.

Jones, M. A., Botsko, M., & Gorman, B. S. (2003). Predictors of psychotherapeutic benefit of lesbian, gay, and bisexual clients: The effects of sexual orientation matching and other factors. *Psychotherapy: Theory, Research, Practice, Training*, 40(4), 289–301.

Kagan, N. (1984). Interpersonal process recall: Basic methods and recent research. In D. Larson (Ed.), *Teaching Psychological Skills: Models for Giving Psychology Away* (pp. 229–244). Monterey, CA: Brooks/Cole.

Karlsson, R. (2005). Ethnic matching between therapist and patient in psychotherapy: An overview of findings, together with methodological and conceptual issues. *Cultural Diversity and Ethnic Minority Psychology*, 11 (2), 113–129.

Kingdon, D., Tyrer, P., Seivewright, N., Ferguson, B., & Murphy, S. (1996). The Nottingham study of neurotic disorder: Influence of cognitive therapists on outcome. *British Journal of Psychiatry*, 169(1), 93–97.

Klein, D. N., Schwartz, J. E., Santiago, N. J., Vivian, D., Vocisano, C., Castonguay, L. G., et al. (2003). Therapeutic alliance in depression treatment: Controlling for prior change and patient characteristics. *Journal of Consulting and Clinical Psychology*, 71, 997–1006.

Klerman, G. L., Weissman, M. M., Rounsaville, B. J., & Chevron, E. (1984). *Interpersonal Psychotherapy of Depression*. New York: Basic Books.

Lafferty, P., Beutler, L. E., & Crago, M. (1989). Differences between more and less effective psychotherapists: A study of select therapist variables. *Journal of Consulting and Clinical Psychology*, 57(1), 76–80.

Lambert, M. J., & Bergin, A. E. (1994). The effectiveness of psychotherapy. In A. E. Bergin & S. L. Garfield (Eds.), *Handbook of Psychotherapy and Behavior Change* (4th ed., pp. 143–189). Oxford, England: John Wiley & Sons.

Leon, S. C., Martinovich, Z., Lutz, W., & Lyons, J. S. (2005). The effect of therapist experience on psychotherapy outcomes. *Clinical Psychology & Psychotherapy*, 12(6), 417–426.

Lieberman, M. A., & Golant, M. (2002). Leader behaviors as perceived by cancer patients in professionally directed support groups and outcomes. *Group Dynamics: Theory, Research and Practice*, 6, 267–276.

Lieberman, M. A., Yalom, I. D., & Miles, M. B. (1973). *Encounter Groups: First Facts*. New York: Basic Books.

Luborsky, L. (1984). *Principles of Psychoanalytic Psychotherapy: A Manual for Supportive-Expressive Treatment*. New York: Basic Books.

Luborsky, L., Crits-Christoph, P., Mintz, J., & Auerbach, A. (1988). *Who Will Benefit from Psychotherapy? Predicting Therapeutic Outcomes*. New York: Basic Books.

Luborsky, L., McLellan, A. T., Diguer, L., Woody, G., & Seligman, D. A. (1997). The psychotherapist matters: Comparison of outcomes across twenty-two therapists and seven patient samples. *Clinical Psychology: Science and Practice*, 4(1), 53–65.

Luborsky, L., Rosenthal, R., Diguer, L., Andrusyna, T. P., Berman, J. S., Levitt, J. T., Seligman, D. A., & Krause, E. D. (2002). The dodo bird verdict is alive and well—mostly. *Clinical Psychology: Science and Practice*, 9(1), 2–12.

Lutz, W., Leon, S. C., Martinovich, Z., Lyons, J. S., & Stiles, W. B. (2007). Therapist effects in outpatient psychotherapy: A three-level growth curve approach. *Journal of Counseling Psychology*, 54, 32–39.

Martin, D. J., Garske, J. P., & Davis, M. K. (2000). Relation of the therapeutic alliance with outcome and other variables: A meta-analytic review. *Journal of Counseling and Clinical Psychology*, 68, 438–450.

Martino, S., Ball, S. A., Nich, C., Frankforter, T. L., & Carroll, K. M. (2008). Community program therapist adherence and competence in motivational enhancement therapy. *Drug and Alcohol Dependence*, 96(1–2), 37–48.

McLennan, J. (1995). Counselor conceptual level and counseling: A reappraisal. *Journal of Psychology: Interdisciplinary and Applied*, 129(6), 651–663.

McLennan, J., Twigg, K., & Bezant, B. (1993). Therapist construct systems in use during psychotherapy interviews. *Journal of Clinical Psychology*, 49(4), 543–550.

Messer, S. B., & Wampold, B. E. (2002). Let's face facts: Common factors are more potent than specific therapy ingredients. *Clinical Psychology: Science and Practice*, 9(1), 21–25.

Miller, W. R., & Mount, K. A. (2001). A small study of training in motivational interviewing: Does one workshop change clinician and client behavior? *Behavioural and Cognitive Psychotherapy*, 29(4), 457–471.

Miller, W. R., & Rollnick, S. (2002). *Motivational Interviewing: Preparing People for Change* (2nd ed.). New York: Guilford Press.

Miller, W. R., Yahne, C. E., Moyers, T. B., Martinez, J., & Pirritano, M. (2004). A randomized trial of methods to help clinicians learn motivational interviewing. *Journal of Consulting and Clinical Psychology*, 72(6), 1050–1062.

Milne, D. L., Baker, C., Blackburn, I., James, I., & Reichelt, K. (1999). Effectiveness of cognitive therapy training. *Journal of Behavior Therapy and Experimental Psychiatry*, 30(2), 81–92.

Multon, K. D., Kivlighan, D. M., Jr., & Gold, P. B. (1996). Changes in counselor adherence over the course of training. *Journal of Counseling Psychology*, 43(3), 356–363.

Najavits, L. M., & Strupp, H. H. (1994). Differences in the effectiveness of psychodynamic therapists: A process-outcome study. *Psychotherapy:* Theory, Research, Practice, Training, 31(1), 114–123.

Najavits, L. M., Ghinassi, F., Van Horn, A., Weiss, R. D., Siqueland, L., Frank, A., Thase, M. E., & Luborsky, L. (2004). Therapist satisfaction with four manual-based treatments on a national multisite trial: An exploratory study. *Psychotherapy: Theory, Research, Practice, Training*, 41(1), 26–37.

Norcross, J. C. (2002). Empirically supported therapy relationships. In J. C. Norcross (Ed.), *Psychotherapy Relationships that Work: Therapist Contributions and Responsiveness to Patients* (pp. 3–16). New York: Oxford University Press.

Okiishi, J., Lambert, M. J., Nielsen, S. L., & Ogles, B. M. (2003). Waiting for supershrink: An empirical analysis of therapist effects. *Clinical Psychology & Psychotherapy*, 10(6), 361–373.

O'Malley, S. S., Foley, S. H., Rounsaville, B. J., Watkins, J. T., Sotsky, S. M., Imber, S. D., & Elkin, I. (1988). Therapist competence and patient outcome in interpersonal psychotherapy of depression. *Journal of Consulting and Clinical Psychology*, 56(4), 496–501.

Orlinsky, D. E., & Howard, K. I. (1976). The effects of sex of therapist on the therapeutic experiences of women. *Psychotherapy: Theory, Research & Practice*, 13(1), 82–88.

Paivio, S. C., Holowaty, K. A. M., & Hall, I. E. (2004). The influence of therapist adherence and competence on client reprocessing of child abuse memories. *Psychotherapy: Theory, Research, Practice, Training*, 41(1), 56–68.

Perepletchikova, F., Treat, T. A., & Kazdin, A. E. (2007). Treatment integrity in psychotherapy research: Analysis of the studies and examination of the associated factors. *Journal of Consulting and Clinical Psychology*, 75(6), 829–841.

Reese, R. J., Usher, E. L., Bowman, D. C., Norsworthy, L. A., Halstead, J. L., Rowlands, S. R., & Chisholm, R. R. (2009). Using client feedback in psychotherapy training: An analysis of its influence on supervision and counselor self-efficacy. *Training and Education in Professional Psychology*, 3(3), 157–168.

Ricks, D. F. (1974). Supershrink: Methods of a therapist judged successful on the basis of adult outcomes of adolescent patients. *Life History Research in Psychopathology: III*. Minneapolis: University of Minnesota Press.

Rogers, C. R. (1951). *Client-Centered Therapy*. Oxford: Houghton Mifflin.

Rosen, A., & Proctor, E. K. (1981). Distinctions between treatment outcomes and their implications for treatment evaluation. *Journal of Consulting and Clinical Psychology*, 49(3), 418–425.

Safran, J. D., & Muran, J. C. (2000). *Negotiating the Therapeutic Alliance: A Relational Treatment Guide*. New York: Guilford Press.

Saunders, S. M., Howard, K. I., & Orlinsky, D. E. (1989). The Therapeutic Bond Scales: Psychometric characteristics and relationship to treatment effectiveness. *Psychological Assessment*, 1, 323–330.

Schoener, E. P., Madeja, C. L., Henderson, M. J., Ondersma, S. J., & Janisse, J. J. (2006). Effects of motivational interviewing training on mental health therapist behavior. *Drug and Alcohol Dependence*, 82(3), 269–275.

Shaw, B. F., Elkin, I., Yamaguchi, J., Olmsted, M., Vallis, T. M., Dobson, K. S., Lowery, A., Sotsky, S. M., Watkins, J. T., & Imber, S. D. (1999). Therapist competence ratings in relation to clinical outcome in cognitive therapy of depression. *Journal of Consulting and Clinical Psychology*, 67(6), 837–846.

Shechtman, A., & Toren, Z., (2009). The effect of leader behavior on process and outcomes in group counseling. *Group Dynamics: Theory, Research, and Practice*, 13, 218–233.

Sholomskas, D. E., Syracuse-Siewert, G., Rounsaville, B. J., Ball, S. A., Nuro, K. F., & Carroll, K. M. (2005). We don't train in vain: A dissemination trial of three strategies of training clinicians in cognitive-behavioral therapy. *Journal of Consulting and Clinical Psychology*, 73(1), 106–115.

Smith, M. L., & Glass, G. V. (1977). Meta-analysis of psychotherapy outcome studies. *American Psychologist*, 32(9), 752–760.

Sterling, R. C., Gottheil, E., Weinstein, S. P., & Serota, R. (1998). Therapist/patient race and sex matching: Treatment retention and 9-month follow-up outcome. *Addiction*, 93(7), 1043–1050.

Sterling, R. C., Gottheil, E., Weinstein, S. P., & Serota, R. (2001). The effect of therapist/patient race- and sex-matching in individual treatment. *Addiction*, 96(7), 1015–1022.

Stevens, S. E., Hynan, M. T., & Allen, M. (2000). A meta-analysis of common factor and specific treatment effects across the outcome domains of the phase model of psychotherapy. *Clinical Psychology: Science and Practice*, 7(3), 273–290.

Stewart, R. E., & Chambless, D. L. (2007). Does psychotherapy research inform treatment decisions in private practice? *Journal of Clinical Psychology*, 63, 267–281.

Sue, S., Fujino, D. C., Hu, L., Takeuchi, D. T., & Zane, N. W. S. (1991). Community mental health services for ethnic minority groups: A test of the cultural responsiveness hypothesis. *Journal of Consulting and Clinical Psychology*, 59(4), 533–540.

Svartberg, M., & Stiles, T. C. (1994). Therapeutic alliance, therapist competence, and client change in short-term anxiety-provoking psychotherapy. *Psychotherapy Research*, 4(1), 20–33.

Trepka, C., Rees, A., Shapiro, D. A., Hardy, G. E., & Barkham, M. (2004). Therapist competence and outcome of cognitive therapy for depression. *Cognitive Therapy and Research*, 28(2), 143–157.

Truax, C. B., & Carkhuff, R. R. (1967). *Toward Effective Counseling and Psychotherapy: Training and Practice*. Hawthorne, NY: Aldine Publishing Co.

Wampold, B. E., Mondin, G. W., Moody, M., Stich, F., Benson, K., & Ahn, H. (1997). A meta-analysis of outcome studies comparing bona fide psychotherapies: Empirically, "all must have prizes." *Psychological Bulletin*, 122(3), 203–215.

Webb, C. A., DeRubeis, R. J., & Barber, J. P. (2010). Therapist adherence/competence and treatment outcome: A meta-analytic review. *Journal of Consulting and Clinical Psychology*, 78, 200–211.

Wogan, M. (1970). Effect of therapist-patient personality variables on therapeutic outcome. *Journal of Consulting and Clinical Psychology*, 35, 356–361.

Yalom, I., & Lieberman, M. (1971). A study of encounter group casualties. *Archives of General Psychiatry*, 25, 16–30.

Yamamoto, J., Acosta, F. X., Evans, L. A., & Skilbeck, W. M. (1984). Orienting therapists about patients' needs to increase patient satisfaction. *American Journal of Psychiatry*, 141(2), 274–277.

Zlotnick, C., Elkin, I., & Shea, M. T. (1998). Does the gender of a patient or the gender of a therapist affect the treatment of patients with major depression? *Journal of Consulting and Clinical Psychology*, 66(4), 655–659.

12

Conclusions: A Phase-Specific Model for Psychotherapist Development

Robert H. Klein, Harold S. Bernard, and Victor L. Schermer

In this, our concluding chapter, we wish to propose a generic, comprehensive, phase-specific schema or framework that can be used to think about psychotherapist development. To accomplish this task, we will attempt to integrate information and insight from four separate sources: (1) specific ideas advanced by our authors, (2) our understanding of the available literature in the field, (3) our own ideas about psychotherapist development, and (4) our view of the current context within which psychotherapists develop and practice their craft. Following this presentation, the remainder of the chapter will be devoted to a series of recommendations regarding (1) the selection of candidates for psychotherapist training, (2) the optimal content for training programs in terms of (a) didactic preparation and (b) the nature of clinical experiences, (3) therapist self-care, and (4) continued professional growth.

Preliminary Considerations

As a preface to providing our own integrative schema, we think it is worthwhile to make several initial comments. To begin with, our schema is not based upon extensive data systematically collected from a diverse, large international sample. An excellent example of such an approach can be found in the reports of the collaborative research team assembled under the auspices of the Society for Psychotherapy Research (Orlinsky & Ronnestad, 2005; Skovholt & Ronnestad, 1995). That team of researchers studied the responses to a comprehensive questionnaire from a sample of more than 5,000 psychotherapists, only 375 of whom (less than 8%) were senior psychotherapists with more than 25 years of clinical experience.

In contrast, the chapters in this volume are based primarily on the thoughts and reflections of a limited number of (mostly male) senior psychotherapists (psychiatrists and psychologists) who were trained and now practice in the United States. From this perspective, our work more closely resembles that of Skovholt and Jennings (2004), who studied the careers of 10 senior therapists To be sure, the ideas presented here have been influenced and augmented by our substantial levels of clinical experience, our collective knowledge of the relevant literature, our joint long-term commitments to cross-disciplinary psychotherapist education and training, and our shared concerns about how well we are preparing the next generation of psychotherapists to practice effectively. Nevertheless, some readers may conclude that our perspective is relatively narrow and our ideas have only limited generalizability, although we do not believe this to be the case.

In addition, it is important to note that psychotherapist development is not a linear process. Our views echo those of Orlinsky and Ronnestad (2005), who noted that psychotherapist development is characterized by concurrent positive and negative cycles or phases. They maintain that every therapist experiences various levels and degrees of "healing involvement," when the therapist maintains personally invested, effective, and affirming relationships with patients, and "stressful involvement," when the therapist feels ineffective, experiences anxiety and boredom, and relies upon avoidant styles of coping with difficulties. These features are associated with periods of growth and depletion, all which are reflected in the therapist's practice patterns. As a result, practice patterns also vary from effective, to challenging, to disengaged or even distressing. These phases interface with each other, making development nonlinear and cyclic in nature. Positive cycles or phases are characterized by therapists' experiencing what they describe as "high healing involvement" and patterns of "effective practice." During these periods psychotherapists report that they are currently experiencing growth, satisfaction and success in their therapeutic work, and a high level of morale. Such periods also tend to be marked by heightened personal reflection, coupled with high motivation for new learning (Orlinsky & Ronnestad, 2005).

By contrast, during negative cycles or phases therapists report low healing involvement, limited growth, and practice patterns that are more distressing. They report an eroding sense of therapeutic mastery, experience therapeutic work as unsatisfactory, and suffer from feelings of depletion and low morale. Often there is limited support available through the work setting for psychotherapists whose work generally feels boring, oppressive, or unfulfilling (Orlinsky & Ronnestad, 2005). Effective and highly involved psychotherapists experience such cycles from time to time. We may feel confused, discouraged, or stymied by diagnostic as well as treatment issues, encounter problems working with other professionals, or find it difficult to work in an agency where caseloads may be oppressive or supervision may be unavailable. Or, some of us simply feel tired, physically run down or sick/injured, preoccupied with family or personal issues, concerned about financial issues, and so forth. When these periods do not quickly resolve, we may feel demoralized and temporarily disillusioned, or even lose faith in what we are doing. Extended periods like this can lead to "burnout" (e.g., Maslach & Leiter, 1997). We believe that it is important for us as psychotherapists to acknowledge these sorts of cycles as well as those that promote growth and effectiveness.

Furthermore, it is clear that psychotherapists repeatedly return to previous developmental tasks as they become more seasoned and experienced. In other words, certain tasks are an essential part of clinical practice and therefore continue to recur: for instance, engaging and assessing a patient to arrive at a diagnosis and to formulate a treatment plan. This task might be construed as a relatively early developmental task to be addressed and mastered. But psychotherapists continue to address this fundamental recurring task throughout their careers. Each time they return to tasks like this, they bring with them a different level of skill, clinical experience, interest, enthusiasm, emotional sensitivity, and so on.

Other broader tasks, such as learning how to make effective and creative use of the self during the treatment process, are lifelong tasks. Those tasks at the interface between personal and professional development are never completely resolved: for instance, the task of finding a balance between personal, family, and professional needs. These sorts of tasks instead tend to occupy us at some level throughout our careers and over an entire lifetime. But again, the ubiquitous nature of these complex tasks enables psychotherapists to have multiple fresh looks at them as they repeatedly struggle for deeper levels of understanding and integration of personal and professional development. This process provides successive opportunities for new learning to occur. Ideally, over time, this results in cumulative levels of increasing skill and mastery, which in turn permit the application of more finely honed, sensitive, flexible, and sophisticated skills for conducting clinical work.

The same line of reasoning, of course, can be extended to embrace not just the practical implementation of treatment, but also how we think about psychotherapy: that is, our theoretical approaches. Most psychotherapists continue to examine and to modify how they think about psychotherapy over the course of their entire careers. A look at the trajectories of the co-editors of this volume reveals that our theoretical positions have changed as we have gained clinical experience, engaged in education and training activities, kept abreast of recent contributions to the literature, and continuously re-examined the quality of our work and our current professional growth. In fact, as we reflected upon the changes in our own thinking, spurred in large part by theoretical developments involving intersubjective co-construction notions about psychotherapy as a process, we decided to do a book in the area of therapist development! This gradual articulation, evolution, and refinement of one's theoretical approach, we believe, is not atypical for most clinicians.

A Five-Phase Model for Psychotherapist Development

At this point, we want to turn our attention to articulating a general model of psychotherapist development. Here we will focus on positive growth as a therapist. This model is based upon the notion that psychotherapist development reflects both personal and professional growth, and that such growth takes place within a particular context or larger social system. These three components, the personal, professional, and contextual, can be arranged in the form of a triangle in which each component reciprocally affects the others, and each has both an historical and contemporary aspect.

While recognizing that development is nonlinear and cyclical, we wish to focus on the central developmental tasks of each phase, the means by which these tasks are accomplished, the learning processes involved, and the developmental pathways that are forged. We will present a five-phase model of development: (1) the pre-professional stage, (2) mastering the basics, (3) consolidating, augmenting, and refining clinical skills and working style, (4) finding one's own voice, and (5) retrenchment, winding down, and preparing for retirement. We will now take up each in turn.

Phase 1: Pre-Professional Phase

The central developmental tasks of this period involve the acquisition of what could be called basic relational skills (Orlinsky & Ronnestad, 2005) that enable engagement, and the capacity for resilience. As O'Leary (Chapter 2) makes clear, many of the most important characteristics that therapists bring to their work begin to develop well before they decide to pursue their training in one of the mental health professions. Of course, many people who develop these characteristics pursue other kinds of work, and these characteristics probably serve them well in whatever vocation they pursue. But if they choose to become mental health professionals, they begin on their developmental path well equipped to become proficient, if not gifted, in what they do.

Let us briefly describe some of these traits or characteristics, and then discuss how they develop. As Stirman and Crits-Christoph (Chapter 11) point out, therapist characteristics such as personality factors, cultural background, gender, training and experience, attitudes, personal history, and personal experience in psychotherapy have been the subject of research for several decades, and many have been linked with positive treatment outcomes (e.g., Bergin & Garfield, 1994; Garfield & Bergin, 1990; Lambert, 2004). In this context, however, we would like to focus on basic relational skills. These skills involve several different but interrelated traits or characteristics. First there is the ability to empathize: to get outside of one's own skin and to understand and experience the world as one's patients do, a characteristic that has been found to be positively related to treatment outcome (Anderson et al., 2009; Starcevic & Piontek, 1997; Anderson, Ogles, Patterson, Lambert, & Vermeersch, 2009). This requires the development of a number of interrelated skills: the ability to listen carefully, to accurately determine what the other person is feeling, to put words to the feeling, and to accurately convey an understanding of the other person's experience. This process enables a therapist to establish an emotional connection with the patient, and permits the patient to feel understood.

A related human characteristic is altruism, the interest in being helpful to others. While there is almost always self-interest involved in the decision to become a therapist, it is best if it is grounded in the wish to give to others and to be helpful. Therapists get a great deal back from their patients in addition to their fee, but the therapeutic relationship is first and foremost one in which therapists give what they can in order to benefit their patients as much as possible.

Still another characteristic, closely related to the ability to empathize and to the altruistic motive, is the capacity to trust others sufficiently to risk personal exposure and vulnerability. Again, people who have been damaged and have not successfully worked through these experiences often lack this ability. A successful therapeutic relationship is one in which patient and therapist learn to trust one another. If and when this trust is called into question, the working-through process ideally leads to a strengthening and solidification of the relationship bond, and our patients emerge from their relationships with us with a greater capacity to (selectively) trust others than when they began their treatment.

While psychological-mindedness is ideally stimulated and strengthened by one's training and early experiences as a therapist, this, too, is a characteristic that almost always begins to be developed well before someone enters one of the mental health professions. In fact, it is hard to imagine someone deciding he or she wants to be a therapist, and entering the field, unless he or she has developed the beginnings of this characteristic. What is meant by psychological-mindedness? There are many components to this trait: among them are an interest in discovering the meaning of things, a curiosity about human motivation, a capacity for introspection, an interest in latent as well as manifest content, and a fundamental curiosity about what makes people tick. Another way to describe this characteristic is to say that some people develop what has come to be called "emotional intelligence": the ability to grasp the emotional meaning of events (Goleman, 1995). Closely related to these qualities is what O'Leary describes as a powerful interest in storytelling and fascination with the genuine drama of "told" experience.

A passion for new learning, marked by curiosity and determination, is yet another characteristic often found among successful psychotherapists (Ackerman & Hilsenroth, 2003). This characteristic generally appears early in life, propelling children toward growth and discovery. It later enables therapists to sustain a commitment to lifelong learning. For the developing psychotherapist, it is this passion that results in a relentless quest for new knowledge, both objective, externally based knowledge and subjective, internally based knowledge. O'Leary suggests a shift of focus from pathology and woundedness to the examination of positive inborn and acquired characteristics such as trust, relational competence, and a passion for new knowledge.

It is these characteristics that help to keep therapists fresh, vibrant, and invested in the practice of psychotherapy.

To be able to maintain long-term engagement in the practice of psycho-therapy also requires tolerance for ambiguity (Vardy & Kay, 1982). In our introduction to this volume, we stated that psychotherapy itself remains a craft, an amalgam of science and art. Unlike the work of the physical scientist or the mathematician, the work of the psychotherapist is often unclear and inexact. Every therapist must choose between multiple, often competing, theories, methods, modalities, and techniques. There is no single, universally agreed upon correct way to treat patients (e.g., Luborsky et al., 2002; Wampold et al., 1997). And, of course, every patient is unique, as is every therapist and, therefore, every therapeutic relationship. In addition, when it comes to measuring progress or overall outcome as a result of treatment, this, too, is inexact and laden with ambiguity. This is especially the case when it comes to psychodynamically-based treatment that does not specifically aim at symptom reduction or remission, but rather more typically pursues broader goals of improving patients' self-awareness, self-esteem, and quality of inter-personal relationships. Unless therapists can tolerate the ambiguities inherent in clinical practice, they will often feel frustrated and even despairing about the work they are doing.

Because of the ambiguity associated with the practice of psychotherapy, we would add yet another characteristic to those of the effective therapist: a capacity for delayed and partial gratification. Change takes time; with most patients it is a slow and gradual process that may be, as mentioned, difficult to measure accurately. Furthermore, unlike the scenarios depicted in stereo-typical cinematic portrayals of therapy, it usually does not follow immediately on the heels of an "Aha!" moment: that is, a sudden flash of insight and enlightenment. Instead, working through to achieve a more comprehensive understanding of whatever is discovered in order to be in a position to alter how one thinks, feels, and behaves is a complex and lengthy process. Furthermore, most participants in therapy, both patients and therapists, would agree that psychotherapy rarely, if ever, resolves all the patient's prob-lems, including the transference–countertransference matrix. Typically, only more delayed, partial, and incomplete resolutions are achieved. Tolerance of these realities is necessary if therapists are to feel content with themselves and take pride in the work they are doing.

Finally, there is the matter of emotional resilience. As Rice elaborates in Chapter 8, the experience of being wounded is a universal one for all of us during our formative years. What distinguishes people with resilience is their ability to overcome these wounds by mobilizing their resources, developing adaptive coping strategies, and healing their wounds. Bouncing back from or overcoming emotionally difficult or painful experiences permits the therapist to achieve a deeper empathic understanding and connection with the patient and to convey a sense of hope, both of which are essential ingredients for successful therapy.

Thus, there are a number of characteristics, many of them closely related to each other, that clearly have their beginnings well before someone decides to pursue one of the mental health professions. Among them are basic relational skills, a capacity for tolerating ambiguity, the ability to accept delayed or partial gratification, a passion for new learning, and resilience (Jennings & Skovolt, 1999). Why do these interests, skills, and capacities develop much more fully in some individuals and not others? While there are surely differences between and among people, it is safe to say that it involves some combination of genetic endowment, environmental influence, and early life experience. Regardless of how it happens, possessing these characteristics means that an individual choosing to pursue a career as a psychotherapist has the capacity for establishing and maintaining relationships, and for creating opportunities for personal growth. It also means that such individuals are better able to tolerate the nonlinear cyclic nature of psychotherapist development. For those who do not possess these relational skills and characteristics, it is probably unlikely they will choose a career as a psychotherapist, but if they do they will have much more work to do if they are to become effective as helping agents.

Phase 2: Mastering the Basics

The essential developmental tasks of this period include acquiring basic knowledge; learning how to make proper use of relational skills and characteristics; learning about the process of change and psychotherapy, the roles and responsibilities of the therapist, and the limitations of treatment; early exploration of issues of technique; and beginning to establish a professional identity and a core set of ethical standards, values, and beliefs.

Cultivating a Sound, Flexible, and Open-Ended Knowledge Base for Psychotherapy

As discussed by Schermer in Chapter 4, crucial for the therapist during the early phase of development is a well-rounded education plus specialized knowledge of normal development, psychopathology, and the role of cultural influences regarding the treatment process. Observational skills must be sharpened and one must learn how to organize, evaluate, and convey information that is gathered. This general background needs to be bolstered by the development of a working knowledge of therapy theory, process, and technique; what treatment is and is not; an understanding of assessment, diagnosis, and treatment planning; the contract process; how to establish a therapeutic alliance; different types and modes of intervention; as well as a thorough understanding of the ethical considerations upon which treatment rests. Schermer also points out that specialized learning and continuing education are of increasing importance today because the "basics" change more rapidly as a function of new knowledge and more diverse approaches to treatment.

Learning How to Make Emotional Contact

As noted by Stirman and Crits-Christoph, there is considerable research evidence to suggest that much of the effectiveness of psychotherapy, regardless of theoretical orientation, is attributable to common or nonspecific factors (Ahn & Wampold, 2001; Kazdin, 2005; Lambert, 2004; Messer & Wampold, 2002). A core aspect of these common factors is the nature of the therapeutic relationship (Bachelor & Horvath, 1999; Norcross, 2002; Wampold & Brown, 2005), a critical part of which is the working alliance (Ackerman & Hilsenroth, 2003; Crits-Christoph et al., 2006; Horvath & Luborsky, 1993; Martin, Garske, & Davis, 2000). To establish this relationship, the therapist must be able to make contact emotionally with the patient. Building this relationship requires basic relational skills, the maintenance of certain underlying values, a shared understanding of treatment processes and goals, plus resilience in order to persevere in the face of difficulties and/or setbacks in the work.

The therapeutic relationship involves a combination of objectivity and concern. This is expressed in the way the therapist relates to the patient at all levels, whether in specific interventions and interpretations, the respect and care shown in the consulting room, and/or the therapist's responses to the patient's life dilemmas and crises. Acquisition of these traits and honing of these skills occurs throughout life. Interferences with them that disrupt effective therapist functioning can also occur at any time, as when a therapist becomes preoccupied with a personal problem or has a strong countertransference reaction. A significant component of supervision, as discussed by Leszcz in Chapter 6, involves learning how to make appropriate emotional contact with the patient, and then monitoring and investigating fluctuations in these components of the therapeutic interaction. Leszcz highlights other developmental tasks during this phase that are facilitated by the supervisory process: feeling permission to have personal reactions to patients and figuring out how to prevent them from getting in the way of the treatment process, or even beginning to make use of them; beginning to develop the capacity to self-reflect; beginning to develop a core set of values as a treating professional; and beginning to synthesize an identity that balances one's professional and personal selves.

Personal psychotherapy and mentoring experiences, as described by Phillips (Chapter 7) and Gayle (Chapter 3) respectively, also tend to promote the development and use of these essential skills as well as the values they embody. If one has engaged in a successful supervisory, personal psychotherapy or mentoring relationship, one ideally learns and internalizes qualities that are useful for promoting engagement and for doing the work of psychotherapy, via modeling and identification at the least. In addition, through the examination of parallel process, Leszcz points out that the process of establishing and maintaining a supervisory alliance permits the ready transfer of knowledge about oneself as well as the conditions and processes required for doing psychological work to one's own work with patients. He describes the impact of effective supervision on both therapist growth and development and improved patient outcomes. Phillips points out, however, that personal psychotherapy, in contrast to supervision, does not involve an evaluation of professional competence. Consequently, successful integration of personal and professional development may best be accomplished through personal psychotherapy without fear that personal exposure may lead to lower evaluations. Her detailed consideration of why, when, and with whom therapists seek personal psychotherapy leads her to conclude that, regardless of theoretical orientation, the experience enhances the personal and professional development of therapists. For certain therapeutic orientations, such as psychodynamic intervention, whether with a family, couple, or group, Phillips argues that personal therapy is necessary for effective intervention.

During this phase the budding psychotherapist is likely to be exposed to a variety of theoretical orientations. As suggested by Stirman and Crits-Christoph in their discussion of the implications of psychotherapy research for optimal psychotherapist development and competence, the particular school of thought and approach/working style that therapists tentatively adopt should fit with who they are and should be both satisfying to them and have a sound empirical and theoretical basis. Therapists should have a common vocabulary and knowledge to communicate effectively with their colleagues and should be able to compare their work with standards and research in the field. They should develop the ability to use their knowledge in ways that allow them to address each patient as a unique individual with a particular set of needs. Mastering the process of engagement and the application of sound technique becomes a central task. Therapists must learn how to apply their knowledge in a disciplined way while at the same time staying open to new possibilities, concepts, and levels of understanding. In addition, therapists should find ways to critically appraise the empirical literature and make use of it to guide their practice. It is important to emphasize here that the choice of both theoretical approach and working style made by the therapist at this phase of development is initially tentative and is often subject to modification as the result of cumulative clinical growth and experience, increased levels of self-awareness, and relevant developments in the field.

Gans (Chapter 5) describes how, during this period of professional development, psychotherapists are likely to encounter certain universal difficulties (e.g., lateness, missed or cancelled sessions, suicidality, therapeutic impasses, threats of unilateral termination, erotic transference and countertransference reactions) and are likely to make common mistakes. These experiences often highlight the relevance and importance of objective and theoretical knowledge versus subjective awareness of self and other. Gans emphasizes the importance of providing basic concepts that will help beginning psychotherapists respond in a more therapeutic fashion, and suggests that the lessons learned from these clinical experiences play an important role in professional development. He enumerates many of the clinical skills that begin to develop during this phase, including learning to tolerate perturbations in the therapeutic relationship, and even beginning to use them for therapeutic advantage; developing the capacity to tolerate the loneliness and isolation that characterizes the life of the therapist; learning to tolerate and work with very powerful affect; developing the capacity to weather patients' criticisms and even rejection; and learning how important it is to address early signs that there are issues between therapist and patient, rather than waiting until they explode into some form of acting out.

Strong Professional Identity and Values

Equally important during the early phase of development is that the therapist should acquire and maintain a professional and ethical stance with patients. This emerges early in life through identifications with significant others, becomes more focused during the educational process and personal psychotherapy, and is supported and strengthened by interactions with colleagues, mentors, and supervisors. It rests upon a growing awareness and appreciation of the laws and ethical standards that apply to the work. A good sense of boundaries is important to this dimension of therapist development. In fact, developing the capacity to monitor transactions at the boundaries in working with patients and to intervene when necessary is essential. How to make such interventions in a way that can be heard becomes an important task to be addressed.

Therapists also need to become aware of their strengths and limitations, what they can and cannot do for patients, the respective rights and responsibilities of patient and therapist, and how to set limits that respect the patient and preserve the work of treatment (e.g., Bike et al., 2009; Norcross & Guy, 2005). Gans suggests that new therapists often have inflated views of the changes they can effect with their patients, and emphasizes that an important developmental task is to come to grips with the limits of what one can accomplish without becoming despairing or feeling completely ineffectual. In this connection, knowledge of authority relations and the proper exercise of expertise and authority is critically important. This comes both from the professional side but also from the building of character that begins early in life and continues throughout the life cycle. Achieving a strong sense of professional identity and values rests upon the therapist's capacity to engage in and to maintain ongoing introspection and self-monitoring activities. From our point of view, the therapist only begins to establish a sense of professional identity during this phase of development; this identity subsequently becomes solidified through continued clinical experience and personal growth. The same line of reasoning suggests that most psychotherapists during this phase begin to form a rudimentary, basic set of beliefs, values, and ethical standards that are consolidated and integrated later in their development.

Phase 3: Consolidating, Augmenting, and Refining Clinical Skills and Working Style

The essential developmental tasks of this period include consolidating, augmenting, and refining one's clinical skills, one's style of working, and one's professional identity while learning how to manage the stress inherent in the profession. These tasks are navigated primarily through additional experiences with patients, acquisition of new knowledge and personal growth, the processes of ongoing introspection and critical examination of the quality of one's work, and the continuing development of one's core set of values and sense of professionalism. Accomplishment of these tasks lays the groundwork for increased differentiation, autonomy, and authenticity of the therapist.

Skillful Use of Self in the Consulting Room

No matter how sound the therapist's technique, therapy is a human process that requires a good deal of insight about oneself and adaptability to pursue properly. As noted by Schermer in Chapter 4, trainees often find it difficult to apply what they have learned in their didactic training to the ongoing clinical situation. A good therapist learns to follow the maxim "know thyself," and how to use various aspects of self in responding to the patient, couple, family, or group. For this purpose, one's own personal or training therapy can be of inestimable value. Yalom (2002) suggests that there is no better way to learn about psychotherapy than by being a patient. Useful, too, is the frequent review of case material with supervisors and peers. Therapists must also know about and heal their rigidities and defenses so they may be more appropriately responsive to patients and situations. They must address any serious impairments in their lives and functional capacities. Leszcz highlights the value of supervision in helping to expand supervisees' knowledge of themselves and to identify modes of coping and defense. Similarly, Phillips recommends personal psychotherapy not only to promote personal growth and self-awareness, but also because these ingredients augment the quality of therapeutic work. During this period psychotherapists also should seek to develop a rich vocabulary, drawn from personal experience, the arts, and literature to talk to the patient about feelings and experiences in meaningful ways.

In our opinion, learning how to make most effective use of the self constitutes a major developmental task that begins early in one's career, as the fundamentals of conducting psychotherapeutic work are being mastered, and remains salient throughout it. Skill as a therapist can often be measured in terms of how well and creatively therapists can draw upon themselves to implement and operationalize their theoretical approach and their style of working. This is true regardless of theoretical orientation. As Neuhaus explicates in his chapter on cognitive-behavioral approaches to treatment (Chapter 10), cognitive-behavioral therapists learn that the treatment outcome is very much affected by their relationships with their patients, and that they need to bring themselves into their clinical encounters if they are to maximize their effectiveness as therapists. Learning how to make most effective use of oneself as a therapist requires refining and expanding how one works, and developing increasing levels of self-awareness, skill, and effectiveness, largely through learning how to use one's own unique assets and limitations. This type of self-knowledge can guide therapists in selecting their theory and practical approach, as well as in patient selection to better promote therapeutic process and outcome, and to keep themselves open, alive, refreshed, and committed.

Over time the therapist must learn how to become increasingly authentic within role (Billow, 2009, 2010a, 2010b). The process of becoming increasingly authentic in role involves grappling with a complex, evolving developmental task that assumes additional importance as the therapist continues to practice. To accomplish this, therapists must acquire more advanced relational skills such as how to effectively monitor themselves and their own reactions, as well as the patient's reactions to them, and theirs to the patient. They must develop the capacity to accurately monitor moment-to-moment shifts in the process of treatment, and be able to experience and understand more deeply evolving transference and countertransference reactions. They must then learn how to use these experiences creatively in the service of pursuing the agreed-upon therapeutic goals.

Ability to Work with Difficult Situations and Patients

A variety of problematic situations and patients confront the therapist during this phase of development. These may range from engaging a new patient in treatment, to practical concerns like timeliness of payment and missed sessions, to resistances and stalemates, to powerful countertransference emotions and conflicts, to encountering unfamiliar dynamics and difficulties. Schermer recommends that didactic preparation for psychotherapists should provide technique and skills for working with difficult patients, whether borderline, "at risk," narcissistic, or psychotic. Gayle suggests that mentoring facilitates the use of intersubjectivity and metaphors (myth, story) in helping more concrete patients to be able to think about their experience in a relational context like psychotherapy.

Rice's chapter (Chapter 8) is especially relevant here. Difficult patients can often trigger the deepest levels of conflict and trauma in the therapist. Vicarious traumatization is an ever- present danger in the consulting room (e.g., Saakvitne & Pearlman, 1995; Klein & Schermer, 2000; Phillips, 2004; Saakvitne & Pearlman, 1995). One cannot do well with difficult patients unless one overcomes personal difficulties that could interfere with treatment. Working effectively with difficult patients may at times require judicious self-disclosure of the therapist's countertransference and personal events that may be affecting the treatment process. Rice thoughtfully discusses psychotherapists' relationships to their own injuries and their understanding or lack of understanding of that relationship and how it affects patients' troubles and the transference–countertransference, inter-projective and inter-projective identification matrices that arise, and ultimately the intersubjective fields they create or destroy.

It should be clear that there is no formulaic way to acquire the ability to work with difficult patients: it has an existential component. O'Leary might argue that the early life experience of therapists has a lot to do with this, whether their families had a manner of living that was resilient and courageous, or whether they found healthy adaptations in the midst of difficulties in development. Trust in oneself and the patient is important. Role models, in the form of supervisors or mentors, are often crucial. Having weathered one's own personal trauma can be very helpful as well.

Equally important in this phase is learning how to say difficult/challenging things to patients in ways that they can hear without becoming overly defensive and emotionally unavailable for engagement or learning. The skill required to be able to confront such sensitive or difficult issues in an honest, direct, and authentic fashion without jeopardizing the working alliance takes years of clinical experience to acquire and to refine.

During this phase of development, psychotherapists need to cultivate and maintain flexibility and range in their modes of intervention, a firm grasp of their limitations and biases, and an awareness and appreciation of what other mental health professionals have to offer. Treatment of complex cases often involves the use of different treatment modalities administered by different treaters. Developing one's ability to work across different treatment modalities and to work collaboratively with other mental health professionals, frequently on a cross-disciplinary basis, is often crucial (Ellison, 2005; Patterson et al., 2006; Sperry, 1995). It also often falls to the psychotherapist to ensure that there is adequate ongoing treatment integration, and that this essential task is not left exclusively to the patient, the person who is generally least able to provide it.

In addition, it is becoming clear, as Schermer points out, that in recent years psychotherapists are being called upon to work with an increasingly diverse population of patients. Psychotherapists must develop cultural competence—that is, sensitivity to the role of cultural factors and how these affect patients' initial presentations as well as their willingness to enter into, and their responses to, treatment. Furthermore, psychotherapists who choose to enter the arena of delivering public mental health services following a disaster, for example, must develop their capacities to offer such services outside of the typical office setting. They will be called upon to provide a broader variety of services, not just traditional psychotherapy, under a broader variety of circumstances and settings, to a broader contingent of people in need of mental health services, not just folks who come to our offices and identify themselves as "patients." In the immediate aftermath of a disaster, for example, it may be far more timely and beneficial for psychotherapists to provide group-based public education sessions rather than individual psychotherapy. As discussed by Phillips, all of these changes from traditional modes of practice require considerable new learning, supervision, and emotional support for most psychotherapists.

Commitment to Lifelong Learning

To avoid becoming stagnant, establishing and maintaining a commitment to lifelong learning is essential during this phase of therapist development. Such a commitment involves looking inwardly as well as outwardly. Gaining and consolidating new knowledge about the self, whether through supervision and/or personal therapy, must be accompanied by a willingness to remain open to learning about new approaches to therapeutic work, the importance of cultural variables, and theoretical advances. The chapters by both Theobald McClendon and Burlingame (Chapter 9) and Stirman and Crits-Christoph (Chapter 11) point to the growing significance of evidentiary evaluations of therapeutic processes and outcomes. In their chapter, Theobald McClendon and Burlingame argue that practice-based evidence is a tool that promotes clinical awareness and development in the form of lifelong learning, while permitting clinicians to creatively integrate the more humanistic elements of treatment with the requirements for a more scientific approach to therapy. Therapists who fail to appreciate the contributions from research as well as the growing insistence on evidence-based approaches to treatment may find themselves out of touch with the recent trends in the field. Staying appropriately informed can be accomplished through reading and discussion, teaching, and participating in professional conferences, and via supervisory activities, both as supervisee and supervisor. Schermer emphasizes the increasing importance of updating one's knowledge and skills on a regular basis. Mentoring, as noted by Gayle, helps to firm up this commitment. Working with one's own wounds, as suggested by Rice, is a lifetime process, especially as stress and life crises in the therapist can always affect the therapist and hence the treatment process.

Finding a Balance: Resilience and the Ability to Manage Life and Work Stress

Therapy work is stressful, as is life itself. Therapists are not immune to the effects of stress. It is how they deal with it that counts. This, too, is a lifelong developmental task. What we experience as stressful and our ways of coping with stress are continuously evolving. The combination of early life experiences and therapist education and training plus personal therapy tends to establish long-lasting patterns of coping with stress.

As therapists gain in life experiences and clinical skill, they face new challenges. One of the most important is finding a balance between their personal and professional lives; another involves finding a balance between their own emotional needs and those of their families. Therapists routinely help patients to assess what matters most to them, and how to channel their energies and apportion their commitments accordingly. Therapists, too, must learn to continuously assess their needs and priorities, as well as those of their families, and to carefully examine their own strengths and limitations. Such balances continue to shift and change over the life cycle as our needs, capacities, and wishes change, and as the world around us changes. Because therapists pay an emotional price for doing this work, we need to learn in an ongoing fashion what it takes for us to feel revitalized and renewed so that we are able to maintain a sense of passion and commitment to doing this work. An over-emphasis on work at the expense of play and self-care can come from family and cultural background and can be reinforced by the rigors of education and training. So, too, can dedicating oneself to working with difficult-to-treat patients. We know, for example, that treatment of trauma can induce vicarious traumatization in therapists (Klein & Schermer, 2000; Phillips, 2004; Saakvitne & Pearlman, 1995), who need to resolve such traumatic reactions in themselves, and also should have a lifestyle and support system that allows them to be resilient in managing stress factors in their lives. The chapters by O'Leary and Rice (Chapters 2 and 8) address some aspects of therapist stressors in greater detail.

Ability to Work Productively in the Current Health Care Environment

The current health care environment imposes increasing external pressures on therapists. Psychotherapists need to be trained to manage the stress of the occupation, adapt to changing circumstances, and maintain their core identities and values—all while learning to make a living! Few can afford the luxury that British analyst Ronald Fairbairn had of practicing on his own in "splendid isolation" for years in Edinburgh, Scotland, doing his "thing" and making a good living (Sutherland, 1993).

Theobald McClendon and Burlingame characterize the manner in which managed care has subtly influenced, as well as overtly regulated, the mental health field. In the current context, therapy is increasingly monitored and paid for through managed care and the insurance industry, which maintains an allegiance to "evidence-based" treatment models. The number of sessions and the amounts of payments are limited by insurance coverage. Insurance and managed care companies have an ever-increasing role in regulating what is considered acceptable treatment, by whom it can be provided, and for how long. Complicated HIPAA regulations must also be observed; laws regarding recordkeeping and collegial communication are more stringent. In addition, there is increasing competition in the marketplace, with more and more people calling themselves "therapists." Early in their careers psychotherapists may have relatively little choice about participating in managed care and insurance companies in order to make a living. Many younger therapists feel that, to survive economically, they have to belong to preferred provider networks. During later phases of their development, however, when therapists are no longer as economically dependent upon them, choosing when and how to relate to managed care and insurance companies becomes an important issue.

In addition, the current health care environment features the development of newer, reportedly more effective psychotropic medications, with fewer side effects, for the treatment of mood and anxiety disorders, among other syndromes. There are many studies based on randomized controlled trials that support their efficacy. Such medication advances are extensively marketed to cost-conscious insurance companies and managed care operations, as well as to the consumer public. This has led to further questioning of the utility and value of psychotherapy itself, although a recent comprehensive review concludes that there is ample research evidence to support the efficacy of psychodynamic psychotherapy and that patients in psychotherapy continue to improve after treatment has ended (Shedler, 2010). Nevertheless, using medications alone, without psychotherapy, may indeed be best suited for certain patients, and clearly holds considerable appeal for those seeking simple, cost-efficient solutions to complex human problems. The goals for psychodynamic psychotherapy go far beyond symptom reduction or remission, and frequently involve exploring how and why the person developed such symptoms, what purposes they may be serving, how to cope more effectively with the underlying difficulties, and more fundamental learning about oneself and one's relationships through the process of treatment. Psychotherapy, from this perspective, takes more time and is costlier.

Theobald McClendon and Burlingame argue that the current requirements for accountability may lead to greater therapist anxiety or, conversely, to therapist awareness and growth. The ability to handle these requirements and pressures is facilitated by how we see ourselves as professionals, how we view the therapeutic process, and how we learn to identify and make use of available supports and resources. The latter include continuing education workshops, support of colleagues, a talent for handling bureaucratic systems (or getting help with it), and eclectic knowledge of techniques and approaches that allow for successful shorter-term interventions. Since managed care and evidence-based treatment seem here to stay, psychotherapists must learn how to deal with managed care and the demands for accountability, develop short-term strategies, define measurable outcomes, and incorporate research findings into their practices.

It is important to emphasize that, during this phase, psychotherapists must continue to develop their core set of fundamental beliefs, values, and ethical standards, plus a firm sense of professional identity to anchor this level of flexibility. This is another lifelong task—one that is relevant at each level of development and that continues to unfold over the entire course of one's career as a psychotherapist. Without these internal guidelines, it is easy to mistakenly overestimate one's ability to intervene effectively, to become caught up in the demands associated with current fads and obsessions, or to lose sight of one's ethical and moral responsibilities: for instance, to do no harm, to observe patients' rights to confidentiality, and to critically address one's role in the treatment process.

Phase 4: Finding One's Own Voice

The central developmental task of this phase is continuing differentiation and further integration at both the personal and professional levels, leading to increasing individuation, authenticity, and integrity (Billow, 2009, 2010a, 2010b; Skovholt & Jennings, 2004; Vinton, 2008). To a significant extent, much of this is accomplished by refining one's skills through continued personal and professional growth; ongoing reassessment of one's strengths, limitations, and preferences; continuing to pursue new learning opportunities; learning and refining how best to use oneself in the treatment process; continuing to learn how to effectively care for oneself; and the philanthropic notion of "giving back." Much of this is mediated through ongoing self-reflection; cumulative clinical experience; discovering and creatively using one's unique set of assets to augment treatment, teaching, research, and/or other professional efforts; experiences as both supervisor and supervisee; serving as a mentor; participating in and conducting continuing education; and using available resources to stimulate, refresh, and renew. Gayle, in her chapter about mentoring (Chapter 3), points out that a critical aspect of the role of mentor is to stimulate and encourage the mentee to find his or her own voice. The intersubjective process she describes is designed to enable therapists to find their own voices in the mentoring process and in their careers.

The specific content of this phase of development is probably the most difficult to articulate. There is, in our opinion, considerable overlap in the tasks associated with phase 3 and this phase. Much of the developmental work involves a reworking, reintegrating, and refining of earlier accomplishments. However, the focus shifts during this phase from consolidation to individuation. Regardless of specific content, the aim of the tasks that make up this phase is similar: to promote differentiation/individuation, authenticity, and integrity in conducting the work of therapy. It is during this phase that one truly solidifies one's theory of therapy and one's style of working. A clearer, individualized, distinctive focus characterizes one's work as a psychotherapist. The work that was barely begun during phase 2 (mastering the basics) on how to best use oneself as a person in the work of psychotherapy, and gradually became more prominent during phase 3 (consolidating, augmenting, and refining clinical skills and working style), now becomes a primary focus. One's overall sense of professional identity becomes more clearly defined and one's personal satisfaction is most likely to peak during this phase (Orlinsky & Ronnestad, 2005; Ronnestad & Skovholt, 2001; Skovholt & Jennings, 2004).

These developments affect not only clinical work, but also a variety of other professional activities. For some, opportunities to assume a leadership role in professional circles may increase, along with opportunities to give back to the profession in some capacity. It is during this phase that those in academic positions may become sought-after collaborators, writers, and/or researchers; invitations to present one's ideas or to nurture exploration of them may abound. Other senior psychotherapists simply take pleasure in their accomplishments, continue to practice effectively, and keep striving to augment their knowledge base and to polish their clinical skills. Less experienced younger colleagues in need of mentoring or supervision may seek out such well-regarded senior clinicians. Patient referrals often tend to increase. Thus, this phase for some is marked by heightened professional visibility and prominence, coupled with opportunities for enhancing the growth and development of younger colleagues and one's profession.

This can be "heady stuff" that poses a variety of challenges. Among these is developing the capacity to say "no." This applies to patient referrals just as much as to invitations to write, supervise, or present. Maintaining a balance (described earlier) becomes more difficult, but more important, especially as one gets older. One needs to be mindful of changing needs and capacities, attend carefully to activities that promote renewal and reinvigoration, continue to maintain a lifelong commitment and openness to new learning and personal growth, and exercise critical judgment in taking on additional professional demands.

Finding one's own voice (Vinton, 2008), however, is not without dangers. Foremost among these is the danger associated with balancing personal narcissistic gratification with a broader and deeper allegiance to the ethical standards of patient care. Let us briefly describe what we mean. People do all kinds of things in the privacy of their offices with the justification that they know what is best for their patients. It is not at all farfetched to imagine a therapist having sex with a patient and saying that he did so because he was convinced that it would be best for the person in question. This, unfortunately, constitutes one of the most common ethical violations. Precisely because clinical work is highly personal and intimate, it is essentially unmonitored. We work in the privacy of our own offices, behind closed doors. Unless we or our patients report what occurs there, no one ever knows. While we believe that it is indeed desirable to find one's "voice" (i.e., develop an individualized way of working), we ultimately need to rely upon the self-monitoring that therapists do of themselves. More specifically, we need to rely upon their primary allegiance to maintain ethical standards, the strength of their own superegos, their capacities not to self-delude, their abiding interests in helping those they treat and doing no harm, and their commitments not to use patients to gratify their own needs and wishes. Because these factors will never be present in 100% of the practitioners out there, there is and will continue to be a percentage of people who act destructively and do harm to patients, rationalizing that they are conducting themselves consistent with their own "voices."

Phase 5: Retrenchment, Winding Down, and Preparing for Retirement

While many psychotherapists never fully retire, the work of this phase involves reassessing one's limits, preferences, and priorities. Typically this is associated with reducing one's clinical hours and more thoughtful selection of any new patients. The extent of one's overall professional activities and commitments must be carefully monitored. Exploration and discussion with patients who require longer-term care must be initiated. Referral arrangements with colleagues must be organized. Supervisory and teaching responsibilities must also be reviewed. One must learn to make the best use of available supports and resources, and begin devoting additional time to self-care activities.

What is especially challenging about the tasks of this developmental period is that this sort of "winding down" must also be accomplished while one tries to remain open to new learning and appropriately in touch with new methods, theories, and research in the field. Just as one tries, as one ages, to maintain physical flexibility and stamina, preserving intellectual and emotional flexibility and stamina remains equally important. Sustaining a level of commitment, passion, and vitality is that much more difficult when a significant aspect of this phase is associated with loss. More specifically, approaching the end of one's career involves coming to terms with losses and wounds and altering one's pattern of attachments and lifelong pursuits. Many are reluctant to face these losses and maintain that they will be "carried out" of their offices, feet first! But as the Kikkuu tribe of Africa reminds us, "No one escapes this world alive." One way or another, termination is inevitable.

A Talmudic saying fits well here: "As soon as a man is born, he begins to die." One is preparing for the end from the very beginning. From this perspective one might argue that the entire educational process, supervision, mentoring, and personal therapy ultimately should be partially geared toward facilitating a good termination. Aging with grace and dignity while honoring commitments to self, family, patients, friends, and colleagues is no easy feat. Perhaps, as psychotherapists, we need to focus more on endings, including our own. Worthy of note is that far more attention has been devoted to managing endings with patients (e.g., Joyce et al., 2007) than to the ending of our own careers.

During phase 4 we begin to think about the developmental tasks that Erikson (1968) addressed in his seminal work, *Identity Youth and Crisis*; others, too, have since investigated tasks and phases of adult development (e.g., Levinson, 1978; Vaillant, 1977). These matters become much more central for us during phase 5. Erikson, for example, described the penultimate developmental stage as "generativity vs. stagnation." Generativity refers to our legacies: what (if anything) we will be leaving to future generations as we pass from the scene. Some of us write books, some of us become mentors to younger people, and others of us take solace in the way we believe we are helping our patients to live more satisfying lives going forward. There is a sense of satisfaction if we feel we have been generative; conversely, there is a feeling of "stagnation" (lack of satisfaction) if we do not.

Feeling satisfied on this front leads to the last of Erikson's eight stages: "ego integrity vs. despair." As we understand it, ego integrity refers to feeling at peace with ourselves. We feel content with where we have been and where we are, and fulfilled in relation to what we feel we have accomplished with our lives. Such a feeling may derive from our professional accomplishments, or it may derive from other endeavors we have engaged in: avocational pursuits, the kind of spouse or parent we feel we have been, or something else entirely. What is important is that if we feel this sense of "integrity," we are free to decide how we want to lead the last years of our lives, however few or many they may be. We may choose to devote some of our time to continuing to work, or we may decide that we want to invest our energies in other pursuits. We are in a much better position to make these decisions for ourselves if we have achieved this feeling of integrity as opposed to the alternative: "despair."

Recommendations

At this point we would like to turn our attention to putting forth a set of recommendations based on what we have learned about psychotherapist development. More specifically, we will present our recommendations about: (1) the selection of candidates for psychotherapist training, (2) the optimal content for training programs in terms of (a) didactic preparation and (b) the nature of clinical experiences, (3) therapist self-care, and (4) continued professional growth.

Selection

We believe that a great deal of what has been written in this book has implications for the selection of people to be trained for work as psychotherapists. To some degree such people are self-selected: that is, people choose to pursue this kind of work. At the same time, there are people charged with choosing whom to admit to training programs. The comments that follow, therefore, are meant both for those who are contemplating becoming psychotherapists, and those who are responsible for deciding whom to admit to training programs.

There are a host of characteristics that are desirable for people who are entering one of the mental health professions and planning to be psychotherapists.

The following list of desirable characteristics is comprehensive but by no means exhaustive. An optimal candidate to become a psychotherapist should demonstrate:

1. Good relational skills: empathy, altruism, the ability to trust, and psychological-mindedness (Anderson et al., 2009; Starcevic & Piontek, 1997)
2. A passionate interest in ongoing learning
3. A tolerance for ambiguity
4. A capacity for delayed gratification and partial gratification (we often wish we had accomplished more even with those we feel we have helped)
5. An ability to be flexible and to overcome difficulties, which we have called "resilience" (Ackerman & Hilsenroth, 2003)
6. Character makeup that is likely to result in a set of attitudes, beliefs, and values compatible with conducting one's practice in an ethical way (Vardy & Kay, 1982)

Let us be clear: we do not believe that one must possess all of these characteristics in order to be an appropriate candidate for a career as a psychotherapist. Rather, we think that the closer one comes to this personality profile, the more natural is the fit for such a career. The less of these characteristics that candidates possess, the harder they will have to work if they are to become effective treating agents. If one is self-selecting into the field, we believe it would be useful to consider to what degree you believe you possess these characteristics; to the extent that you do not, we would suggest considering how interested you are in developing them, and how feasible you believe it is that you can do so.

Let us now turn to the issue of selection of candidates for training programs, and begin by asserting that it is our unmistakable impression that the assessment of candidates along these dimensions is usually not the focus of interviews of candidates and the deliberations of training committees. Rather, our sense is that for the most part what occurs is what might be called "negative screening": attempting to rule out those who are grossly inappropriate candidates for our field. It is our view that while this is important, it is not nearly enough. We believe we should be making the effort to find the most appropriate candidates to become psychotherapists, not just ruling out the grossly inappropriate ones.

In looking at the list of characteristics we have enumerated, one might think that what we are advocating is an in-depth personality assessment, perhaps including a battery of psychological tests as well as a series of probing, in-depth interviews. While this might be desirable in an ideal world, we are aware that it is not practical. So, then, what are we suggesting? We believe that interviewers and committees should keep these desirable characteristics in mind as they evaluate potential candidates, and do the best they can to select people who are as promising as possible. It is simply not the case that "just anybody" can be an effective therapist as long as there is nothing terribly wrong with him or her. It is the responsibility of those who choose the next generation of practitioners to make their selections as conscientiously as possible; to not do so is a dereliction of their duty to protect the public who will be served by these practitioners.

This responsibility does not end with the selection of candidates for training programs: it extends to whom we allow to graduate, and then beyond. It is our impression that once someone is admitted to a training program, he or she is allowed to graduate and become credentialed unless he or she does one or more things that are so egregious that the program has no alternative but to terminate him or her. We do not believe this is a high enough standard. We have a responsibility to graduate only those who meet a reasonably high standard of competence and character to qualify them to practice.

This is part of a much larger matter that extends well beyond training. We are aware that the comments that follow go beyond the discussion of the selection of candidates for training in one of the mental health professions, and the issue of who is allowed to graduate from such training programs. However, we believe it follows from what we have said thus far, and that it is important for our field to come to grips with the reality of what transpires in the world of clinical practice.

It is vital for our field to acknowledge that a great deal of what goes on behind the closed door of the therapist's consultation room is unacceptable. Some of it is demonstrably poor practice that most clinicians would agree (if they knew what was occurring) was beneath a reasonable standard of professionalism. Some of it is even worse: unethical practices that have a high degree of likelihood of being harmful to those on the receiving end of the treatment. Having sex with one's patients, which occurs all too often, is only one form of unethical practice. There are many others, too numerous to delineate in this chapter. The result is that patients are harmed and, when these practices become public, the mental health professions suffer (deservedly) in the public's eye.

The first response to the notion that "something must be done about this" is that monitoring what professionals do behind closed doors is impossible. While it must be acknowledged that it would be very difficult to do so to a greater degree than currently occurs, we do not believe it is impossible. Further, we believe that the mental health professions have been, and continue to be, negligent in not attending sufficiently to this issue.

So what can be done about it? In a word, greater efforts need to be made to monitor what psychotherapists do, and to discipline those who do not do work that is adequately competent and consistent with the ethical and professional precepts of the field. There need to be clearly identified and readily accessible mechanisms that allow consumers and other professionals to raise questions about the practices of psychotherapists, and to have those questions investigated. At present, there are such mechanisms in the form of discipline-specific (e.g., psychology) professional review boards available at a state level to investigate allegations of professional misconduct. These allegations are weighed against national professional and ethical standards articulated by each of the mental health disciplines. However, the existence of such review boards may not be well known outside of the professions, and, therefore, they may not be easily accessible to patients. Increasing their visibility and accessibility might prove useful. Furthermore, in most states anyone can call himself or herself a "therapist" without having had any formal training within one of the traditional mental heath disciplines. Such "therapists," of course, may not be subject to review by a discipline-specific state board. It is beyond the scope of this book to specify just what other mechanisms might look like, but they would certainly need to be reasonably cost-efficient in terms of the time and money that would be required. Any system would of course be less than perfect, and would not ensure that unprofessional and unethical practices would no longer occur. But greater effort needs to be made for the mental health professions to monitor themselves or, failing that, to be monitored by external entities, because the current state of affairs leaves the consuming public without adequate protection from the abuses and substandard practices that some of our fellow professionals engage in.

Optimal Content of Training Programs

Didactic Preparation

The optimal content of training programs for mental health professionals has been the subject of concern and debate for many years. Training curricula have been developed, assessed, and modified for each of the major mental health disciplines. Reviews of the relevant literature for psychology, for example, can be found elsewhere (e.g., Kendall, 2005; McFall, 2006; Ritschel, 2005).

In general, such training programs endeavor to provide the new professional with the specialized knowledge and experiences necessary to enter the chosen mental health profession. Our purpose here is not to provide another comprehensive review of the training offered by each discipline; rather, it is to emphasize the aspects of current training that seem most important to reassess and address differently. We will look first at didactic preparation and then turn our attention to clinical experiences.

More specifically, with regard to the content of didactic preparation, we would emphasize the importance of providing trainees with a broad didactic knowledge base that appropriately recognizes current trends in the field. Trainees should be exposed not only to the more traditional areas of study (e.g., psychopathology, assessment and diagnosis, theories of therapy) but also to the relatively newer areas of inquiry (e.g., process and outcome research on psychotherapy, short-term and evidence-based approaches to treatment, neurobiology, and psychopharmacology). It is these areas of research that are the most rapidly growing, generating new ideas and methods of treatment, and stimulating a good deal of controversy. The information explosion in these areas is truly staggering, but potentially quite useful. How to evaluate this information and incorporate it into ongoing clinical practice is one of the most significant challenges facing practitioners (APA, 2006; Hunsley, 2007; Kazdin, 2008). Properly training tomorrow's clinicians to be able to do so effectively is, in our opinion, critical. Increased early exposure to clinical research and evidence-based approaches to treatment, for example, will ideally help trainees to experience increased comfort and familiarity in using and applying these approaches, overcome elements of resistance, and recognize the implications of research for clinical practice (Bauer, 2007; Cook & Coyne, 2005; Kivlighan, 2008; Leffingwell & Collins, 2008). This, in turn, can reduce what Theobald McClendon and Burlingame refer to as to the "essential tension" between the creative patient–therapist interconnection versus the technical, more easily measured aspects of psychotherapy outcome.

Making this a priority item in today's training programs would also enable trainees to remain more responsive to the growing demands for accountability associated with evidence-based practice (Burlingame et al., 2004; Burlingame & Beecher, 2008; Spring, 2007). These demands are likely to increase, not diminish, in the future. Similarly, teaching trainees more about how to implement shorter-term approaches to treatment may make it easier for them to cope with managed care and insurance companies, whose influence is also growing stronger. As noted earlier, the political power and influence associated with these forces most directly affects the abilities of younger therapists to earn a living, since it is they who often cannot survive on the basis of their reputations but have to rely more upon becoming members of preferred provider networks to sustain their clinical practices. Addressing these challenges as part of training might better prepare new professionals for coping with these sociopolitical and economic realities and provide new opportunities for bridging research and practice, enhancing the knowledge base, and improving patient care (Hunsley, 2007; Kazdin, 2008; Klein, 2009).

Exposure to research and empirical data needs to be complemented by exposure to alternative theoretical models and approaches as well. Newer theoretical models of the treatment process, especially those that focus on intersubjectivity and the importance of understanding the person of the therapist, need to be presented and explicated (Aron, 1996; Fosshage, 2003; Mitchell, 1988; Ogden, 1994; Stolorow & Atwood, 1992; Ogden, 1994; Aron, 1996; Fosshage, 2003). It is clear that these models, which are gaining more and more adherents, introduce important new perspectives for understanding the treatment process. More traditional conceptualizations about transference and countertransference are being reevaluated and are undergoing significant modification. The intersubjective focus on the co-creation of the therapeutic relationship is receiving much-needed attention. This focus is also consistent with the renewed research interest in how the characteristics of the therapist affect both the therapeutic relationship and the outcome of treatment (Norcross, 2002). Training new clinicians to devote more attention to their contributions to the process and outcome of therapy will be valuable no matter what treatment models they eventually adopt.

Our examination of therapist development also underlines the value of early exposure of trainees to a wide variety of different treatment models and modalities. This gives them at least some familiarity with a broader range of possible treatment interventions. Equipping them with an expanded knowledge of possible therapeutic interventions may promote increased flexibility of response and allow them to formulate more individually tailored treatment regimens. Such knowledge may also better equip trainees to practice with a broader variety of patients under a broader variety of conditions (e.g., outside of the traditional office setting following a disaster). Results from the most comprehensive study of psychotherapist development (Orlinsky & Ronnestad, 2005) indicate that therapists who use multiple treatment modalities (e.g., individual and group therapy) report increased levels of clinical competence and greater resistance to depleting, negative practice cycles.

Closely related to this issue is that of devoting increased didactic preparation to issues of cultural diversity (Brinson & Cervantes, 2003; Comas-Dias, 2005; Poe-Davis & Coleman, 2001; Robinson & Howard-Hamilton, 2000; Sue & Sue, 1999; Comas-Dias, 2005; Brinson & Cervantes, 2003). To be able to practice effectively with the broader range of patients who now seek treatment, as well as those who are increasingly likely to do so in the future, will require increased awareness and sensitivity to differences as a function of age, race, gender, socioeconomic status, religion, and culture. How patients present for treatment and how they respond to treatment are both significantly influenced by these variables. Lack of adequate knowledge and sensitivity to these issues may render treatment efforts by unprepared clinicians less than useful, or even unwanted and irrelevant. Training the scientist-practitioner for the 21st century requires paying closer attention to these variables and how they affect the entire treatment process (Drabick & Goldfried, 2000; Hunsley, 2007). The responses of both patients and clinicians need to be monitored. Furthermore, from a pedagogical perspective, we need to establish how best to train new professionals to become more culturally aware and sensitive. Some training programs for psychologists, for example, are already trying to do this (Canter & Fuentes, 2008). Didactic training alone may well be insufficient. Rather, as suggested by Gans in Chapter 5, this may require some combination of didactic training plus carefully selected and supervised clinical experience, or it may require personal psychotherapy and/or group process experiences, as noted by Phillips in Chapter 7.

Clinical Experience

Developing competence in working effectively with patients requires ongoing clinical experience coupled with appropriate supervision. It is not enough to know about the precepts of various theories or the diagnostic criteria for different psychiatric disorders; one must also learn how to apply what one has learned to real-world experiences with actual patients. Hence, we would argue that there is considerable value in training programs making a sustained effort to ensure that trainees are exposed to as broad a variety of patients as possible. This not only leads to the development of an increased range of clinical skills; it also augments trainees' levels of comfort, familiarity, and security in coping with new patients.

In addition, trainees should have opportunities to implement a variety of treatment models, methods, and modalities with these patients. There are many effective ways by which to provide treatment or intervention. Expanding trainees' range of treatment responses and options is likely to result in more sensitive and thoughtful engagements with patients. Furthermore, as noted earlier, trainees should be encouraged to learn how to use these approaches both inside and outside the confines of the office. Those who choose to work with trauma may well have many more opportunities to conduct some forms of intervention and/or treatment in the community, outside of the traditional office setting. They will, however, also require additional training and support to enable them to come to terms with their own emotional responses, as well as those of their patients, and thereby reduce the likelihood of compassion fatigue, burnout, and vicarious traumatization (Edelwich & Brodsky, 1980; Farber, 1990; Maslach & Leitner, 1997; Klein & Schermer, 2000; Maslach & Leitner, 1997; Phillips, 2004; Saakvitne & Pearlman, 1995; Edelwich & Brodsky, 1980; Farber, 1990).

In the course of gaining clinical experience with a broad variety of patients, problems, and approaches to treatment, training programs should ensure that their trainees also learn about what other mental health professionals have to offer. When might couples or family therapy be useful, and who can provide that? For whom might medications prove helpful? These and related questions often need to be asked when providing treatment for complex cases. Most importantly, trainees need to learn not only what other professionals do, but also how to work collaboratively with them as part of a treatment team (Sperry, 1995; Ellison, 2005; Patterson et al., 2006; Sperry, 1995). Furthermore, successful treatment integration rests upon knowledge of what others can provide, a shared view of what is needed by the patient, and a mutual appreciation for how best to work together.

From our point of view, none of the trainees' patient care experiences should ever be provided without careful supervision. By supervision, we are referring to the relationships and processes described by Leszcz in Chapter 6. Such supervisory activity is characterized by mutual respect, honesty, and the willingness to try to examine the interpersonal processes involved in both trainees' work with their patients and their work with their supervisors. The creation of a safe, non-defensive atmosphere in supervisory sessions that emphasize introspection and self-disclosure can improve the trainee's understanding of the process of psychotherapy and the use of self to do the work. Participation in such supervisory activities benefits not only the trainee, but the supervisor as well. Each of the participants experiences multiple opportunities to learn and to grow.

Clinical experience and supervision are consistently identified as major, formative components of professional development, along with personal psychotherapy (Orlinsky & Ronnestad, 2005). Thoughtful and appropriate supervision can provide invaluable support, encouragement, modeling, mentoring, and permission to examine one's own emotional reactions. It is through these processes, which serve as the parallel for working with patients, that trainees often learn their most memorable clinical lessons. The supervisory context challenges trainees to learn how to use their relational and introspective skills to carefully examine both the therapeutic and supervisory process. Personal psychotherapy certainly provides such opportunities, as might a mentoring relationship. But not every trainee obtains personal psychotherapy or mentoring before or during training. Hence, we would argue that it is difficult to overestimate the value of good supervision.

In addition, working closely in a supervisory and/or mentoring relationship with a more senior clinician can also be extremely useful in assisting trainees to begin to articulate and develop their own sense of professional ethics and identity. This is a critical area of professional development that helps to sustain one as a clinical professional throughout a career, despite fluctuating levels of success and satisfaction. It allows one to thoughtfully decide how to deal with managed care, for example, and how to identify instances that may compromise the integrity of one's work. Establishing a sound ethical basis for clinical practice, coupled with a strong sense of professional identity, acts as a safeguard that protects us as therapists, our patients, and the communities we serve. This area certainly merits systematic attention and examination during the period of training; it is far too important to leave to chance.

Consideration of professional identity and ethics should be dealt with both through the didactic and clinical experience components of training. The supervisory relationship provides an excellent context in which to explore these issues. So, too, does the mentoring relationship. However, training programs often apportion relatively little in the way of faculty resources to promoting and cultivating mentoring connections. For the most part, this task receives limited attention and tends to be left entirely to the trainees, without active faculty involvement. In our opinion, establishing mentoring relationships also warrants further attention as an important aspect of training.

In our earlier discussion of characteristics that identify successful therapists we mentioned, among other things, psychological-mindedness. There are several components that make up psychological-mindedness. One is curiosity; another is introspection. We want to emphasize here that we regard these qualities as essential for continuing personal and professional growth and development. One's ability, interest, and willingness to engage in ongoing self-scrutiny and monitoring is linked to providing effective clinical care and participating in successful supervision and/or mentoring activities. All of these require the courage to look honestly at oneself and to risk personal exposure.

Both one's warts and one's beautiful parts, one's errors and one's insightful contributions, can be subjected to examination and exploration. Without that courage there can be only limited growth. Training programs may need to reassess how much attention they pay to encouraging, stimulating, and rewarding introspection and self-scrutiny among their trainees.

Last, with regard to sustaining growth and development, we believe that trainees should be encouraged to seek supervision and consultation after they complete their training, not simply during their training. In other words, seeking supervision or consultation should not be regarded as a sign of diffi-culty or that the therapist needs some sort of remedial help. Instead, we should be training the next generation of clinicians to recognize supervision and consultation as opportunities to build one's capacity for establishing the deeper, more authentic, and trusting relationships that are associated with more effective clinical work.

Therapist Self-Care and Continuing Growth

Therapist Self-Care

Doing the work of psychotherapy is stressful and demanding. Furthermore, it can feel quite lonely and isolating, since most of our work is done alone with our patients. In many instances, however, it goes well and is a source of satisfaction that promotes further personal and professional growth. But we also know that therapist success and development is nonlinear and includes cycles that can be discouraging and depleting. It is, therefore, important for therapists to learn how to take care of themselves in order to sustain their own well-being over the long haul, and to ensure that they maintain a high stan-dard of clinical care with patients (e.g., Kottler, 1999, 2003; Norcross, 2000). We would suggest that it is crucial for therapists to (a) learn how to continu-ously monitor their own reactions, (b) acknowledge that these affect their work, (c) figure out what they need to remain engaged, committed, passion-ate, authentic, and refreshed in conducting the work, and (d) devote suffi-cient time and energy to identifying and gratifying their own personal needs outside the treatment setting.

This seems like a simple enough formula to follow, yet it is surprising how many therapists do not take proper care of themselves. This happens despite our collective admonitions to those we treat to be sure to take proper care of *themselves*! Perhaps we should accompany such statements with the old parental adage: Do what I say, not what I do. Few senior therapists would debate the fact that we caretakers can be a testy lot. Many of us are so used to taking care of others that we overlook our own needs and do not devote nearly the same level of care to ourselves as we do to others. Getting older, of course, does have a way of reminding us to do just that. But we think it is important for new professionals, as well, to recognize the importance of this task. Failure to pay proper attention to therapists' needs is not good for either therapists or their patients. Both, in fact, are much more likely to benefit when therapists feel content and fulfilled with their work and their lives outside of the consulting room.

Continuing Growth and Development

As has been emphasized at various points in this volume, good psychotherapists are committed to life-long, or at least career-long, growth and development. There is no such thing as having "arrived" as a psychotherapist. There is always more to learn, both because the knowledge base in the field is always expanding, and because each developmental stage for the therapist provides new challenges and new opportunities for learning. Even in the last of the five phases we delineate in this chapter (retrenchment, winding down, and preparing for retirement), there are new challenges to wrestle with and learn about. Our learning, growth, and development ends only when we stop working altogether.

Learning How Best to Use Oneself in the Therapeutic Process

Earlier we alluded to certain "lifetime tasks" that face psychotherapists. Among those are the tasks of lifelong learning, finding a balance between competing needs and priorities, and promoting self-care and replenishment. One more item on this list merits further discussion: the task of learning how to creatively and effectively use oneself in the treatment process. Tackling this task is both extremely challenging and extremely rewarding. It requires ongoing introspection and self-monitoring. Only by developing the capacity, the courage, and the commitment to maintain ongoing introspection and self-monitoring can one refine and expand how one works, develop increasing levels of self-awareness, skill, and effectiveness, and learn how best to use one's own unique assets and limitations. Therapists' knowing themselves and how to use themselves to accomplish the work of therapy enables them to maintain their integrity and to grow in an authentic fashion (Billow, 2009, 2010a, 2010b). It leads them to more carefully frame their theories and clinical approaches, to realistically recognize their strengths and limitations, and to select patients they are more likely to be able to treat effectively. Finally, searching to discover how to use oneself creatively and effectively in the treatment process ensures more positive growth cycles in their personal and professional development that allow them to remain open, passionate, and committed.

While it is easy for us to get caught up in completing our responsibilities every day (or week, or month, or year), it is not sufficient. We need to go beyond this and be sure to set aside time for professional development. Fortunately, there are many ways that we can accomplish this. We can and should read as much as we can: at least a few of the many journals that are published multiple times a year, and selected books that strike us as interesting and/or important. There are professional development events available all the time: lectures, seminars, workshops, and conferences. Such events can be expensive, both in terms of registration fees and in terms of lost practice time. But if we do not make the time to attend such events at least occasionally, our work can become stale, and we can end up serving our patients less well. In addition, in recent years more and more professional development activities have become available online, so that we can learn a great deal now without ever having to leave our offices or homes.

Worthy of note in this connection are opportunities to participate as a member of a small intensive experiential group that is part of some professional conferences. The American Group Psychotherapy Association and the American Association of Psychotherapy are two professional organizations among several that conduct such events. These small groups, led by a senior clinician, may convene over several days during a conference, or may meet on a regular basis during successive annual conferences. As group members, mental health professionals can learn about group dynamics and perhaps more importantly can use these opportunities to address their own personal needs. Participants generally report that these experiences enable them to emotionally reconnect with colleagues, to better understand themselves and their relationships, and to feel a sense of renewal and revitalization.

Another opportunity for ongoing professional growth and development is that of supervision. The traditional form of supervision, in which a more junior person discusses his or her work with a more senior person, is discussed at length by Leszcz in Chapter 6. The experience of supervising one or more junior therapists is often a valuable growth experience for the supervisor as well as the supervisee(s). Another form of supervision that is very widespread is peer supervision (or consultation), in which professional peers get together and discuss their own and each others' clinical work, without the presence of a more senior "expert." This is obviously a less expensive alternative (no money changes hands), and for some it is easier to disclose errors and confusion to a group of peers than to a so-called expert. The process of regularly reviewing one's work with others, and opening oneself up to others' perspectives about one's patients and what is happening in the therapist–patient matrix, can be invaluable.

Still another source for professional as well as personal growth and development is when therapists choose to enter treatment themselves. While many therapists do so while they are being trained, there is no need for it to end there. In fact, the model of engaging in treatment for a period of time, finishing one's work, and never going back for additional work is increasingly passé. More and more frequently, patients return for treatment periodically through the life cycle, particularly if their experiences have been positive ones. This is, or should be, no less true for therapists. While treatment is always grounded in personal concerns that reach a point where one decides to begin or resume treatment, personal psychotherapy has an additional benefit for mental health practitioners. They have the opportunity to model those characteristics of their therapists that fit for them, and more generally to learn about what treatment (one hopes, good treatment) is all about. They inevitably bring these lessons back to the work they do with their own patients, even if they are not always aware that they are doing so. Thus, personal treatment can be another important source of professional growth and development.

Work as a psychotherapist is inherently stressful, both because of the nature of the material we work with day in and day out, and because of the isolation and loneliness that so often characterizes the clinician's day-to-day life. Clinicians who are committed to doing the best work they can do make a life-long commitment to good self-care and professional replenishment, and use some or all of the options mentioned above to ensure that they remain current, fresh, and vital as they treat those who come to them for help with their various struggles.

References

Ackerman, S. J., & Hilsenroth, M. J. (2003). A review of therapist characteristics and techniques positively impacting the therapeutic alliance. *Clinical Psychology Review*, 23, 1–33.

Ahn, H., & Wampold, B. E. (2001). Where oh where are the specific ingredients? A meta-analysis of component studies in counseling and psychotherapy. *Journal of Counseling Psychology*, 48, 251–257.

American Psychological Association (APA) Presidential Task Force on Evidence-Based Practice. (2006). Evidence-based practice in psychology. *American Psychologist*, 61, 271–285.

Anderson, T., Ogles, B. M., Patterson, C. L., Lambert, M. J., & Vermeersch, D. A. (2009). Therapist effects: Facilitative interpersonal skills as a predictor of therapist success. *Journal of Clinical Psychology*, 65(7), 755–768.

Aron, L. (1996). *A Meeting of Minds: Mutuality in Psychoanalysis*. Hillsdale, NJ: Analytic Press.

Bachelor, A., & Horvath, A. (1999). The therapeutic relationship. In M. A. Hubble, B. L. Duncan, & S. D. Miller (Eds.), *The Heart and Soul of Change: What Works in Therapy* (pp. 133–178). Washington, D.C.: American Psychological Association.

Bauer, R. M. (2007). Evidence-based practice in psychology: Implications for research and research training. *Journal of Clinical Psychology*, 63, 685–694.

Bergin, A. E., & Garfield, S.L. (Eds.) (1994). *Handbook of Psychotherapy and Behavior Change* (4th ed.). New York: Wiley.

Bike, D. S., Norcross, J. C., & Schatz, D. (2009). Processes and outcomes of psychotherapists' personal therapy: Replication and extension 20 years later. *Psychotherapy Theory, Research, Practice, Training*, 46(1), 19–31.

Billow, R. M. (2009). Modes of leadership: Diplomacy, integrity, sincerity, and authenticity. In R. H. Klein, C. A. Rice, & V. L. Schermer (Eds.), *Leadership in a Changing World: Dynamic Perspectives on Groups and their Leaders*. Lanham, MD: Lexington Books.

Billow, R. M. (2010a). Modes of therapeutic engagement: Part I: Diplomacy and integrity. *International Journal of Group Psychotherapy*, 60, 1–28.

Billow, R. M. (2010b). Modes of therapeutic engagement: Part II: Sincerity and authenticity. *International Journal of Group Psychotherapy*, 60, 29–58.

Brinson, J. &Cervantes, J. (2003). Recognizing ethnic/racial biases and discriminatory practices through self-supervision. In J.A. Kotter &W.F. Jones (Eds.). *Doing better*. New York: Brunner/Routledge.

Burlingame, G. M., & Beecher, M. (2008). New directions and resources in group psychotherapy (Special Issue). *Journal of Clinical Psychology*, 64(11), 1197–1205.

Burlingame, G. M., MacKenzie, K. R., & Strauss, B. (2004). Small group treatment: Evidence for effectiveness and mechanisms of change. In M. J. Lambert (Ed.), *Bergin and Garfield's Handbook of Psychotherapy and Behavior Change* (5th ed., pp. 647–696). New York: Wiley.

Cantor, D. W., & Fuentes, M. A. (2008). Psychology's response to managed care. *Professional Psychology: Research and Practice*, 39, 638–645.

Comas-Diaz, L. (2005). Becoming a multicultural psychotherapist: the influence of culture, ethnicity, and gender. *Journal of Clinical Psychology*, 61(8), 973–981.

Cook, J. M., & Coyne, J. C. (2005). Re-envisioning the training and practice of clinical psychologists: Preserving science and research orientations in the face of change. *Journal of Clinical Psychology*, 61, 191–196.

Crits-Christoph, P., Connolly Gibbons, M.B., & Hearon, B. (2006). Does the alliance cause good outcome? *Psychotherapy: Theory, Research, Practice, Training*, 43, 280–285.

Drabick, D. A., & Goldfried, M. R. (2000). Training the scientist-practitioner for the twenty-first century: Putting the bloom back on the rose. *Journal of Clinical Psychology*, 56, 327–340.

Edelwich, J., & Brodsky, A. M. (1980). *Burn-out*. New York: Human Sciences Press.

Ellison, J. M. (2005). Teaching collaboration between psychopharmacologist and psychotherapist. *Academic Psychiatry*, 29, 195–202.

Erikson, E. (1968). *Youth Identity and Crisis*. New York: W. W. Norton.

Farber, B. A. (1990). Burnout in psychotherapists: Incidence, types, and trends. *Psychotherapy in Private Practice*, 8(1), 35–44.

Fosshage, J. L. (2003). Contextualizing self psychology and relational psychoanalysis: Bi-directional influence and proposed syntheses. *Contemporary Psychoanalysis*, 39, 411–448.

Garfield, S. L., & Bergin, A. E. (Eds.) (1990). *Handbook of Psychotherapy and Behavior Change* (4th ed.). New York: Wiley.

Goleman, D. (1995). *Emotional Intelligence: Why It Can Matter More Than IQ*. New York: Bantam Books.

Horvath, A. O., & Luborsky, L. (1993). The role of the therapeutic alliance in psychotherapy. *Journal of Consulting and Clinical Psychology*, 61(4), 561–573.

Horvath, A. O., & Symonds, B. D. (1991). Relation between working alliance and outcome in psychotherapy: A meta-analysis. *Journal of Counseling Psychology*, 38, 139–149.

Hunsley, J. (2007). Addressing key challenges in evidence-based practice in psychology. *Professional Psychology: Research and Practice*, 38, 113–121.

Jennings, L., & Skovholt, T. M. (1999). The cognitive, emotional and relational characteristics of master therapists. *Journal of Counseling Psychology*, 46, 3–11.

Joyce, A. S., Piper, W. E., Ogrodnicizuk, J. S., & Klein, R. H. (2007). *Termination in Psychotherapy; A Psychodynamic Model of Processes and Outcomes*. Washington, D.C.: American Psychological Association.

Kazdin, A. E. (2005). Treatment outcomes, common factors, and continued neglect of mechanisms of change. *Clinical Psychology: Science and Practice*, 12, 184–188.

Kazdin, A. E. (2008). Evidence-based treatment and practice: New opportunities to bridge clinical research and practice, enhance knowledge base, and improve patient care. *American Psychologist*, 63, 146–159.

Kendall, P. C. (2005). Clinical psychology in the twenty-first century: The wheel remains. *Journal of Clinical Psychology*, 61, 1083–1086.

Kivlighan, D. M. Jr. (2008). Overcoming our resistances to "doing" evidence-based group practice: A commentary. *Journal of Clinical Psychology: In Session*, 64, 1284–1291.

Klein, R. H. (2009). Toward the establishment of evidence-based practices in group psychotherapy. *International Journal of Group Psychotherapy*, 58(4), 441–454.

Klein, R. H., & Schermer, V. L. (Eds.) (2000). *Group Psychotherapy for Psychological Trauma*. New York: Guilford Press.

Kottler, J. A. (1999). *The Therapist's Workbook: Self-Assessment, Self-Care, and Self-Improvement Exercises for Mental Health Professionals*. San Francisco: Jossey-Bass.

Kottler, J. A. (2003). *On Being a Therapist* (rev. ed.). San Francisco: Jossey Bass.

Lambert, M. L. (2004). *Bergin and Garfield's Handbook of Psychotherapy and Behavior Change* (5th ed.). New York: Wiley.

Leffingwell, T. R., & Collins, F. L. Jr. (2008). Graduate training in evidence-based practice in psychology. In R. G. Steele, T. D. Elkin, & M. C. Roberts (Eds.), *Handbook of Evidence-Based Therapies for Children and Adolescents: Bridging Science and Practice*. New York: Spring Science+Business Media.

Levinson, D. J. (1978). *The Seasons of a Man's Life*. New York: Knopf.

Luborsky, L., Rosenthal, R., Diguer, L., Andrusyna, T. P., Berman, J. S., Levitt, J. T., Seligman, D. A., & Krause, E. D. (2002). The dodo bird verdict is alive and well—mostly. *Clinical Psychology: Science and Practice*, 9(1), 2–12.

Martin, D. J., Garske, J. P., & Davis, M. K. (2000). Relation of the therapeutic alliance with outcome and other variables: A meta-analytic review. *Journal of Counseling and Clinical Psychology*, 68, 438–450.

Maslach, C., & Leiter, M. P. (1997). *The Truth About Burnout*. San Francisco: Jossey-Bass.

McFall, F. M. (2006). Doctoral training in clinical psychology. *Annual Review of Clinical Psychology*, 2, 21–49.

Messer, S. B., & Wampold, B. E. (2002). Let's face facts: Common factors are more potent than specific therapy ingredients. *Clinical Psychology: Science and Practice*, 9(1), 21–25.

Mitchell, S. A. (1988). *Relational Concepts in Psychoanalysis*. Cambridge: Harvard University Press.

Norcross, J. C. (2000). Psychotherapist self-care: Practitioner-tested, research-oriented strategies. *Professional Psychology: Research and Practice*, 31, 710–714.

Norcross, J. C. (Ed.) (2002). *Psychotherapy Relationships that Work*. New York: Oxford University Press.

Norcross, J. C., & Guy, J. D. (2005). The prevalence and parameters of personal therapy in the United States. In J. D. Geller, J. C. Norcross, & D. E. Orlinsky (Eds.), *The Psychotherapist's Own Psychotherapy: Patient and Clinician Perspectives*. New York: Oxford University Press.

Ogden, T. H. (1994). The analytic third: Working with intersubjective clinical facts. *International Journal of Psycho-Analysis*, 75, 3–19.

Orlinsky, D. E., & Ronnestad, M. H. (2005). *How Psychotherapists Develop: A Study of Therapeutic Work and Professional Growth*. Washington, D.C.: American Psychological Association.

Patterson, J., Albala, A. A., McCahill, M. E., & Edwards, T. M. (2006). *The Therapist's Guide to Psychopharmacology: Working with Patients, Families, and Physicians to Optimize Care*. New York: Guilford Press.

Phillips, S. B. (2004). Countertransference: Effects on the group therapist working with trauma. In B. Buchele & H. Spitz (Eds.), *Group Interventions for Treatment of Psychological Trauma*. New York: American Group Psychotherapy Association.

Ritschel, L. A. (2005). Reconciling the rift: Improving clinical psychology graduate training in the twenty-first century. *Journal of Clinical Psychology*, 36, 1111–1114.

Ronnestad, M. H., & Skovholt, T. M. (2001). Learning arenas for professional development: Retrospective accounts of senior psychotherapists. *Professional Psychology: Research and Practice*, 32(2), 181–187.

Saakvitne, K. W., & Pearlman, L. A. (1995). *Trauma and the Therapist*. New York: Norton.

Shedler, J. (2010). The efficacy of psychodynamic psychotherapy. *American Psychologist*, 65(2), 98–109.

Skovholt, T. M., & Jennings, L. (Eds.) (2004). *Master Therapists: Exploring Expertise in Therapy and Counseling*. Boston: Allyn & Bacon.

Skovholt, T. M., & Ronnestad, M. H. (1995). *The Evolving Professional Self: Stages and Themes in Therapist and Counselor Development*. New York: Wiley.

Sperry, L. (1995). *Psychopharmacology and Psychotherapy: Strategies for Maximizing Treatment Outcomes*. New York: Psychology Press.

Spring, B. (2007). Evidence-based practice in clinical psychology: What it is, why it matters, what you need to know. *Journal of Clinical Psychology: In Session*, 63, 611–631.

Starcevic, V., & Piontek, C. M. (1997). Empathic understanding revisited: Conceptualization, controversies, and limitations. *American Journal of Psychotherapy*, 51(3), 317–328.

Stolorow, R. D., & Atwood, G. E. (1992). *Contexts of Being: The Intersubjective Foundations of Psychological Life*. Hillsdale, NJ: Analytic Press.

Sue, D.W. & Sue, S. (1999). *Counseling the culturally different*. New York: Wiley.

Sutherland, J. D. (1993). *Fairbairn's Journey to the Interior*. London: Free Association Press.

Vaillant, G. E. (1977). *Adaptation to Life*. Boston: Little Brown.

Vardy, M. M., & Kay, S. R. (1982). The therapeutic value of psychotherapists' values and therapy orientations. *Psychiatry*, 45(3), 226–233.

Vinton, E. A. (2008). Finding a voice of one's own: The development of a unique, authentic manner as retrospectively reported by highly experienced relational psychoanalysts. *Dissertation Abstracts*.

Wampold, B. E., & Brown, G. S. (2005). Estimating variability in outcomes attributable to therapists: A naturalistic study of outcomes in managed care. *Journal of Consulting and Clinical Psychology*, 73, 914–923.

Wampold, B. E., Mondin, G. W., Moody, M., Stich, F., Benson, K., & Ahn, H. (1997). A meta-analysis of outcome studies comparing bona fide psychotherapies: Empirically, "all must have prizes." *Psychological Bulletin*, 122(3), 203–215.

Yalom, I. D. (2002). *The Gift of Therapy*. New York: Harper Perennial.

Index

Abraham, Gunther, 72–73
Abraham, Karl, 72
Academy of Cognitive Therapy, 229
accountability, viii, 186, 284, 292
Ackerman, S., 128
Ackerman, S. J., 254, 259
Acosta, F. X., 250
ADDRESSING (age, disability, religion, ethnicity, social class, sexual orientation, indigenous heritage, national origin, and gender/sex), 157
Adler, Alfred, 169
advertising, 11
Aesculapius, 76
affect, 104
African Americans, 250
Agazarian, Yvonne, 77
aging, 287–88
Alcoholics Anonymous, 170
alienists, 171
Allen, L. B., 217
Allen, M., 255–56
alliance-fostering therapy, 259
Alonso, A., 115, 133
altruism, 37–38, 273
ambiguity
   in didactic preparation, 77–78
   tolerance for, 274
American Association of Psychotherapy, 298
American Group Psychotherapy Association, 298
American Psychological Association (APA), 14
   "Guidelines for Providers of Psychological Services to Ethnic, Linguistic, and Culturally Diverse Populations," 43

Anna O, 69
anxiety disorders, 217
APA. See American Psychological Association
apologies, 110–11
Applebaum, S. A., 36
archetypes, 166
Asklepios, 167
Ast, G., 176
Atlantic City, 73
Atwood, G., 90
Auerbach, A., 245–46, 252
Australian Psychological Society, 132
authority role, 80

bachelor's degree, 78
Baldwin, S. A., 253
Bales, Robert, 82
Ball, S. A., 253, 254
Balzano, J., 194
Bambling, M., 128
Bandler, R., 190–91, 207
Barber, J. P., 260
Barlow, D. H., 217, 247
Barnett, J., 57
Basco, M. R., 224–25
Bauer, R. M., 194–95
Bazron, B., 129
Beck, A. T., 224–25, 260
Beck, Aaron, 79, 82
Beecher, M., 194, 195
Beecher, M. E., 207
Behavioral Tech, LLC, 229
Beidel, D. C., 219–20, 224, 232
Benedek, T., 155–56
Bergin, A. E., 19, 256
Bernal, M., 43–44

Bettelheim, Bruno, 40
Beutler, L. E., 247, 252
bias, 44, 45, 109–10, 111
    classist, 43
    in supervision, 131
bibliotherapy, 134
Bike, D. S., 146, 147, 150
Binder, J. L., 260
Bion, W. R., 91
Blatt, S. J., 246
Bonanno, G. A., 39
Bonney, W., 30, 31
borderline personality disorder, 217,
    233–34
Bordin, E. S., 252, 259
Boswell, J., 126
Botermans, J., 146, 147
boundaries, 98, 106
    management of, 107–9, 278
    for mentors, 57
    in supervision, 118, 121–22, 133–34
    with wounded healer, 182–84
Bowman, D. C., 260
Brandt, S., 119
Breuer, Josef, 69
Brigham Young University, 197
Brightman, B., 90
British Psychoanalytic Institute and
    Society, 83
Brodsky, A., 99
Brodsky, A. M., 184
Brown, Laura, 157
Bufka, L. F., 247
Buie, J., 196
Bukloh, L. M., 196
Burkard, A., 136
Burlingame, G., 194, 195, 201
burnout, 81, 99, 270
Burns, David, 82
Butler, S. F., 260

Campbell, J., 166
cancellation, 97, 98
Carkhuff, R. R., 258
Carroll, K. M., 253, 254
Castonguay, L., 126
Catholics, 171
cause and effect, 86
CBT. See cognitive-behavioral therapy
CBT Triangle, 215f
Celenza, A., 158
certification, CBT, 229
Chan, A., 62
change

in didactic preparation, 74–76
in health care, 84–85
in patients, 74–75, 274
in psychotherapy, vii–viii, 74–75,
    84–85, 274
Charcot, Jean-Martin, 69, 72
Chen, E. C., 194
childhood, of psychotherapists, 31,
    54–55, 62–63, 169
children, of psychotherapist, 145
China, 129–30
Chiron, 167, 174–75
Chisholm, R. R., 260
Chittams, J., 260
Choate, M. L., 217
Christie, Agatha, 178
CL. See conceptual level
Clark, A., 191
Clark, J., 121
classist bias, 43
Clemence, A., 128
Clemence, A. J., 259
clinical intuition, 18
clinical psychology, 85–86
cognitive-behavioral therapy (CBT), 5, 87
    adherence to, 255
    certification for, 229
    in context, 213–14
    continuing education in, 229–30
    countertransference with, 224–25,
        235–36
    evidence-based treatments in, 217–18,
        220
    goals, 232–33
    group therapy, 227–28
    homework, 234–35
    internship in, 226–28
    outcomes with, 225
    panic disorder in, 247
    patient classification in, 216–17
    for personality disorders, 233–334
    personal role in, 212–13, 219, 222–23,
        225, 229, 230, 231–34, 235, 236,
        237, 238t, 239–40, 239t, 279–80
    personal treatment and, 152–53
    principles of, 215–16, 215f
    self-practice in, 224
    self-reflection in, 231–32, 279–80
    self-selection with, 226, 228
    Socratic method in, 76
    standards for, 238t, 239t
    subdivisions of, 214–15
    supervision with, 228–29, 230, 232,
        233, 235–36

therapeutic alliance in, 218–19, 220–22, 236–37, 239–40
training in, 223–24, 225–30, 231–33, 237, 238*t*, 239*t*, 259, 260
treatment adherence with, 236–37
unconscious in, 22
Cohen, B., 60
Collings, A., 120
collusion, 61
communication
    of empathy, 19
    nonverbal, 85, 177
    skills of, 281
    training in, 75–76
community, 12
compassion fatigue, 149
competence
    in ethics, 132
    outcomes with, 254–55
conceptual frameworks, 73–74
conceptual level (CL), 258–59
confidentiality
    with HMOs, 196
    in personal treatment, 159–60
conflict of interest, 56
conflict resolution, 98
Connolly Gibbons, M. B., 259
Connor, K. A., 147, 158
containment, 60, 78
continuing education, 78, 82, 282, 297–98
    in CBT, 229–30
    delivery of, 85
    in didactic preparation, 83–84
Counseling the Culturally Diverse (Sue and Sue), 43
countertransference, 19
    with CBT, 224–25, 235–36
    experience of, 94
    Freud, S., and, 89, 168, 174
    personal treatment for, 152–53, 155
    self-disclosure of, 280
    sublimation of, 77
    supervision and, 122, 127, 135, 137, 155
    trauma response of, 149–50, 280, 283, 294
    use of, 108–9, 117
    in wounded healer, 177–78
Crago, M., 247, 252
Crits-Christoph, K., 259
Crits-Christoph, P., 245–46, 252, 253, 254, 259, 260

Cross, T., 129
cultural competence, 42–45. *See also* diversity
    definition of, 129
    mentors and, 61–63
    need for, 12, 30, 87, 281, 293
    personal treatment and, 157–58
    with research-supported treatment, 194
    self-reflection for, 157, 158
    in supervision, 128–31
    training for, 88
culture, 128–31
culture of origin, 62–63
curiosity, 273
A Curious Calling (Sussman, M.), 30, 33–34

DBT (dialectical behavior therapy), 83, 218, 229, 234
Delworth, U., 116
Dennis, K., 129
DeRubeis, R. J., 255
despair, 178, 179, 288
Deutsch, F., 89
Development of Psychotherapists Common Core Questionnaire (DPCCQ), 146
didactic preparation, 4
    ambiguity in, 77–78
    change process in, 74–76
    conceptual frameworks in, 73–74
    continuing education in, 83–84
    defining, 71–72
    ethics in, 76
    impact of, 88–89
    insufficiency of, 293
    phase I: graduate or medical school, 79–81
    phase II: internship or residency, 81–82
    phase III: specialty training, 82–83
    research on, 291–92
    scientific method, 76–77
    skills from, 280
    stages of, 78–83
digitalization, 85
Dilthey, Wilhelm, 64
disaster, 12, 16, 281–82
disease, 86
dissociation, 105
dissociative identity disorder, 89
diversity, 42–45, 87–88
    with mentors, 61–62
    prejudice and, 110, 111

Dora, 89
Dostoevsky, Fyodor, 36
double bind, 59
DPCCQ, 146
dreams, 174–75
Driver, S., 38
dual relationships, 56

Ebersole, G. H., 127–28
EBP. *See* evidence-based practice
EBT. *See* evidence-based treatment
eclecticism, 75
Edelwich, J., 99
Edwards, L., 136
efficacy, 14, 245, 246–49, 292
ego-ideal, 99–102
ego integrity, 288
Ellenberger, H. F., 169
Elman, N., 159
EMDR (eye movement desensitization
    reprocessing), 83
Emery, G., 216
emotional intelligence, 273
empathy
    communication of, 19
    outcomes with, 252
    in psychological-mindedness, 36–37
    Socratic method without, 76
empirically supported treatment (EST),
    191, 192, 193–94
"Empirically Validated Psychotherapy"
    (Greening), 200–201
empowerment, 61
Enlightenment movement, 173
Erikson, E., 39, 287–88
erotic transference, 105–6
Esau, 167
essential tension, 207, 292
EST. *See* empirically supported treatment
ethics
    with boundaries, 109
    competence in, 132
    identity with, 286–87
    mandated personal therapy, 158–60
    of motivation, 76
    review boards, 290–91
    supervision, 132, 295
    training, 76
Ethics of our Fathers, 114
ethnicity, matching, 250
Evans, L. A., 250
evidence-based practice (EBP), 13–14,
    16, 191
    development of, 197–98

evidence-based treatment and, 193–94
    information-gathering in, 193
    process of, 192–93
    resistance to, 201–3
evidence-based treatment (EBT), 4–5, 191
    in CBT, 217–18, 220
    defining, 14
    empirically supported treatment,
        193–94
    evidence-based practice and, 193–94
exemplarity, 58
"experience-near-experience," 64
experiential-humanistic perspective, 153

Fairbairn, Ronald, 283
Faltus, F. J., 151
Farber, B., 36, 39
feedback, 123, 260
Feeley, M., 255
felt sense, 55
feminization, viii
Fenster, S., 145
Fisher, G., 193
Fleming, J., 155–56
Fliess, Wilhelm, 169
Flowers, J. V., 192, 200
Forehand, R., 62
Forrest, L., 159
Fort Hood, Texas, 149
Foster, J., 123
Fowles, John, 207
Frank, A., 260
Freeman, A., 222, 225
Freud, Amanda, 168
Freud, Anna, 79, 83
Freud, Jacob, 167, 168
Freud, Sigmund, 3–4
    Anna O consultation, 69
    Charcot and, 69, 72
    countertransference and, 89, 168, 174
    divergence from, 86
    family of, 167–68
    on hierarchy, 137
    on personal treatment, 152
    on psychotherapy, 70
    self-scrutiny of, 29
    on transference, 174
    as wounded healer, 168–69, 173–74
Friedberg, R. D., 219–20, 224, 232
Friedman, R. A., 144
friendship, 102
Fujino, D. C., 250
Fussell, F., 30, 31
"future shock," 84, 86, 90

Gallop, R., 253, 254, 259
Ganzarian, Ramon, 78
Ganzer, C., 54
Garfield, S. L., 19
Gelso, 127
gender, 61–62, 88
    matching, 249–50, 251
    self-disclosure by, 137
    shamanism and, 166
generativity, 288
Gestalt therapy, 70
Gibbard, Graham, 82
The Gift of Therapy (Yalom), 147
Gioe, Vincent, 78
God, 167–68
Goldberg, C., 172
Gonsalvez, C., 117
Goodheart, C. D., 195
"good therapist," 18–20
Gorman, A. A., 219–20, 224, 232
Gorman, J. M., 247
graduate school, 79, 80
Greben, S., 126
Greeg, W. F., Jr., 176
Greening, T., 200–201
grief, 88
Grinder, J., 190–91, 207
group therapy, 127
    CBT, 227–28
    leadership styles with, 248
    peer, 185–86
    research on, 245–47
    for resilience, 38
    wounded healer and, 170, 175,
        178–79, 185–86
    Yalom on, 154
Grunebaum, H., 152
guided imagery, 55–56
"Guidelines for Providers of Psychological
    Services to Ethnic, Linguistic,
    and Culturally Diverse
    Populations," 43
Guy, J. D., 146–48

Halifax, J., 166
Halstead, J. L., 260
*Handbook of Psychotherapy and Behavior
    Change* (Garfield and Bergin), 19
Handler, L., 128, 259
Hasan, N. T., 190
"Have you ever been in psychotherapy,
    Doctor?" (Friedman), 144
Hayes, 127
Hayes, S. C., 193

Hays, P. A., 157
*Healing Together After Trauma: A Couple's
    Guide to Coping with Trauma and
    Post-Traumatic Stress* (Phillips and
    Kane), 145–46
health care
    agendas of, 85
    change in, 84–85
    managed, viii, 9, 16, 195–96,
        283–84, 292
    system of, 8–9
health maintenance organization
    (HMO), 191, 195–96
Heffron, M., 55
Heidegger, M., 64
helplessness, 178, 179
Henry, W. E., 171
Henry, W. P., 260
Heracles, 167
Herman, J., 132
hermeneutical growth, 50, 57
hermeneutic method, 63–65
Heru, A., 137
Hess, S., 119
Hetherly, V., 115, 124
hierarchy
    Freud, S., on, 137
    mentors and, 52, 55, 57, 62
    of supervision, 52, 120, 133, 156
Hill, C., 119
Hill, C. E., 258
Hilsenroth, M., 128
Hilsenroth, M. J., 254, 259
HIPAA (Health Insurance
    Portability and Accountability
    Act of 1996), 83
Hippocrates, 167
HMO. *See* health maintenance
    organization
Holloway, E. L., 258
Howard, F., 116
How I Became a Therapist
    (Reppen), 29
How Psychotherapists Develop
    (Orlinsky and Ronnestad), 150
HRT. *See* human relations
    training
Hu, L., 250
human relations training (HRT), 258
Hunsley, J., 193
Huppert, J. D., 247
Hynan, M. T., 255–56
hypnotic suggestion, 76
hysteria, 69

idealization, 61, 126, 183
identity
    dissociative identity disorder, 89
    with ethics, 286–87
    of psychotherapists, 118, 278, 284–87
    sexual abuse and, 286
    from training, 83
    victim, 170
Identity Youth and Crisis (Erikson),
    287–88
Imel, Z. E., 253
incest, 185
"Independent School," 83
individuation, 31–32, 285
inflation, 61
Inman, A., 130, 131
Inskipp, F., 116
interconnectedness, 191
internship, 81, 226–28
interpersonal context, ix, 58–60,
    61, 116
interpersonal process recall (IPR), 258
intersubjective field, 178–81, 184
intimacy, 36, 184
intrapsychic dynamics, 60
introspection, 36
intuition, 18, 80
IPR. *See* interpersonal process recall
Isaacs, M., 129
isomorphy, 122, 127
Ivey, A. E., 258
Ivins, B., 55

Jacob, 167
Jacobi, M., 51
Jennings, L., 269
Jesus, 167–68
Johnson, B., 57
Jolly, B., 116
Jonsson, C., 126
Joseph, S., 150
Jung, Carl, 166, 168, 169

Kagan, N., 258
Kakkad, D., 194
Kane, D., 145
Karlsson, R., 250
Kazdin, A. E., 193, 196, 197
Khan, Masud, 83
Kikkuu, 287
Kilminster, S., 116
King, R., 128
Kivlighan, D. M., Jr., 201
Klein, Melanie, 83

Kluft, Richard, 89
Knox, S., 119, 136
Kobasa, S. C., 39
Kuhn, T. S., 207

Ladany, N., 115, 136
Lafferty, P., 247, 252
Laireiter, A.-R., 225, 232
Lambert, M. J., 206, 247, 256
Lambert, W., 128
Langs, R., 182
language, matching, 250
Latin Americans, 250
Lawrence, D. H., 36
Leahy, R., 222
legislation, 62
Lehrman-Waterman, D., 136
Leiderman, P. H., 127–28
Leszcz, M., 120
Levant, R. F., 190, 195
Levenson, H., 121
licensure, 12–13, 62, 70, 76, 79, 80, 281
Lichtenberg, J., 123
Liese, B., 260
life coaching, 13
Linehan, Marsha, 217
Linley, P. A., 150
literature, 78, 134
local clinical scientists, 198
London, S., 192–93
Longfellow, H. W., 172
Luborsky, L., 245–46, 252, 260
Ludgate, J. W., 224–25

magic, 190–91, 208
The Magus (Fowles), 207
Malle, Louis, 73
Manevich, I., 39
manualized treatment, 10, 256
Mark, D., 260
Martino, S., 253, 254
Masten, A. S., 39
matching, 249–51
Matthews, K., 115, 124
McAuley, M., 61
McClendon, D. T., 197, 198
McCloskey, R. D., 222, 225
McLennan, J., 258–59
McLeod, H., 117
McNeill, B., 116, 126
"medical model," 86
medical school, 79
Mentoring Functions Questionnaire-9, 51
mentors, 4, 35

boundaries for, 57
career support from, 52
case study, 53–57, 59, 60, 62–63,
    64–65
cultural competence and, 61–63
defining, 49
functions of, 51–52
hierarchy and, 52, 55, 57, 62
interpersonal aspects with, 58–60, 61
intrapsychic dynamics with, 60–61
as people, 57, 60–61
qualities of, 57
relational/intersubjective theory with,
    53, 57, 58, 61
research on, 51
as role models, 58
in training, 56, 295
transference with, 61
Mercer, D., 260
Merleau-Ponty, M., 72
metaphoric exercises, 59–60
Metzger, 39
microcounseling, 258
Miller, W. R., 76
Mintz, J., 245–46, 252
mirror neurons, 74
Mitchell, S., 54
MMPI, 248
motivation, 33, 34
    to help, 37–38
    of patient, 76
    in psychotherapy, 76
Muran, J. C., 253
Murphy, L., 120
Mutual Psychological Development
    Questionnaire, 51
Myers-Briggs Temperament Indicator,
    32, 33

Najavits, L. M., 260
Narducci, J., 259
narrative, 37, 40, 57, 60, 63
Native Americans, 88
Nazis, 76
negative screening, 289
neuroscience, 10, 74
neuroticism, 247
New York Times, 144
Nielson, S. L., 206, 247
Norcross, J. C., 146–48, 150, 151, 152, 158
Norsworthy, L. A., 260
Northern Ireland, 171
Notes from Underground (Dostoevsky), 36
Nuttall, J., 199

object-relations, 58
observation
    by psychotherapist, 275
    in supervision, 138, 261
oedipal complex, 173
Ogles, B. M., 206, 247
Ogren, M., 126
Okiishi, J., 206, 247
Onken, L. S., 260
Orchowski, L., 30
Orlinsky, D. E., 17, 150, 270
Orthodox Jews, 110
outcomes
    CBT, 225
    competence, 254–55
    empathy, 252
    feedback, 260
    matching, 249–51
    psychotherapist personality, 249
    resilience, 74
    supervision, 125, 126, 127–28
    therapeutic alliance, 89, 118,
        252–54, 259
    training, 259–60
over-dependence, 61

Padilla, A. M., 43–44
panic disorder, 247
parallel process, 122
participant-observation model, 101
patience, 274
patients, 4, 19. *See also* transference;
        countertransference; therapeutic
        alliance
    affect towards, 104
    backgrounds, 12
    change in, 74–75, 274
    classification, 216–17
    identified, 281–82
    intimacy with, 184
    matching with, 249
    monitoring, 195
    motivation, 76
    psychotic, 106
    requests by, 102–4
    responsibility, 96
    supervision by, 107
    traumatized, 149, 280–81
    wounded healer and, 176–77,
        182–83
payment, 94, 96, 97, 98, 99
PBE. *See* practice-based evidence
PBT. *See* practice-based treatment
Pearson, James, 77

peripatetic school, 73
personality disorders, 233–334
personal treatment, 4, 21–22, 119,
    144–45
  benefits of, 150–51, 160, 298–99
  CBT, 152–53
  confidentiality in, 159–60
  for countertransference, 152–53, 155
  cultural competence and, 157–58
  experiential-humanistic perspective, 153
  family or couple therapy as, 154
  group perspectives, 154
  mandated, 158–60
  across orientations, 146–47
  prevalence of, 146, 148
  psychodynamic perspective, 152–53,
    277
  psychotherapist for, 151–52, 160
  reasons for, 147–48, 279
  supervision and, 154–57, 277
  systems theory perspective, 154
personhood, 74
Persons, J. B., 220, 221
persuasion, 76
Peyton, V., 123
Phillips, Suzanne B., 145–46
philosophy, 78, 216
Physicians Health Services, 186
Physician Substance Abuse Monitoring,
    186
Pilkonis, P. A., 246
Poirot, Hercule, 178
Polanyi, Michael, 91
Pope, K., 121
Pope, K. S., 150
post-traumatic stress disorder (PTSD),
    79, 81, 84
practice-based evidence (PBE), 190, 197
  as co-therapist, 200–207
  data from, 204–6, 208
  HMO use of, 195–96
  measures in, 198–99
  problems with, 206–7
  resistance to, 201–3
practice-based treatment (PBT), 191, 195
practice guidelines, 14
pre-professional phase, 272–75
President's New Freedom Commission on
    Mental Health Final Report, 13
Price, M., 137
principle-based approach, 218
privilege, 109, 158
Proctor, B., 116
protocol-based approaches, 217, 219–20

pseudoshrinks, 206
psychoanalysis, 69
  decline of, 85
  subjectivity of, 90–91
psychodynamic perspective
  ambiguity in, 274
  goals, 284
  personal treatment in, 152–53, 277
  on unconscious mechanisms, 177
psychological-mindedness, 35–38, 273,
    295–96
psychology
  behaviorist, 86–87
  clinical, 85–86
  evolution of, 86
  humanistic, 86
  paradigms in, 86–87
Psychology Code of Ethics, 159
psychopharmacology, 10–11, 284
psychotherapists. See also continuing
    education; countertransference;
    didactic preparation; personal
    treatment; supervision; training;
    wounded healer
  affect of, 104
  aging, 287–88
  as blank screens, 7, 15
  burnout, 81, 99, 270
  career choice, 31–35
  childhoods, 31, 54–55, 62–63, 169
  children, 145
  communication skills, 281
  conceptual level, 258–59
  creativity, 199
  cycles, 270
  demographics, 42–43, 87
  developmental stages, 31–32, 270,
    271–88
  efficacy, 14, 245, 246–49, 292
  ego-ideal, 99–102
  expertise, 193, 207–8
  exposure, 293–94
  "good," 18–20
  with group therapy, 170
  hostility, 117, 135
  identity, 118, 278, 284–87
  individuation, 31–32, 285
  influence of, 8, 30
  influences on, 3–4, 17–18, 20, 199
  integration of, 199, 201
  interviews with, 39–42
  licensure, 12–13, 62, 70, 76, 79, 80,
    281
  marginalization of, 171–72

married, 148
matching with, 249–51
modalities, 271, 277, 293
motivation, 33, 34, 37–38, 76
pathology, 33–34, 158, 171–72
as people, 15, 17, 18, 19, 33–34,
    39–42, 151, 199, 212–13, 249, 279
for personal treatment, 151–52, 160
predatory, 158, 184, 185
pre-professional phase, 272–75
professional self, 6–7, 80–81, 280
psychological-mindedness of, 35–38
qualities of, 95–96, 135, 288–90
relational skills, 272–73
research on, 5–6, 29, 31–32, 245–46,
    269
resilience, 38–39
responsiveness, 107
rigid, 98, 106–7
selection of, 288–90
self-care, 296–97
self-reflection, 16–17, 30, 111–12, 117,
    172, 174–75, 199, 201, 284, 286,
    295–96, 297
self-training, 134
senior, 269–70, 286
shame, 100, 120, 121, 124, 133, 135,
    136
stress f, 77, 81, 282–83, 299
suicide rates, 172
teams, 234, 294
trauma work by, 38–39, 149–50,
    179–81, 280–81, 294
treatment integration by, 281
"type A," 246
unilateral termination of, 104–5, 250
values, 278–79
vulnerability, 35, 108–9, 158–59, 172,
    199
psychotherapy. See also communication;
    outcomes; specific therapies
accountability, viii, 186, 284, 292
adherence to, 256
after disasters, 12, 16, 281–82
basis of, 95
change in, vii–viii, 74–75, 84–85, 274
craft of, 80
defining, 13
exploration vs action in, 102–4
framework of, 96–99
intersubjective approach to, 7–8
magic equated with, 190–91, 208
modification of, 106–7
motivation in, 76

as praxis, 70
prevalence of, 148
process of, 94
with psychopharmacology, 11, 12
for psychotic patients, 106
reasons for, 148
resilience from, 38
resistance, 96–98
settings, vii–viii
techniques, 251–56
theories, 31–32, 75
time-limited, 9, 10, 16, 196, 260
treatment integration, 281
unilateral termination of, 104–5, 250
psychotic disorders, 217
PTSD. See post-traumatic stress disorder
Putsche, L., 59

racism, 109–10, 111
randomized controlled trial (RCT), 191,
    216–17, 225
"range of possibility," 63
Rappaport, E., 145
rationalization, 76
Raue, P., 128
RCT. See randomized controlled trial
Recupero, P., 137
Reese, R. J., 260
reinforcement, 76
rejection, 104–5
Relational Health Index-Mentor, 51
relational/intersubjective theory, 53, 57,
    58
relational model, 45
religion, 110
Reppen, Joseph, 29, 34–35
research, 5–6, 29, 31–32, 269
    on didactic preparation, 291–92
    on group therapy, 245–47
    on matching, 249–50
    on mentors, 51
    on outcomes, 248–56
    on technique, 251–56
    training and, 81, 258–59, 291–92
    on treatment choice, 257
    on wounded healer, 186
research-supported treatment (RST), 191.
    See also evidence-based practice
    cultural competence, 194
    empirically supported treatment and,
        193–94
resilience, 38–39, 74, 274, 281
resistance, 96–98, 201–3
resistance analysis, 76

retiring, 287
Ricks, D. F., 245
Riess, H., 132
Roberts, M. C., 196
Rock, M. H., 156
Roget, N., 193
role model, 58
Romantic movement, 173
Ronnestad, M. H., 17, 31, 32, 145, 146,
    147, 150, 270
Rosalynn Carter Symposium on Mental
    Health Policy, 13
Roth, S., 95
Rowlands, S. R., 260
RST. See research-supported treatment
Rush, J. A., 216
Rutter, M., 39

Salvendy, J., 120
Sanislow, C. A., 246
Saypol, E., 39
Schacht, T. E., 260
Schamberger, M., 259
Schatz, D., 146, 147, 150
Schermer, V., 60
Schlosser, L., 136
Schover, L., 121
Schultz, J., 119
Schwartz, B., 192, 200
Schweitzer, R., 128
scientific method, 76–77
The Secret of the Sea (Longfellow), 172
self
    -awareness, 173–75, 181–82, 186–87
    -care, 296–97
    -practice, 224
    professional, 6–7, 80–81, 280
    -reflection, 16–17, 30, 111–12, 117,
        156, 172, 174–75, 199, 201,
        231–32, 279–80, 284, 286, 295–96,
        297
    in relational/intersubjective theory, 54
    -scrutiny, 29
    -selection, 226, 228
    sense of, 52
    -training, 134
    use of, 53–54
self-disclosure
    of countertransference, 280
    by gender, 137
    in supervision, 119–20, 133, 134,
        135–37
    of wounded healer, 179, 181–82
sensitizers, 39
SES. See socioeconomic status

sexual abuse
    identity and, 286
    matching with, 251
    in supervision, 121
    by wounded healer, 184–85
Sexual Boundary Violations (Celenza), 158
sexuality. See also erotic transference
    incest, 185
    matching, 249–50
shamans, 166, 186
shame, 100, 120, 121, 124, 133,
    135, 136
Shanfield, S., 115, 124
Sharpe, Ella Freeman, 79
Shaw, B. F., 216
Shear, M. K., 247
"sheepskin psychosis," 81
Sims, J. H., 171
Siqueland, L., 260
Skilbeck, W. M., 250
Skovholt, T. M., 17, 31, 32, 145, 269
slippery slope, 106, 134
Sloan, L., 119
Smith, J., 136
social constructivist viewpoint, 59
social professions, 32–33
society, 186
Society for Psychotherapy Research, 6,
    269
socioeconomic (SES) status, 250–51
Socratic method, 76
soul, 86
Spray, S. L., 171
SPR Collaborative Research Network,
    146, 147
Spring, B., 194
SSI. See Supervisory Style Inventory
stagnation, 288
Standards and Guidelines for the Practice of
    the Psychotherapies, 132
standardized testing, 32–33
"Status of minority curricula and training
    in clinical psychology" (Bernal and
    Padilla), 43
Steinbock, A., 58
Stevens, S. E., 255–56
Stoic philosophers, 216
Stolorow, R., 90
Stoltenberg, C., 116
Storrs, D., 59
Stossel, S., 151
Strasser, S., 64
Strassle, C., 128
Strassle, C. G., 259
Strauser, D. J., 151

Strong, D., 137
Strong Interest Inventory, 32
Structure of Magic (Bandler and Grinder), 190–91
Strunk, 255
Strupp, H. H., 260
Strupp, Hans H., 151
student-teacher bonding, 73
Studies on Hysteria (Breuer and Freud), 69
substance abuse, 70–71, 80, 249
Sue, D., 43, 44
Sue, D., 43, 44
Sue, S., 250
suicide, 99–102, 172
suicide contract, 99, 100
Sundin, E., 126
supershrinks, 206, 245
supervision, 4, 95, 103
    accessibility of, 257, 296
    attachment in, 122–23
    bias in, 131
    boundaries in, 118, 121–22, 133–34
    with CBT, 228–29, 230, 232, 233, 235–36
    competency model of, 116
    countertransference and, 122, 127, 135, 137, 155
    cultural competence in, 128–31
    developmental integrated model of, 116–17
    developmental model of, 115, 123–24
    efficacy, 125–26
    ethics from, 132, 295
    expectations in, 118
    hierarchy of, 52, 120, 133, 156
    idealization in, 126
    importance of, 114–15, 294–95
    improvement from, 126–28, 295
    with internships, 227
    interpersonal model of, 116
    liability in, 137–38
    models of, 114–16, 128, 137
    negative experiences in, 119–21, 124–25, 134, 156
    objectives of, 134–35
    observation in, 138, 261
    outcomes with, 125, 126, 127–28
    by patients, 107
    peer, 298
    personal treatment and, 154–57, 277
    proximity in, 137–38
    responsibility of, 117–18
    self-disclosure in, 119–20, 133, 134, 135–37

    self-reflection in, 156
    sexual abuse in, 121
    standards for, 131–33
    systems model of, 115–16
    tasks of, 116
    therapeutic alliance in, 122, 124–25, 131, 136, 156, 276–77
    of wounded healer, 183
Supervisory Style Inventory (SSI), 120
Sussman, M. B., 171–72
Sussman, Michael, 30, 33–34, 36
systematic reviews, 193
systems theory perspective, 154

Tabachnik, B. G., 150
Takeuchi, D. T., 250
Tarasoff, 137
Taylor, A., 59
TDCRP, 249
Temes, C. M., 253, 254
Thase, M. E., 224–25, 260
therapeutic alliance, 19
    alliance-fostering therapy, 259
    in CBT, 218–19, 220–22, 236–37, 239–40
    as factor, 89
    honesty in, 110
    as motivation, 76
    outcomes with, 89, 118, 252–54, 259
    suicide with, 100
    in supervision, 122, 124–25, 131, 136, 156, 276–77
    training for, 259
    trust in, 273
therapeutic contract, 96–99
therapeutic relationships, 19
The Therapist's Pregnancy: Intrusion in the Analytic Space (Phillips, Fenster and Rappaport), 145
The Third Reich in the Unconscious (Volkan), 176
Toren, Z., 248
training. *See also* didactic preparation
    in ambiguity, 77–78
    CBT, 223–24, 225–30, 231–33, 237, 238t, 239t, 259, 260
    clinical experience in, 293–95
    in communication, 75–76
    for cultural competence, 88
    curricula for, 291
    didactic, 71–91
    ethics in, 76
    formal, 12–13, 79, 80
    in helping skills, 258
    identity from, 83

training. *See also* didactic preparation (*cont'd*)
    mentors in, 56, 295
    outcomes with, 259–60
    research and, 81, 258–59, 291–92
    in scientific method, 76–77
    selection for, 289
    self-, 134
    specialty, 70, 82–83, 256–57, 292–93
    for therapeutic alliance, 259
trance states, 166
transference, 45
    erotic, 105–6
    Freud, S., on, 174
    with mentors, 61
trauma
    countertransference with, 149–50, 280,
        283, 294
    resilience with, 38–39, 281
    wounded healer and, 179–81
Treatment of Depression Collaborative
    Research Program, 246
Truax, C. B., 258
trust, 39, 273
truth, 72
tuberculosis, 173
Tummala-Narra, R., 44

unconditional positive regard, 61
unconscious, 22
unconscious mechanisms, 176–77
understanding, implicit, 64
unified treatment approach, 217
unilateral termination, 104–5, 250
University of Pennsylvania, 151
University of Toronto, 118
Usher, E. L., 260

Varra, A. A., 193
victim identity, 170
Vinton, E. A., 199, 201
vocation, 32–33
Volkan, V. D., 176

Walker, B. B., 192–93
Walker, R., 121
Wampold, B. E., 195, 253, 258
Warren, A., 38
Watkins, C. J., 115
Werner, E. E., 39
Weston, D., 55
White, B., 38
white privilege, 109

Why I Became a Psychotherapist (Reppen),
    34–35
William Alanson White Institute, 20
Willutzki, U., 146, 147, 225, 232
Winnicott, Donald, 83
Wiseman, H., 146, 147
Wogan, M., 248
Wolf Man, 89
Wolpe, Joseph, 79
Woods, S. W., 247
Woody, G., 253, 254, 260
World War II, 173
worried well, vii, 12
Worthen, V., 126
wounded healer, 4, 22, 36, 165
    boundaries with, 182–84
    countertransference in, 177–78
    damage from, 182–83, 187
    fear of, 30
    Freud, S., as, 168–69, 173–74
    group therapy and, 170, 175, 178–79,
        185–86
    health workers as, 171, 175–76
    history of, 166–69
    idealization of, 183
    intersubjective field of, 178–81, 184
    Jung as, 169, 173–74
    patients and, 176–77, 182–83
    research on, 186
    risk from, 169–70
    self-awareness of, 173–75, 181–82,
        186–87
    self-disclosure of, 179, 181–82
    sexual involvement by, 184–85
    supervision of, 183
    trauma and, 179–81
    universality of, 171–72, 186, 274
Wright, J. H., 224–25
Wright, James, 90

Yalom, Irvin, 49–50, 119, 127–28, 147
    on group therapy, 154
    on personal therapy, 144, 279
Yamamoto, J., 250
YAVIS syndrome (young, attractive,
    verbal, intelligent, and successful), 12
Y-OQ. *See* Youth Outcome Questionnaire
Youth Outcome Questionnaire (Y-OQ),
    197, 198*f*

Zane, N. W. S., 250
Zuroff, D. C., 246